Research-Based Practices for Teaching Common Core Literacy

Research-Based Practices for Teaching Common Core Literacy

EDITED BY

P. David Pearson
Elfrieda H. Hiebert

Foreword by Nell K. Duke

TEACHERS COLLEGE PRESS

TEACHERS COLLEGE | COLUMBIA UNIVERSITY
NEW YORK AND LONDON

INTERNATIONAL
LITERACY
ASSOCIATION
Newark, Delaware

Published by Teachers College Press, 1234 Amsterdam Avenue, New York, NY 10027

The International Literacy Association (ILA) is a global advocacy and membership organization dedicated to advancing literacy for all through its network of more than 300,000 literacy educators and experts across 75 countries. With 60 years of experience in the field, ILA believes in the transformative power of literacy to create more dynamic societies, prosperous economies, and meaningful lives. ILA collaborates with partners across the world to develop, gather, and disseminate high-quality resources, best practices, and cutting-edge research to empower educators, inspire students, and inform policymakers. ILA publishes several peer-reviewed journals, including *The Reading Teacher*, *Journal of Adolescent & Adult Literacy*, and *Reading Research Quarterly*. For more information, visit literacyworldwide.org.

Library of Congress Cataloging-in-Publication Data is available at loc.gov

Research-based practices for teaching common core literacy / edited by P. David Pearson, Elfrieda H. Hiebert.
pages cm
Includes bibliographical references and index.
ISBN 978-0-8077-5644-7 (pbk. : alk. paper)
ISBN 978-0-8077-5645-4 (hardcover : alk. paper)
ISBN 978-0-8077-7373-4 (ebook)
1. Literacy—Study and teaching (Elementary)—United States. 2. Literacy—Study and teaching (Secondary)—United States. 3. Reading (Elementary)—United States. 4. Reading (Secondary)—United States. 5. Common Core State Standards (Education) I. Pearson, P. David, editor of compilation. II. Hiebert, Elfrieda H.
LC151.R435 2015
372.6--dc23   201500318

ISBN 978-0-8077-5644-7 (paper)
ISBN 978-0-8077-5645-4 (hardcover)
ISBN 978-0-8077-7373-4 (ebook)

Printed on acid-free paper
Manufactured in the United States of America

22   21   20   19   18   17   16   15   8   7   6   5   4   3   2   1

Contents

Foreword

A few years ago I proposed a professional book on the Common Core State Standards (CCSS) called Read the Core. Each page of the book would say simply "Read the Core." I was joking, but only kind of. The joke was born of a very real frustration that so many people talking and writing about the Common Core—from bloggers to legislators to administrators to even some classroom teachers—don't seem to have actually read it. They were discussing, critiquing, even "implementing" the Common Core based on very little understanding of what it actually involves or expects.

A related phenomenon I have observed I call "standards stereotyping." In this phenomenon, people boil the Common Core down to just a few ideas: the Common Core is about complex text and close reading, or the Common Core is about informational text and disciplinary literacy. Simplification is a natural human instinct, but in the case of the Common Core State Standards, it is dangerous. There is no doubt that the Common Core does deal with complex text, reading closely, informational text, and disciplinary literacy, but it deals with many areas within and beyond those topics—unprecedented emphasis on ascertaining the meaning of unfamiliar words, for example; groundbreaking expectations for the use of digital tools for writing; and the call to integrate verbal, visual, and quantitative information. The Common Core also addresses a number of areas, such as specific expectations for knowledge of sound—letter relationships and grammatical constructions in oral language, that are not new or 'sexy,' but are, nonetheless, deeply deserving of our attention.

The contributors to this volume have read the Common Core, closely. The editors have put together a text that goes way beyond stereotypes and polemics about the Common Core, taking a deep and measured dive into a wide range of essential topics within the Standards, including those that have garnered relatively little attention. I read a lot, and I can't think of the last time I read anything about the CCSS as engaging and thought provoking as this. Space certainly does not permit me to discuss all of the thoughts incited, but the following are three aspects of the volume I see as especially worthy of our thinking. First, *Research-Based Practices for Teaching Common Core Literacy* offers a historical perspective in a number of chapters. We all recognize the value of a historical perspective, but it has all too rarely been applied in discussions of the Common Core. The historical context offered in this book will enrich your thinking. Second, many chapters discuss the research base, or lack thereof, underlying specific facets or interpretations of the Common Core. For example, some aspects of close reading, such as those that involve carefully analyzing the structure of a text, have a deep history in research, whereas others, such as limiting textual analysis to literal meaning, do not. There is a danger of getting so swept up in practices that come immediately to mind in reading the Common Core that we forget what we have known long before the Common Core came to be. We owe the Common Core attention, but we owe a long-standing and robust research base attention, too. Third, a number of chapters highlight what is unsaid, as well as what is said, in the Core. For example, John T. Guthrie's chapter reminds us that the Common Core is essentially mute around literacy motivation and engagement, and yet motivation and engagement are inarguably entailed in actually meeting standards as cognitively demanding as these.

I encourage you to take *Research-Based Practices for Teaching Common Core Literacy* as an opportunity to read between and outside the lines of the Common Core, as well as within them. Thank you to the editors and contributors of this complex text. And wishing engaged reading to all of you.

—Nell K. Duke
University of Michigan

Preface

> Those who do not remember the past are condemned to repeat it.
>
> —George Santayana

This volume is based on the premise that remembering what we've learned is fundamental to designing solutions to current problems. As a field, we have produced a wealth of knowledge about reading development over the past half century. In this volume, a generation of scholars, all of whom have contributed to that record of productivity, reflects on what this knowledge offers for educators as they work to implement a new generation of policies, specifically those spawned by the Common Core State Standards (CCSS) (NGA Center for Best Practices & CCSSO, 2010).

This volume focuses on the period from 1965 to 2014. We begin with 1965 because that was the year that President Lyndon Johnson signed into law the Elementary and Secondary Education Act. The first section or "title" of the act had to do with financial assistance to schools for educating low-income students in reading and mathematics. Soon thereafter, the number of university faculty in reading education increased as states and districts required specialties in reading education for Title I teachers. The passage of Title I was followed by the establishment of an agency within the U.S. Department of Education—The National Institute of Education—that was devoted to funding research programs in education. Research on reading was a focus with the funding of the Center for the Study of Reading in 1975. During the 1970s and 1980s, the increase in the number of research publications was phenomenal. A hint at the volume of research comes from a Google n-gram analysis of the phrase "reading research." Relative to all of the two-word phrases used in English texts for a particular year, the use of the phrase "reading research" increased tenfold from 1960 to 1985.

The authors in this volume represent a core group of individuals who were involved in the reading research enterprise during this period. Their roles were those of contributors to the literature and of mentors and advisors to graduate students. One author—S. Jay Samuels—began his prolific career at the University of Minnesota in 1965. Other contributors were graduate students, classroom teachers, or even high-school students at the beginning of the period. But by the late 1970s, all of the primary contributors were actively contributing to the research literature. Each chapter represents the culmination of decades of involvement by a researcher and his or her colleagues on a topic critical to practice and policy.

AN OVERVIEW OF THE VOLUME

We attend to three aspects of the reading research enterprise: frameworks, content, and context. Within the extensive scholarship on reading education over the past 50 years, our understandings about critical processes of learning and instruction have grown considerably. The previous generation of reading scholars—individuals such as David Russell, Nila Banton Smith, Emmett Betts—had strong ideas about the content of reading instruction. But they didn't always have a strong rationale to justify what they believed worked well. The work on theory and frameworks over the past 50 years has meant clear ideas of why particular practices should be emphasized and others eliminated and why still other practices should be added to the curriculum. The scholarship of the past 50 years has also brought to the fore the need to attend to the context of instruction. The reading experiences of students are embedded in and influenced by a myriad of contexts—communities, schools, classrooms, the publishing industry, and also the expectations and opportunities for teachers.

Frameworks and Processes

Learning from text or comprehension is the ultimate purpose of reading. As P. David Pearson and Gina N. Cervetti show in the volume's introductory chapter, substantial progress has been made over the past 50 years in understanding the nature of comprehension. Pearson and Cervetti identify the Four Resources Model as a synthesis of the views of reading comprehension processes and practices that takes into account the text, reader, and context and, in so doing, provides a way to engage all readers in thinking and learning from and with text.

The volume of research over the past 50 years owes a great deal to the involvement of the U.S. Department of Education in educational funding and policy. As Barbara Kapinus and Richard Long describe in their chapter, the relationship between scholarship and federal policy is often tenuous but the proliferation of federal policies on reading education and the stance of these policies have influenced the face of reading education substantially.

Perspectives on learning and teaching, whether labeled as frameworks, models, or guidelines, influence the enactment of reading instruction in classrooms. Drawing on a review of models of reading, Michael L. Kamil concludes that the implicit model of the CCSS expands upon conventional definitions of literacy. He argues for making the model explicit so that additions, potential deletions, and changes can be made to the Standards in disciplined ways.

Reading is first and foremost a language process, and in her chapter Rosalind Horowitz reviews research that substantiates the critical role of oral language in literacy development. To support even greater attention to oral language in literacy than present in the CCSS, Horowitz concludes her chapter with a set of evidence-based principles for fostering oral language's role in literacy.

Content

This section epitomizes the commitment of a generation of scholars to evidence-based reading experiences in public schools. The instructional solutions include the gamut of comprehension instruction to the development of fluent reading skills. And it is to the credit of this generation of scholars that they continue to ask questions about new phenomena, such as the comprehension of multiple texts and formative assessment.

Joanna P. Williams' chapter revisits the cognitive-strategy approach, which attends to the specific elements of comprehension tasks and readers' mental processing. As Williams emphasizes, these strategies serve as a means, not an end in themselves. The emphasis on authors' craft and the structure of the text within the CCSS reflects this perspective.

Jay S. Blanchard and S. Jay Samuels address an aspect of literacy instruction that has not been as integral to previous Standards documents as it is in the CCSS—comprehending ideas across texts, including the texts of media. Blanchard and Samuels present the rationale for a view of multiple-source comprehension and highlight sources that provide classroom practitioners in supporting this proficiency in students.

Unless students are engaged in reading, any number of instructional suggestions or frameworks will contribute little to the vision of a populace that is able to learn from complex text. Guthrie examines the interplay of reading skills and motivations from grades 3 to 7. To truly support the goal of engaged, knowledgeable individuals in society, Guthrie demonstrates that educators must attend to what is "under the hood"—that is, the motivations that support students' engagement in reading.

The ability to recognize the meanings of words in text is a strong indicator of comprehension. Michael F. Graves describes how knowledge about the ways instruction can support students' vocabulary has grown and identifies the particular dimensions of instruction that support this growth. Much is known about vocabulary instruction, but Graves concludes that more work is needed to create comprehensive programs that show effects on comprehension.

Rasinski, Paige, and Nageldinger address a topic that was not discussed extensively in reading education at the beginning of the 50-year period of focus—fluency. Rasinski et al. show that there is a sufficient research foundation to have oral reading fluency as an integral part of the reading curriculum but, in many classrooms, this activity does not get its due. When evidence-based practices happen significant improvements in students' overall reading proficiency levels will follow.

How much students read matters, a message that Richard L. Allington has reminded educators of since his 1977 "If they don't read much, how they ever gonna get good?" article. With colleagues Monica T. Billen and Kimberly McCuiston, Allington asks why reading volume wasn't in the foreground of the CCSS. To mitigate possible wrong steps and misinterpretations of the CCSS, Allington et al. offer a series of instructional solutions that will ensure that students get the experiences that are required to read complex texts.

In the final chapter of a long and influential career, Robert Calfee has left us with the message that what we teach is influenced by evidence and that the best evidence comes from the reflections of the participants (i.e., teacher and students) on learning in everyday classroom activities. With co-authors Barbara Kapinus and Kathleen M. Wilson, Calfee shows how formative assessment can be a tool for improving teaching and learning in reading.

Context

Prior to the mid-1960s, the contexts of learning to read were not often considered. Beginning in the 1960s and increasing in importance in every decade thereafter, context has become a major issue in reading policy and practice at every level of analysis: Readers are situated within classrooms, classrooms within schools, schools within districts, and districts within states, states within a federal system of governance. In this volume, we focus on three aspects of the context of schooling that are especially germane to creating equitable contexts for students, especially those who live in high-poverty communities: the school context, the texts used for instruction, and teachers.

Barbara M. Taylor reminds us that high-level literacy outcomes discussed in the first section (e.g., comprehending complex texts, engagement in reading as a sustained habit) do not occur as a result of the experiences in a single classroom of a single grade. High levels of literacy are created through the efforts of a school team. Taylor emphasizes that enactment of the CCSS ideals will only occur if schools and districts embed the CCSS as part of a broader multiyear process of collaborative school reform.

Perhaps the most significant difference in the CCSS from previous Standards is the presence of the staircase of text complexity with its assumption that text complexity needs to be accelerated from grades two onward. The chapter by Elfrieda H. Hiebert and Leigh Ann Martin examines this fundamental assumption of the CCSS. They also describe ways in which teachers can respond to the mandates for increased text complexity, especially in light of the number of struggling readers that were identified prior to an acceleration of text complexity.

Over the 50-year period of focus, published programs have offered increasingly more guidance for teachers. James V. Hoffman and P. David Pearson consider the increased amount of guidance provided in programs relative to the evidence that shows that teachers are the distinguishing factor in classrooms where students learn. But Hoffman and Pearson remain optimistic, identifying ways in which the imbalance can be corrected and greater trust can be placed in the expertise of teachers.

OUR HOPE FOR THIS VOLUME

Our vision of this volume—and also that of Jean Ward, acquisitions editor at Teachers College Press who has enthusiastically supported the project from the first moment we described it to her—is that it serves as a context for learning and reflection by teachers, educational leaders such as supervisors and coaches, and researchers. Hopefully, the conclusions and suggestions offered by this group of scholars can serve as grist for study groups of teachers, graduate and undergraduate courses, professional development sessions, and also conversations among colleagues.

However, we have an additional hope for this volume: that it illustrates a form of summarizing and curating knowledge in our field. During this 50-year period, meta-analyses became popular. But the reflections of senior scholars on their area of specialty relative to new directions and policies, as exemplified in this volume, illustrate another form of knowledge curation. We are hopeful that the foundation provided by this volume will inspire others to continue this tradition of curating knowledge. And we're not at all suggesting that we have to wait for 50 years. Within the increasingly flat world of the 21st century, periodic updates are useful.

EHH & PDP

Acknowledgments

We owe a debt to S. Jay Samuels. It was Jay who had the vision for this book and who talked extensively with us in its conceptualization. It is no accident that the 50 years covered by this book begin with the very year that Jay began his professional career at Minnesota—an institution (indeed the *only* institution) at which he taught, advised, and conducted research for most of this 50-year period. What is unique about Jay is that he conducted research within all three of the frames (framework, content, and context) that we have used to conceptualize this book. Jay was a builder of models and theories—indeed the LaBerge and Samuels Model brought to the field the all-important construct of automaticity—a key component in all viable models of reading since Jay and David LaBerge introduced it in the 1970s. But he was powerfully interested in pedagogy—conducting instructional experiments on a range of pedagogical issues—the role of alphabet knowledge, the impact of pictures on word identification and comprehension, decoding, fluency (his repeated-readings work is still widely cited and used to shape practice), and even the effect of teaching text structure on comprehension. And he dealt with context in his work promoting effective models of professional development (he edited a late 1980s book for the International Reading Association) and setting research policy (he was most notably a member of the National Reading Panel). The greatest honor, of course, is to have Jay as one of our authors for the very volume he viewed as essential to the needs of our current policy situation.

PART I

PROCESSES AND FRAMEWORKS

CHAPTER 1

Fifty Years of Reading Comprehension Theory and Practice

P. David Pearson and Gina N. Cervetti

The history of reading comprehension during the period between the elections of President Kennedy and President Obama includes major shifts in the ways that literacy educators and educational psychologists think about reading comprehension, both as a basic intellectual process and as an instructional responsibility for teachers and schools.

We begin this chapter by unpacking the history of reading comprehension to illuminate major developments in theory and practice over that 50-year period. Next, we focus on current construction-integration models of comprehension and their impact on policy and practice, giving special emphasis to the impact of these models on the development of the Common Core State Standards ([CCSS]; National Governors Association Center for Best Practices [NGA Center] & The Council of Chief State School Officers [CCSSO], 2010).

We represent the history of this period of time as a series of shifts in the relative importance of three factors—(1) the text, (2) the reader, and (3) the context—that have been used to explain reading comprehension. This chapter suggests that one or another of these three factors has dominated during different periods. Within our description of each period of time, we highlight what it meant to foreground one factor over the others. In the end, we suggest ways to conceptualize reading comprehension that moderate the less productive extremes of this history, recognizing that there are many ways to read a text and many resources to bring to meaning-making and interpretation.

A SHORT HISTORY OF READING COMPREHENSION

To document and explicate the history of reading comprehension, we analyze the relative salience of the three factors above—text, reader, and context—through a simple visual model. This trio of factors has been used by reading theorists for over a century to account for the degree of readers' comprehension achievement (e.g., Huey, 1908). We start with a hypothetical model[1] based on the assumption that these three factors influence reading comprehension to about the same degree. Hence in this model, reader, text, and context are represented as three *equal* circles whose intersection represents reading comprehension (see Figure 1.1). Over the past 50 years, each of these factors has had its moment in the spotlight, serving as the leading explanation for proficient comprehension. Therefore, in each of our visual representations, the *size* of each of these circles shifts to signify the relative salience of each factor during different periods.

Pre-1965: A Text-Centric Era

Prior to the mid-1960s, comprehension was all about the text. The dominant theoretical perspective in all of psychology, including cognitive psychology, was behaviorism, which was born in the early 1900s, in the work of E. L. Thorndike (1910) and J. B. Watson (1913), and maintained through the 1950s and beyond by B. F. Skinner (1957). Behaviorists believed that useful theories relied upon observation; as a result, the unobservable contents and processes of the brain (the "black box") fell outside the purview of psychology, leaving only the inputs (mainly text and task) and outputs (recall, answers to questions, blanks filled in, or perhaps eye movements or other physical correlates) as psychologically relevant explanatory phenomena. One could observe stimuli and responses; everything else was just speculation, a practice best left to philosophers.

In the behaviorism-dominated milieu, the text ruled the comprehension process, and its features determined the nature and degree of comprehension any given reader achieved. Reading was a largely perceptual process. First, the reader visually analyzed the relevant features of letters until those letters were identified. Next, the letters were mapped onto sounds to pronounce strings of sounds (including words). Finally, the reader listened to the output—either externally during oral reading or internally during silent reading—and achieved understanding. This model of reading earned the label of *bottom-up*, suggesting

Figure 1.1. Reader, Text, and Context

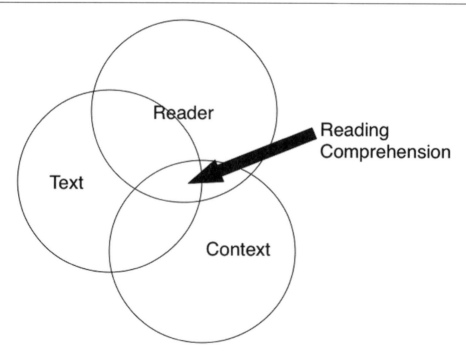

that lower-level processes, such as the visual features (of letters), are analyzed along the way to higher-level processes, such as semantic processing (deciding where a concept fits in one's memory store) or reading comprehension. Others used the label *outside-in*, to capture the sense that the comprehension process starts outside of the reader (i.e., in the text). Another label attached to these models is "the simple view" (Gough & Hillinger, 1980), which relies on the fundamental claim that Reading Comprehension = Listening Comprehension x Decoding (RC = LC x D). The assumption there is that meaning is *in the text*, and our job as readers is to use the text's visual features to dig out that meaning.

The parallel paradigm in literary theory was the text-centric movement known as New Criticism (Brooks & Warren, 1938/1960; Richards, 1929), which favored close reading of a "text qua text" as the key to understanding its meaning. Readers were admonished to keep their *top-down* (or, if you prefer, *inside-out*) knowledge resources at bay, to suppress individual responses to text, and to defer to the bottom-up processes that allowed the text to speak to the reader. Learning from text was largely a receptive process; students literally received the information that emerged from this close, analytic reading process. In many ways, New Criticism and close reading were responses to a fascination with approaches to literary criticism that focused on the historical and personal contexts in which writers did their work (Catterson & Pearson, in preparation; Ransom, 1937; Young, 1976). Before the rise of New Criticism, according to Ransom (1937), literary analyses were far too subjective and speculative, too steeped in a kind of pseudo-historicism in which writers could not escape the bounds of the times and context in which they wrote. New Criticism did not involve personal responses to literature, historical study, or linguistic or moral analysis that dealt with the abstract character of the text.

The fact that New Criticism was a response to other approaches implies that there were alternative views, and indeed there were. Most notably, there were strongly historical perspectives represented during the first third of the 20th century, even approaches that put the reader at the center of the process, such as Rosenblatt's (1938) reader-response perspective. But New Criticism, close reading, and the centrality of the text won the day (at least until sea changes swept through both psychology (Gardner, 1985) and literary criticism (Tompkins, 1980) in the 1970s and 1980s (Lockhart, 2012).

In Figure 1.2, text's leading role is depicted as a giant "text" circle in comparison with smaller "reader" and "context" circles. The instructional approaches of this period reflected the emphasis on text. Establishing accuracy of word recognition on the way to automaticity on the way to fluency and, eventually, to comprehension was the dominant pedagogical model. Text-based questions with right answers—what Pearson and Johnson (1978) called text-explicit question-answer relationships—were the order of the day. Textual readings were privileged across text genres, as evidenced by examples of questions from the Brooks and Warren classic, *Understanding Poetry* (1938/1960): "Can you find any principle of progression in the poem? Some good poems do work, in part at least, by accumulation, but the accumulation should lead to a significant impression. Do you find such an impression?" (p. 289). The term *close reading* was often applied to this approach, which implied that readers should stick close to the text as they tried to generate understanding.

The Era of the Reader: 1970s–1980s and Beyond

The late 1960s and early 1970s ushered in the cognitive revolution in psychology (Gardner, 1985). Once again, it became respectable for psychologists to speculate about what might be going on inside the black box, as scholars such as Huey (1908) had done in the days before behaviorism captured the field. Theories were developed about the nature of the processes that played out inside the brain during reading comprehension, as well as the nature of the storage mechanisms in memory. Elaborate accounts of knowledge acquisition during reading and of the organization of knowledge in memory became primary frameworks for understanding comprehension. At the same time, the reader became the centerpiece of the reading comprehension process. Kolers (1969), in an article written during the early phases of the cognitive revolution, chose the provocative title "Reading Is Only Incidentally Visual." Although no one besides Kolers stated it in quite these terms, this expression is an apt characterization of the new cognitive perspectives, which privileged a top-down orientation where higher-order resources, such as the semantic processing of prior knowledge, were used to minimize reliance on lower-order resources such as features and letters.

There was a re-emergence of the long-suppressed reader-response paradigm, marked by the rediscovery of Louise Rosenblatt's transactional theories of reading literature (Rosenblatt, 1938, 1968). Reader-response theories emphasize "readerly" readings that begin with the "apprehension" of understanding inside the reader and then move outward to the text as an evidentiary source to corroborate or temper the reader's internal musings. Interpretation emerges from the interaction between the reader and text, meaning that no two readers can ever be expected to interpret a text in exactly the same way, though their personal models of meaning typically bear a sufficiently strong family resemblance to allow for negotiating a social meaning through discussion. Figure 1.3 depicts these shifts, with a large circle for "reader" and relatively smaller circles for "text" and "context." The reader in the foreground, as illustrated in Figure 1.3, is evident in the three cognitive-based approaches to the study of reading comprehension that dominated this period.

The first cognitive-based approach involved efforts to explain how readers come to understand texts through their knowledge of the underlying structures of texts. Readers' story schemata—or schemata for textual organizational frames—were viewed as a dominant force that drove comprehension. Text-focused scholars offered structural accounts of the nature of narratives and expository texts, complete with predictions about how knowledge of those structures enhances both text understanding and memory (Kintsch, 1974; Mandler & Johnson, 1977; Meyer, 1975; Rumelhart, 1977; Stein & Glenn, 1979). Because the structure-oriented analyses were concerned with readers' knowledge of *text*, they honored knowledge of text over knowledge of the world and/or the topics that were described in the texts. Although their accounts did provide some explanation for how readers understood text, the focus on text structure failed to get to the heart of comprehension—understanding ideas.

The task of explicating comprehension fell to the second dominant cognitive-based approach of this period: schema theory (Anderson & Pearson, 1984). Schema theory emphasizes the role of the reader's existing topical and world knowledge in comprehension, examining how readers bring that knowledge to bear on text comprehension. The metaphors of "constructing meaning" (Tierney & Pearson, 1983) and the reader as "builder" (Pearson, 1992) capture the dominant view of reading comprehension in the schema theory model.

A third major strand of research that emerged from this period focused more on processes and practices than on knowledge. Dubbed "metacognition" (see Baker & Brown,

Figure 1.2. Text-centric Models of Reading Comprehension in the 1960s:
   Meaning Is Largely in the Text

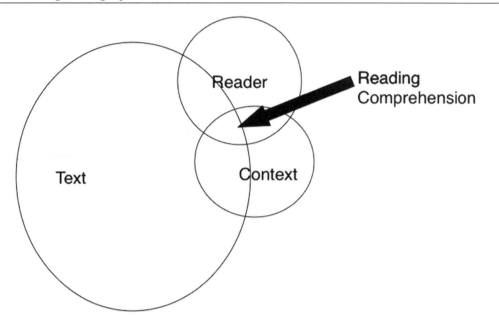

Figure 1.3. Reader-centric Models of Reading Comprehension of the 1970s:
   Meaning Is Largely in the Reader

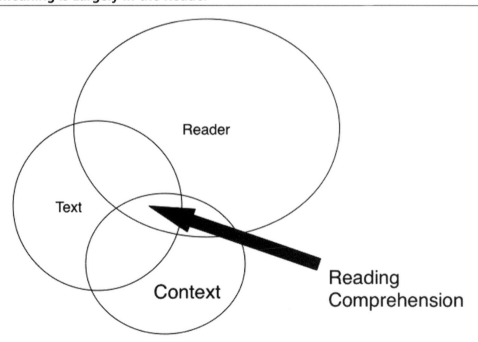

1984, for a contemporary review of this research), the work emphasized all of the intentionally activated strategies that readers use to monitor their comprehension ("Does my current model of what the text means make sense?") and repair breakdowns in comprehension ("How can I get my comprehension back on track?"). If schema theory evoked the metaphor of the reader as builder, then metacognitive work gave equal status to the reader as "fixer," who must always be willing to repair the fragile process of meaning-making when it goes wrong.

Movements in pedagogy paralleled these theoretical developments in psychology and literary theory. This was a period rampant in constructivist learning models (students must build knowledge for themselves) and equally constructivist pedagogies (teachers must avoid "telling" students what they need to know and instead arrange conditions and activities to allow students to discover through systematic inquiry what they need to know to complete an activity, performance, or project) (see Pearson & Johnson, 1978). Aesthetic reader response became the cornerstone of literary reading. Personal, aesthetic, expressive response prevailed over, or at the very least preceded, more efferent (work-like) forays into the comprehension of ideas and examinations of the author's craft. The question about text shifted from the New Criticism version of meaning: "What is the meaning of the text?" to the reader-response version: "How do readers make meaning from a text?" (Tompkins, 1980).

Instructional activities changed as well, moving away from a steady diet of literal, text-based questions toward an explicit process of relating the "new to the known" (Pearson & Johnson, 1978). Students were encouraged to integrate what they gained from reading into their existing knowledge structures in memory (i.e., schemata) (Anderson & Pearson, 1984). Teachers were encouraged to ask, "What do students already know, and how can I exploit that to help them access new ideas in the text that I would like them to learn?" Numerous instructional routines emerged that reflected the broad commitment to the centrality of reader knowledge. These included Ogle's (1986) K-W-L routine and Raphael's Question-Answer-Relationships (QARs) (Raphael & Pearson, 1985; Raphael & Wonnacott, 1985). These two popular examples typify the broad-based commitment to the centrality of reader knowledge in driving the comprehension process.

Other interventions hearkened back to earlier research on the role of text structure in shaping reading comprehension. They focused on teaching students to use their knowledge of text structure to understand, learn, and remember information, particularly from informational texts (see Pearson & Camparell, 1981, for a review from this early period). The most ambitious of these interventions (see Armbruster, Anderson, & Ostertag, 1987, and Bartlett, 1978) involved teaching students to think of text structures as architectural "frames" into which authors could position key content.

In a classic instructional study, Palincsar and Brown (1984) operationalized the advances in metacognitive approaches to reading comprehension in the pedagogical routine Reciprocal Teaching. The full title of that landmark study is "Reciprocal Teaching of Comprehension-fostering and Comprehension-monitoring Activities." This title is significant because it suggests that both awareness (the builder) and repair (the fixer) of sense-making can be achieved by intentionally applying strategies (summarizing, questioning, clarifying, and predicting). Reciprocal Teaching was originally validated with struggling readers, many of whom had learning disabilities, at the middle school level. Reciprocal Teaching has spread over the past 30 years to virtually every level of K–16 education and to a wide range of disciplinary settings (see Palincsar, 2007). In many ways, it touches on all the themes of this reader-based era. In addition, with its socially based, Vygotskian roots, Reciprocal Teaching anticipated the context-centric era that lay just ahead.

The Era of Context: 1985 and Beyond

To assign time frames to movements in reading comprehension, as we have done for the text- and reader-centric periods, necessarily oversimplifies both their origins and their legacies. Nowhere is that oversimplification more evident than with the models of comprehension that privilege context. Assigning them to the years 1985 and beyond obscures their much earlier roots. The sociocultural turn in literacy theory (Bloome & Green, 1984), and to a lesser degree in psychology (J. S. Brown, Collins, & Duguid, 1989; Cole, 1996), started to gather momentum in the 1970s, but it was not until the late 1980s and early 1990s that it became a dominant paradigm—and even then, this occurred only in the field of literacy. In terms of our dynamic visual model, the dominance of context and situation is represented by a large circle for "context" and small circles representing "reader" and "text" in Figure 1.4.

Theoretical roots of context-centric approaches. Within psychology, the situated cognition movement emerged from the work of J. S. Brown et al. (1989) and A. L. Brown and J. C. Campione (1994). These researchers argued that approaches to nurturing cognitive development were too abstract and divorced from the "authentic activity" that they were designed to facilitate. In their zeal to develop context-free, transferable concepts and skills, reading educators had inadvertently and inappropriately focused on the teaching and learning of explicit but abstract rules and conceptual features. What was needed, contextualists argued, was a "situated" view of cognition and epistemology. To help learners develop useful models of meaning for text or experience, teachers would need to design activities that situate students in the specific and authentic rather than the abstract. Situated perspectives ultimately sought generalizable knowledge and practices, but the underlying principle was that the best way to learn what is abstract, general, and context-free is for learners to behave as though all that matters is to understand phenomena as they exist within their natural settings, including in the text at hand. The irony of this perspective is that the particular is the surest path to the general.

Others (e.g., Harste, Woodward, & Burke, 1984) put forward more socially oriented critiques, championing constructs such as the social construction of meaning, which viewed cognition of all sorts as being distributed within a community rather than encapsulated within the individuals of a community.

This same period of time also witnessed the rediscovery of the Russian psychologist Vygotsky (1978) and Russian literary theorist Bakhtin (1975/1981). Following Vygotsky's lead, reading researchers fixed their attention on the social nature of learning and the key role that teachers and students' peers play in facilitating learning for an individual. Possibly the most influential learning construct in the 1980s was Vygotsky's "zone of proximal development," which represents the difference between the learning a child can accomplish on her own and what she can accomplish with the help of others (such as a teacher, mentor, parent, or knowledgeable peer).

Figure 1.4. Context-centric Models of Reading Comprehension from the 1980s and 1990s: Meaning Is Largely in the Context

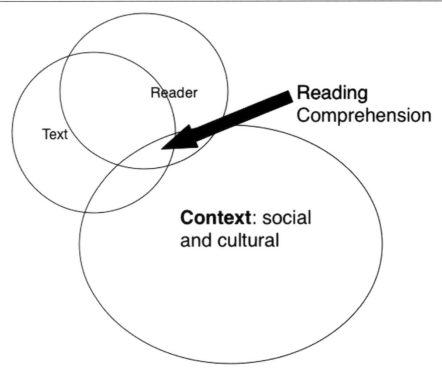

From Bakhtin's (1975/1981) dialogical perspective, scholars forged a new, intertextual view of reading comprehension and adopted the basic premise that readers understand each new "text"—written, oral, or experiential—in relation to *all* the previous "texts" that they, and the culture in which they construct meaning, have experienced. By the mid-1990s, these new constructs had shifted the attention of reading researchers from the reader and the text to the situational context and the interpretive community surrounding the act of reading.

Pedagogically, this new perspective suggested approaches favoring close analysis of the contextual (rather than the textual or reader) features that shape the ways in which teachers and students negotiate the meaning of text:

- The social construction of meaning, most likely in rich conversational settings around text (more likely, multiple texts) in which students interact freely and voluntarily
- Critical analysis of the devices (structures and tools) that authors use to shape the meaning they want readers to take away from a text
- Thorough examination of the subtexts that accompany text, including a close analysis of ideas and language that reveal which groups (along with their ideologies and voices) are either privileged or silenced by both the text and the surrounding conversation

Classroom applications of context-centric approaches. In the classroom, critical approaches have involved students in problematizing and interrogating (or, in everyday parlance, closely analyzing and questioning) texts and textbooks (Freebody & Luke, 1990; Lewison, Flint, & Van Sluys, 2002). Students are encouraged to ask questions about how the world is being portrayed in a text, whose voices and experiences are represented, and how these portrayals benefit particular groups in society (Lankshear, 1997). They might, for example, read for evidence of ethnocentric interpretations of history. They might also analyze how an author's decisions around language position readers to identify with particular characters or ideologies in literature. Students also develop counternarratives that include less dominant perspectives on issues and texts (Lewison et al., 2002). Questions for a discussion might include: Whose interests are served by this text? Whose interests and views are marginalized or absent? What ideological assumptions does the author make?

Although it extends beyond critical literacy, Freebody and Luke's widely used Four Resources Model was developed during this period when literacy theory and practice took a sociocultural turn (Freebody & Luke, 1990; Luke & Freebody, 1999). Freebody and Luke suggest that, depending on a wide range of contextual variables (e.g., pedagogical context, purpose, perceptions of consequences), readers engage with text by taking on four roles:

- *Code breaker*: cracks the code or cipher by working from the material form of the text, such as print-symbol-sound relations and punctuation, mapping spellings to sounds and vice versa, and associating a representation of the word form with its common meaning
- *Meaning-maker*: generates and integrates the communications of a text into a message, including the knowledge required to understand it
- *Text user*: focuses on the pragmatics of use—what function a text serves in the social contexts in which reading occurs
- *Text critic* (originally called "text analyst"): takes a critical stance, unpacking the social, economic, ideological, moral, emotional, and political assumptions behind a text and the consequences of using it

These roles hearken back to periods in our history that have emphasized particular resources in comprehension. Two of the roles, the code breaker and meaning-maker, remind us of the text-centric and reader-centric eras, respectively; the text user and text critic stances are solidly in the context-centric camp of critical literacy and other more socially driven models. The text critic role, in particular, acknowledges the social dimensions of comprehension by taking into account the fact that authors—text makers—operate from particular perspectives and that seeing those perspectives at work in texts is an important part of making and reworking meaning.

A MODERN ERA OF BALANCE: CONSTRUCTION-INTEGRATION MODELS

Even as more socioculturally oriented models were earning their theoretical and practical stripes in the world of reading theory and pedagogy, cognitive models from the 1970s that made reader and text variables more prominent did not disappear; to the contrary, these models underwent constant revision and refinement on another theoretical plane throughout the 1980s and 1990s. The newer models achieved a greater balance between reader and text variables than did earlier text- or reader-centric models. Thus, they avoided the critiques that had begun to be leveled at schema theory from both inside (McNamara, Miller, & Bransford, 1991) and outside (McVee, Dunsmore, & Gavalek, 2005) the field of cognitive psychology.

Over the past 3 decades, reading comprehension theory has been dominated by a quest to understand how readers construct multiple representations of what a text means (Graesser, Wiemer-Hastings, & Wiemer-Hastings, 2001). This quest has resulted in a number of cognitive models that make somewhat different claims about the construction of these representations and about the particulars of inference-generation in the process of construction. Despite differences in their details, these theoretical cognitive models are rather consistent in many respects (e.g., Goldman, Graesser, & van den Broek, 1999; Ruddell & Unrau, 2004). For this reason, in this chapter, we have adopted the language and constructs of Kintsch's (1998) Construction-Integration (C-I) model to illustrate the principles of these kinds of models in general. Because we will claim that the C-I model has become dominant in both cognitive psychology and applications to reading pedagogy, curriculum, and assessment, we will examine it in more detail than we have done for its ancestors.

The Nature of Reading in the C-I Model

In comparison with the text-, reader-, and context-centric models of earlier eras, the C-I model seems to us to be more balanced in terms of reader and text factors, with a lesser nod to contextual factors. The sizes of the circles in Figure 1.5 reflect this balance of attention to reader and text factors and the decreased dominance of context.

In this class of cognitive models, readers are viewed as actively seeking to create coherent mental representations of a text (Graesser, Singer, & Trabasso, 1994; van den Broek, 2010). As they create coherence, readers traverse three levels of text representation: (1) a *surface form*, (2) a *textbase*, and (3) a *situation model* (Kintsch, 1988, 1998).

The *surface form* captures the linguistic structure of the text, the actual words and phrases. It tends to be the result of accurate decoding, is short-lived in memory, and is not strongly related to comprehension per se, because it contains little semantic information.

The construction phase (the first of the two-phase model) is text-based and bottom-up. In this *textbase* phase, textual information activates the reader's background knowledge in an associative and relatively uncontrolled, almost automatic, manner (see also the memory-based model; Gerrig & O'Brien, 2005).

The initial activation is followed by the second phase—the integration phase— and is decidedly top-down; in this phase, activated knowledge and the information in the *textbase* are integrated into a coherent mental representation of the text. The product of this integration phase is the *situation model*. During integration, background knowledge supports connections between and to ideas from the text and provides the foundation for inferences. As readers proceed through a text, they generate many relevant and irrelevant inferences, but the semantic relations represented in the text constrain the process, activating only that knowledge needed to build a situation model and deactivate irrelevant inferences (Kintsch & Welch, 1991). That is, when text propositions and inferences align, they strengthen each other to build a coherent representation of the text. In this aspect of

Figure 1.5. Depiction of the Relative Salience of Reader, Text, and Context in Kintsch's Construction-Integration Model

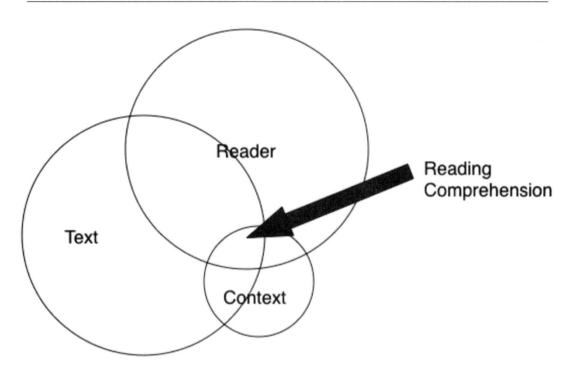

comprehension—the process of integrating prior knowledge and text—the C-I model departs from earlier schema theory views in which knowledge, or schemata, guide readers' interpretations of text and scaffold the assimilation of information from text into their working memory and ultimately into their long-term store of semantic memory. In the C-I model, schemata also help constrain the chaotic process of inference-generation that occurs during the construction phase of comprehension. This subtle but important distinction is what prevents C-I models from the criticism of runaway inference-generation leveled at schema theories in the 1990s (see, e.g., McNamara et al., 1991).

Much research has been dedicated to identifying the processes, strategies, skills, and background knowledge that readers must have to arrive at a coherent situation model of the text. One important insight is that, although much of the processing that results in text representations is automatic, readers can exert more conscious coordination and leverage strategic problem solving when comprehension breaks down. In those instances, readers may strategically search and reactivate information from the preceding text (from memory or by reinspecting the actual text), and/or they may strategically search for and activate background knowledge (van den Broek, 1990). Effective readers know when their efforts to comprehend require such strategic interventions and what appropriate corrective steps might be (Baker & Brown, 1984; Cote, Goldman, & Saul, 1998). However, individuals vary considerably in their control over the corrective steps needed to repair comprehension when it goes awry, and many readers need instruction to learn to use strategies effectively (Kintsch, 2004). Hundreds of correlational and intervention studies have demonstrated that students who are explicitly taught to use comprehension strategies can apply them to new texts, leading to improved comprehension (National Institute of Child Health and Human Development, 2000). The inclusion of more comprehension-strategy instruction in reading programs attests to the influence of the C-I model (Block & Pressley, 2002; Dole, Duffy, Roehler, & Pearson, 1991; Rapp, van den Broek, McMaster, Kendeou, & Espin, 2007).

Although the C-I model appears at first glance to focus mainly on the interaction between reader and text, implementation of the skills and processes required for the development of situation models is also influenced by the context—for example, the text genre, the discipline of the text (history vs. physics or literature), and the reader's goals (Kintsch, 1998). Some C-I models also include somewhat more explicit attention to context. For example, Graesser, Millis, and Zwaan (1997) add two levels of representation to Kintsch's model—(1) a text-genre level involving the nature of information and the way information is presented in accordance with different text genres, and (2) a pragmatic-communication level, which refers to the communicative context of the text and the intentions of its author. Texts that are written to convey information might prompt different reader stances from those written to amuse readers. Even so, in C-I models, compared with the role of context in sociocultural models, context plays a modest role.

The Impact of C-I Models on Policy and Practice

The C-I model, as Kintsch (1998) and others (e.g., Linderholm, Virtue, van den Broek & Tzeng, 2004; Perfetti, 1999) have explicated it, has become the dominant paradigm in explaining conceptualizations of both basic processes and pedagogical practices for reading comprehension. To test this claim, we examine three important policy contexts—(1) the RAND report produced in 2002 as a seminal account of our knowledge of reading comprehension, (2) the latest reading framework of the National Assessment of Educational Progress (NAEP; National Assessment Governing Board—NAGB, 2008), and (3) the model of comprehension underlying the Common Core State Standards for English Language Arts (CCSS ELA; NGA Center for Best Practices & CCSSO, 2010).

RAND Model

As Rumelhart (1977) and Lipson and Wixson (1986) did in their interactive models, the RAND (2002) panel defined reading comprehension as "the process of simultaneously extracting and constructing meaning through interaction and involvement with written language" (p. 11). The panel went on to suggest that comprehension entails three primary elements:

- The *reader* who is doing the comprehending
- The *text* that is being comprehended
- The *activity* in which comprehension is a part (p. 11)

The reader and text factors are very similar to those we have discussed in examining C-I models. Significantly, the RAND panel acknowledged that the interaction of the three primary elements occurs within a sociocultural context "that shapes and is shaped by the reader and that interacts with each of the three elements" (p. 11) (see Figure 1.6.). The RAND definition emphasizes the salience of both the text (extracting meaning) and the reader (constructing meaning) through interaction with written language (the activity). The position of the text in the RAND report is telling: "We use the words extracting and constructing to emphasize both the importance and the insufficiency of the text as a determinant of reading comprehension" (p. 11).

The factors of reader, text, and activity are familiar in the strong cognitive traditions of the 1970s and 1980s and in the current C-I models. However, attention to context in contemporary models provides some twists to our analysis of comprehension that show a strong trace of the sociocultural turn of the 1990s. In characterizing the RAND view of sociocultural context, Pearson, Valencia, and Wixson (2014) argue that context extends to physical location (school, work, or home), discipline (science, literature, or social studies), and purpose (reading to learn, to be entertained, or for insight, or reading for gist or details).

The NAEP Framework

The recent framework developed for the reading assessment of the *National Assessment of Educational Progress* (NAGB, 2008) puts forward three key cognitive targets that must be assessed: (1) *locate and recall*, (2) *integrate and interpret*, and (3) *critique and evaluate*. The types of activities assigned to the *locate and recall* category are decidedly text-based and correspond roughly to the sort of activities we identified as dominant in the text-centric period before the cognitive revolution. The *integrate and interpret* activities bear an uncanny resemblance to those we associated with the reader-centric models of the 1970s and 1980s and seem consistent with the practices in which readers engage in the creation of a situation model in the integration phase of C-I models. Not surprisingly, the NAEP tasks that earn the *critique and evaluate* label fall more naturally into the activities associated with critical literacy as it emerged in the 1990s, complemented by examinations of author's craft tasks that have always been associated with literary analyses of text. There is no exact counterpart for *critique and evaluate* in the C-I model; however, such activities seem to carry the sense of *using* or *applying* knowledge that is stored in memory, at least in part as a result of having placed new knowledge acquired from reading (and learning from) text into memory. And, of course, the metaphor of the reader as a *text user* or *text critic* is implicated strongly in almost all instantiations of critical literacy (e.g., Freebody & Luke, 1990), including the NAEP's target, *critique and evaluate*. In a sense, the NAEP framework, at least in its three cognitive targets, embodies the history of reading comprehension over the past half-century. That said, its links to the C-I models from the cognitive tradition are more transparent and stronger than its links to other models from other eras.

The Common Core State Standards for English Language Arts

A surface-level analysis of the reading standards in the CCSS ELA permits the conclusion that its anchor standards for reading are consistent, at least in broad strokes, with current C-I models of reading comprehension (note: we omitted Standard 10 on text complexity from the CCSS ELA to focus on comprehension). Broadly speaking, the CCSS' parsing of

Figure 1.6. The 2002 RAND Model of Reading Comprehension

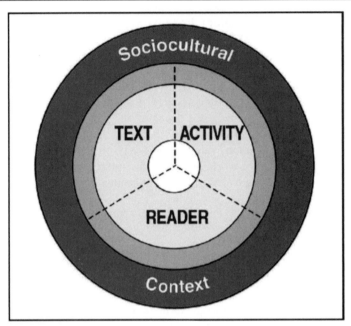

Note: In contrast to earlier diagrams, context is now in the surround and activity (the tasks in which we ask students to engage) has been added as a key variable at the core of comprehension.

the nine reading comprehension standards into three overarching categories (Key Ideas and Details, Craft and Structure, and Integration of Knowledge and Ideas) (see Table 1.1) roughly corresponds to the three NAEP categories, but the mapping is a little tricky.

Examination of the CCSS. The standards in the Key Ideas and Details category bear a close family resemblance to NAEP's first cognitive target: locate and recall. But the standards in the Craft and Structure category bear more resemblance to NAEP's third cognitive target (critique and evaluate) than they do to the second NAEP target (integrate and interpret). Conversely, the standards in the CCSS category Integration of Knowledge and Ideas are a better match for the second NAEP cognitive target (integrate and interpret). What students are asked to do in the Key Ideas and Details standards sounds very much like a C-I description of constructing a textbase. And most of the tasks outlined in the Craft and Structure and Integration of Knowledge and Ideas standards represent things readers would do either (1) in the integration phase of C-I (where readers create the situation model), or (2) using the knowledge, most likely gained as a result of creating the situation model, to apply to a new issue or problem. Pearson (2013) found that the mapping to the C-I model was distributed across the three CCSS categories in complicated ways. So, for example, Standards 1–3, 5, and 8 focus on a close reading of the content on the page—a text-based orientation. Standards 2, 7, and 9 foreground the integration of ideas (1) within and across texts and (2) with existing knowledge—classic situation model work. Still other standards focus more on analysis and interpretation (e.g., comparing the text at hand with prior texts in Standard 9, critiquing text-based arguments in

Table 1.1. College and Career Readiness Standards from the Common Core State Standards for English Language Arts

Cluster	Standard
Key Ideas and Details	1. Read closely to determine what the text says explicitly and to make logical inferences from it; cite specific textual evidence when writing or speaking to support conclusions drawn from the text.
	2. Determine central ideas or themes of a text and analyze their development; summarize the key supporting details and ideas.
	3. Analyze how and why individuals, events, and ideas develop and interact over the course of a text.
Craft and Structure	4. Interpret words and phrases as they are used in a text, including determining technical, connotative, and figurative meanings, and analyze how specific word choices shape meaning or tone.
	5. Analyze the structure of texts, including how specific sentences, paragraphs, and larger portions of the text (e.g., a section, chapter, scene, or stanza) relate to each other and the whole.
	6. Assess how point of view or purpose shapes the content and style of a text.
Integration of Knowledge and Ideas	7. Integrate and evaluate content presented in diverse media and formats, including visually and quantitatively, as well as in words.
	8. Delineate and evaluate the argument and specific claims in a text, including the validity of the reasoning as well as the relevance and sufficiency of the evidence.
	9. Analyze how two or more texts address similar themes or topics in order to build knowledge or to compare the approaches the authors take.

Standard 8, or inferring point of view in Standard 6); they have the look and feel of what NAEP would classify as examples of the *critique and evaluate* target and what Freebody and Luke (1990) call text user or text critic standards.

Another strong but often overlooked connection between C-I models and the CCSS is the centrality of knowledge acquisition. The whole point of the C-I model is to describe how readers transform the information represented by words on a page into a semantic code that allows it to be integrated into long-term semantic memory, where it will endure as knowledge that is available for all sorts of cognitive enterprises, including guiding future text-based construction and situation model integration efforts. In accounting for the role of knowledge in the standards, Cervetti and Hiebert (2015) note that the CCSS developers call for a curriculum that is "intentionally and coherently structured to develop rich content knowledge within and across grades" (NGA Center & CCSSO, 2010, p. 10), because a foundation of knowledge in core subjects makes students better readers and writers across content areas.

Entailments and interpretations of the CCSS. Clearly, we are convinced that many, and perhaps most, of the recent developments in reading policy and practice—most notably, the RAND report, NAEP framework, and the CCSS—have been heavily and positively influenced by the C-I model of reading comprehension. However, when one shifts attention away from the official CCSS to documents that have been developed to guide interpretation and implementation of the standards (e.g., S. Brown & Kappes, 2012; Coleman & Pimentel, 2012), the mapping is less transparent and more complex. The Publishers' Criteria (Coleman & Pimentel, 2012), in particular, a document written by the main CCSS-ELA authors to advise publishers on how to craft new materials to implement the standards, seem to have found a way to undermine the standards themselves. A review of these criteria, all of which point to construction of a text base, leaves one wondering what happened to the integration phase of the C-I model. For example, the criteria state that a significant percentage of the tasks and questions that students encounter should be text-dependent, meaning they "do not require information or evidence from outside the text or texts; they establish what follows and what does not follow from the text itself" (p. 6). Further, the criteria specify that publishers should "make the text the focus of instruction by avoiding features that distract from the text . . . [and] should be extremely sparing in offering activities that are not text based" (p. 10).

We find these developments in the implementation work of the CCSS quite discouraging: They represent an intellectual betrayal of the commitment the standards make to theory and research about the comprehension process—namely, the *balance* among tasks that promote the development of three related capacities:

- Constructing a solid text base
- Building a rich situation model that permits integration with knowledge and the building of new knowledge
- Using what you know to engage in a range of critical thinking and application tasks around text

We can only hope that voices championing the absolutely essential balance among construction, integration, and use (almost a "what the text says, means, and does" philosophy) will prevail in the process of implementing these standards. Whether they will remains to be seen.

SUMMARY, REPRISE, AND PROJECTIONS INTO THE NEAR FUTURE

To summarize this journey through the past half-century, we end with a bold claim—namely, that a conceptualization of reading exists that actually provides a kind of grand synthesis of the various historically important views of reading comprehension processes and practices that we have unpacked in this chapter. We think Freebody and Luke's Four Resources Model has the right balance of reader, text, task, and context to serve both as a summary of our journey and as a tool for crafting sensible, research-based curricula (see Underwood, Yoo, & Pearson, 2007).

The Importance of the Four Resources Model

In their model, Freebody and Luke (1990) assert that readers assume four very different roles or stances as they read—the code breaker, meaning-maker, text user, and text critic—and that each role emphasizes a particular resource—the reader, the text, the task environment, or the sociocultural context (hence, the label: Four Resources). Luke and Freebody (1999) analyze each of these resources (or roles, as they sometimes label them) as "descriptions of the normative goals of classroom literacy programs." In enacting these four roles, readers:

- *Break the code* of written texts by recognizing and using fundamental features and architecture, including alphabet, sounds in words, spelling, and structural conventions and patterns
- Participate in understanding and composing *meaningful* written, visual, and spoken texts, taking into account each text's interior meaning systems in relation to the reader's available knowledge and experience of other cultural discourses, texts, and meaning systems
- *Use texts* functionally by traversing and negotiating the labor and social relations around them—that is, by knowing about and acting on the different cultural and social functions that various texts perform inside and outside school and understanding that these functions shape the texts' structure, tone, degree of formality, and sequence of components
- *Critically* analyze and transform texts by acting on knowledge that texts are not ideologically neutral—that they represent particular points of views while silencing others and influence people's ideas—and that text designs and discourses can be critiqued and redesigned in novel and hybrid ways

The four resources provide a rough summary of the historic shifts in theoretical views of the reading process we have outlined in this chapter. Prior to the mid-1970s, the field of reading education was dominated by "perceptual" views of reading that emphasized the idea that reading comprehension is the product of decoding and listening comprehension. In this "simple view," reading is essentially a process of decoding print to speech and listening to the product to achieve understanding. This is the reader's role as *code breaker*.

The 1970s brought to center stage psycholinguistic and cognitive perspectives (see Anderson & Pearson, 1984; Pearson & Stephens, 1993) and, with them, the idea of the reader as *meaning-maker*. What mattered most was the reciprocal relationship between knowledge and comprehension. Readers use their knowledge in active ways to control the reading process, always seeking congruence between what they know and what passes before their "eyes" in reading. Knowledge is the cause and the consequence of comprehension.

The sociolinguistic perspectives of the 1980s and 1990s (see Heath, 1983; Wells, 1986) championed functional views of reading—how the social and cultural *contexts* in which the reading actually occurred shaped the sense of what was "appropriate." Thus, retelling a story to a friend who asks what a book is about requires a different "performance" from giving a formal "plot-theme-characters" retelling in a 9th-grade literature class. In the *text user* role, the reader literally has to learn to "read context" as well as reading text.

Although there have been critical perspectives that challenge the structuralist assumptions in "modern" views of epistemology and ontology for centuries, it was not until the 1990s that postmodern perspectives (Foucault, 1980; Giroux, 1991) assumed a dominant role in the discourse of reading education. By that time, the term *reading* had been nearly universally replaced by the broader and more contextualized term *literacy* (see Gee, 1987). A key understanding is that texts are inherently "interested"; that is, they are written by individuals (or groups) with intentions, conscious or unconscious, that are conveyed through text. Furthermore, it is "interested" individuals, who bring their own histories to the act of reading at many levels—idiosyncratic, social, and cultural. Hence, all acts of literacy—in addition to being verbal acts of communication—are social, political, or economic. In the role of *text critic*, the reader asks: In whose interests is this text written? Who are the champions? Who are the villains? Who is invisible?

We think the power of the Four Resources Model is in its implication that it is not only unnecessary, but also unwise, to make a choice among the resources that are available to readers as they try to make sense of text. Our view is that when readers approach a text, they bring all four stances, all four resources, to the task. And within a given text, there will be stretches where one reads as if code-breaking matters most, especially when the text is dense, the words unfamiliar, and the graphemic patterns obscure. In other stretches, readers will put most if not all of their cognitive energies into making connections with whatever knowledge bases they carry in their long-term memory. In those instances, understanding what's new in terms of what they already know—and then asking themselves what they learned to enhance their current knowledge base—will be what really matters. There will also be other stretches when readers emphasize the uses and functions of text to try to see how authors do their magic of persuading readers to take their messages seriously. In such cases, the reader emphasizes both function (What is the author trying to say?) and form (What tools of the craft is the author using to achieve her ends?). Finally, in other stretches, readers will focus almost entirely on critique, evaluation, and subtext, and will ask: What is the author's ulterior motive? What assumptions does she make? And how can the reader talk back to those assumptions? Each of the four resources is necessary, but not sufficient, to contend with the reading demands of schooling and citizenship.

All of these resources, along with the stances they bring with them, are part of what it means to be a complete reader. Until and unless educators realize this, they are likely to be doomed to a lifelong cycle of repeating each of these models in serial fashion. Each of the resources deserves pedagogical emphasis in classrooms, but ultimately they all need to be brought together for learners into a coordinated meaning-making process. What the literacy education profession should begin to do is to build pedagogy and curriculum that emphasizes flexible, nimble approaches to reading that encourage students to view texts from different stances, depending on their purposes and on how they read the opportunities and obstacles all around them.

Implications for Schools and Classrooms

Clearly, we are committed to the multiperspective view that comes with accepting the Four Resources Model. But the question for educators at the district, school, and classroom level is whether acceptance of a model like this will affect and, we hope, improve the ways in which they facilitate and teach comprehension. We think it will; in fact, we would not have written this chapter if we didn't think so. The question is, how?

First and foremost, reading comprehension instruction, when implemented with the Four Resources Model as the driving force, demands that students use all of the available resources to make sense of text and learn to take more than one stance toward text, if not in a single lesson then definitely across lessons. There is no one right way to understand either a single text or text in general; all of the stances in the Four Resources Model have a place in making meaning during reading and, therefore, in the curriculum designed to help students make sense of texts. Which stance a teacher emphasizes on a particular day or in a given moment will depend on the teacher's purpose for the students in the precise situation.

The Four Resources Model suggests that there is more than one stance from which to make sense of a text. If this is true, then it follows that for any given question, task, or practice, there is always more than one *right* answer, or at least more than one *plausible* answer. Interestingly, this implication that questions always have more than one right answer can be derived as easily from a perspective that suggests that text-based, reader-based, and context-based conceptualizations of comprehension all have something to offer the classroom teacher in terms of helping students negotiate the meaning of texts they encounter. Thus, classroom discussions of text must be open to multiple interpretations of a text—and even multiple interpretations of a question asked about a character's motives or the real purpose behind an author's point of view. Another implication is that when teachers are reading students' assignments, they need to look not for the one answer they think is correct or best for a given question but for the quality of the reasoning students provide when they explain their answers. A marginal answer with a great line of reasoning behind it might (and we think should) deserve a higher score than a technically correct answer with no rationale for why it is a good answer. (We acknowledge, of course, that a highly plausible response that also has a great line of reasoning would be even better!) In terms of the CCSS-ELA, a focus on quality of reasoning is desirable precisely because quality of reasoning that links a student's claim to evidence is more important than just giving the right answer. And this isn't just a criterion for middle and high school students; it applies equally to conversations and assignments in kindergarten or 1st grade.

Earlier, we discussed the high likelihood that implementation efforts for the CCSS had actually betrayed the intent of the standards themselves, particularly when it comes to understanding the role that prior knowledge plays when students build models of meaning for texts or deciding what counts as close reading of a text. That likelihood bears grave consequences for instruction around text, particularly instruction designed to ensure that kids get a real chance to explore the text as

- a resource for enhancing one's knowledge,
- a source of evidence for supporting opinions about a character's motives or claims about how a scientific process works, and
- an opportunity to evaluate how an author is manipulating language and perspective to persuade readers to accept her point of view on an environmental issue.

One final point: If we as a profession accept the Four Resources Model—and along with it, a commitment to examine reading from the perspectives of the text, reader, *and* context—then we must find a way to engage *all* readers, not just our most able readers, in traversing *all* four of the resources every day and every week. We must avoid the trap of assuming that there is a hierarchy or an order of acquisition to the resources—that students must first master the code breaker stance before they get opportunities to engage text as a meaning-maker, a text user, or a text critic. It would be easy, and even appealing, to assume that each resource was logically a prerequisite to its successor. If we fell into that trap, we would end up implementing a kind of basic skills conspiracy of good intentions. The conspiracy goes like this: First, you have to get the *words right* and the *facts straight* before you can do the *what if's*, *I wonder what's*, and the *says who's* of text understanding. The problem with the basic skills conspiracy is that students on the low end of the performance continuum will end up spending most of their school careers getting the *words right* and the *facts straight*—and they'll never get to the *what if's*, *I wonder what's*, and the *says who's*. Putting an end to this inequitable conspiracy would be an important step toward bringing opportunities for richer engagement with text to all students.

NOTE

1. We use the term *model* as a metaphor for a general framework for organizing and describing factors that influence the phenomenon under examination—in this case, reading comprehension. For a more refined treatment of models of reading, see Chapter 3 by Michael L. Kamil in this volume.

REFERENCES

Anderson, R. C., & Pearson, P. D. (1984). A schema-theoretic view of basic processes in reading comprehension. In P. D. Pearson, R. Barr, M. L. Kamil, & P. Mosenthal (Eds.), *Handbook of reading research* (pp. 255–291). New York, NY: Longman.

Armbruster, B. B., Anderson, T. H., & Ostertag, J. (1987). Does text structure/summarization instruction facilitate learning from expository text? *Reading Research Quarterly, 22,* 331–346.

Baker, L., & Brown, A. L. (1984). Metacognitive skills and reading. In P. D. Pearson, R. Barr, M. L. Kamil, & P. Mosenthal (Eds.), *Handbook of reading research* (pp. 353–394). New York, NY: Longman.

Bakhtin, M. (1981). *The dialogic imagination: Four essays* (Trans. M. Holquist & C. Emerson). Austin, TX: University of Texas Press. (Original work published 1975)

Bartlett, B. J. (1978). *Top-level structure as an organizational strategy for recall of classroom text.* (Unpublished doctoral dissertation). Arizona State University, Tempe, AZ.

Block, C., & Pressley, M. (Eds.). (2002). *Comprehension instruction: Research-based best practices.* New York, NY: Guilford Press.

Bloome, D., & Green, J. (1984). Directions in the sociolinguistic study of reading. In P. D. Pearson, R. Barr, M. L. Kamil, & P. Mosenthal (Eds.), *Handbook of reading research* (pp. 395–452). White Plains, NY: Longman.

Brooks, C., & Warren, R. (1960). *Understanding poetry* (3rd ed.). New York, NY: Holt, Rinehart, & Winston. (Original work published 1938)

Brown, A. L., & Campione, J. C. (1994). Guided discovery in a community of learners. In K. McGilly (Ed.), *Classroom lessons: Integrating cognitive theory and classroom practice* (pp. 229–270). Cambridge, MA: MIT Press.

Brown, J. S., Collins, A., & Duguid, P. (1989). Situated cognition and the culture of learning. *Educational Researcher, 18*(1), 32–42.

Brown, S., & Kappes, L. (2012). *Implementing the Common Core State Standards: A primer on "close reading of text."* Washington, DC: The Aspen Institute.

Catterson, A. K., & Pearson, P. D. (in preparation). Close reading: Historical antecedents and current consequences.

Cervetti, G. N., & Hiebert, E. H. (2015). Knowledge, literacy, and the Common Core. *Language Arts, 92*(4), 256–269.

Cole, M. (1996). *Cultural psychology: A once and future discipline.* Cambridge, MA: Harvard University Press.

Coleman, D., & Pimentel, S. (2012). *Revised publishers' criteria for the Common Core State Standards in English language arts and literacy, grades 3–12.* Washington, DC: National Governors Association Center for Best Practices & The Council of Chief State School Officers. Available at www.corestandards.org/assets/Publishers_Criteria_for_3-12.pdf

Cote, N., Goldman, S. R., & Saul, F. U. (1998). Students making sense of informational text: Relations between processing and representation. *Discourse Processes, 25,* 1–53.

Dole, J., Duffy, G. G., Roehler, L. R., & Pearson, P. D. (1991). Moving from the old to the new: Research on reading comprehension instruction. *Review of Educational Research, 61,* 239–264.

Foucault, M. (1980). *Power/knowledge: Selected interviews and other writings, 1972–1977.* London, UK: Harvester Press.

Freebody, P., & Luke, A. (1990). Literacies programs: Debates and demands in cultural context. *Prospect: Australian Journal of TESOL, 5*(7), 7–16.

Gardner, H. (1985). *The mind's new science: A history of the cognitive revolution.* New York, NY: Basic Books.

Gee, J. P. (1987). What is literacy? *Teaching and Learning, 2,* 3–11.

Gerrig, R. J., & O'Brien, E. J. (2005). The scope of memory-based processing. *Discourse Processes, 39,* 225–242.

Giroux, H. A. (1991). *Postmodernism, feminism, and cultural politics: Redrawing educational boundaries.* Albany, NY: State University of New York Press.

Goldman, S. R., Graesser, A. C., & van den Broek, P. (1999). Essays in honor of Tom Trabasso. In S. R. Goldman, A. C. Graesser, & P. van den Broek (Eds.), *Narrative comprehension, causality, and coherence* (pp. 1–10). Mahwah, NJ: Erlbaum.

Gough, P. B., & Hillinger, M. L. (1980). Learning to read: An unnatural act. *Bulletin of the Orton Society, 30,* 179–196.

Graesser, A. C., Millis, K. K., & Zwaan, R. A. (1997). Discourse comprehension. *Annual Review of Psychology, 48,* 163–189.

Graesser, A. C., Singer, M., & Trabasso, T. (1994). Constructing inferences during narrative text comprehension. *Psychological Review, 101,* 371–395.

Graesser, A. C., Wiemer-Hastings, P., & Wiemer-Hastings, K. (2001). Constructing inferences and relations during text comprehension. In T. Sanders, J. Schilperoord, & W. Spooren (Eds.), *Text representation: Linguistic and psycholinguistic aspects* (pp. 249–271). Amsterdam, The Netherlands: Benjamins.

Harste, J. C., Woodward, V. A., & Burke, C. L. (1984). *Language stories and literacy lessons.* Portsmouth, NH: Heinemann.

Heath, S. B. (1983). *Ways with words: Language, life, and work in communities and classrooms.* New York, NY: Cambridge University Press.

Huey, E. B. (1908). *The psychology and pedagogy of reading.* New York, NY: Macmillan.

Kintsch, W. (1974). *The representation of meaning in memory.* Hillsdale, NJ: Erlbaum.

Kintsch, W. (1988). The use of knowledge in discourse processing: A construction-integration model. *Psychological Review, 95,* 163–182.

Kintsch, W. (1998). *Comprehension: A paradigm for cognition.* Cambridge, UK: Cambridge University Press.

Kintsch, W. (2004). The construction-integration model of text comprehension and its implications for instruction. In R. B. Ruddell & N. J. Unrau (Eds.), *Theoretical models and processes of reading* (5th ed., pp. 1270–1328). Newark, DE: International Reading Association.

Kintsch, W., & Welch, D. M. (1991). The construction-integration model: A framework for studying memory for text. In W. E. Hockley & S. Lewandowsky (Eds.), *Relating theory and data: Essays on human memory* (pp. 367–385). Hillsdale, NJ: Erlbaum.

Kolers, P. A. (1969). Reading is only incidentally visual. In K. Goodman & J. Flemming (Eds.), *Psycholinguistics and the teaching of reading* (pp. 8–16). Newark, DE: International Reading Association.

Lankshear, C. (1997). *Changing literacies.* Philadelphia, PA: Open University Press.

Lewison, M., Flint, A. S., & Van Sluys, K. (2002). Taking on critical literacy: The journey of newcomers and novices. *Language Arts, 79*(5), 383–392.

Linderholm, T., Virtue, S., van den Broek, P., & Tzeng, Y. (2004). Fluctuations in the availability of information during reading: Capturing cognitive processes using the landscape model. *Discourse Processes, 37,* 165–186.

Lipson, M. Y., & Wixson, K. K. (1986). Reading disability research: An interactionist perspective. *Review of Educational Research, 56,* 111–136.

Lockhart, T. (2012). Teaching with style: Brooks and Warren's literary pedagogy. In M. B. Hickman & J. D. McIntyre (Eds.), *Rereading the New Criticism* (pp. 195–218). Columbus, OH: Ohio State University Press.

Luke, A., & Freebody, P. (1999). Further notes on the four resources model. *Reading Online.* Available at http:www.readingonline.org/research/lukefreebody.html

Mandler, J. M., & Johnson, N. S. (1977). Remembrance of things parsed: Story structure and recall. *Cognitive Psychology, 9,* 111–151.

McNamara, T. P., Miller, D. L., & Bransford, J. D. (1991). Mental models and reading comprehension. In R. Barr, M. L. Kamil, P. B. Mosenthal, & P. D. Pearson (Eds.), *Handbook of reading research* (Vol. 2, pp. 490–511). New York, NY: Longman.

McVee, M., Dunsmore, K., & Gavalek, J. (2005). Schema theory revisited. *Review of Educational Research, 75*(4), 531–566.

Meyer, B. J. F. (1975). *The organization of prose and its effects on memory.* Amsterdam, The Netherlands: North Holland Publishing.

National Assessment Governing Board (NAGB). (2008). *Reading framework for the 2009 National Assessment of Educational Progress.* Washington, DC: National Assessment Governing Board, U.S. Department of Education.

National Governors Association Center for Best Practices & Council of Chief State School Officers. (2010). *Common Core State Standards for English language arts and literacy in history/ social studies, science, and technical subjects.* Washington, DC: Authors. Available at www. corestandards.org/assets/CCSSI_ELA%20Standards.pdf

National Institute of Child Health and Human Development (NICHD). (2000). Report of the National Reading Panel. *Teaching children to read: An evidence-based assessment of the scientific research literature on reading and its implications for reading instruction* (NIH Publication No. 00-4769). Washington, DC: U.S. Government Printing Office.

Ogle, D. (1986). K-W-L: A teaching model that develops active reading of expository text. *The Reading Teacher, 39*, 564–570.

Palincsar, A. S. (2007). The role of research, theory, and representation in the transformation of instructional research. *National Reading Conference Yearbook*, vol. 67, 41–52.

Palincsar, A. S., & Brown, A. L. (1984). Reciprocal teaching of comprehension-fostering and comprehension-monitoring activities. *Cognition and Instruction, 1*(2), 117–175.

Pearson, P. D. (1992). Reading. In M. C. Alkin (Ed.), *Encyclopedia of educational research* (6th ed., Vol. 3, pp. 1075–1085). New York, NY: Macmillan.

Pearson, P. D. (2013). Research foundations of the Common Core State Standards in English language arts. In S. Newman & L. Gambrell (Eds.), *Quality reading instruction in the age of Common Core State Standards* (pp. 237–262). Newark, DE: International Reading Association.

Pearson, P. D., & Camparell, K. (1981). Comprehension of text structures. In J. Guthrie (Ed.), *Comprehension and teaching* (pp. 27–54). Newark, DE: International Reading Association.

Pearson, P. D., & Johnson, D. D. (1978). *Teaching reading comprehension*. New York, NY: Holt, Rinehart & Winston.

Pearson, P. D., & Stephens, D. (1993). Learning about literacy: A 30-year journey. In C. J. Gordon, G. D. Labercane, & W. R. McEachern (Eds.), *Elementary reading: Process & practice* (pp. 4–18). Boston, MA: Ginn Press.

Pearson, P. D., Valencia, S., & Wixson, K. (2014). Complicating the world of reading assessment: Toward better assessments for better teaching. *Theory into Practice, 53*, 236–246.

Perfetti, C. A. (1999). Comprehending written language: A blueprint of the reader. In C. Brown & P. Hagoort (Eds.), *The neurocognition of language* (pp. 167–208). New York, NY: Oxford University Press.

RAND Reading Study Group. (2002). *Reading for understanding: Toward an R&D program in reading comprehension*. Santa Monica, CA: RAND.

Ransom, J. C. (1937). Criticism, Inc. *Virginia Quarterly Review, 13*(4). Available at www.vqronline.org/essay/criticism-inc-0

Raphael, T. E., & Pearson, P. D. (1985). Increasing students' awareness of sources of information for answering questions. *American Educational Research Journal, 22*, 217–236.

Raphael, T. E., & Wonnacott, C. A. (1985). Heightening fourth-grade students' sensitivity to sources of information for answering comprehension questions. *Reading Research Quarterly, 20*(3), 282–296.

Rapp, D. N., van den Broek, P., McMaster, K. L., Kendeou, P., & Espin, C. A. (2007). Higher-order comprehension processes in struggling readers: A perspective for research and intervention. *Scientific Studies of Reading, 11*, 289–312.

Richards, I. A. (1929). *Practical criticism*. New York, NY: Harcourt, Brace & Company.

Rosenblatt, L. M. (1938). *Literature as exploration*. New York, NY: Appleton-Century, Inc.

Rosenblatt, L. M. (1968). *Literature as exploration* (2nd ed.). New York, NY: Noble & Noble.

Ruddell, R. B., & Unrau, N. J. (Eds.). (2004). *Theoretical models and processes of reading* (5th ed.). Newark, DE: International Reading Association.

Rumelhart, D. E. (1977). Toward an interactive model of reading. In S. Dornic (Ed.), *Attention and performance VI* (pp. 573–603). Hillsdale, NJ: Erlbaum.

Skinner, B. F. (1957). *Verbal behavior*. New York, NY: Appleton-Century-Crofts.

Stein, N. L., & Glenn, C. G. (1979). An analysis of story comprehension in elementary school children. In R. Freedle (Ed.), *New directions in discourse processing* (Vol. 2, pp. 53–120). Norwood, NJ: Ablex.

Thorndike, E. (1910). The contribution of psychology to education. *Journal of Educational Psychology, 1*(1), 8.

Tierney, R. J., & Pearson, P. D. (1983). Toward a composing model of reading. *Language Arts, 60,* 568–580.

Tompkins, J. P. (1980). *Reader-response criticism: From formalism to post-structuralism.* Baltimore, MD: Johns Hopkins University Press.

Underwood, T., Yoo, M. S., & Pearson, P. D. (2007). Understanding reading comprehension in secondary schools through the lens of the four resources model. In L. S. Rush, A. J. Eakle, & A. Berger (Eds.), *Secondary school literacy: What research reveals for classroom practice* (pp. 90–116). Urbana IL: National Council of Teachers of English.

van den Broek, P. (2010). Using texts in science education: Cognitive processes and knowledge representation. *Science, 328,* 453–456.

van den Broek, P. W. (1990). The causal inference maker: Towards a process model of inference generation in text comprehension. In D. A. Balota, G. B. Flores d'Arcais, & K. Rayner (Eds.), *Comprehension processes in reading* (pp. 423–446). Hillsdale, NJ: Lawrence Erlbaum Associates.

Vygotsky, L. S. (1978). *Mind in society.* Cambridge, MA: Harvard University Press.

Watson, J. B. (1913). Psychology as the behaviorist views it. *Psychological Review, 20,* 158–177.

Wells, C. G. (1986). *The meaning makers: Children learning language and using language to learn.* Portsmouth, NH: Heinemann.

Young, T. D. (1976). *The New criticism and after.* Charlottesville, VA: University of Virginia Press.

CHAPTER 2

The Use of Research in Federal Literacy Policies

Barbara Kapinus and Richard Long

This chapter identifies the scope of federal educational policy and practices related to literacy from 1965 to the present. At the beginning of this period, the federal government provided resources to schools to compensate for an inadequate tax base, leaving states a great deal of discretion in how to allocate those funds. Individuals in government recognized that students needed improved reading opportunities if they were to escape the cycle of poverty in their communities—and reading opportunities required resources. Fifty years later, there is a far different federal role as the federal Congress and executive branch directs many state-level policies and practices that impact classrooms across the nation. For example, federal funding or the withholding of funds is used to compel states to adopt and enforce more complex standards, processes for the evaluation of teachers and principals based on student assessments, and use of data to make key decisions.

Our focus in this chapter is on federal policies that have to do with reading and literacy. As will become evident as we progress through our review of the federal government's evolving role during this 50-year period, many acts of Congress related to literacy have claimed underpinnings in the research of the literacy community, such as the scholars whose work fills this volume for example. However, what research is selected and how it is interpreted can take unique forms in the arena of federal policy (see also Goodman, Calfee, & Goodman, 2013).

THE RELATIONSHIP BETWEEN POLICY AND RESEARCH

Policymakers deal with what can be described as the art of the possible and practical, whereas academic researchers deal with explanations and connections that require re-examination and cautions about conclusions. The difference in perspective between policymakers and researchers is evident in an anecdote from Roller and Long (2001). One of the authors put a senior administration official in touch with a literacy researcher to provide an answer to a pressing policy question related to the proverbial phonics questions (how much, what kind?). At the end of a 20-minute phone call between the official and the literacy expert, the official said, "I really hate myself. That guy has spent his whole life studying and understanding this complex issue. He was very nicely willing to share the nuances and to help me craft an insightful decision. Unfortunately, I just needed to know yes or no" (p. 708). This anecdote highlights the stance of policymakers: Through politics, ideas and perspectives about education and instruction are translated into decisions about the use of resources, procedures for resource distribution, and measurement of the outcomes. Thus, when policymakers are working on federal and even state policies, the decisionmaking rule is simple: It is yes or no.

Frequently, policymakers recognize a need (often based on the work of journalists, economists, and/or public complaints) and seek a solution before education researchers have gathered solid evidence on how the need might be successfully addressed. This is evident in policies regarding high-stakes testing and teacher accountability that have—in our opinion as well as those of longtime experts in testing (Baker, Barton, Darling-Hammond, Haertel, Ladd, Linn, Shavelson, & Shepard, 2010)—been put into place without research evidence to support them.

REVIEW OF HISTORIC FEDERAL LEGISLATION SUPPORTING READING EDUCATION

The past 50 years have seen policymakers becoming increasingly involved in shaping instructional practice. A timeline of critical federal activities related to reading education appears in Figure 2.1. In the sections that follow, we describe some of these activities, especially those that set the stage for the implementation of the Common Core State Standards (CCSS; National Governors Association [NGA] Center for Best Practices & Council of Chief State School Officers [CCSSO], 2010).

Elementary and Secondary Education Act

The signing of the Elementary and Secondary Education Act (ESEA) in 1965 helped shape the federal role in creating national policy about the basic education of children in high-poverty settings and/or with home languages other than English. At the time the ESEA was passed, legislators and government officials were focused on whether inputs and outputs were equal for all students. The federal government was not collecting data on or evaluating what was actually happening to students in schools. Instruction was considered the realm of states and local educational agencies. Living in a home with incomes below the poverty threshold and/or where the dominant language was one other than English was viewed as a potential challenge to students' acquisition of a basic education. The evidence used to structure ESEA was simply that students in certain schools seemed to lack access to basic education. In most states, school funding was tied to state and local taxes. Schools in poverty-impacted communities had fewer resources than schools in wealthier communities. Policymakers at the federal level believed that providing funds for additional resources in these lower-income communities would solve the problem of lower achievement. Figuring out how to provide the instruction that would lead to improvement was left to local schools and states. When discussing the structure of the first ESEA, Wayne Morse, a U.S. senator from Oregon who has been a Republican, Independent, and Democrat during his 30 years in the Senate, stated, "We thought that all schools needed was money, that they knew what was needed to help high need students" (Cross, 2010, p. 21).

Figure 2.1. A Timeline of Critical Federal Activities Related to Reading Education

Selected Activities	Year
Elementary and Secondary Education Act (ESEA)	1965
National Assessment of Education Progress (federal funds)	1968
Education for All Handicapped Children Act (EHA)	1975
Nation at Risk	1983
Charlottesville Summit	1989
Comprehensive School Reform	1998
Reading Excellence Act	1998
National Reading Panel	1999
No Child Left Behind (ESEA Reauthorization)	2002
Reading First	2002
Individuals with Disabilities Education Act (EHA reauthorization)	2004
Race to the Top (stimulus act)	2009
Promised Neighborhood Act	2010

The basic concept of the original ESEA program was that compensatory programs could provide resources to fill the needs or gaps in certain schools that lacked books, staff, and curriculum resources they needed to give all their students access to a solid, basic education. There was little direct evidence that this was the correct intervention strategy or that it would even work.

Indeed, by the later part of the 1960s and early 1970s scholars and analysts who were studying evidence from ESEA came to believe that the approach was inappropriate or, at the very least, inadequate (Jencks, 1974). However, with minor changes, the idea of compensatory education, with its remedial thinking, remained the central focus of the ESEA for almost 40 years as Congress renewed the act six times. But when the act appeared before Congress for the seventh time in 2001, the focus of the act was changed and given a new name, the No Child Left Behind Act (NCLB).

REA and CSRD

Not everything was static in the period between the initial passage of ESEA and the enactment of NCLB in 2002. Change had been encouraged by the landmark report *A Nation At Risk* (Gardner, 1983). This report, commissioned by the U.S. Secretary of Education, concluded that the nation's very well-being was linked to the quality of its schools, not simply equal access to resources. The national discussion of education policy focused on the idea that providing access alone (equity) was no longer the sole feature for successful federal programming; rather, quality needed to be included in program provisions, along with access and quality.

As the undersecretary and acting deputy secretary of the U.S. Office of Education from 1993 through 2000, Marshall Smith was instrumental in crafting and supporting the passage of two acts that would provide a foundation for the NCLB legislation. Smith and his associates called for an examination of the contents of Title I, a section of ESEA, and its alignment with critical research findings (Marshall Smith, personal interview, 2009, as reported in Long & Selden, 2011). Reports commissioned by the U.S. Office of Education (e.g., Rotberg, 1993) brought expert recommendations from policy analysts and researchers. These recommendations were later used in the rationale for the Reading Excellence Act (REA) that was passed in 1998 through a major lobbying effort by Reid Lyon at the National Institute of Child Health and Human Development. This law required schools to use scientifically research-based reading, which culminated in the appropriation of the term *scientifically based reading research* (REA, 1998). The notion of scientifically based reading research would become even more central in the Reading First component of the NCLB legislation. Over time, the construct of scientifically based reading research would be extended and clarified in the concept of evidence-based education (Whitehurst, 2002). These developments introduced a new criterion for the use of federal funding through Title I of ESEA; instructional practices selected for use in federally funded programs had to be based on empirically validated research.

An additional legislative act passed in 1998, the Comprehensive School Reform Demonstration (CSRD) Act, was similar to the REA. It helped lay the foundation for the policies of NCLB. According to the CSRD, a school district's allocation of ESEA funds would no longer be based simply on its demographics and the submission of a plan. The CSRD stipulated how schools could spend funds, and it also required districts submit plans to the U.S. Department of Education for the use of the federal funds to support both instruction and professional development. Moreover, these proposal efforts needed to be based on evidence—that is, research involving experimental or quasi-experimental design.

No Child Left Behind (NCLB)

In 2002, NCLB built on the ideas that underlay the REA and CSRD. First was the idea of scientifically based reading research of REA, which would be represented prominently in the Reading First portion of NCLB (see McCardle & Chhabra, 2004; Whitehurst, 2002). The second idea was the CSRD notion that schools should be held accountable for the progress of groups of high-need students, not just the "average" progress of students in a school. This meant giving increased attention to assessments and analyses of student outcomes on these assessments, especially for economic and cultural subgroups.

With the NCLB legislation, the federal government put in place two tools to ensure that particular types of changes were occurring in schools receiving federal funding. Based on views held by the senior democratic and republican education committee leaders that previously legislated programs had led to insufficient improvement in reading and mathematics, NCLB had a detailed and extensive accountability mechanism. Recipients of NCLB funds would not be responsible for monitoring their own progress. Instead, the act required states and districts receiving Title I funds to meet particular adequate yearly progress (AYP) goals for their total student populations and for specified demographic subgroups, including major ethnic/racial groups, economically disadvantaged students, limited English proficient (LEP) students, and students with disabilities. Schools that failed to meet AYP goals for 2 or more years would be classified as "in need of improvement" and would face steadily escalating consequences. These consequences included school transfer options: Parents of students in a school could choose to transfer a child to another school, one that was not identified as being in need of improvement. After 3 or more years of failing to meet AYP, supplemental services (tutoring or other extra education services that provide academic aid to students) would be provided. After 4 consecutive years of failing to meet AYP, corrective actions, such as replacing school staff, implementing new curriculum, or extending the school year or school day, would be put in place. After 5 consecutive years of failure to meet AYP, a school needed to be restructured with alternative plans; some of these plans include the reopening of a school as a public charter school or replacing all or most of the school's staff, including the principal. Federal funding for states, districts, and schools was contingent upon an agreement between the federal government and the states to accept the legislative requirements. All of these directives marked a major shift in the role of the federal government and the U.S. Department of Education in the conduct of schooling at the state and local levels.

It is notable that there was more focus on research-based evidence in the Reading First portion of NCLB than in the other parts of that legislation, such as testing and adequate yearly progress. The guidelines for Reading First required states (and their districts) to adopt an entire process for reading education based on the interpretation of research by a particular group of researchers and educators. This group, known as the National Reading Panel (NRP), reviewed a large body of research on learning to read and distilled it into five essential elements of reading that schools and classroom should address: (1) phonics, (2) phonemic awareness, (3) vocabulary, (4) fluency, and (5) comprehension. This work appeared as the *Report of the National Reading Panel Teaching Children to Read* (National Institute of Child Health and Human Development, 2000).

The NRP's findings were strongly questioned when they were first published (Calfee, 2014; Pressley, 2005; Pearson, 2004). But at the time of the release of the NRP's report, officials within the Reading First management and subsequently leaders and policymakers in states, districts, and schools, mandated compliance with the five elements or, as they came to be called, the five pillars required for success in learning to read. There are indications that U.S. Department of Education officials and some experts reviewing state applications for Reading First pressured states and districts to adopt specific programs, curriculum materials, and assessment tools, contrary to the legislation's directives that prohibited the U.S. Department of Education from making curriculum decisions (Manzo, September 7, 2005, November 9, 2005). In September 2006, an internal review by the Department of Education's Office of Inspector General (OIG) found that the Reading First program exhibited conflicts of interest. Some of the consultants hired by the Department of Education to train teachers and state department of education personnel were also coauthors of certain reading programs. After publishing a series of seven reports on the mismanagement of Reading First—and referring the matter to the Justice Department—the OIG requested the U.S. Congress to clarify what was meant by "scientifically based" and whether it was enough for a program to contain elements that have been researched or if a program itself had to have been researched.

The Common Core State Standards

Since 2010, another development within the policy arena has added to how decisions on curriculum and instruction are made and who makes them: the creation of the CCSS, which were adopted by 45 states, the District of Columbia, the Department of Defense Education Activity, and 3 U.S. territories by December 2013 (NGA Center for Best Practices & CCSSO, 2010). As of the writing of this chapter (June 2014), a number of states have either reversed their adoption of the CCSS and/or dropped out of the CCSS-aligned assessment consortia (Partnership for Assessment of Readiness for College and Careers [PARCC] and Smarter Balanced Assessment Consortium [SBAC]), declaring their intention to create their own standards and assessments. The motivation for this shift appears to be concerns about retaining educational control by stakeholders within individual states (Gewertz, 2014; Ujifusa, 2014). The guidelines found in the CCSS are more inclusive than the NRP or NCLB when it comes to what evidence is considered critical for defining and achieving successful reading competency.

Background for the Standards. The impetus for the CCSS can be traced to the initiation of state-by-state comparisons on the National Assessment of Educational Progress (NAEP), which began in 1992 measuring the number of students reading on grade level. State-by-state comparisons made it possible to see how a representative sample of students in a particular state performed relative to students in other states. When the majority of students in some states were found to be proficient in reading according to their state assessments but many of those same students failed to attain proficient status on the NAEP, educational scholars and analysts began to question the standards individual states were using to assess their students. The National Center for Education Statistics (NCES) conducted an analysis of proficiency standards in states and on the NAEP (Bandeira de Mello, Blankenship, McLaughlin, & Rahman, 2009). Bandeira de Mello et al. reported that 31 states set standards for proficiency in grade 4 reading that were lower than the cut point for the basic performance level on the NAEP. For grade 8 reading, 15 states set lower standards of proficiency than the basic performance level on the NAEP.

The federally mandated assessment, NAEP, may have been an impetus, but the work of creating a common set of standards emanated from state policymakers—both governors and chief state school officers. Variable standards became a topic of conversation at meetings of the NGA and the CCSSO. As chair of the NGA in 2006–2007, then-governor of Arizona Janet Napolitano wrote an initiative, as other chairs of the association had done before (and have continued to do since). Napolitano's initiative emphasized improving math and science education and the workforce. To remain competitive in the global economy, Napolitano argued, the United States needed an internationally competitive education system. Particular countries that showed high performances on international assessments, such as the Programme for International Student Assessment (PISA) and the Programme for International Reading Literacy Study (PIRLS) (e.g., New Zealand and Singapore), had national standards for education. Analysts have not been able to make a causal link between national standards and high achievement on international assessments because there is not sufficient control over data collection. However, at the time, the Napolitano argument resonated with many education policymakers who believed that for students to have the opportunity to compete in world markets, the United States needed similar high-level standards across the country, not just in certain localities.

Another compelling argument for common standards was the apparent lack of preparedness among U.S. students for college and career after high school graduation (Rothman, 2011). A 2004 study by ACT, an organization producing college admissions tests, found that alarmingly low percentages of students were ready for college courses or the demands of the workplace.

Following the early discussions on the need for national standards, Napolitano created a task force that consisted of chief state school officers, governors, corporate chief executive officers, and experts in higher education. In December 2008, this task force released a report (NGA, CCSSO, & Achieve, 2008) that called for common standards for U.S. schools and served as the foundation for efforts to develop what would eventually become known as the Common Core State Standards.

Shortly thereafter, the NGA, the CCSSO, and a nonprofit group called Achieve came together to bring the recommendations of the report into policy and practice. These three organizations were at the center of the effort, and they hired a group from Student Achievement Partners to write the Standards based on broad input from several committees and groups. Other national organizations, including the International Reading Association and the two largest teachers' unions (the American Federation of Teachers and National Education Association), were asked for input. Drafts of the standards were posted online, and organizations and individuals were invited to respond. According to one report, the CCSS development team received 10,000 responses to drafts of the standards (Bidwell, 2014).

Once the standards were completed in the spring of 2010, state legislatures began to adopt them. As noted earlier, by December 2013, 45 states, the District of Columbia, and 3 U.S. territories had adopted the CCSS. The initiative was not federal, although, as President Obama suggested in his 2013 State of the Union Address, federal Race to the Top funds[1] had been used to persuade almost every state to develop "curricula and higher standards" (Obama, 2013). Adopting the CCSS saved states the effort of doing the complex standards development work on their own. Further, the U.S. Department of Education showed support for the CCSS through the funding of two consortia to design and implement assessments that were aligned with the Standards. The consortia themselves were run by states, but a major portion of the original funding (approximately $330 million) came from the federal government in the form of Race to the Top funds (U.S. Department of Education, September 2010).

The relationship between research and the Standards. The membership of the team that was contracted to write the Standards—Student Achievement Partners—was not similar in background to the membership of the panel responsible for the report of the NRP that provided the rationale for at least some of the policies within NCLB. Of the 13 members of the Standards Development Work Team, three came from nonprofits and one came from a university (retired) (NGA, 2009). The remainder of the team came from for-profit entities. At the same time that the formation of the Standards Development Work Team was announced, a feedback team was also announced. Of this group of 18 members, 15 were researchers from universities, including two who had been members of the NRP (NGA, 2009). The other three members of the feedback group included a teacher and two individuals from nonprofit education think tanks.

In English language arts, the Standards Development Work Team developed a broad set of 10 goals for reading and 10 goals for writing that described what students should know and should be able to do at the end of high school to be prepared for college or a career-entry job. These were termed the *anchor standards*. The grade-level standards for reading and writing were developed from these anchor standards. There were similar anchor standards for listening and speaking. The grade-level standards were designed to reflect progressions of skills and knowledge across the grades, a development in classroom practice that included formative assessment, curriculum maps, and carefully articulated sequences in student learning, referred to as "learning progressions" (Heritage, 2010; Jacobs, 1997; Popham, 2008). This was a departure from previous standards and frameworks that simply listed skills that should be addressed at each grade level.

The CCSS were intended to reflect research, but some people questioned whether important research had been considered (Pearson, 2013; Rothman, 2011). For example, the call to increase the complexity of texts was based on two studies—one based on texts from the 1950s through 1970s (Chall, Conard, & Harris, 1977) and the other summarizing text features from the early 1900s through the 1980s (Hayes, Wolfer, & Wolfe, 1996). The need for more complex texts for students in middle and high school was supported by research indicating that high school texts were often written at a low level that did not reflect the complexity in college texts. However, the idea of using complex texts, at least with beginning and early readers, was not based on a clear body of research (Gamson, Lu, & Eckert, 2013; Hiebert & Mesmer, 2013).

FEDERAL POLICY RELATED TO ASSESSMENT OF STUDENT ACHIEVEMENT

The federal government's involvement in both mandating and funding particular assessment programs has had substantial consequences for reading education over the past 50 years. From a period when there were no federal mandates regarding assessments to the present where state assessments through the two CCSS-aligned consortia have been developed with federal funds, the role of the federal government in the assessments that millions of schoolchildren take annually has brought about major changes in the daily lives of teachers and students in American classrooms.

The National Assessment of Educational Progress

From 1968 until 1992, the federal government provided an assessment of reading achievement nationwide, the NAEP. The results were based on assessments of representative samples of students conducted every 4 years. A group of experts and test developers created the assessment tasks. The NAEP in reading has collected and reported information on achievement gaps among socioeconomic groups. It also has used surveys of students, teachers, and administrators to provide data on resources and instructional practices in classrooms and schools. In that reporting, it raised early concerns about whether all students had equal access to effective education.

The development of the 1992 NAEP. In 1988, Congress mandated that NAEP results in reading would include voluntary, state-by-state reporting for grade 4 (National Assessment Governing Board [NAGB], 1992). The purpose was to determine whether states were supporting the achievement of all students, including those who were poor or from minority groups. At the same time that Congress approved the reporting of state-level scores on NAEP, it also established a group to oversee the development of NAEP assessments and the reporting of the scores. This group was called the National Assessment Governing Board (NAGB). It included appointees by the president and Congress. Along with the National Center for Educational Statistics (NCES), which was part of the U.S. Department of Education. NAGB made final decisions on test design and reporting. In the early days of NAGB, efforts were made to have its members represent a wide range of perspectives. In our opinion, over time the members seemed to become more representative of the incumbent president and his advisors.

Because the 1992 NAEP in reading was supposed to report scores by state level, the development of that NAEP was highly publicized. Hoping to prevent partisan politics and specific ideologies from dominating the process, NAGB, working with Congress and the U. S. Department of Education, created panels with input from education organizations such as CCSSO. The purpose of one panel was to provide general guidance, while the second panel was responsible for creating the assessment. The composition of the groups was driven by the intention of using consensus among diverse stakeholders and experts to develop an assessment that was acceptable, and even attractive, to a broad range of informed stakeholders.

The resulting assessment made several changes in design from the previous NAEP reading assessments that were planned to enhance its appeal to those who were skeptical of state-by-state reporting and also to increase its construct validity. Longer texts, open-ended questions, and the NAEP Reader (a form of the test where students picked from an array of stories and answered general, open-ended questions about the story) were all attempts to reflect sound classroom practice in reading.

Research and the NAEP. The NAEP for 1992 reflected some specific research and practice. Research indicated that usually when proficient students read through longer texts, they develop understandings in a recursive sequence—forming a general idea of what the text conveys, building increasing understanding, and finally considering how and why an author created the text (Langer, 1990). Research also indicated that certain reading activities—such as summarizing and making inferences—were especially important in becoming a proficient reader (Dole, Duffy, Roehler, & Pearson, 1991). The design and questions of the NAEP were also influenced by research that suggested students do not "get the meaning of text" but instead create an understanding based on what they already know and what the text conveys (NAGB, 1992).

Some reading research and practices were addressed in special studies conducted at the time the 1992 assessments were administered. These included determining how well students read orally as well as gathering information on the type of instruction they received and what kind of reading they did both in and out of school. These special studies were partly a way to examine aspects of reading that were not usually included in large-scale assessments because of technical, time, and financial constraints. They also were a means of gaining support from diverse groups in the education and policy communities. Subsequent NAEP reading assessment designs have changed the taxonomy but have not moved away from the general notion of reading being the process of constructing meaning from text. In addition, changes in NAEP reading designs have not had the broad-based input and review that the first state-by-state version in 1992 had.

Assessment and the CCSS

In 2010, as part of the federal Race to the Top funding effort, the U.S. Department of Education held a competition for funds to develop assessments to measure achievement of the CCSS. The developers were to be consortia of states. Two groups received funding: SBAC and PARCC. The federal guidelines required that the assessments being developed (1) be delivered on a computer-based platform, (2) be valid and reliable, and (3) be designed for use in teacher evaluation. The assessments were to be part of systems that include interim or formative assessment and professional development. Although the assessments are being developed by consortia of states, the federal role in framing the assessments is substantive, with regular monitoring of the progress and design of the tests.

Characteristics of the funded assessments. SBAC's effort includes computer adaptive summative assessments with performance or research simulation tasks as well as both constructed and selected response items. Most of the constructed response items are to be scored using artificial intelligence. The SBAC system will include optional, interim assessments delivered via computers that can be used by classroom teachers to monitor progress across the school year. There will be a digital library with professional development components on such topics as assessment literacy, formative assessment practices, and instruction related to the CCSS. The digital library will also include information on the summative assessment tasks, resources for using formative assessment, prototypes of instructional activities, and tools for using data from the summative assessments.

PARCC is developing a similar system. The summative, end-of-year assessment is delivered via computer but is not computer adaptive. It has optional diagnostic and mid-year assessments. It will include student research simulations, like SBAC's system, but it will be administered about three-quarters of the way into the school year and will be more extensive than those on SBAC. PARCC is also developing teacher resources.

If the majority of the states use SBAC and PARCC—assessments that are aligned to the CCSS and have features quite similar to the NAEP (such as long passages and open-ended responses)—then one could say that the original aims of NAEP (to provide a barometer of student performance in the nation as a whole) have been addressed. However, there is little, if any, public discussion of this issue, and the current departure of some states from the two federally funded assessment consortia make such a scenario unlikely in the near future.

Research and CCSS-related assessments. The SBAC and PARCC assessments are connected directly to the CCSS. The intent was not to create assessments that reflect transparent recommendations or findings from research on literacy and language, per se; instead the link to research was through the CCSS. Since the CCSS were themselves research-based, so goes the argument, a link to the CCSS is a link to scholarship (see Pearson, 2013, for a different tale about the strength of the research base for the CCSS). Perhaps because the CCSS were promoted as research-based, there has not been much consideration of additional research related to the construct of reading being used to develop the assessments.

An important distinction to note—one that has been ignored by several policymakers and journalists in recent comments—is that the CCSS, in both design and content, can have a major impact on assessment design but not necessarily on assessment policy. Current federal policy requires all students in grades 3 through 8 to be tested and also requires the use of student test scores in evaluating teacher effectiveness (Layton, 2014; U.S. Department of Education, April, 2010). States can use either the new assessments being developed by the consortia or their own assessments. This assessment requirement is not a result of the standards; rather, it is a continuation of federal policy and policies that were in place in some states before the standards were even developed. The CCSS call for (1) integration of language arts, with reading and writing being closely linked; (2) close reading of texts; (3) providing text evidence of inferences; (4) complex texts; (5) expository texts; and (6) the use of language arts in research (especially integrating information across text in producing writing). Most of these skills cannot be adequately assessed using multiple-choice questions. Consequently, students are being asked to do research simulations, to construct as well as select responses to questions, to provide text evidence for their responses, and to produce relatively long writing that integrates information from multiple texts.

The passages used in the new assessments under development, especially the SBAC assessments, are not necessarily naturally occurring texts as in NAEP. This is partly because of the large number of test items required and the highly limited development time allowed by the Race to the Top funding guidelines. On the SBAC assessment, many of the stimulus texts are being written as part of the assessment development. This has been an essentially financial and logistical decision rather than a reflection of research. PARRC is trying to use naturally occurring texts, but deadlines and resources could prevent them from doing so.

Politics and Economics of the New Assessments of the CCSS

Teacher accountability is a major goal of many, and possibly most, education policymakers who are making decisions about funding and general guidelines for assessments that have recently been developed by the states or are under construction by the assessment consortia. Accountability has become a major factor in assessment design. The new assessments must allow teacher effectiveness to be calculated based partly (sometimes as much as 50%, depending on state-level policy) on the scores of students taking the new assessments. This has made psychometricians cautious about planning the types of items allowed on the assessments, the scoring of items, and the reporting of results. It also has made the groups guiding the design of the assessments cautious about using innovation. Consequently, most items are multiple-choice, although items are more complex than the types of multiple-choice items that have been used in previous assessments.

Financial constraints at the state level have also influenced the design of the new assessments, mandating efficient administration and scoring of assessments. Originally, SBAC (2011, 2012) indicated that there would be a substantive number of constructed response items on the summative assessment that would assess the "full range" of the CCSS and that teachers would be involved in the scoring. This practice would have provided teachers with a working knowledge of what students need to understand and do to be successful. Some states balked at the additional cost of this approach, so it was decided to create open-ended questions that mainly could be scored using artificial intelligence. This greatly limited the types of open-ended questions that could be included and also affected the depth of processing or thinking that the items could require as well as the range of standards that could be assessed. For example, an open-ended question could be scored for the correct use of propositions, but not for the logic displayed.

Looking back, we can identify three trends since the 1988 legislation that changed NAEP into a state-by-state assessment. First, the focus has increasingly moved from national patterns to patterns among states. Second, state legislators, members of state boards of education, superintendents, and state department of education staff have become increasingly involved in the design of assessments at both the national and state levels. Third, there has been an increased effort to involve experts and stakeholders with a range of perspectives and interests. Language-minority groups and experts, special-needs advocates and experts, parents, and businesspeople have been asked to provide input. The current assessment consortia have invested numerous resources to meet the requirement that students with disabilities be accommodated and to attend to the needs of students for whom English is a second language. The involvement of a broader community stands in stark contrast to assessments from NAEP's development in 1968 and to state assessments of that time. During that period, the NAEP was essentially the product of advice from a relatively small group of experts (as few as a handful of scholars in the 1960s and 1970s to approximately a dozen in the late 1980s who worked with the staff of an organization (initially the CCSSO and later Educational Testing Service [ETS]) with input from the U.S. Department of Education through its NCES. By 1992, the NAEP had a steering committee of 15 members, had a planning committee of 15 members, and was subject to extensive review by state department of education staff.

There is even broader involvement of stakeholders in the current assessment consortia, SBAC and PARRC, which have numerous committees and work groups developing and reviewing the assessment design and items. More than a hundred teachers have been involved in each consortium in some aspect of the assessment work.

OBSERVATIONS AND THOUGHTS ABOUT THE FUTURE

This review of federal legislation of the past 50 years of education shows that research can be used as a tool in developing and implementing education policy. At the beginning in the early and mid-60s, research provided the impetus for legislation. For example, the impetus for the original ESEA legislation was research indicating that children who lived in high-poverty social communities were not performing as well as their counterparts from higher socioeconomic groups. Government leaders at the time believed that equity was a major goal of general policy and that education was the tool to achieve it. Directing how education was conducted was not the goal or the purpose of this early federal funding.

During the first four reauthorizations of Title I of ESEA (1964, 1966, 1968, and 1974) the *content* of instruction and the method of delivering content (including professional development to ensure that the appropriate content was delivered in the appropriate manner) were not the focus. Even as goals and definitions of reading shifted (e.g., REA, 1998), the structure and the traditional policies of the federal system itself restricted the government from prescribing precisely how teachers should teach. The government made recommendations and implied general goals but did not specify the components of the curriculum.

This perspective changed with the passage of the NCLB in 2001. Specifically, the Reading First sections created a new interpretation of federal education law. The requirement was that to use the federal funds, both the appropriate content (e.g., the five pillars of reading) and ways to deliver this content (e.g., specification of particular amounts and kinds of professional development and types of materials to be used) were much more specific and had to pass federal muster before the funds were released to the states. What constituted research was defined in the statute, and not all research was treated equally; some was considered to be unuseable because of its methodology, while a highly specified type of research was viewed as "valid" because of its methodology.

By the end of the Obama administration's first term in 2011, federal education policy was built around the concept that internationally benchmarked college and career ready standards would deliver the changes in education needed to make a difference. But where is the evidence that this focus on college and career and more prescriptive policy will work? What about the specifics that are being prescribed? Local autonomy is a major feature of many of the education systems, such as Finland's, that outperform the U.S. system on international assessments.

In terms of specific instructional factors, the education research community has developed many key ideas. For example, they suggest that having students focus on problem solving and inferences is more important than reciting facts; reading and writing are better taught together than separately; and scaffolding or the manipulation of reading contexts can support the performance of less able readers (Donavan & Pelligrino, 2004; Guthrie, 2003; McCardle, Chhabra, & Kapinus, 2008; Snow, Griffin, & Burns, 2005). These (and other elements) should be supported by policies that allow the necessary teacher flexibility in how instruction is provided to students. Unfortunately, policies are not providing information that is directly useful to change instruction. Ideally, for example, assessments should be promoted that require questions that allow students to reflect on and analyze the information being provided to demonstrate their cognitive ability. All of these elements have been the subject of years of research and analysis, but, at least within public policies, they have not been integrated into the mandated assessment systems.

Comings (2013) observed that educators cannot seem to bring to scale demonstration or research efforts on school improvement. Policymakers might better devote their energies to finding ways to bring to scale solutions that support high levels of learning among the 21 million children who are enrolled in Title I, the 7 million in special education, and the 1 million who are receiving instruction to help them learn English, in addition to the millions of students who are performing adequately but not at the levels required for full participation in the international marketplace of the 21st century.

As reading educators who have worked on national and state projects for a combined total of over 90 years, we have witnessed people who have little or no knowledge of education or education research creating policy based on selective use of evidence. At times, economic and political factors have trumped sound practice and research. More important, policymakers have not yet determined how to support access to sound education for all students without getting in the way of continuous growth in the quality of schooling. The lack of the use of evidence and the lack of progress in improving learning would support the hypothesis that federal policy is often more about policymakers holding on to their offices rather than providing the education that our children need to become leaders and preserve our democracy.

NOTE

Race to the Top was a new type of program where USDE initiated states to apply for funds to support programs that USDE was focused on. From the beginning it was clear that not all states would receive a share of the funding available; in short, it was a competitive grant program.

REFERENCES

American College Test (ACT). (2004). *Crises at the core: Preparing all students for college and work.* Iowa City, IA: ACT.

Baker, E. L., Barton, P. E., Darling-Hammond, L., Haertel, E., Ladd, H. F., Linn, R. L., Shavelson, R. J., & Shepard, L. A. (2010). *Problems with the use of student test scores to evaluate teachers* (EPI Briefing Paper No. 278). Washington, DC: Economic Policy Institute.

Bandeira de Mello, V., Blankenship, C., McLaughlin, D., & Rahman, T. (2009). *Mapping state proficiency standards onto NAEP scale: 2005–2007 (Research & Development Report).* Washington, DC: U.S. Department of Education, Institute of Education Sciences, National Center for Education Statistics.

Bidwell, A. (2014, February 27). The history of Common Core State Standards. *US News.* Available at http://www.usnews.com/news/special-reports/articles/2014/02/27/the-history-of-common-core-state-standards

Calfee, R. C. (2014). Introduction: Knowledge, evidence, and faith: How the federal government used science to take over public schools. In K. S. Goodman, R. C. Calfee, & Y. M. Goodman (Eds.), *Whose knowledge counts in government literacy policies? Why expertise matters* (pp. 1–17). New York, NY: Routledge.

Chall, J. S., Conard, S., & Harris, S. (1977). *An analysis of textbooks in relation to declining SAT scores.* Princeton, NJ: College Entrance Examination Board.

Comings, J. (2013, August/September). Reading to change: The indispensable step for taking education innovations from small scale to large scale success. *Reading Today, 31*(1) 6.

Common Core State Standards Initiative. (2014). Available at www.corestandards.org/about-the-standards/development-process

Cross, C. T. (2010). *Political education: National policy comes of age.* New York, NY: Teachers College Press.

Dole, J. A., Duffy, G. G., Roehler, L. R., & Pearson, P. D. (1991). Moving from the old to the new: Research on reading comprehension instruction. *Review of Educational Research, 61*(2), 239–264.

Donavan, M. S., & Pelligrino, J. W. (2004). *Learning and instruction: A SERP research agenda.* Washington, DC: The National Academies Press.

Gamson, D. A., Lu, X., & Eckert, S. A. (2013). Challenging the research base of the Common Core State Standards: A historical reanalysis of text complexity. *Educational Researcher, 42*(7), 381–391. doi:10.3102/0013189X13505684

Gardner, D. P. (1983). *A nation at risk.* Washington, DC: The National Commission on Excellence in Education, U.S. Department of Education.

Gewertz, C. (2014, July 9). Lawmakers assert role in standards Common Core sparks bills. *Education Week, 33*(36), 1, 32–33.

Goodman, K. S., Calfee, R. C., & Goodman, Y. M. (Eds.). (2013). *Whose knowledge counts in government literacy policies? Why expertise matters.* New York, NY: Routledge.

Guthrie, J. T. (2003). Concept-oriented reading instruction. In A. P. Sweet & C. E. Snow (Eds.), *Rethinking reading comprehension* (pp. 115–140). New York, NY: Guilford Press.

Hayes, D., Wolfer, L., & Wolfe, M. (1996). Schoolbook simplification and its relation to the decline in SAT-Verbal scores. *American Educational Research Journal, 33*(2), 489–508.

Heritage, M. (2010). *Formative assessment in practice: A process of inquiry and action.* Cambridge, MA: Harvard Education Press.

Hiebert, E. H., & Mesmer, H. A. (2013). Upping the ante of text complexity in the Common Core State Standards: Examining its potential impact on young readers. *Educational Researcher, 42*(1), 44–51.

Jacobs, H. H. (1997). *Mapping the big picture: Integrating curriculum and assessment K–12.* Alexandria, VA: Association for Supervision and Curriculum Development.

Jencks, C. (1974). Comment on Inequality in occupational status and income. *American Educational Research Journal, 1*(1), 169–175.

Langer, J. A. (1990). The process of understanding: Reading for literary and informative purposes. *Research in the Teaching of English,* 229–260.

Layton, L. (2014, July 24). Glenn Beck takes to theatres to criticize Common Core. *The Washington Post,* A3.

Long, R. M., & Selden, R. (2011). How reading research and federal policy on reading instruction have interrelated over the past 35 years. In S. J. Samuels & A. E. Farstrup (Eds.), *What research has to say about reading instruction* (4th ed., pp. 448–462). Newark, DE: International Reading Association.

Manzo, K. K. (2005, September 7). States pressed to refashion Reading First designs. *Education Week, 25*(2), 1, 24–25.

Manzo, K. K. (2005, November 9). Inspector general to conduct broad audits of Reading First. *Education Week, 25*(11), 10.

McCardle, P., & Chhabra, V. E. (2004). *The voice of evidence in reading research.* Baltimore, MD: Brookes Publishing Co.

McCardle, P, Chhabra, V., & Kapinus, B. (2008). *Reading research in action: A teacher's guide for student success.* Baltimore, MD: Brookes Publishing Co.

National Assessment Governing Board. (1992). *Reading framework for the 1992 National Assessment of Educational Progress.* Washington, DC: U.S. Government Printing Office.

National Governors Association. (2009, July 1). *Common Core State Standards Development Work Group and Feedback Group announced* (Press release). Available at www.nga.org/cms/home/ news-room/news-releases/page_2009/col2-content/main-content-list/title_common-core- state-standards-development-work-group-and-feedback-group-announced.html

National Governors Association (NGA) Center for Best Practices & Council of Chief State School Officers (CCSSO). (2010). *Common Core State Standards for English language arts and literacy in history/social studies, science, and technical subjects.* Washington, DC: Authors. Available at www.corestandards.org/assets/CCSSI_ELA%20Standards.pdf

National Governors Association, Council of Chief State School Officers, & Achieve (2008). *Benchmarking for success: Ensuring U.S. students receive a world-class education.* Washington, DC: National Governors Association.

National Institute of Child Health and Human Development. (2000). *Report of the National Reading Panel: Teaching children to read: An evidence-based assessment of the scientific research literature on reading and its implications for reading instruction: Reports of the subgroups.* Bethesda, MD: National Institute of Child Health and Human Development, National Institutes of Health.

Obama, B. (2013). State of the union message. Available at www.whitehouse.gov/the-press-office/2013/02/12/remarks-president-state-of-the-union-address

Pearson, P. D. (2004). The reading wars: The politics of reading research and policy—1988 through 2003. *Educational Policy, 18*(1), 216–252.

Pearson, P. D. (2013, January). *Research and the common core: Can the romance survive?* Webinar. Available at www.textproject.org/professional-development/webinars

Popham, W. J. (2008). *Transformative assessment.* Alexandria, VA: Association for Supervision and Curriculum Development.

Pressley, M. (2005, December 14). The rocky road of Reading First: Another chapter in the long history of complaints about federal reading efforts. *Education Week, 25,* 24–25.

Reading Excellence Act (REA). (1998). Available at www.gpo.gov/fdsys/pkg/BILLS-105hr2614eas/pdf/BILLS-105hr2614eas.pdf

Roller, C. M., & Long, R. M. (2001). Critical issues: Sounding like more than background noise to policy makers: Qualitative researchers in the policy arena. *Journal of Literacy Research, 33*(4), 707–725.

Rotberg, I. C. (1993). *Federal policy options for improving the education of low-income students* (Vols. 1 & 3). Santa Monica, CA: RAND & Institute on Education & Training.

Rothman, R. (2011). *Something in common the Common Core Standards and the next chapter in American education.* Cambridge, MA: Harvard Education Press.

Smarter Balanced Assessment Consortium. (2011). *Overview.* Available at www.Smarterbalanced.org/wordpress/wp-Overview-Presentation.pdf

Smarter Balanced Assessment Consortium. (2012). *Theory of action.* Available at www.Smarterbalanced.org/wordpress/wp-Theory-of-Action.pdf

Snow, C. E., Griffin, P., & Burns, M. S. (Eds.). (2005). *Knowledge to support the teaching of reading: Preparing teachers for a changing world.* San Francisco, CA: Jossey-Bass.

Ujifusa, A. (2014, July 9). Louisiana standards showdown: Governor vs. state chief, board. *Education Week, 33*(36), 1, 32–33.

U.S. Department of Education. (2010, April). *Race to the Top Assessment program: Notice inviting applications.* Washington, DC: U.S. Department of Education.

U.S. Department of Education. (2010, September). Press release. Available at www. ed.gov/news/press-release/US-Secretary-duncan-announces-winners-competition-improve-student-asse

Whitehurst, G. J. (2002). Evidence-based education (EBE). Available at www2.ed.gov/nclb/methods/whatworks/eb/evidencebased.pdf

CHAPTER 3

Relevance of Models of Reading for Common Core State Standards

Michael L. Kamil

This chapter provides an explanation of models and their uses as an introduction to the implicit model undergirding the Common Core State Standards (CCSS; National Governors Association [NGA] Center for Best Practices & Council of Chief State School Officers [CCSSO], 2010). The chapter also explores the importance of this implicit model for the implementation, extension, and evaluation of the CCSS. In addition, it elaborates some of the variables that are lacking, both in conventional models of reading and in the CCSS model. Please note that although the CCSS emphasize the full panoply of communication skills, including writing and oral language, the topics I discuss here will focus primarily on reading.

MODELS AND THEORIES OF READING

Models of reading have a long history, extending to the very beginnings of reading research (cf. Huey, 1908). At one level, the term *model* can be used interchangeably with the term *theory*. To do so, however, obscures important differences between models and theories. A theory is a logically organized set of ideas or facts that attempts to formalize a domain. The intent of a theory is to derive new propositions (sometimes labeled *hypotheses* or *predictions*) that can be tested in future research. Theories are a cornerstone of the scientific method. If predictions of a theory are not borne out by future research, then the theory needs to be changed. By contrast, models are devices used to help simplify, illustrate, visualize, or otherwise comprehend a set of abstract data, findings, or a theory. Models can be either *explicit* or *implicit*. Some models present relationships among variables directly; these are referred to as explicit models. In some contexts, the model that was used must be inferred; these are referred to as implicit models.

Uses of Models

To summarize, models are used to simplify a body of knowledge, typically of research findings, whereas theories attempt to represent all the complexities of a domain with the intent of allowing testable propositions to be derived. (For general discussions of the uses of models in science and research, see Bergmann [1953] or Lachman [1960], among many others.) The myriad of variables involved in reading often require some simplification, and models provide that kind of generality. Models also have been used to guide organizational structures—for example, when an organization chart shows a simplified version of lines of authority. In addition, models can be used to inform instruction by providing an explicit rendition of the most important variables that should be accounted for in instruction—a task that I explicitly undertake later in this chapter. Another important use of models is as a guide for policymaking. Again, the importance of models for developing policies is that they highlight the important variables that must be addressed in order to implement the practice or principle in question.

Most models of reading focus on either the reading process or the process of knowledge acquisition. Few, if any, are models of instruction; instead, the models of the processes are used to move from the processes to instruction. Huey (1908) is one of the few authors to address explicitly matters of instruction based on the research he presented. However, his review of instruction is less grounded in extensive research than is common today, and it is not explicitly presented as a model.

How Do Models Relate to Standards?

In the field of education, standards are specific skills or content that students must perform at an appropriate level within a particular domain. Standards for reading, both in the CCSS and in earlier standards documents, typically outline the skills that students must acquire, not the content they must learn, or they suggest ways to implement instruction to help students meet those standards. The CCSS make this last point explicitly: "The Standards define what all students are expected to know and be able to do, not how teachers should teach" (NGA Center & CCSSO, 2010, p. 4). I elaborate on this reluctance to specify instruction more fully in the section on the limitations of the CCSS.

Models of reading are usually developed from research. Consequently, models are fertile sources for the development of standards. The danger of following this process lies in the fact that not all models are equally useful, nor are they equally well grounded in the research. In the following section, I address some of the better-known models of reading, how they were developed, and the instructional implications that were drawn from them.

THE "GOLDEN AGE" OF MODELS

The 1970s and 1980s saw a profusion of models with different emphases, which have been summarized in a number of reviews (e.g., Kamil, 1978; Ruddell, Ruddell, & Singer, 1994; Samuels & Kamil, 1984; Singer & Ruddell, 1976, 1985; Singer, Ruddell, & Holmes, 1970; see also Pearson & Cervetti, Chapter 1, this volume). Although these models informed both sides in the "reading wars" of the late 1980s and early 1990s, the debates turned on disagreements over what often became a social/political difference rather than disagreements over scientific facts. (See Kamil, 1995, and Stanovich, 1990, for a summary of some of the reading wars debates.)

In the following discussion, I characterize in general terms what several models from the "golden age" emphasized. Bear in mind that each model is far more complex than this brief discussion can capture.

Context

In the 1960s, Goodman (1967) published a model of reading that he referred to as a psycholinguistic guessing game. He and his colleagues elaborated the model, but its base assumptions suggested that readers relied heavily on context to determine the meanings of words. The Goodman model and others related to it became known as top-down models, which referred to the idea that readers were assumed to start with comprehension and work "down" to decoding only when it was necessary. The importance of this approach was its emphasis on comprehension as opposed to decoding. Some of the evidence for this model came from miscue research (e.g., Brown, Goodman, & Marek, 1996; Goodman, 1969). Goodman and others emphasized the meaningful nature of miscues (errors of translation from text to speech). Because students' miscues very often make some semantic sense, Goodman argued, and his model reflected, the proposition that making meaning was guiding reading. An instructional implication of this model was that students should not be subjected to intensive and isolated decoding.

Decoding

In the early 1970s, Gough (1972) developed a model of reading in which he attempted to show what happens during a single second of reading. This model assumed that readers used decoding to translate text into ever-larger language units—letters to words to sentences, and so on. This and similar models came to be known as bottom-up models because they emphasized decoding as the first step in reading. Gough and his colleagues conducted many studies to validate the steps of the model. An instructional implication drawn from this model was that decoding should be the first skill set students are taught.

Automaticity

LaBerge and Samuels (1974) used extensive research from cognitive psychology to develop a reading model that focused on a central concept called "automaticity." Automaticity is related to the cognitive psychological idea of attention. Simply put, all cognitive tasks require attention, or a focus on performing a mental operation. An assumption among proponents of this model is that for an individual, attention is fixed in its capacity. The amount of attention required to complete a task depends on how complex the task is and how automatic the performance of that task is. The familiar example is trying to do more than one thing at a time. If one task is automatic, then the other can be performed simultaneously. If both tasks require much attention, however, then performance suffers. In terms of reading, LaBerge and Samuels identified two critical tasks: decoding and comprehension. They suggested that decoding was necessary and that it was the initial driver of reading. However, if decoding was not automatic, it required large amounts of cognitive attention. Comprehension also required attention, but it was less likely to be automated because it entails more deliberate processes, such as requiring readers to look up word meanings in their mental lexicons and parse the logic of the syntax of complex sentences. Consequently, a lack of automaticity in decoding could lead to difficulties in comprehension. The more automatic decoding becomes, the more attention can be devoted to comprehension. That said, as students fine-tune their reading skills, learn the meanings of more words, and become more efficient language processors, even comprehension can become highly automated.

Instructional implications of this model were based on the notion that students had to become fluent decoders before they could become proficient comprehenders. Decoding also had to occupy the central role in reading instruction early in the reading curriculum. The focus needed to be not simply on decoding but on *automatic* decoding.

Balanced Approach

Stanovich (1980) developed a reading model that he termed *interactive-compensatory*. This assumes that there are various sources of knowledge that can be used in the process of making sense of text. For example, decoding is one route to making meaning, but it is only effective if the reader knows the vocabulary of the text. Encountering unknown words might create comprehension difficulties for readers unless they can invoke a knowledge source, such as context clues, prior knowledge, topic knowledge, expectations, or a host of other sources that can assist in decoding and comprehending. Proficient readers seem to shift back and forth among their various knowledge sources as they make sense of text. Stanovich's perspective on the cognitive processes involved in reading suggested a balance between emphasizing decoding and comprehension in reading instruction.

The contrast between the Goodman and Gough models is one of the factors that led to the reading wars, but not the only one. As the debate became more heated, the Stanovich model was a welcome alternative to Goodman's and Gough's models, largely because Stanovich posited that readers could operate in *either* a bottom-up or top-down mode, depending on a range of reader (knowledge or interest) and text (topic and linguistic complexity) variables.

Insufficient specification was (and indeed, continues to be) a big issue in building models (Mosenthal & Kamil, 1991). Often, there is such a great number of variables that not all of them can be incorporated into a model. Ultimately, this exclusion of variables becomes a problem because it is a source of error that will eventually lead to erroneous predictions. Insufficient specification was at least one of the motivations for the trend toward systematic reviews of research that were undertaken on a large scale during the late 1990s—namely, the National Academy of Science effort dubbed Preventing Reading Difficulties (Snow, Burns, & Griffin, 1998) and the report of the National Reading Panel (NICHD, 2000). The purpose of the reviews was to consider more of the variables than most models could (or did) incorporate. In the next section, I consider these two reviews, along with others.

REVIEWS OF RESEARCH

The outcomes of the reading wars were not a series of clear-cut choices among the extant models, but rather a focus on reviews of the research literature that could be quantified—for example, by using meta-analysis. The literature had expanded exponentially during the period of the reading wars, consisting, by 1999, of more than 100,000 published journal articles (NICHD, 2000). To make sense of this massive amount of information required systematic reviews.

Approaches to Research Reviews

Reviews of research can be conducted in three ways: One way is by achieving consensus, where a panel of experts reviews the research and arrives at a conclusion. Another way is evidence-driven: attempts to examine the research comprehensively and then quantify the results to reach conclusions. The third way of reviewing research combines the first two approaches.

Consensus reviews do not *necessarily* have to account for all the data, nor do they have to be systematic in the review procedures they use. The expert knowledge of the reviewers is the driving force in analyzing the research, and the implicit assumption is that the expertise of the reviewer(s) acts as a validity and quality control filter in determining the relative weight accorded to different research studies. Evidence-driven reviews must follow established procedures for gauging quality control and the relative weight of each research study; once those procedures have been established, matters of quality and weight do not depend on the opinions of experts. As noted earlier, statistical methods such as meta-analysis compare and analyze research from different research studies.

Significant Published Reviews

Three influential publications have presented extensive reviews of the literature from the time period. Each publication illustrates one of the three approaches. *Preventing Reading Difficulties* (Snow, Burns, & Griffin, 1998) is a consensus review; it represents a set of conclusions based on the opinions of a convened panel of experts about the interpretation of a body of relevant research. The National Reading Panel report (NICHD, 2000) is based on an evidence-driven synthesis, reaching conclusions on the basis of a comprehensive analysis of the research literature related to reading instruction for K–12 students. The NRP review employed meta-analyses where possible and used other quantitative analyses when meta-analyses were inappropriate. Finally, *The Handbook of Reading Research, Volume III* (Kamil, Mosenthal, Pearson, & Barr, 2000) represents a combination of the two methods. Expert authors were invited to review specific topics and were then free to choose how to conduct the reviews. (This tradition has continued with *The Handbook of Reading Research, Volume IV* [Kamil, Afflerbach, Moje, & Pearson, 2011].)

These were not the only reviews of research conducted around 2000. However, they do represent the different ways in which conclusions about the research can be reached. The CCSS document is the result of building on these as well as subsequent reviews.

Notable in its effect on the creation of the CCSS is the review of research guiding the development of the *Reading Framework for the 2009 National Assessment of Educational Progress* (NAEP; National Assessment Governing Board [NAGB], 2008). This research defines reading as an active and complex process that involves students in

- understanding written text;
- developing and interpreting meaning; and
- using meaning as appropriate to the type of text, purpose, and situation.

What is important about this definition is that it emphasizes comprehension rather than alphabetics or decoding. This is not to say that the processes related to alphabetics or decoding are irrelevant. Rather, it can be said that for *most* students, the code aspects of reading have been mastered by 4th grade. The definition also was used to guide the development of an assessment framework that would measure how well 4th-, 8th-, and 12th-grade students could read.

The NAEP framework emphasized the use of informational text over literary text, included a strong vocabulary component, and placed a stronger emphasis on comprehension skills than previous NAEP frameworks had done. A look at the framework's definition of advanced-level reading illustrates this perspective. It reads:

> Twelfth-grade students performing at the Advanced level should be able to analyze both the meaning and the form of the text and provide complete, explicit, and precise text support for their analyses with specific examples. They should be able to read across multiple texts for a variety of purposes, analyzing and evaluating them individually and as a set. (NAGB, 2008)

Although there is no explicit model in the NAEP framework, it is possible to infer an implicit model by examining the lists of text characteristics that are included at each of the grade levels. Similarly, as noted earlier, there is no *explicit* underlying model for the CCSS. Instead, the standards' developers relied on many assumptions derived from research to determine the specific directions and forms of individual standards. Some of these assumptions are simply offered without any research-based evidence for their support, while others have some support that can be derived from work conducted after the CCSS document was published.

THE COMMON CORE STATE STANDARDS FOR ENGLISH LANGUAGE ARTS

As the latest entry into the policy arena and a leading candidate for an initiative that could direct education policy at the state and local levels for years to come, the Common Core State Standards for English Language Arts (CCSS ELA) deserve careful analysis. In the following sections, characteristics of the CCSS will be examined in order to uncover the implicit model. The discussion will consider the underlying assumptions for the whole set of standards, as well as the anchor standards, the skills that are recommended as part of CCSS, and instructional implications. In addition, the benefits and limitations will be discussed with reference to the model on which CCSS is based.

Underlying Assumptions of CCSS

The implicit model that supports the CCSS derives from a key set of assumptions. One important assumption is that throughout their school years, students should receive instruction that will allow them to complete high school with the skills they need to succeed in either college or a career. The work of Carnevale, Smith, and Strohl (2010) suggests that the requirements needed for college and career are converging. This is important because it represents something of a departure from earlier thinking that assumed the skills for college were different from those required for the workplace. Researchers do not suggest that the two skill sets are identical, only that there is a substantial and increasing overlap in the skills. The CCSS reflect awareness that this overlap is substantial. The model for student skills commonly needed for college and work include the following:

- Building knowledge in different subject areas or domains
- Becoming proficient in new content areas or disciplines
- Reading purposefully
- Being able to refine and share knowledge

These skills are related to the need for individuals to be flexible during their lives after high school, choosing college or work and participating in a number of different careers. A small body of studies supports the appropriateness of this CCSS assumption (e.g., Conley, Drummond, Gonzalez, Rooseboom, & Stout, 2011).

The CCSS stress rigorous content and the application of knowledge through high-order skills in order to move student achievement beyond present levels. Given that the proportion of advanced readers has not changed across the history of the NAEP assessments (National Center for Education Statistics, 2013), this is a real priority.

Rather than develop an entirely new set of standards, however, CCSS developers assumed that there already were good exemplars of state standards and decided to build upon the strengths and lessons of those standards. The CCSS document was also informed by reading standards and policies in top-performing countries.

Perhaps the most important assumption underlying the CCSS is that there is sufficient evidence to support the inclusion of many or most of the anchor standards. There is less evidence for the inclusion of many of the grade-by-grade specifications (see Pearson, 2013).

A General Model of Student Skills

The CCSS were developed to reflect four explicit principles that affect their form and character. The standards were to be (1) research- and evidence-based, (2) aligned with college and career expectations, (3) rigorous, and (4) internationally benchmarked.

A key aspect of the standards is the assumption that all four communication skills (reading, writing, listening, and thinking) in language arts are important. To meet the requirements of the entire set of standards, students must be able to perform in speaking, listening, reading, and writing. In addition, students must be able to apply these skills across a variety of texts, levels of difficulty, and different disciplines. The following brief sketches of these skills, strategies, and dispositions indicate what students should be able to do in order to meet the standards:

- *Demonstrate independence.* Among other skills, the CCSS assume that students should be able to comprehend and evaluate complex text across disciplines. In addition, they assume that students should be able to construct effective arguments and convey multifaceted information, and they should be able to do this on their own, without outside assistance.

- *Build strong content knowledge.* The CCSS require students to be able to establish a base of knowledge across a wide range of subject areas by engaging with reading materials of quality and substance. They should be able to become proficient in new areas through research and study. In addition, they must read purposefully to gain both general knowledge and discipline-specific expertise. Another key aspect of building content knowledge is that students should be able to refine and share their knowledge.

- *Respond to demands of audience, task, and discipline.* At a somewhat more specific level, the standards hold that students must be able to understand and respond to different text and task demands and recognize how these demands change across disciplines. Some of these skills apply to many disciplines, such as being able to consider context or appreciate nuances, while other skills are specific to individual disciplines, such as knowing that different disciplines use different text structures and kinds of evidence. Here, again, audience is critical in reading purposefully and being able to refine and share knowledge.

- *Critique as well as comprehend.* This skill set is the central CCSS focus. It is designed to produce open-minded, skeptical readers. To present effective critiques, students first must have the ability to understand what authors are saying. Once they determine this, they must be able to determine and question the authors' assumptions. Another facet of this set of skills is the need to assess the veracity of the authors' claims and how those claims might color the content of the text.

- *Privilege evidence.* The CCSS require students to be able to cite text evidence for their interpretations. This skill is related to comprehending and critiquing text. In addition, students must be able to make their reasoning about the meaning of the text clear, particularly when the meaning goes beyond the text evidence. Finally, students must be able to evaluate others' use of evidence in order to do principled critiques of texts.

- *Use technology strategically and capably.* This set of skills supports the students' ability to employ technology thoughtfully to enhance their reading. Students tailor their searches online to acquire useful information efficiently, and they integrate what they learn using technology with what they learn offline. Students should know the strengths and limitations of various technological tools and mediums and be able to select and use those best suited to their communication goals.

- *Understand other perspectives and cultures.* These skills are often not acknowledged explicitly in previous sets of standards as they are in the CCSS. Through reading and listening, students should be able to communicate effectively with and understand the perspectives of people from varied backgrounds. In addition, students should be able to evaluate other points of view critically and constructively.

Other assumptions related to what students must be able to do that are subsumed in those that I have listed include the following:

- *Care about precision.* A major aspect of precision is related to understanding the selection of specific vocabulary as well as the impact of vocabulary choices. Students should also be able to distinguish among choices in vocabulary items and be able to compare differences in meanings. Almost equally important is the ability of students to determine when precision matters and when it doesn't.
- *Attend to the craft and structure of texts.* On a more specific level, students should attend to structure when they are reading. At the very least, structure is a very important clue to meaning in text. More important, students must be able to understand that craft and structure play a major role in presenting information in different disciplines.
- *Understand how an author's craft relates to setting and plot.* Although the CCSS focus primarily on informational text, they also promote the development of skills that relate specifically to understanding literary texts. Both text types are important, and the skills to identify and use the differences in their structure need to be part of the overall skill set students should master. Some of the skills required for understanding literary texts are analogs of those found in informational texts, such as attending to structure and understanding differences in presentations of different literary genres.

In summary, this is a general, albeit implicit, model of reading and literacy that is elaborated in successive stages—first by anchor standards, and then by detailed standards in grades and grade-level bands. In the next section, I describe some general instructional implications that the model entails.

Instructional Implications

The CCSS do not explicitly specify instructional strategies for providing students with skills they need for success in college and career. However, they do imply some elements of instruction. The developmental nature of the standards is an element of instruction.

Without specifying a set reading curriculum, the standards make it clear that students need to be exposed to more complex text in terms of quantity, quality, and difficulty. In addition, the CCSS stress the goal of preparing students to read and comprehend materials across disciplines—history/social studies, science, and technical subjects—an idea not considered in many sets of standards. The importance that the CCSS place on informational text reflects the emphasis seen in the NAEP *Reading Framework* (NAGB, 2008). Some differences do exist between the NAEP framework and the CCSS in the proportions of text genres used at various grade levels, but this is a result of the differing definitions of informational text used by the developers. For example, the CCSS count literary nonfiction as informational text, whereas NAEP considers it literary text.

The CCSS do not put forth any specific instructional strategies. Implicitly, the model suggests that students need to be taught how to read text in different disciplines. However, there are two documents that address instructional recommendations for publishers (Coleman & Pimentel, 2012a, 2012b). Despite this set of recommendations, the original Standards document is clear that instructional decisions should be the province of the teacher (NGA Center & CCSSO, 2010).

The CCSS are meant to apply to all students, including English language learners (ELLs). However, these ELL students may require and should be provided with additional time, appropriate instructional support, and aligned assessments. The CCSS are also meant to apply to students with disabilities. The additional instructional support includes using universal design principles wherever possible. Students with disabilities should also have an individualized educational plan (IEP) and instruction from high-quality teachers and other professionals who have special expertise in working these students. Accommodations that do not change the CCSS are also recommended, as are assistive technologies that provide access to both the general curriculum and the standards (NGA Center & CCSSO, 2010).

Anchor Standards

As discussed earlier in this book (see Chapter 2, this volume), to get at the various skills the CCSS expect students to possess, the document provides 10 anchor standards. Each of these standards is subdivided into more specific standards that lay out what students should understand and be able to do by the end of each grade level, or grade band (NGA Center & CCSSO, 2010; for a list of the anchor standards, see Table 1.1, Chapter 1, this volume). These grade-level standards are sufficiently detailed to guide a curriculum that fulfills the CCSS goals. Although the individual standards are important for the elaboration of the implicit model, it is beyond the scope of this chapter to deal with each one individually. Instead, the following are some examples to illustrate the finer grains of the standards as they specify the implicit model at upper grades. Standards at lower grade levels are specified at a more general or simpler level of sophistication. At higher grade levels the standards require more complex comprehension:

- For grade 3, a standard reads "Use information gained from illustrations (e.g., maps, photographs) and the words in a text to demonstrate understanding of the text (e.g., where, when, why, and how key events occur)." (National Governors Association Center for Best Practices, 2010, p. 14)
- At grades 6–8, a standard for reading science and technical material requires students to be able to "Determine the central ideas or conclusions of a text; provide an accurate summary of the text distinct from prior knowledge or opinions." (National Governors Association Center for Best Practices & CCSSO, 2010, p. 62)
- At grades 9–10, a standard for history and social studies calls for students to be able to "Cite specific textual evidence to support analysis of primary and secondary sources attending to such features as the date and origin of the information." (National Governors Association Center for Best Practices & CCSSO, 2010, p. 610)

Limitations of the CCSS

The CCSS have clear limitations for the overall goal of creating students who are prepared for college and career. The CCSS acknowledge some of these limitations as follows (implying, of course, that they are not so much limitations as they are conscious decisions about issues that could and should be left to the discretion of the states, districts, or schools that adopt the standards):

1.   The standards define what all students are expected to know and be able to do. They do *not* specify how teachers should teach.
2.   The standards specify some particular forms of content, but they do *not* indicate all or even most of the content that students should learn. A content-rich curriculum consistent with the expectations laid out is needed for successful implementation. Even the examples provided are meant to illustrate the types and levels of texts that could be used at different levels; they are not meant to be a canon.
3.   The standards do not describe everything that can or should be taught. A great deal is left to the discretion of teachers and curriculum developers. This is most obvious in preparation for the workplace. Every occupation has somewhat different literacy demands. It would be impossible to include *all* of those differences in the standards.
4.   The standards do not specify advanced work for students who currently meet the standards. Advanced work should provide students with opportunities to move beyond the college and career readiness baseline laid out in the CCSS. This advanced work should be consistent with the models that undergird the standards.
5.   The standards offer no specification for the intervention methods or materials that are necessary to support students who are progressing at below-average rates. This is because no set of grade-specific standards can fully reflect the large variety in abilities, needs, learning rates, and achievement levels of students in any given classroom. However, the standards are intended for all students, and failure to progress at reasonable rates should be evidence that interventions are required.
6.   The CCSS do not define the full range of supports appropriate for ELL students and for students with special needs. For these students, it is possible to meet the standards in reading, writing, speaking, and listening without displaying native-like control of conventions and vocabulary, as long as there are instructors who are able to provide appropriate instruction and assessment of performance. The standards should also be read as allowing for the widest possible range of students to participate fully from the outset and as permitting appropriate accommodations to ensure the maximum participation of students with special education needs, although the details of the supports are not specified in the standards.
7.   The standards describe English language arts and some content-area literacy components. These areas are critical to college and career readiness, but they do not define the whole of such readiness. Students require other aspects of academic performance, including social, emotional, and physical development and approaches to learning. Similarly, the standards define literacy expectations in history/social studies, science, and technical subjects, but literacy standards in other areas, such as mathematics and health education, consistent with the implicit model contained in the current

standards, are necessary to create a complete set of standards for use in a comprehensive literacy program.

There are some other limitations as well. For example, the standards do not specify the sort of preparation that teachers need to become proficient in the kind of instruction that enables students to meet the standards. Being able to apprehend the model underlying the CCSS would certainly help instructors learn how to make principled decisions about what and how to teach. Another limitation is in materials. The CCSS dictate a change in levels of complexity and in the distribution of text types. Most of the materials currently available would not align with the standards. A great deal of work will be needed to bring about the needed alignment.

In addition, existing assessments used to track performance of students are not aligned with the CCSS. Two consortia, the Smarter Balanced Assessment Consortium (SBAC) and the Partnership for Assessment of Readiness for College and Careers (PARCC), are now completing assessments to match the CCSS (http://www.smarterbalanced.org/; http://www.parcconline.org/.) (For further discussion, see Blanchard & Samuels, Chapter 6, this volume.)

Finally, and perhaps most seriously, the specific progressions of standards across grade levels are only generally supported by research. The overall principle seems to be that the complexity of standards should increase across levels. It is clear that not all of the progressions can be derived from extant research.

So Why Worry About Models?

It is important to understand the implicit model for the CCSS in order to be certain that there is consistency among the various elements of implementation, instructional materials, assessments, and the like. This can best be accomplished by making the implicit model more visible and explicit. The CCSS allow for states to customize the standards by as much as 15%. A model would certainly help determine whether any additions are consistent with both the extant standards and future research and instructional results.

Models, or at least models more elaborate than those now available, are needed to flesh out some elements of the CCSS. For example, a fully elaborated model of disciplinary reading would be helpful to ensure that the standards for history, science, and technical material are on target. In addition, if standards for other disciplines are developed, such a model would help ensure that the new standards are consistent with the main body of standards. In this regard, Alexander and Jetton (2000) provide a solid review of early work on disciplinary literacy and learning from text. Much more work on developing a description of disciplinary literacy needs to be done, and when that work is complete, it will need to be incorporated into the CCSS. One important distinction to be drawn in this work is that reading and learning become interwoven as readers do more extended reading in disciplines.

Text complexity is another concept that needs a great deal more elaboration. The CCSS include three types of variables in complexity:

- Qualitative evaluation of texts (levels of meaning, structure, language conventionality and clarity, and knowledge demands)

- Quantitative evaluation of the text (readability measures and other measures of text complexity)
- Match of reader to text and task (reader variables such as motivation, knowledge, and experiences; and task variables such as purpose and the complexity generated by the task assigned and the questions posed)

The definition of complexity in CCSS is clouded by the fact that the examples given in the document and appendices seem to rely almost completely on quantitative measures (e.g., The Lexile® Framework for Reading) despite an explicit reference to qualitative criteria for assessing complexity. Recent work on this issue by Pearson and Hiebert (2014 and Preface, this volume) comes down on the side of emphasizing qualitative evaluation of complexity.

Some work on this topic has been used to justify the base model presented in the CCSS documents (e.g., Nelson, Perfetti, Liben, & Liben, 2012). More recent scholarship has called into question at least some of the basic assumptions that were used to justify the increase in complexity that is evident in the CCSS as they are currently presented (Gamson, Lu, & Eckert, 2013; Hiebert & Mesmer, 2013; Pearson, 2013). The evidence for and against the assumptions about text complexity marshalled in these papers is somewhat mixed. Gamson et al. (2013) and Hiebert and Mesmer (2013) find the evidence lacking; the latter isolate three assumptions about text complexity:

1. Many current high school graduates are not prepared to read the texts of college and the workplace (p. 46).
2. K–12 texts have decreased in complexity (p. 47).
3. Increasing the complexity of texts from the primary grades onward can close the gap between the levels of texts in high school and college (p. 47).

Pearson (2013) concludes that there is at least some support for the first two assumptions. The third assumption involves an important unresolved question as to whether instruction in the lower grades can decrease the gap between the entry-level literacy skills needed for college or work and the CCSS exit level for 12th grade. This is a crucial issue because the standards were derived from a set of assumptions about the requirements of work and college and were "backmapped" from those assumptions. Williamson, Fitzgerald, and Stenner (2014) have recently suggested that there are at least three different models for closing the gap, and only one of them involves starting the gap-closing efforts in the primary grades.

Research on text complexity is proceeding at an increasing pace. Incorporating new research into the existing research base about the CCSS will be an important priority to augment the explication of the implicit model underlying the CCSS. It will be even more important as a contribution to practice. Many new perspectives on the issues surrounding text complexity have been explored in a special issue of *Elementary School Journal* (2014, December).

A model of reading electronic and multimedia text would also be useful as a way to expand the definition of text. Although a few standards now exist for these types of texts, a more elaborated set of standards is required as these texts are becoming increasingly common.

Finally, a theory of assessment that matches the new standards is critically important. Given the expanded and elaborated definition of literacy embodied in the CCSS, older assessments may not be able to measure students' success or failure in meeting them. Although the approaches being used by the two consortia working on CCSS-related assessments are intended to be practical developmental efforts, a model would be helping in guiding their development. Concerns such as learning progressions, item sampling, difficulty of text in items, and even the types of items should be addressed in a principled way by an explicit model.

CONCLUSION

The Common Core State Standards are the most rigorous set of education standards produced to date in the United States (Conley et al., 2011). It is clearly worth the effort to make all the details of the implicit model underlying these standards more obvious and explicit. It is also worth the effort to continue to elaborate and expand the current standards to account for new research findings and new forms of communication.

The implicit model that I have detailed in this chapter will be useful in guiding much of the activity surrounding the CCSS, helping to make the model consistent with the aims of the standards. The model will also be useful in evaluating new additions to the Standards for consistency. There can be precedence of the Standards over research, or vice versa. Often, certain areas of instruction are valued, even if there is not a sufficiently deep research base to justify that emphasis. In these cases, it is possible that the development of new standards could drive research. It is critical for all standards be evidence-based, so acceptance should be contingent on there not being negative evidence in the research literature.

It will take substantial effort to implement the CCSS, but the promise they hold is great. The standards are based on a model that expands conventional definitions of literacy and seems likely to lead to greater student capabilities. When stakeholders can see the organization of the standards as an explicit model, implementation will be far more efficient.

Although models of reading have often been viewed as academic exercises, this chapter has shown how they can affect the ways in which reading and reading instruction are viewed and practiced. Models of reading (and, of course, more generally of literacy) are crucial to the continued evolution of the CCSS in principled ways. They will provide the organization and discipline for new additions, potential deletions, and necessary changes. If the underlying models for standards cannot be made explicit, then the development and refinements of standards will be a far less efficient process.

REFERENCES

Alexander, P. A., & Jetton, T. L. (2000). Learning from text: A multidimensional and developmental perspective. In M. L. Kamil, P. B. Mosenthal, P. D. Pearson, & R. Barr (Eds.), *Handbook of reading research* (Vol. 3, pp. 285–310). Mahwah, NJ: Erlbaum.

Bergmann, G. (1953). Outline of an empiricist philosophy of physics. In H. Feigl & M. Brodbeck (Eds.), *Readings in the philosophy of science* (pp. 262–287). New York, NY: Appleton-Century-Crofts.

Brown, J., Goodman, K., & Marek, A. (Eds.) (1996). *Studies in miscue analysis: An annotated bibliography*. Newark, DE: International Reading Association.

Carnevale, A., Smith, N., & Strohl, J. (2010). *Help wanted: Projections of jobs education requirements through 2018*. Available at www9.georgetown.edu/grad/gppi/hpi/cew/pdfs/FullReport.pdf

Coleman, D., & Pimentel, S. (2012a). *Revised publishers' criteria for the Common Core State Standards in English Language arts and literacy, grades K–2*. Available at http://achievethecore. org/page/227/publishers-criteria-for-k-2-ela-literacy-detail-pg

Coleman, D., & Pimentel, S. (2012b). *Revised publishers' criteria for the Common Core State Standards in English Language arts and literacy, grades 3–12*. Available at http://achievethecore. org/page/228/publishers-criteria-for-3-12-ela-literacy-detail-pg

Conley, D., Drummond, K., Gonzalez, A., Rooseboom, J., & Stout, O. (2011). *Reaching the goal: The applicability and importance of the Common Core State Standards to college and career readiness*. Eugene, OR: EPIC. Available at www.epiconline.org/publications/documents/ ReachingtheGoal-FullReport.pdf

Gamson, D., Lu, X., & Eckert, S. (2013). *Challenging the research base of the Common Core State Standards: A historical reanalysis of text complexity. 42*(7), 381–391.

Goodman, K. (1967). Reading: A psycholinguistic guessing game. *Journal of the Reading Specialist, 6*, 126–135.

Goodman, K. (1969). Analysis of oral reading miscues: Applied psycholinguistics. *Reading Research Quarterly, 9*, 9–30.

Gough, P. B. (1972). One second of reading. In J. F. Kavanagh & I. G. Mattingly (Eds.), *Language by ear and by eye* (pp. 331–358). Cambridge, MA: MIT Press.

Hiebert, E. H., & Mesmer, H. A. (2013). Upping the ante of text complexity in the Common Core State Standards: Examining its potential impact on young readers. *Educational Researcher, 42* (1), 44–51.

Huey, E. B. (1908). *The psychology and pedagogy of reading*. New York, NY: Macmillan.

Kamil, M. L. (1978). Models of reading: What are the implications for instruction in comprehension? In S. Pflaum-Connor (Ed.), *Aspects of reading education*. Chicago, IL: National Society for Studies in Education.

Kamil, M. L. (1995). Some alternatives to paradigm wars. *Journal of Reading Behavior, 27*, 243–261.

Kamil, M. L., Afflerbach, P., Moje, E., & Pearson, P. D. (Eds.). (2011). *Handbook of reading research* (Vol. IV). New York, NY: Routledge.

Kamil, M. L., Mosenthal, P. B., Pearson, P. D., & Barr, R. (Eds.). (2000). *Handbook of reading research* (Vol. 3). Mahwah, NJ: Erlbaum.

LaBerge, D., & Samuels, S. J. (1974). Toward a theory of automatic information processing in reading. *Cognitive Psychology, 6*, 293–323.

Lachman, R. (1960). The model in theory construction. *Psychological Review, 67*, 113–120.

Mosenthal, P., & Kamil, M. L. (1991). Research in reading and writing: A model of progress. In R. Barr, M. Kamil, P. Mosenthal, & P. D. Pearson (Eds.), *Handbook of reading research* (Vol. 2, pp. 1013–1046). New York, NY: Longman.

National Assessment Governing Board. (2008). *Reading framework for the 2009 National Assessment of Educational Progress*. Washington, DC: Author.

National Center for Education Statistics. (2013). *The nation's report card: Trends in academic progress 2012* (NCES2013 456). Washington, DC: U.S. Department of Education.

National Governors Association Center for Best Practices & The Council of Chief State School Officers. (2010). *Common Core State Standards for English language arts and literacy in history/*

social studies, science, and technical subjects. Washington, DC: Authors. Available at www.corestandards.org/ELA-Literacy

National Institute of Child Health and Human Development. (2000). *Report of the National Reading Panel: Teaching children to read: An evidence-based assessment of the scientific research literature on reading and its implications for reading instruction: Reports of the subgroups.* Washington, DC: Author.

Nelson, J., Perfetti, C., Liben, D., & Liben M. (2012). *Measures of text difficulty: Testing their predictive value for grade levels and student performance.* Washington, DC: Council of Chief State School Officers. Available at www.achievethecore.org/content/upload/nelson_perfetti_liben_measures_of_text_difficulty_research_ela.pdf

Pearson, P. D. (2013). Research foundations of the Common Core State Standards in English language arts. In S. Neuman & L. Gambrell (Eds.), *Quality reading instruction in the age of Common Core State Standards* (pp. 237–262). Newark, DE: International Reading Association.

Pearson. P. D., & Hiebert, E. (2014). The state of the field: Qualitative analyses of text complexity. *Elementary School Journal, 115,* 479–500.

Ruddell, R. B., Ruddell, M. R., & Singer, H. (1994). *Theoretical models and processes of reading* (4th ed.). Newark, DE: International Reading Association.

Samuels, S. J., & Kamil, M. L. (1984). Models of the reading process. In P. D. Pearson, P. Mosenthal, M. Kamil, & R. Barr (Eds.), *Handbook of reading research* (pp. 184–224). New York, NY: Longman.

Singer, H., & Ruddell, R. B. (Eds.). (1976). *Theoretical models and processes of reading* (2nd ed.). Newark, DE: International Reading Association.

Singer, H., & Ruddell, R. B. (1985). *Theoretical models and processes of reading* (3rd ed.). Newark, DE: International Reading Association.

Singer, H., Ruddell, R. B., & Holmes, J. A. (Eds.). (1970). *Theoretical models and processes of reading.* Newark, DE: International Reading Association.

Snow, C., Burns, M., & Griffin, P. (1998). *Preventing reading difficulties in young children.* Washington, DC: National Academy Press.

Stanovich, K. E. (1980). Toward an interactive-compensatory model of individual differences in the development of reading fluency. *Reading Research Quarterly, 16,* 32–71.

Stanovich, K. E. (1990). A call for an end to the paradigm wars in reading research. *Journal of Reading Behavior, 22*(3), 221–231.

Williamson, G. L., Fitzgerald, J., & Stenner, J. (2014). Student reading growth illuminates the Common Core text-complexity standard: Raising both bars. *Elementary School Journal, 115,* 230–254.

CHAPTER 4

Oral Language

The Genesis and Development of Literacy for Schooling and Everyday Life

Rosalind Horowitz

Oral language is crucial to human daily life. It is also crucial to learning and to the development of literacy in school settings. There is scarcely an educational activity at any grade level that is not propelled and sustained by oral language. Through oral language, humans acquire new information in every discipline and explore infinite possibilities for advancing their knowledge and thinking. Students share ideas in a variety of ways orally and co-construct meanings and interpretations of content as they pursue school topics and content through their day-to-day life interactions.

The influential role of oral language in human linguistic, social, and cognitive development received important recognition in the United States in 2010 with the publication of the now widely adopted CCSS (Common Core State Standards for English Language Arts and Literacy, History/Social Studies, Sciences and Technical Subjects [CCSS; National Governors Association (NGA) Center for Best Practices & Council of Chief State School Officers (CCSSO), 2010]). What is distinguishable and different about the CCSS is that they identify oral language as a significant proficiency that merits attention in all of the disciplines in which we expect students to apply literacy practices—literature, science, and social studies. Also, the CCSS writers for mathematics recognized the critical role that oral language serves in mathematical development in the Common Core State Standards Initiative for Mathematics (2014). Inclusion of oral language within standards documents is a relatively new development in the United States. To add to the mix, the recently published Next Generation Science Standards (NGSS) are replete with references to language and literacy, with the lion's share of emphasis going to oral language (NGSS Lead States, 2013). Before these developments in the CCSS and the NGSS, oral expression was emphasized within regional and national curricula in other English-speaking nations, such as Canada, the United Kingdom (with standards for sign language), Australia, and New Zealand. Furthermore, Norway, a non-English-speaking country with a high literacy rate, has incorporated oral language standards for many years. Effective use of language in oral communication is recognized as essential if American students are to attain the competencies they will need for academic literacy and communicative expertise in the global workplace. In this chapter, I develop the thesis that the relationship between oral language and literacy—reading and writing—is critical both to American schooling and to everyday personal or work life in the 21st century. Based on a review of research, I argue that educators will benefit from a solid knowledge of the theory and research that complements the CCSS and even goes beyond the ideas expressed in the standards. With understanding of theory and research about oral language development and oral discourse processes of the classroom, teachers will be better able to apply this knowledge with sophistication and precision to discipline-based curricula, published pedagogical materials, or teacher-designed materials.

This chapter has three sections: The first section is an overview of scholarship on oral language and its relation to literacy. Included in this section are both historical perspectives about this relationship and research findings. The second section considers how oral language and literacy lay the foundation for the primary premises treated in the CCSS—namely, that oral language, along with reading and writing, is a fundamental tool for promoting the acquisition of knowledge and inquiry in all the disciplines of schooling. Oral language issues that are not sufficiently addressed within the CCSS are also explored. The final section presents a set of principles for the use of oral language to build and interface with literacy activities, drawn from research that supports teachers in their classroom implementation and augmentation of the CCSS.

THE ORAL LANGUAGE AND LITERACY CONNECTION

In this chapter, the term *oral language* refers to the sounds, words, utterances, sentences, and discourse structures used in dialogic communication. Oral language uses registers, styles of talk, dialects, culture-based vocabulary or syntax, and organizing macro-structures—all of which are strategically suited to one's intentions, the tasks at hand, audiences, or social contexts. *Literacy* refers to the effective language processing of printed texts—the reading and writing of extended text sources—that may be also at some point be incorporated with a range of additional media and technology. However, issues of discourse and register, for example, are implicated in literacy as well as in oral language—whether we are considering academic or everyday language in communication contexts.

Historical Roots of Oral Language and Literacy Development

Linguists have demonstrated how children's oral and written language may follow paths that reproduce elements of the evolution of language dating back some 50,000 generations, at least (Halliday, 1985, p. 9). References to oral language as an object, a symbolic system, and as a process predate current work by centuries, going back to ancient Greek scholars, who addressed communication and rhetoric in oratory. Among Greek scholars, oral language was fundamental to the art of composing, examined through the concept of *topoi*—topics or thesis-like statements used for invention and structure in writing (Dick, 1964; Thomas, 1989). Further, knowledge of features of oral language, such as the organization and presentation of ideas, has been regarded as essential for writing, reading, and, above all, reasoning and clarity of expression.

Relationships between oral language development and reading habits were described in substantial detail over a century ago in speech-rhetoric circles, as well as in the classic work *The Psychology and Pedagogy of Reading* by Edmund Burke Huey (1908). An interest in oral language, particularly inner speech (self-reflection or metacognition) during reading, has persisted in some measure throughout the latter half of the 20th and into the 21st centuries. Over time, oral language instruction has continued to be incorporated into the pedagogy of reading in the American classroom, based on language processing by ear and eye, with teachers using oral language activities to support the development of decoding skills, phonemic awareness, vocabulary knowledge, and sentence construction (Kavanagh & Mattingly, 1972; Smith, 1934/1965). However, there has been less attention given by researchers to larger language units, the cognitive structuring of ideas or the logic needed to process procedural or persuasive information in specific everyday situational or academic contexts.

Until recently, we have seen little research about the role of oral language in listening comprehension, reading, and writing. However, research on listening comprehension and its relationship to the development of reading comprehension proficiency, especially in English as a Second Language (ESL) instruction, is increasing given the large numbers of immigrant, mobile citizens (Hakuta, 2014; Lund, 1991).

Research Overview

Research on oral language has focused on five areas that appear to have influenced the CCSS writers. As this brief review of research indicates, each of the areas has implications for the role of oral language in reading and writing instructional design and implementation.

Everyday language development. At a young age, children develop skill at expressing their thoughts orally, progressing from single-word utterances to more complex, complete conversational constructions (Ervin-Tripp & Strage, 1985; Halliday, 1987). In some families and cultures, parent language practices expand a child's language, cognitive awareness, thinking, and reasoning. Bernstein's (1971) research on elaborated and restricted codes in the United Kingdom showed that talk was limited in families of low socioeconomic means. He argued that the talk that did occur in mother-child interactions in low-income families was often truncated, telegraphic, or abbreviated. The talk did not elicit oral responses or reasoned thinking on the part of the children. For example, a mother's directives might include: *Close the door. Eat your supper. Go to bed.* These examples lack information about intentionality or purpose and provide no oral explanations of the consequences for not following through, which prevent children from learning *if-then* constructions and, above all, beyond the linguistics of these constructions, the situational motivation and reasoning needed for human action.

In families that use what Bernstein (1971) described as an elaborated code, the form of elaboration and explanation varies considerably from that within the restricted code. Imagine, for instance, a parent talking with a child who is reluctant to go to bed. Rather than saying, "Go to bed," a parent using the elaborated code would provide information about the consequences of staying up late on the next day's activities. The parent might say, "If you do not go to bed, you will not be able to get up on time. You'll be tired and late for school. You'll also be too tired to do well in school." This extension of language, with the incorporation of actions that follow a situation, would give the child several logical reasons for following the parent's request. The differences between the two codes, according to Bernstein, carried significant implications for differential performance in school settings by students in different socioeconomic classes.

At the time this work was published, Bernstein's (1971) research was the subject of international attention, including heated criticism for discriminating against low-income families. In the more than 40 years since its publication, however, Bernstein's work has come to be regarded as offering valuable insights (Moore, 2013).

Relatedly in the United States, Heath (1982) examined the practice of storybook reading in homes, especially prior to bedtime. She concluded that in the homes of the low-income families where bedtime adult-child reading and corresponding talk were rare, young children missed out on language and listening experiences that support their understanding of narrative and story lines and influence later reading habits.

Hart and Risley (1995) reported that children who lack access to particular types of oral language experiences in their homes are not well equipped to acquire new content knowledge and forms of discourse in school. They examined children from 7 months to 3 years of age who were from welfare, working-class, or professional families. Children from the welfare families heard 32 million fewer words than children from professional families. "In four years, an average child in a professional family would accumulate experience with almost 45,000,000 words, an average child in a working-class family 26,000,000 words, and an average child in a welfare family 13,000,000 words" (Hart & Risley, 1992, p. 9). This would suggest that the children in welfare homes had an alarming 32-million-word gap. The consequences of these findings are dramatic. And the evidence is overwhelming that this oral vocabulary knowledge predicts reading comprehension and school success (Dickinson et al., 2010; McKeown, Beck, Omanson, & Perfetti, 1983; Snow, Burns, & Griffith, 1998). E. D. Hirsch (2014) extends this research by arguing that oral vocabulary is, ultimately, the culprit in producing social inequality in our society.

In addition to vocabulary exposure, Hart and Risley note that parent styles of talk, parents' efforts at encouraging interaction with their children, and valence—the tone parents use with children—are all factors that contribute to a child's language development and ultimately performance in school settings. Parental imitations of a child's talk—a high form of compliment—as well as a parent's repetition of the child's expressions and ideas provide affirmative feedback that builds a child's sense of confidence; these activities are frequent in professional families' interactions. Disapprovals are distinctly avoided in professional homes but were found to be exercised frequently in the welfare homes Hart and Risley studied.

Research beginning in the 1960s has had a consistent theme: Oral language and literacy develop best when children acquire important skills and practices through the processes of child-adult conversations (Snow, 1983). A section of the CCSS (2010) entitled "Stay on Topic Within a Grade and Across Grades" recognizes the foundational role oral language plays in literacy acquisition. This section of the CCSS states that "children in the early grades (particularly K–2) should participate in *rich structured conversations* with an adult in response to the written texts that are read aloud, orally comparing and contrasting as well as analyzing and synthesizing" (p. 33; italics added). Above all, children acquire many language and cognitive skills through structured conversation, including the ability to listen and respond effectively. Through conversation, children also become skilled at discerning speakers' purposes in speaking, as well as the purposes and points of view of the authors of written texts.

Oral language in listening and reading comprehension. Typically, children begin school with speaking and listening skills they have gained from interacting in their homes and communities. Once children enter school, this oral language foundation is built on and extended in school activities (Resnick & Snow, 2009; Sticht & James, 1984). Both receptive and expressive vocabulary knowledge in oral language influence beginning reading skill acquisition (Scarborough, 2001; Wise, Sevcik, Morris, Lovett, & Wolf, 2007). But the relationship between oral language and learning in content areas and of written language proficiencies is not unidirectional. That is, levels of oral language do influence children's learning of content and of written language and thinking skills but, at the same time, students' oral language capabilities are enriched and extended as a result of learning new content and becoming literate. For example, Feitelson and colleagues showed that listening to story reading had significant effects on the language development and reading comprehension of children in the early grades (Feitelson, Goldstein, Iraqui, & Share, 1993; Feitelson, Kita, & Goldstein, 1986).

After an extensive review of existing research that compared listening and reading comprehension, Sticht, Beck, Hauke, Kleiman, and James (1974) concluded that listening comprehension and reading comprehension are highly interrelated. Sticht et al. have gone so far as to argue that listening and reading comprehension depend on the same general comprehension processes. The perspective that Sticht and colleagues take is that listening proficiency facilitates and even predicts the level of skill that will be achieved in reading (Sticht et al., 1974; Sticht & James, 1984).

Numerous studies substantiate this unitary process view, that listening and reading engage many of the same underlying processes (e.g., Curtis, 1980; Kintsch & Kozminsky, 1977; Sinatra, 1990). According to the unitary perspective (Sticht et al., 1974; Sticht & James, 1984), once students have mastered decoding, they should be performing fairly consistently across listening and reading tasks. Sticht et al. (1974) based this conclusion on the studies they identified in their comprehensive review of the existing research at the time. Up to grade 7, performance in listening comprehension was generally higher than performance in reading comprehension. In adulthood, the direction of the difference was reversed. Diakidoy, Stylianou, Karefillidou, and Papageorgiou (2005) have confirmed a pattern of decreasing differences in listening and reading performances as students move through the grades. This unitary processing may be altered—that is, modified by dual processing as a result of text complexity and school tasks in secondary and higher education, when students recognize the benefits of rereading and close analysis of content that are much more difficult to achieve in the listening mode.

For poorer readers, the ability to comprehend through listening can serve as a compensatory scaffold. Horowitz and Samuels (1985) examined the reading processing and recall of informational text with 38 6th-graders who exhibited both good and poor reading skills. Students were asked either to listen or to read aloud easier or harder informational text passages in a counterbalanced design. Students immediately retold what they read or heard and answered multiple-choice comprehension questions about the passage content. Poor readers demonstrated better listening comprehension with the easy text than the good readers who listened to the same text. This suggested that the poor readers were compensating for their poor reading skills by using listening comprehension skills, but this was not the case with hard texts, on which better readers demonstrated superior comprehension. Extending this research, Rubin, Hafer, and Arata (2000) studied college student listening and reading by varying the mode of processing with text types. They found that listening comprehension increased when students listened to an oral-based discourse (over a literate-based text) and reading comprehension increased when reading a more literate-based discourse (over an oral-based discourse). In unison, this research suggests that the mode of processing is related to the text language and text type.

Schreiber (1987) argued that reading comprehension is more difficult than listening comprehension because the written text lacks prosodic elements of speech that help with the comprehension and interpretation of discourse. Schreiber's research with children who were learning to read in the early grades demonstrated that spoken words offer clues about stress, intonation, and duration of intonations that are important in recognizing sentence structure. Children listened to tape-recorded sentences that were spliced and altered for prosodic features (stress, intonation, pauses, and so on). Schreiber found that children of ages 6, 7, and 8 relied on prosody more than adults. This study showed that perceptual processing of sentence structures of speech is influenced by elements of sound. These sound counterparts are not readily recognized in silent text reading, which poses a text-processing difficulty for many children.

Substantial time should be devoted to oral reading and listening to talk and texts in classrooms to help children move from auditory processing to the visual processing of language that is required for advanced learning with varying texts (Horowitz, 1991). Not only is this useful for advanced learning and teaching, but students often prefer the oral expression of text content. Ninth-graders in a Texas magnet school revealed in a survey that they preferred a teacher's oral reading of no-narrative, expository/informational sources over silent reading so that they could more effectively focus and concentrate on the meaning of the text.

Talk about text. When students read texts in school settings, guided by effective instruction, we know that they don't just read; they also talk about the texts. And we have learned a great deal about the role that talk plays in promoting participation (e.g., Soter et al., 2008) and comprehension (e.g., Murphy et al., 2009; Nystrand, 2006). A recurrent theme in this line of inquiry is that classroom teachers who employ more interpretive and critical foci (what we might refer to as "higher-order" or "deeper" questioning) promote higher levels of participation (Murphy et al., 2009; Soter et al., 2008). Less consistently, the trend is for these sorts of probes to promote higher levels of reading comprehension (e.g., Applebee, Langer, Nystrand, & Gamoran, 2003; McKeown Beck, Blake, 2009; Taylor, Pearson, Peterson, & Rodriguez, 2003). Chinn, Anderson, and Waggoner (2001) used an approach that emphasized text-based collaborative reasoning about challenging mores and ethical questions related to stories. They found that the approach increased critical thinking about these issues to a greater degree than did more recitation-style (known-answer) questions. Collaborative reasoning has also been shown to elicit long-term improvements in the quality of arguments and writing produced by students (Dong, Anderson, Kim, & Li, 2008). Van den Branden (2000) found that even primary grade students improve their comprehension when they are required to collaborate to negotiate a consensus meaning for a text by explaining their reasoning to one another. In short, there is good reason to promote rich, dialogic talk about texts in classrooms.

The CCSS (2010) have implicitly acknowledged this body of work on the role of talk in literacy development by recommending, for example, that students listen to

young learners preferred more difficult over less difficult texts—namely, a book on robotics, a more difficult book, over one on space travel, an easier book. Further, discussion as an instructional strategy can widen the range of possible meanings and interpretations that students consider when they are reading a text; ideas occur to them in collaboration with their peers that may never have arisen in private readings. How students comprehend speech acts and topics collectively can influence their ability to understand and develop arguments independently.

Presently, much of the research on classroom discussions and reading is largely correlational or single-case studies of discourse in a given classroom or individuals or a set of speakers in the case of one-on-one instruction (Nystrand, 2006). There is precious little empirical research that compares using such discussion practices as a predictor of improved reading comprehension; a notable exception is the elaborate meta-analysis of the experimental effects of discussion on comprehension discussed earlier (Murphy, Wilkinson, Soter, Hennessey, & Alexander,2009) or participation (Soter et al., 2008).

During the past 50 years, research studies of oral language have identified the development of linguistic constructions as reflections of psychological and social knowledge across preschool, primary, and elementary grades. Without a doubt, we know more about the genesis of oral language outside of school than we do about the development of oral language in academic contexts and among adolescents (Schleppegrell, 2001, 2004). The CCSS cite Graff (2003) as indicating that only 20% of students entering college are prepared to use arguments and engage in argumentation, in either oral or written language. Achugar, Schleppegrell, and Oteiza (2007) note that writing in the academic register requires complex and abstract thinking. They believe students will benefit from explicit teaching of language analysis, which will help build reasoning and argumentation skills.

ORAL LANGUAGE AND THE DEVELOPMENT OF LITERACY WITHIN THE CCSS

The primary goal of the CCSS is to create a body of educational standards that unify and create consistency among state educational objectives. Through the implementation of the standards, proponents of the CCSS hope to raise performance and proficiency levels of students across the United States. Advocates also hope students will become more internationally competitive. As Chapter 2 in this volume by Kapinus and Long suggests, the links between research and recommendations within any policy document such as the CCSS can be tenuous or nonexistent. Such a tenuous relationship between research, practice, and policy is not unique to the CCSS, as Kim (2008) has illustrated with other educational initiatives. This would suggest that a volume like this one as well as teacher training are needed to provide the links among theory, research, practice, and policy to facilitate implementation of CCSS.

CCSS Recognition of the Importance of Oral Language Development

The CCSS (2010) suggest that oral language activity is completely intertwined with reading, writing, and participation in academic tasks. The standards treat language use and functions as cognitive and reasoning processes and include relevant benchmarks for each grade. The CCSS also remind us that different domains of knowledge utilize different types of text patterns and oral discourse structures. Thus, as previously mentioned, a text on history may use cause-and-effect structures. In contrast, science may incorporate problem-solution and cause-and-effect structures that are used differently from those in history texts (Horowitz, 1985a, 1985b).

The CCSS (2010) call for students to "evaluate a speaker's point of view, reasoning and use of evidence and rhetoric" (p. 22). They also state that students should be able to: "Present information, findings, and supporting evidence such that listeners can follow the line of reasoning, and the organization, development, and style are appropriate to task, purpose, and audience" (p. 22). In addition, the standards identify three kinds of texts that should be addressed in the curricula of different subject areas and across grades K–12: arguments, informative/explanatory texts, and narratives. Of these three types of texts, we know the most about children's reading of narratives and the structures of narratives used in the lower grades in schools. It should be recognized that the CCSS have identified being able to write arguments as essential for academic success, emphasizing this point repeatedly throughout the writing standards. This is no coincidence. Cogent reasoning and use of evidence—basic elements of argumentation—are characterized in the CCSS as essential to a democratic nation.

The CCSS' emphasis on argumentation supports the rationale for teaching argumentation and reasoning, skills that are based on higher-order comprehension and the production of discourse. In addition, the standards view student discussions about texts as an avenue for building social competence. The CCSS (2010) call for increasing collaborative interaction where students learn "to work together, express and listen carefully to ideas, integrate information for oral, visual, quantitative, and media sources" (p. 8). Students are being asked to integrate and evaluate these sources and to work with them strategically and collaboratively, on the plausible grounds that these practices will be needed for life demands and the work world.

The CCSS acknowledge a finding from research—that there are considerable variations within spoken language and written language (Biber, 1991, 2006). The nature of vocabulary and even the grammar that a writer uses in an email to a colleague can vary significantly from the vocabulary and grammar a writer might use in an academic volume. Similarly, the language that a 12-year-old female uses in presenting a book report in English class is dramatically different from the language she would use in lunchroom conversations with her best female friends.

Differences in language use go beyond these variations as a result of formal or informal language contexts. For example, the use of vocabulary differs substantially between narrative and expository texts (Hiebert & Cervetti, 2012). The words that make narrative texts unique are typically words that describe personality traits, emotions, ways of communicating, and the movement of characters across space and contexts. In expository texts, unique words pertain to the topic under discussion and the conceptual clusters into which groups of words fall. They can be as specific as the properties that distinguish between soluble and nonsoluble substances. They constitute what Hirsch (2014) identifies as "domain specificity."

Unique uses of vocabulary go much beyond distinctions between genres. Individual content areas have their own specialized vocabularies (Schleppegrell, 2001). The vocabulary of physics rarely overlaps with the vocabulary of biology, for example. Becoming familiar with the vocabulary of one content area is unlikely to support learning in another (e.g., *centrifugal force* and *inversion* in physics; *cytoplasm* and *mitochondria* in biology). Further, specialties and topics within content areas have their own vocabularies. Within physics, for instance, the vocabulary associated with speed, velocity, and acceleration (e.g., *momentum, projectile motion*) differs from the vocabulary associated with light and optics (e.g., *radiation, incandescence, phosphorescence*). There may well be specialties that combine physics and biology in which vocabulary overlaps (e.g., the vocabulary of argumentation, with words such as *claim, evidence, warrant, assertion, assumption*, and the like), but, at least for students from grades K–12, it will be rare for the specialized vocabulary of disciplines to overlap. And sometimes when it does overlap, the meaning of a particular term may be quite different (e.g., the word *force* in physics vs. *force* in history and civics). Vocabulary in the CCSS (2010) emerges in three areas of language use: reading, writing, and speaking/listening.

Although research on text structures was at its height in the 1970s and 1980s, it did not fully develop in content fields. The CCSS give attention to macro-features (i.e., the larger structures) of written language as well as vocabulary. Among these macro-features are the manner in which the text is organized, the manner in which an argument is developed through a discussion, the manner in which arguments are supported with evidence, and the nature of conclusions (particularly the degree to which these conclusions are supported by evidence).

Language Shortcomings in the Common Core State Standards

The CCSS make some significant contributions toward establishing a common set of standards, across grades K–college, for oral language and listening, reading, and the production of writing. But, from the perspective of research on oral language and its relationship to literacy (Horowitz, 1973, 2007, 2015; Horowitz & Samuels, in press; Lawrence & Snow, 2011), the claim could be made that the CCSS only skim the surface of this topic and, thus, fail to characterize accurately what is already known and what is still needed. More specifically, the previous five research topics are underrepresented in the CCSS and in the national policy conversation about language and literacy.

First, insufficient attention is given to the range of student populations being served in the United States. Most classrooms today are filled with English language learners who are often bilingual and migrant or immigrant populations living in poverty. The CCSS Report (2010) disavows itself of responsibility for these populations, the groups we serve in most urban schools in America. The section entitled "What is Not Covered by the Standards" notes in Item 5 "It is also beyond the scope of the Standards to define the full range of supports appropriate for English language learners and for students with special needs" (p. 6). However, despite this disclaimer of responsibility, they go on to say these populations do in fact need opportunity to learn: "At the same time, all students must have the opportunity to learn and meet the same high standards if they are to access the knowledge and skills necessary in their post-high school lives" (p. 6).

These new immigrant populations come with unique life challenges and language characteristics. They come with oral-based cultures and discourse types, oral narratives, and written language practices used in everyday life beyond schools. These oral-based styles of discourse are significantly different from the talk and particularly the essayist style of academic writing that has been and is increasingly characteristic of schooling

(Horowitz, 2014). Not only are the language and literacy practices of many cultural groups different from those of earlier immigrant groups of the 1920s, but the new immigrant students and their families are also confronted by the changes created by the surrounding world and the digital revolution. Over 30 years ago, Ong (1982/2012) distinguished between orality and the technologies of literacy. Scholars have long hypothesized about the shifts in thinking generated by the transition from orality to literacy, both for individuals and for cultures (see, e.g., Havelock, 1988). Ong described the phenomenon as the "technologizing of the word." Differences in oracies and literacies of students from a variety of cultures may be extensive, and these differences may be exacerbated as bilingual and transnational communities confront the digital-global world. Creating productive learning environments that recognize and build on the oracies and literacies of cultures within classrooms and the demands of literacy in the digital-global age comprises perhaps the biggest challenge for American educators (Bunch, Kibler, & Pimentel, 2012; Hull & Moje, 2012).

Second, save for a token acknowledgment in Reading Standard 7, the CCSS do not address in detail the changing nature of text sources: the use of digital sources, multiple literacies, and multiple modalities—and fast and slow types of cognition. Yet, children and youth now process these on a daily basis both inside and outside of school. Some research suggests that texts are becoming more oral-like and conversational in nature, with a reduction in technical vocabulary, shorter sentence structures, shorter paragraphing, and more easily comprehensible sources. For example, Biber and Finegan (1989) developed an empirically based model of stylistic variation of oral and written English prose across 4 centuries, showing that texts are becoming more personal, experiential, situational, and nonabstract. This would suggest that students would benefit from greater exposure to and practice with a broader range of oral discourses and genres. Oral experiences are not only based on conversations, but also include oral expression within digital media, lectures, and debates. The genesis and development of literacy now has incorporated a variety of forms of symbolic representations. These include oral representations conveyed by multiple media: e-books, smart phones, tablets, videos, charts, graphics, computer imaging, and more. Their impact on literacy needs to be studied more carefully than it has in the past. Standard 5 in speaking and listening calls for the strategic use of digital media—textual, graphical, audio, visual, and interactive elements—resulting in an interaction among multimodal literacies. Even so, there is still so much to learn about these new media that only a sea change in our research and development work will suffice to understand their role in tomorrow's literacy curriculum.

Third, the standards would benefit from greater attention to writing and the vast literature from rhetoric, and its relation to reading. Exposing students to the concept of voice and tone in writing, to the options available for achieving and processing an author's style, and to the various positions of readers and writers as they produce and receive communication, particularly persuasive text would strengthen the CCSS. Writers engaged in the composing act should develop an author's voice and achieve stylistic positioning and a relationship to readers, while crediting sources of evidence that advance reasoning.

Fourth, projections of the kinds of tasks and contexts in which reading, writing, and learning will occur in the 21st century need to be made as states and consortia of states (such as the CCSS) establish standards that will ensure individuals are ready for college and careers. The task requirements for college and workplace success warrant closer attention. What are the future trends for jobs and the literacy uses in the next generation of occupations? What skills in reading or writing will be needed in future careers and professions? What applications of oral language are anticipated in reading and writing?

The CCSS are an attempt to unify educational standards in the United States, although some states have not adopted these standards. Initially, 45 states as well as the District of Columbia, three territories, and the Department of Defense Education Activity endorsed the Standards. Since that time, some states, such as Indiana, Oklahoma, and Mississippi, have reversed their adoption of the standards and/or their participation in the CCSS-aligned assessment consortia (see Kapinus & Long, Chapter 2 this volume). The standards remain controversial to some educators, researchers, and policymakers—and increasingly, the American public (McDonnell & Weatherford, 2013). As has been argued in this chapter, in particular areas, the standards are incomplete, especially in their treatment of key aspects of oral language.

APPLYING THE CCSS ELA ORAL LANGUAGE AND LITERACY PERSPECTIVE

One way of making space for oral language in the CCSS and schools is to adopt a set of principles to serve as supports for teaching practices, student activities, and curricular goals that ensure oral language and literacy development for the populations we serve and the future requirements of higher education and work life. The following statements summarize widely recognized findings about the role of oral language, literacy, and learning from the research literature (e.g., Horowitz, 2007; Lawrence & Snow, 2011).

1. *The development of oral language in young learners' inventive play is the first step to engaging in linguistic creative expression.* Developmentally, oral language—used in storytelling, role playing, poetry, song, and with drawings and dance—is a precursor to reading, writing, and novel thinking. As a precursor, oral language gives children knowledge of the conventions and inventiveness that will also surface in and through written language and may be used in the children's own writing. When used in cooperation, oral and written language may result in a higher level of meaning-making.

2. *Oral language need not be only speech that is voiced aloud. There is evidence that a reader has inner speech characterized by metacognition (thinking about one's own thinking) and self-reflection* (Vygotsky, 1986). Research has shown that good readers report using inner speech while reading (Horowitz & Samuels, 1985; Huey, 1908). This inner speech serves the reader (and writer) well in facilitating engagement with and comprehension of a text. Poor readers often do not utilize inner speech. Beck, McKeown, and Worthy (1995) showed that voicing of text, such as subvocalizing, actually increased the reading comprehension of elementary children. The ability to use outer voicing or inner voicing is influenced by readers' encounters with everyday speech and the vocabulary and syntax they are accustomed to hearing, such as dialogue with parents, peers, and siblings.

3. *Oral language, such as talk that follows a reading activity, allows readers to recompose, reflect, analyze, synthesize, and evaluate the text.* Best done with a teacher or peer, this practice helps readers comprehend and organize their thoughts about the reading as they speak about it. Textbooks and teacher

manuals provide multiple avenues for discussion after reading. This practice is also valuable for remembering and using academic content.

4. *Oral and written language represent distinct symbolic systems that are different modes of making meaning* (Halliday, 1987). Oral and written language modes are not the same, but they do emanate from the same inner wellspring of knowledge and linguistic intentions that children bring to any communicative context. In the best of circumstances, oral and written language complement each other. When used in cooperation, they may result in a higher level of meaning. Students must be attuned to the differences between speech and writing, if they are to process and comprehend written language. Because writing incorporates prosodic features of oral language (pitch, pauses, stress words, rhythm), linguists have shown that writing is an imperfect representation of speech (Chafe & Danielewicz, 1987). This perspective challenges the earlier view of linguists such as Bloomfield (1933) who argued that writing was essentially speech written down. In working with teachers, I have heard teachers proclaim that students should "write as they talk." This conclusion may be misleading under certain circumstances. Numerous scholars have disputed Bloomfield's assertion, demonstrating that writing is not simply speech written down (Akinasso, 1982; Biber, 1991; Chafe & Danielewicz, 1987; Elbow, 2013; Halliday, 1987). Students must be attuned to the differences between speech and writing if they are to process and comprehend written language. These differences present challenges for all students, but also the special populations we serve, who must transpose written cues into the sounds of oral language that are not well represented by the conventions of punctuation, italicization, and other symbolic markings in the text.

The CCSS have taken a small step toward helping districts and schools develop an appreciation of oral language and its role in literacy. Literacy educators and researchers can creatively heighten the role of oral language across the grades by relying on research-based knowledge that expands the development of literacy for schooling and everyday life. Indeed, those who aspire to expand the repertoire of learners' reading and writing expertise would do well to look to speaking and listening as the language and conceptual foundations of literate behavior.

Acknowledgment: This chapter was completed with the diligent and meticulous assistance of Lisa A. Griffith, College of Public Policy, Masters of Public Administration, The University of Texas–San Antonio. Appreciation is also extended to Ellen R. Van Meter for calling to my attention some key parameters of the CCSS and to Traci Kelley, who assisted with the editing of the final copy, both in the College of Education and Human Development at The University of Texas—San Antonio.

REFERENCES

Achugar, M., Schleppegrell, M., & Oteiza, T. (2007). Engaging teachers in language analysis: A functional linguistics approach to reflective literacy. *English Teaching: Practice and Critique,* 6(2), 8–24.

Akinasso, F. N. (1982). On the differences between spoken and written language. *Language and speech*. 25(2), 97–125.

Applebee, A. N., Langer, J. A., Nystrand, M., & Gamoran, A. (2003). Discussion-based approaches to developing understanding: Classroom instruction and student performance in middle and high school English. *American Educational Research Journal*, 40(3), 685–730. doi:10.3102/00028312040003685

Beck, I. L., & McKeown, M. G. (2007). How teachers can support productive classroom talk: Move the thinking to the students. In R. Horowitz (Ed.), *Talking texts: How speech and writing interact in school learning* (pp. 207–220). London, UK, & New York, NY: Routledge/Taylor & Francis.

Beck, I. L., McKeown, M. G., & Worthy, J. (1995). Giving a text voice can improve students' understanding. *Reading Research Quarterly*, 30, 220–238.

Bernstein, B. (1971). *Class, codes and control* (Vol. I). London, UK: Routledge & Kegan Paul.

Biber, D. (1991). *Variation across speech and writing*. Cambridge, UK: Cambridge University Press.

Biber, D. (2006). *University language: A corpus-based study of spoken and written registers*. Amsterdam, The Netherlands: John Benjamins.

Biber, D., & Finegan, E. (1989). Drift and the level of English style: A history of three genres. *Language*, 65, 487–517.

Bloomfield, L. (1933). *Language*. New York, NY: Holt.

Bunch, G. C., Kibler, A., & Pimentel, S. (May 1, 2012). *Realizing opportunities for English learners in the Common Core language arts and disciplinary literacy standards*. Paper presented at the annual meeting of the American Educational Research Association, San Francisco, CA.

Chafe, W., & Danielewicz, J. (1987). Properties of spoken and written language. In R. Horowitz & S. J. Samuels (Eds.), *Comprehending oral and written language* (pp. 83–116). San Diego, CA, & London, UK: Academic Press.

Chinn, C. A., Anderson, R. C., & Waggoner, M. A. (2001). Patterns of discourse in two kinds of literature discussion. *Reading Research Quarterly*, 36(4), 378–411. doi:10.1598/ RRQ.36.4.3

Common Core Standards for Mathematics. (2014, January 1). Common Core State Standards Initiative. Available at www.corestandards.org/math

Common Core State Standards Initiative. (2010). Common Core State Standards for English/ language arts and literacy in history/social studies, science, and technical subjects. Available at www.corestandards.org/the-standards

Conley, D. (2013). *Getting ready for college, careers and the Common Core: What every educator needs to know*. San Francisco, CA: Jossey-Bass.

Curtis, M. E. (1980). Development of components of reading skill. *Journal of Educational Psychology*, 72, 656–669.

Diakidoy, I-A. N., Stylianou, P., Karefillidou, C., & Papageorgiou, P. (2005). The relationship between listening and reading comprehension of different types of text at increasing grade levels. *Reading Psychology*, 26, 55–80.

Dick, R. C. (1964). Topoi: An approach to inventing arguments. *Speech Teacher*, 13, 313–319.

Dickinson, J. K., Goninkoff, R. M., & Hirsh-Pasek, K. K. (2010). Speaking out for language: Why language is central to reading development. *Educational Researcher*, 39(4), 305–310.

Dong, T., Anderson, R. C., Kim, I., & Li, Y. (2008). Collaborative reasoning in China and Korea. *Reading Research Quarterly*, 43(4), 400–424. doi:10.1598/RRQ.43.4.5

Elbow, P. (2013). *Vernacular eloquence: What speech can bring to writing*. Oxford, UK: Oxford University Press.

Ervin-Tripp, S. M., & Strage, A. (1985). Parent-child discourse. In T. Van Dijk (Ed.), *Handbook of discourse analysis* (Vol. 3, pp. 67–78). New York, NY: Academic Press.

Feitelson, D., Goldstein, Z., Iraqui J., & Share, D.I. (1993). Effects of listening to story reading on aspects of literacy acquisition in a diglossic situation. *Reading Research Quarterly, 28*, 70–79.

Feitelson, D., Kita, B., & Goldstein, Z. (1986). Effects of listening to series stories on first graders' comprehension and use of language. *Research in the Teaching of English, 20*, 339–356.

Fiano, D. A. (2014, January, February, March). Primary discourse and expressive oral language in a kindergarten class. *Reading Research Quarterly. 49*(1), 61–84.

Graff, G. (2003). *Clueless in academe.* New Haven, CT: Yale University Press.

Hakuta, K. (2014). Kenji Hakuta on Common Core assessment. Understanding language initiatives at Stanford University. Virtual Institute on assessment at textproject.org

Halliday, M. A. K. (1985). *Spoken and written language.* Victoria, Australia: Deakin University.

Halliday, M.A.K. (1987). Spoken and written modes of meaning. In R. Horowitz & S. J. Samuels (Eds.), *Comprehending oral and written language* (pp. 55–113). San Diego, CA, & London, UK: Academic Press.

Hart, B., & Risley, T. (1995). *Meaningful differences in everyday experiences of young American children.* Baltimore, MD: Brookes.

Hart, B., & Risley, T. R. (2003). The early catastrophe: The 30 million word gap. *American Educator, 27*(1), 4–9.

Havelock, E. A. (1988). *The muse learns to write: Reflections on orality and literacy from antiquity to the present.* New Haven, CT: Yale University Press.

Heath, S. B. (1982, April). What no bedtime story means: Narrative skills in home and school. *Language in Society, 11*(1), 49–76.

Hiebert, E. H., & Cervetti, G. N. (2012). What differences in narrative and informational texts mean for the learning and instruction of vocabulary. In J. Baumann & E. Kame'enui (Eds.), *Vocabulary instruction: Research to practice* (2nd ed., pp. 322–344). New York, NY: Guilford Press.

Hillocks, G. (2011). *Teaching argument writing, 6–12: Supporting claims with relevant evidence and clear reasoning.* Portsmouth, NH: Heinemann.

Hirsch, E. D. (2014, October 6). *The wealth in words: Vocabulary and social inequality.* Available at http://go.turnitin.com/webcast/ssw14/wealth-in-words

Horowitz, R. (1973). *A summary and analysis of recent studies of parent-child interaction with implications for language development.* Unpublished master's thesis. The University of Minnesota–Twin Cities.

Horowitz, R. (1985a). Text patterns. Part I. *Journal of Reading, 28*(5), 448–454.

Horowitz, R. (1985b). Text patterns. Part II. *Journal of Reading, 28*(6), 534–541.

Horowitz, R. (1990). Discourse in oral and written language: Critical contrasts for literacy and schooling. In J. H. A. L. de Jong & D. K. Stevenson (Eds.), *Individualizing the assessment of language abilities* (pp. 108–26). Clevedon Avon, UK: Multilingual Matters.

Horowitz, R. (1991). Orality and literacy and the design of schooling for the 21st century: Some introductory remarks. *Text, 11*(1), i–xvi. Berlin, Germany, Amsterdam, The Netherlands, & New York, NY: Mouton de Gruyter.

Horowitz, R. (Ed.) (2007). *Talking texts: How speech and writing interact in school learning.* London, UK, and New York, NY: Routledge/Taylor & Francis.

Horowitz, R. (2014, November 20). *Literacy and orality: The reconstruction of writing in technologically and culturally evolving contexts.* Meadows Lecture for Excellence in Education. Distinguished Invited Address. The University of North Texas–Denton.

Horowitz, R. (Ed.). (2015). *Orality and literacy in the 21st century: Prospects for writing and pedagogy.* A special themed issue for *Writing & Pedagogy, 7*(2), Shefield, UK, & Bristol, CT: Equinox.

Horowitz, R., & Freeman, S. H. (1995). Robots vs. spaceships: The role of discussion in kindergartners' and second graders' preferences for science text. *The Reading Teacher, 49*(1), 30–40.

Horowitz, R., & Samuels, S. J. (1985). Reading and listening to expository text. *Journal of Reading Behavior, 17*(3), 185–198.

Horowitz, R., & Samuels, S. J. (Eds.). (in press). *The acheivement gap and reading: Complex causes, persistent issues, possible solutions.* New York, NY: Routledge/Taylor & Francis.

Huey, E. B. (1908). *The psychology and pedagogy of reading.* Boston, MA: MIT Press.

Hull, G., & Moje, E. B. (2012, January). *What is the development of literacy the development of?* Paper presented at the Understanding Language Conference, Stanford University, Palo Alto, CA.

Kavanagh, J. F., & Mattingly, I. G. (Eds.). (1972). *Language by ear and by eye. The relationships between speech and reading.* Cambridge, MA: MIT Press.

Kellaghan, T. (2001). Reading literacy standards in Ireland. In G. Shield & U. Delaigh (Eds.), *Reading matters: A fresh start* (pp. 3–19). Dublin, Ireland: Reading Association of Ireland.

Kim, J. S. (2008). Research and the reading wars. In F. J. Hess (Ed.), *When research matters: How scholarship influences education policy* (pp. 89–111). Cambridge, MA: Harvard Education Press.

Kintsch, W., & Kozminsky, E. (1977). Summarizing stories after reading and listening. *Journal of Educational Psychology, 69,* 491–499.

Lawrence, J., & Snow, C. E. (2011). In M. Kamil, P. D. Pearson, E. B. Moje, & P. Afferbach (Eds.), *Handbook of reading research* (pp. 320–337). London, UK: Routledge/Taylor & Francis.

Lund, R. J. (1991). A comparison of second language listening and reading comprehension. *The Modern Language Journal, 75*(2), 196–204.

McDonnell, L. M., & Weatherford M. S. (2013, December). Organized interests and the Common Core. *Educational Researcher, 42*(9), 488–497.

McKeown, M. G., Beck, I. L., & Blake, R. G. K. (2009). Rethinking comprehension instruction: Comparing strategies and content instructional approaches. *Reading Research Quarterly, 44*(3), 218–253.

McKeown, M. G., Beck, I. L., Omanson, R. C., & Perfetti, C. A. (1983). The effects of long-term vocabulary instruction on reading comprehension: A replication. *Journal of Reading Behavior, XV*(1), 3–18.

Moore, R. (2013). *Basil Bernstein: The thinker and the field.* New York, NY: Routledge.

Murphy, P. K., Wilkinson, I.A.G., Soter, A. O., Hennessey, M. N., & Alexander, J. F. (2009). Examining the effects of classroom discussion on students' comprehension of text: A meta-analysis. *Journal of Educational Psychology, 101*(3), 740–764. doi:10.1037/a0015576

National Governors Association (NGA) Center for Best Practices & The Council of Chief State School Officers (CCSSO). (2010). *Common Core State Standards for English language arts and literacy in history/social studies, science, and technical subjects.* Washington, DC: Authors. Available at www.corestandards.org/assets/CCSSI_ELA%20Standards.pdf

National Governors Association (NGA) Center for Best Practices & The Council of Chief State School Officers (CCSSO). (2010). *Common Core State Standards for Mathematics.* Washington, DC: Authors.

NGSS Lead States. (2013). *Next generation science standards: For states, by states.* Washington, DC: The National Academies Press.

Nguyen-Jahiel, K. T., Anderson, R. C., Hom, H., Waggoner, M., & Rowell, B. (2007). Using literature discussions to reason through real-life dilemmas: A journey taken by one teacher and her fourth-grade students. In R. Horowitz (Ed.), *Talking texts: How speech and writing interact in school learning* (pp. 187–220). London, UK, & New York, NY: Routledge/Taylor & Francis.

Nystrand, M. (2006). Research on the role of classroom discussion as it affects reading comprehension. *Research in the Teaching of English, 40*, 392–412.

Ong, W. (2012). *Orality and literacy: The technologizing of the word* (3rd ed.). New York, NY: Routledge/Taylor & Francis. (Original work published 1982)

Rapanta, C., Garcia-Mila, M., & Gilabert, S. (2013). What is meant by argumentative competence? An integrative review of methods of analysis and assessment in education. *Review of Educational Research, 83*(4), 483–520.

Resnick, L., & Snow, C. (2009). *Speaking and listening for preschool through third grade*. Newark, DE: New Standards/International Reading Association.

Reznitskaya, A., Anderson, R., McNurlen, B., Njuyen-Jahiel, K., Archoudidou, A., & Kim, S. (2001). Influence of oral language on written argument. *Discourse Processes, 32*(2 & 3), 155–175.

Rubin, D. L., Hafer, T., & Arata, K. (2000). Reading and listening to oral-based versus literate-based discourse. *Communication Education, 49*(2), 121–134.

Saunders, W. M., & Goldenberg, C. (2007). The effects of instructional conversation on English language learners' concepts of friendship and story comprehension. In R. Horowitz (Ed.), *Talking texts: How speech and writing interact in school learning* (pp. 221–252). London, UK, & New York, NY: Routledge/Taylor & Francis.

Scarborough, H. S. (2001). Connecting early language and literacy to later reading (dis)abilities: Evidence, theory, and practice. In S. G. Neuman & D. K. Dickinson (Eds.), *Handbook of early literacy research* (pp. 97–110). New York, NY: Guilford Press.

Schleppegrell, M. J. (2001). Linguistic features of the language of schooling. *Linguistics and Education, 12*(4), 431–459.

Schleppegrell, M. J. (2004). *The language of schooling: A functional linguistics perspective*. Mahwah, NJ: Erlbaum.

Schreiber, P. (1987). Prosody and structure in syntactic processing. In R. Horowitz & S. J. Samuels (Eds.), *Comprehending oral and written language* (pp. 243–270). San Diego, CA, & London, UK: Academic Press.

Sinatra, G. M. (1990). Convergence of listening and reading processing. *Reading Research Quarterly*, 115–130.

Smith, N. B. (1965). *American reading instruction*. Newark, DE: International Reading Association. (Original work published 1934)

Snow, C. E. (1983). Literacy and language: Relationships during the preschool years. *Harvard Educational Review, 53*(2), 165–189.

Soter, A. O., Wilkinson, I. A., Murphy, P. K., Rudge, L., Reninger, K., & Edwards, M. (2008). What the discourse tells us: Talk and indicators of high-level comprehension. *International Journal of Educational Research, 47*(6), 372–391. doi:10.1016/j. ijer.2009.01.001

Sticht, T. G., Beck, L. J., Hauke, R. N., Kleiman, G. M., & James, J. H. (1974). *Auding and reading: A developmental model*. Alexandria, VA.: Human Resources Research Organization.

Sticht, T. G., & James, J. H. (1984). Listening and reading. In P. D. Pearson, R. Barr, M. L. Kamil, & P. Mosenthal (Eds.), *Handbook of reading research* (Vol. 1, pp. 293–317). White Plains, NY: Longman.

Taylor, B. M., Pearson, P. D., Peterson, D. S., & Rodriguez, M. C. (2003). Reading growth in high-poverty classrooms: The influence of teacher practices that encourage cognitive engagement in literacy learning. *The Elementary School Journal, 104*(1), 3–28. doi:10.1086/499740

Thomas, R. (1989). *Oral tradition and written record in classical Athens.* In P. Burke & R. Finnegan (Eds.), Cambridge studies in oral & written cultureNew York, NY: Cambridge University Press.

Van den Branden, K. (2000). Does negotiation of meaning promote reading comprehension? A study of multilingual primary school classes. *Reading Research Quarterly, 35*(3), 426–443. doi:10.1598/RRQ.35.3.6

Van Der Veer, R. (2007). *Lev Vygotsky* (R. Bailey, series editor, *Continuum Library of Educational Thought*, Vol. 10). London, UK, & New York, NY: Continuum.

Vygotsky, L. (1986). *Thought and language.* (A. Kozulin, Ed. & Trans.) Cambridge, MA: MIT.

Wilkinson, L., & Silliman, E. (2000). Classroom language and literacy learning. In M. L. Kamil, P. B. Mosenthal, P. D. Pearson, & R. Barr (Eds.), *Handbook of reading research* (Vol. 3, pp. 337–360). Mawah, NJ: Lawrence Erlbaum Associates.

Wise, J. C., Sevcik, R. A., Morris, R. D., Lovett, M. W., & Wolf, M. (2007). The relationship among receptive and expressive vocabulary, listening comprehension, pre-reading skills, word identification skills, and reading comprehension by children with reading disabilities. *Journal of Speech, Language, and Hearing Research, 50*, 1093–1109.

PART II

THE CONTENT OF
LITERACY INSTRUCTION

CHAPTER 5

Reading Comprehension Instruction
Moving into a New Era

Joanna P. Williams

Comprehension is the ultimate goal of reading, yet until recently instruction in reading included relatively little emphasis on matters of comprehension. Nor was there much interest in developing comprehension theory until psychology adopted the cognitive paradigm. Over the past few years, however, both theoretical and applied aspects of reading comprehension have been studied extensively.

The recent move toward the Common Core State Standards (CCSS), which puts great emphasis on comprehension and critical thinking, comes at a time when the field of reading is ready to make major advances in comprehension instruction. This chapter reviews the rather brief history of comprehension instruction and discusses ways in which our current thinking can help guide our response to the challenges of the Common Core. It also addresses a particular interest of mine—how the Common Core goals can most usefully be achieved when the students are young and/or at risk for academic failure.

The CCSS initiative is unusual in that when it was first announced, it set proficiency goals for students across grade levels but did not mandate any particular curriculum or instructional methods for teachers to help achieve the goals. Rather, the initiative focused primarily on the nature of instructional texts. The most dramatic change proposed by the CCSS developers is in the substantial increase in the difficulty level of the texts to which students are exposed, starting in the earliest grades. The developers cite two sources as justification for this change: (1) a study by Williamson (2008), which showed that the complexity level of books that high school seniors are expected to read is considerably below the level of the books that they will encounter when they enter college; and (2) the 2006 ACT college entrance examination scores, which revealed that half of the students taking the test did not read well enough to deal with their beginning college courses without remediation. An analysis of the scores indicated that what differentiated the students who did well on the exam and those who did not was not any particular element of comprehension, such as making inferences or finding main ideas. It was the ability to understand complex texts (Adams, 2013).

But in spite of the initial silence from the standards' developers as to instructional choices, the CCSS initiative is not entirely laissez-faire in this area. The primary architects of the English/language arts standards in the CCSS, David Coleman and Sue Pimentel (2012), do put forward an instructional method of choice, one that is new to most teachers:

close reading. This method has been borrowed from a literary theory, the New Criticism (Richards, 1930), that was developed for older, more advanced students (Brown & Kappes, 2012). In close reading, the text at hand is not simply read; it is studied. That is, the reader analyzes the text over many dimensions, with the goal of arriving at its meaning(s) via attention to its word choice, syntax, tone, rhetorical devices, and the like. It may take several readings for all of a text's meaning to be identified (see Allington, Billen, & McCuiston, Chapter 10, this volume, and Pearson & Cervetti, Chapter 1, this volume).

In a close-reading lesson, the teacher guides students through this process, using discussion and questions (Brown & Kappes, 2012), emphasizing questions whose answers are based on information found in the text (Coleman & Pimentel, 2012). Coleman and Pimentel argue that students develop a deep understanding of a text by attending to these kinds of questions. At the same time, students learn how to read text in general (i.e., how to get reliable information from a text by applying critical thinking skills), and how to appreciate and critique logical arguments. Coleman and Pimentel (2012) further argue that, for this instruction to be effective, teachers must make sure students do not digress by talking about personal experiences or other tangential topics. They also raise the issue of boundaries: Unless readers are very precise in their reading, they will not know the difference between what they have read and what they *thought* they read but actually brought to the text from their own background knowledge and experiences.

To address CCSS goals, close reading is supposed to start in the early grades. Coleman and Pimentel indicate that it is to be provided for all students rather than restricted to only the better students, because close reading is a way to develop the disciplinary and world knowledge that is, for the CCSS, just as much a part of the central goal of reading instruction as are mastering basic reading skills and fluency development.

It is important to note that the new instructional demands that the CCSS place on schools are not based on extensive research findings, either theoretical or empirical (Cunningham, 2013). Researchers, of course, have begun to examine the assumptions underlying the standards and to investigate potential outcomes of the implementation of instructional practices that adhere to the standards. At this point, however, these investigations do not point definitely to instructional designs that will best achieve the Common Core goals and do not provide evidence for (or against) the new directives. How should today's teachers respond, given the lack of guidelines?

THE TRANSITION FROM OLD TO NEW: INSIGHTS FROM THE HISTORY OF COMPREHENSION INSTRUCTION

A period of transition to a new way of doing things is an opportunity to get rid of ideas and practices that are no longer productive or that were misguided from the start. At the same time, there is a danger that in our zeal to adopt the new, we, as reading researchers and educators, might turn our backs on ideas and practices that, in fact, have been effective. What can we take from current instruction that might help us achieve CCSS goals in the area of reading comprehension? What might be judged ready to be discarded? A brief review of the evolution of comprehension instruction may help us see what such decisions might entail (for a review of comprehension theory, see Pearson & Cervetti, Chapter 1, this volume).

Serious attention to comprehension came rather late in the history of reading instruction, prompted in part by a highly influential article by Durkin (1978–1979). On the basis of extensive observations, Durkin concluded that almost no comprehension instruction was taking place in elementary school classrooms. Rather, class time was spent on "mentioning" comprehension tasks and having students complete workbook activities. Teachers provided little explanation of how to do the tasks and gave little feedback beyond declaring answers right or wrong.

Information Processing

Durkin's article was well timed. It helped turn attention toward a new theoretical model, information processing, which offered the promise of understanding the nature of higher mental activity. The model defined reading as a cognitive process, or rather, a complex set of cognitive processes, in which several sources of information are integrated. According to this model, not all the information needed to comprehend a text resides within the text itself. A reader is constantly making inferences to fill gaps in the textual information provided. To do this, readers use additional information that comes from whatever prior knowledge they possess about the topic of the text. This latter information source can be parsed more specifically: Although most prior, or background, knowledge relates to content, experienced readers also have some knowledge of the way texts themselves are structured, and this knowledge, too, helps guide their understanding of what they read.

Much of the early empirical work within this cognitive paradigm focused on issues of automatic processing and dealt with mental phenomena measured in milliseconds. This work was not directly relevant to the concerns of educators, who look for opportunities to modify and improve student performance and understanding. But some cognitive psychologists undertook a different type of research, which educators *did* find relevant. Investigators such as Pressley and Afflerbach (1995) asked good readers to describe what they were thinking about as they read. The objective of this work was to determine what it was that expert readers were doing and then teach students to do the same thing. These verbal protocols indicated that good readers employ conscious strategies as they read. From these and other types of studies, specific comprehension strategies that seemed productive and amenable to instruction were identified.

Cognitive Strategies

Some of these strategies looked very much like the skills that were derived from older theories. But these earlier skills-based programs had not solved the problems of struggling readers. A spate of analyses attempted to differentiate skills and strategies, describing skills as being automatic and strategies as being based on conscious attention to the reading task. However, this differentiation is difficult to maintain. The concept of metacomprehension was introduced, highlighting the importance of making students aware of their own cognition processes. The goal here was to teach students to monitor and evaluate their comprehension to make sure they had understood what they had read and to use repair strategies such as rereading when necessary (Jacobs & Paris, 1987).

Cognitive strategy instruction has not been without its detractors. Some have criticized a direct focus on strategies as being a stilted and artificial approach that can interfere with normal fluent reading. Some also have expressed concerns that a focus on their own mental processing can distract students from comprehending the text in front of them (Garcia, Taylor, Pearson, Stahl, & Bauer, 2007; McKeown, Beck, & Blake, 2009).

Over the years, extensive research and classroom practice have made it clear that simply having students acquire and practice strategies in isolation is not conducive to the development of proficient reading, which involves a constant, ongoing adaptation of many cognitive processes. Rather, teachers must be able to respond flexibly and opportunistically to students' needs for instructive feedback as they read, providing instruction on strategies as required (Gersten, Fuchs, Williams, & Baker, 2001). This is not an easy task for many teachers, even experienced ones (Williams, 2002). Moreover, even after all these years, the field of reading comprehension has yet to settle on a short list of essential strategies to teach, let alone how to teach them.

Dialogic Reading

Wilkinson and Son (2011) describe the extensive work that has been done on dialogic reading, a considerably more flexible approach to comprehension instruction that involves strategies but does not put them in such a predominant position. Strategies are invoked as useful tools but are not dealt with as explicit objects of instruction. In the dialogic reading approach, instructional programs are designed to promote not only proficiency in reading comprehension but also the learning of academic content, such as science and social studies. (See Guthrie, Wigfield, & Perencevich, 2004, and Romance & Vitale, 2001, for examples of instruction whose goals are both comprehension proficiency and mastery of academic content.)

Thus, our understanding of comprehension strategies and our recommendations as to how to teach them have evolved dramatically since the 1980s. Nonetheless, strategies remain a prominent part of much of today's reading instruction.

Reader Response

The years following the introduction of the cognitive model as the framework for comprehension research and instruction also saw the rise of reader-response theory (Beach, 1993; Rosenblatt, 1978). The approach arose from literary analysis, but it was similar in conceptualization to the cognitive model. It viewed reading as constructivist—that is, integrating information from various sources was the way knowledge was constructed. Reader response differed from the cognitive model in emphasis, however. It stressed the unique meaning that individual readers take from a text because of their unique history of cognitive development and consequent unique knowledge base. Most constructivist instruction holds that teachers should serve as guides and facilitators and should not impose their own interpretations of texts on their students. It emphasizes personal associations and reactions to textual information. Actual teaching is relatively unstructured, and there is no direct instruction in comprehension strategies. This orientation toward comprehension instruction, as would be expected from its literary-analysis source, first became popular in the higher grades and then moved into the elementary grades. It has waned in popularity in recent years, but it is still somewhat influential.

Summing Up

In 2000, the congressionally mandated National Reading Panel (NRP) issued its evaluation of the existing research on reading instruction (National Institute of Child Health and Human Development, 2000). The panel's criteria for accepting research findings as evidence were stringent: Only sound experimental or at least quasi-experimental studies qualified. (Because reader-response theory had generated little empirical research, the NRP did not examine its effectiveness.) Given the relatively small body of relevant research available at the time, the evidence for effective comprehension instruction was not as strong as that for other areas of reading. However, it was sufficient to determine that teaching certain comprehension strategies was effective. This endorsement further helped support the interest in strategy instruction. Another important contribution of the NRP was the acknowledgment that scientific evidence can and should be used as the basis for instructional development, and that only the outcomes of well-designed studies should be accepted as evidence. In response, funding agencies, which have tremendous power to influence the shape of research, now require advanced research designs and statistical methods. Valuable methodological advances have followed, along with advances in our knowledge of how to teach reading.

Soon after the NRP report was issued, Reading First was launched. This was an important national initiative that put into practice recommendations drawn from the work of the NRP. It led to profound changes in American classrooms. These changes focused primarily on the teaching of alphabetics; a much greater emphasis on phonemic awareness and phonics was seen. With respect to comprehension, strategy instruction was front and center. Unfortunately, the great effort undertaken by the Reading First program led to disappointing results. The performance of students who received Reading First comprehension instruction was judged no better than that of those who had not received the instruction (Gamse, Jacob, Horst, Boulay, & Unlu, 2008).

Perhaps the CCSS has arrived at an opportune time. Some may argue that the comprehension strategies approach has run its course. It has displayed the typical pattern in which an instructional approach is introduced and then pushed as far as it will go. Then, as teachers become experienced with the approach, instantiations of its rigorous, "pure" version gradually disappear. This perspective is playing out in our current, more relaxed approach to direct strategy instruction. It is also implicated in the decreased attention to teaching students to reflect on their own mental activities as they read. And, at this point, there is minimum interest in previously critical theoretical distinctions: There is much less concern about the precise labeling of skills versus strategies, for example.

WHAT HAS BEEN LEARNED?
IMPLICATIONS FOR ACHIEVING CCSS GOALS

When a new approach comes in, the older one is often rejected. It is always the new approach that is deemed active, thoughtful, and higher level (McDonald, 1964). In a successful transition to a new approach, methods and techniques that have been effective remain, though they may be reinterpreted and translated into language that fits the new approach. A less successful transition ignores what has been learned from the past, and effective practices are abandoned. At this time of major transition, we, as reading researchers and educators, should make sure that we do not discard ideas and practices that have, in fact, been effective.

Challenges for the Schools

This is where the field of reading instruction is today. It has become clear that cognitive strategy instruction is not a panacea. Schools are not producing college and career ready students—although cognitive strategy instruction can hardly be blamed for that! The questions to consider are: What will be the result of implementing the CCSS? Will comprehension instruction be successful when students are faced with more challenging texts? Will close reading, which was developed for use with older readers, be effective across the grades? Will what has been learned during the years when the focus was on readers' mental processing be used to help students reach the goals set forth in the CCSS?

Introduction of more complex text. The first and foremost challenge that schools will face is the introduction of more complex text. The CCSS call for an increase in the amount of specifically informational text that students read at each grade. This in itself may not be a very dramatic shift because educators already have made a significant move toward the use of such texts. However, the standards demand high proficiency in reading texts across the spectrum. They also demand proficiency in understanding aspects of text that have been neglected in recent years, especially those that deal with craft and structure. Recent research has acknowledged the importance of text structure, but in no way do our past efforts either in research or practice (e.g., Meyer & Ray, 2011; Williams & Pao, 2013) encompass the broad definition of structure outlined in the CCSS, which includes study of language structures from word to phrase to sentence to text. Vocabulary, of course, has always been a mainstay of reading instruction. But CCSS-endorsed texts also contain complex sentence structures that have patterns that may be unfamiliar to students whose experience with academic language is limited. By reading complex texts, it is expected that students will become aware of the relationship between linguistic patterns and the functions they serve in a text (Wong-Fillmore & Fillmore, 2012), and that this will enhance their overall comprehension.

There is little research to support the introduction of more complex texts as a way to build reading proficiency (Cunningham, 2013). In fact, one of the perennial ideas in reading instruction, which has hardly changed since Betts (1946), is that texts should be selected for instruction (instructional-level texts) that are somewhat above what a student can read on his or her own (independent level), but not very much above that level. When students are asked to read texts beyond this point, they are said to have reached the frustration level. How will students fare when faced with such complex reading material? Many students struggle with the easier texts that they are currently being assigned, and we are far from knowing how to select and sequence texts effectively. Mesmer, Cunningham, and Hiebert (2012) have undertaken the development of a theoretical model of text complexity for the early grades that encompasses word-level, syntax-level, and discourse-level text features. Such a model can serve as a guide for future research on the contribution of various text elements to the complexity of texts and for ways in which this knowledge might be used in the design of early-grade instruction. This could eventuate in an empirically based model of the factors that make for optimal increases in instructional text complexity as readers move through the grades. In a similar vein, Graesser and his colleagues have developed a computer tool, Coh-Metrix, that analyzes texts on many levels of cohesion and language (Graesser, McNamara, Louwerse, & Cai, 2004). This model has the potential of allowing teachers to select texts based on a reader's ability profile. (Fountas & Pinnell's 1996 work on guided reading through leveled texts was an important forerunner of this type of endeavor.)

The CCSS calls for students to acquire content knowledge from the texts they read as they are improving their comprehension. Typically, these have been considered two very different instructional goals, each addressed separately by teachers whose preparation has been oriented toward one or the other, but not both. Content-area teachers usually have not been taught how to teach reading. When it is suggested that they should provide such instruction as needed, they often protest that they have not been trained how to do so. Moreover, over the past few years, instruction in history and science has become less text-dependent. Teachers across content areas are spending more classroom time lecturing, holding discussions, and using video and other media to transmit information. Textbooks are marginalized, and opportunities for students to practice reading are diminished.

For the last few years, content-area teachers have been urged to emphasize the text in their instruction, but such change has been slow in coming. Now, given the CCSS mandate, reading teachers will be required to focus on content acquisition as well as on comprehension development. Moreover, all teachers will be expected to move students toward deeper levels of understanding of texts that are complex both linguistically and conceptually. Classrooms will have to rely on texts more than on discussion or video. Otherwise, students will not meet the advanced standards that involve delineating and evaluating the validity of the reasoning in a text as well as the relevance and sufficiency of the evidence it provides. It is unclear whether the amount of time and attention devoted to a text (or a series of texts that are presented for study as a set) will be sufficient to yield satisfactory retention of content without incorporating additional instructional components.

Emphasis on close reading. The other major challenge for schools is the introduction of the instructional method of close reading. Ideally, the adoption of such instruction will motivate and engage students because they will be learning new and interesting things from worthwhile books. At the same time, learning to read texts in depth will lead students to become proficient and critical readers. But this is the ideal. As I have noted, close reading previously has typically been used only with older students (Brown & Kappes, 2012). How will it be adapted for use in the earlier grades? How will teachers be prepared to teach close reading? Will this method be successful in moving students beyond simply understanding the gist of a text? Students will have to retain the text's content, achieve a thorough comprehension of its arguments, and understand the place of that text in relation to other texts. They will have to learn more about language—morphology, syntax, and figurative language—and how these text features contribute to the meaning of the text. Will students be able to accomplish this? Will what they learn be applicable to new or unusual texts? Most important, how much of what they acquire will transfer from the intensive study of a few texts in school to general reading competence outside the classroom?

Some investigators suggest that close reading will prove so difficult for many students that it will become onerous for them. We know how important it is to keep students motivated and engaged (Guthrie et al., 2004; see also Guthrie, Chapter 7, this volume). Others are concerned about specific aspects of the close-reading method itself, especially the emphasis on text-dependent questions and tasks. The standards require students to determine what the text says explicitly, so that they can base inferences on that information and cite specific textual evidence when drawing conclusions about its message. This is seen as an important corrective to the recent neglect of texts in content-area classrooms. Another argument in favor of having students concentrate on the text at hand is that this procedure will "level the playing field" and reduce the performance gap between students with language- and literacy-poor backgrounds and their more advantaged peers, because the differences in amount of background knowledge among the students will not be so centrally relevant to the instruction.

In Chapter 1, Pearson and Cervetti presented a critique of the CCSS's emphasis on text-dependent questions and tasks. They based their discussion on Kintsch's (1998) comprehension-integration model, which postulates two levels of representation: the textbase, which essentially represents "what the text says," and the situation model, which refers to the coherent mental representation that readers achieve after taking what they have gleaned from the text and integrating it with their own prior knowledge. Though constructing the textbase does involve some use of prior knowledge—for example, in making local inferences—prior knowledge really comes in at the point of constructing the situation model. Without a representation at the level of the situation model, there is no integration of the textual information and one's knowledge base—which is what yields comprehension and drives further learning. Pearson (2013) argues that emphasis on text-dependent questions is misdirected, because invoking prior knowledge as one reads is not under conscious cognitive control. Furthermore, he says the notion of text boundaries—what is in the text and what is outside of it—can become murky. As a reader progresses through a text that is longer than a paragraph or two, Pearson asks at what point the information presented at the beginning of the text becomes part of one's knowledge base. If one follows CCSS recommendations, that information is not to be used in classroom discussions of later portions of text.

Snow and O'Connor (2013) also have expressed concerns about the emphasis on close reading and especially on text-dependent questions. They suggest that this method works against the valuable outcomes promoted by discussion and argumentation, where limiting evidence to what is found in a text (or set of texts) can stultify knowledge-building and intellectual growth. (They also reject the argument that close reading will reduce the performance gap, arguing that it is the lack of background knowledge that is the main reason behind disadvantaged students' struggles with reading, and that close reading ignores this factor.)

These concerns are well founded when one considers students who have mastered the rudiments of reading (although I would suggest that even many high-achieving high school students today could benefit from instruction on the importance of recognizing and respecting text boundaries). However, my opinion of the value of text-dependent questions differs somewhat from the opinions expressed by Pearson (2013) and Snow and O'Connor (2013), partly because my research interests focus on young students and those who are older and less able.

Recommendations for Instruction

Young students, those at risk for academic failure, and students with learning disabilities do well with instruction that is structured, explicit, scaffolded, and intensive; that proceeds systematically from the simple to the complex, and provides substantial practice at each step; and that incorporates meaningful and interesting tasks (Williams, 1998). One additional feature of appropriate instruction, in my opinion, is the use of specially designed training materials (texts, in the case of reading instruction) that provide simple, clear templates that exemplify instructional points (Williams & Pao, 2013). When students are first introduced to something new—structure, strategy, or whatever—they will advance more readily when they are not burdened by the additional demands of distracting complexities.

Focus on story themes. At the time when constructivist ideas were prominent and the reader-response approach was in its prime, I became very much concerned about what would happen to younger and less able students. Constructivist teaching techniques, which are generally unstructured, are not very effective with these groups. I saw that encouraging students to relate story information to their own personal experience pulled the students away from the information in a text. In a study I conducted that involved students with and without learning disabilities matched on standardized reading comprehension scores, some comprehension measures (e.g., the number of acceptable predictions the students made and the number of important idea units they included in their summaries) did not differentiate the two groups (Williams, 1993). However, the students with learning disabilities were less able to identify the theme of the story they read. Also, their summaries contained more idiosyncratic responses that included personal and other irrelevant information. Within each group of students, as the number of idiosyncratic responses increased, the ability to state the story theme decreased. This tendency to import information from outside sources is a threat to achieving an effective mental representation of the text. Associations involving one's own interests and values are, of course, often triggered automatically when reading. But if such irrelevant and inappropriate information is not edited out, it becomes part of the text representation, and one's grasp of the meaning of the text will be compromised. (Inhibition of associations is sometimes impossible, but this is a phenomenon that exists on a very different psychological level. See Gernsbacher, 1993, for further discussion.)

It is up to the teacher to help students recognize the tangential nature of some of their associations and to disregard them as they work through the meaning of the text. To do this, instruction must focus on the information in the text. When I visited classrooms, I was dismayed to see that this was not always the case. Teachers were applying the "background knowledge strategy." Of all the cognitive strategies that have been studied and recommended, this is certainly one of the most widely used. I realized that the great appeal of this strategy probably came about because it provided a concrete and straightforward instantiation of the (very appealing) conceptualization of reading in information-processing terms. Moreover, this strategy was easy to implement. The teacher could make sure that students had the knowledge they needed simply by providing it before students did their reading. Sadly, this led to giving more and more classroom time over to introducing text content by means other than reading and to less concern for what actually appeared in the text.

I designed an instructional program that taught students to identify the themes of stories by having them focus on the text information via a series of generic questions and to recognize these themes in new stories (Williams, 1998). The students also learned to relate story themes to their own experiences. However, the instruction insisted on a strong textual orientation. The program was used successfully by middle school students with learning disabilities and by elementary school students in the 3rd and 4th grades.

Identify text structure. My work also led me to focus on another way in which applying the information-processing paradigm to instruction seemed to be a threat to the quality of instruction for young children. The idea of having 6- and 7-year-olds (or older children, for that matter) reflect on their own thinking processes did not sit well with me. When I turned my attention to expository text, it was with the idea of developing instruction that followed the time-tested principles of learning that I have specified earlier. Our interventions embed text-structure instruction within social studies lessons. Students become familiar with basic rhetorical structures such as compare-and-contrast and cause-and-effect. The goal is twofold: improvement in reading comprehension ability and content acquisition. Our interventions have students address a text by locating clue words in it that signal a particular text structure and then using organizing questions and a graphic organizer specific to that structure to identify the text's central information. The texts we use are short, they contain simple vocabulary and syntax, and, most important, they conform closely to the text structure being taught. These texts provide simple templates for each structure, and students, through analysis of these texts, can abstract the structural patterns. As the lessons progress, the texts become longer and more complex. The idea is that later, when the students approach authentic text, which is typically not well structured—certainly almost never in the rigorous way our training materials are structured—they will be able to identify a text (which may be a portion of a longer or more complex text) as an example of a specific structure. At this point, they will be able to use their mental representation of the structure—their template—to identify and comprehend the important information in the text. I have referred to this procedure as the "close analysis of text structure"—CATS (Williams, Hall, & Lauer, 2004). We are now completing the evaluation of a year-long program for second graders that includes Meyer's (1985) five basic text structures: sequence, compare-and-contrast, cause-and-effect, description, and problem solving. The social studies content describes life in American communities, past and present.

The texts used in our studies are designed to be clear exemplars of a specific structure; there is no ambiguity about their meaning or about how each sentence helps in arriving at the meaning. The students' tasks do not encourage readers to drift beyond the confines of the text. And students are never asked to contemplate their own mental processing. (The program also includes trade books that present the basic social studies content and provide the basis for creating our close-analysis texts. The trade books are used by the teachers for read-alouds and allow for a freer discussion than is permitted during the close-analysis lesson.)

Researchers have not established developmental trajectories that trace progress toward mature comprehension of the various text structures. Such trajectories will help in the design of texts that are optimal for readers at different proficiency levels. (The work of Mesmer et al., 2012, will be of great value here.) From our data, it appears that the level of language at which instruction should focus is different for different structures. Most text-structure research today has focused on a level in which the organization of a series of sentences represents the structure. Our sequence structure warranted that approach (Williams, Stafford, Lauer, Hall, & Pollini, 2009). But causal structure, we found

(Williams et al., 2014), was better dealt with for our 2nd-graders with texts in which the structure was exemplified at the sentence level (i.e., both cause and effect were represented within a single sentence, along with appropriate connective words). Our comparison, description, and problem-solution structures were also organized within single sentences or across sentence pairs.

Our instruction is a long way from fulfilling the CCSS exhortation to introduce students to challenging texts that make them critical readers and thinkers. But children in the first two grades, and perhaps even in 3rd grade, need to spend their time developing a strong foundation in basic reading. This foundation includes both decoding and comprehension. Their comprehension instruction first should be focused on helping them learn the absolute basics of text understanding. Traditionally, this has meant finding the main idea of a text along with its important details, and recognizing what information is irrelevant or tangential to the main idea. This general formulation needs amplification to be applied appropriately to narrative structure and to the several basic structures found in informational text. When students are able and comfortable with this level of comprehension (they needn't have actually mastered it—mastery will come with time and experience), then they are ready to tackle the Common Core standards that go beyond basic understanding to the additional points in the CCSS definition of comprehension. The close-analysis CATS procedure that we have been using seems to follow the spirit of close reading as far as it makes sense to do so with primary grade students.

This does not mean that primary-grade children will thereby be deprived of opportunities to develop their capacity for interpretation and critical thinking and to expand their conceptual horizons. They should be guided in these matters even before formal schooling begins. Parents and teachers can introduce challenging ideas through spoken language. Television and films can provoke thoughtful discussion. *Comprehension* instruction should start long before reading *comprehension* instruction, and neither of these two essential goals, *comprehension* and *reading comprehension*, should be allowed to impede the progress of the other.

CONCLUSION

It is too early to predict how the move to the CCSS will fare, either in terms of implementation or the assessment of student outcomes. Its success will depend on many factors, including outside influences such as national politics. As U.S. schooling shifts toward CCSS as a general policy, it is interesting to reflect on experiences with previous major policy shifts. As always, there is initially a period during which educators try out a variety of things in their attempts to implement a new directive. Some of these fail because they take too extreme a position: They may follow theory too slavishly. Sooner or later things settle down. Teachers figure out feasible ways of translating theory into practice and implementing the policy, some of which will be truly effective. The efforts of researchers yield evidence in support of the new policy, and this persuades some of those who have not yet endorsed the changes.

We should not think of our move into the CCSS era as abandoning our previous vision. For all the problems of the cognitive strategy approach, the advances that we have made since adopting the information-processing paradigm will inform future instruction, no matter what new policies are formulated. That approach led us to address for the first time the question of what comprehension really means, and it has prompted us to identify specific elements of comprehension, analyze comprehension tasks, and simulate readers' mental processing. Much of the successful instruction based on this approach incorporates a series of steps that students must work through to reach their comprehension goal. Students are not expected to perform these steps forever. As they become proficient, the steps drop out, but the comprehension ability remains. In other words, the routines are enacted in a highly orchestrated, almost automatic, manner rather than in a deliberate step-by-step manner. This may sound simple, but sometimes it is difficult to identify and analyze a task, and sometimes it is difficult to determine an effective path for the student to follow. This is genuine instruction, in my view. It is a far cry from the "read it and then take a test on it" approach that Durkin (1978–1979) observed. What it takes is a willingness to go beyond the idea of the "whole." We never made much progress when we saw "reading" or "comprehension" as something so complex that it could not be analyzed. I hope we never hear talk about "the text in its (awesome) complexity."

We should celebrate the great progress we have made. Let's be happy to see the excesses of the cognitive strategy approach on their way out, but let's make sure that the solid core of that approach is not lost. Over the past few years, we have addressed the *reader* and the *task* (RAND, 2002). Now it is the time to address the *text*. All that we have learned so far will help us take up today's new challenges.

REFERENCES

Adams, M. (2013). Common Core State Standards: Productivity is key. In S. B. Neuman & L. B. Gambrell (Eds.), *Quality reading instruction in the age of Common Core Standards* (pp. 204–218). Newark, DE: International Reading Association.

Beach, R. (1993). *A teacher's introduction to reader-response theories. NCTE teacher's introduction series.* Urbana, IL: National Council of Teachers of English.

Betts, E. A. (1946). *Foundations of reading instruction, with emphasis on differentiated guidance.* New York, NY: American Book Company.

Brown, S., & Kappes, L. (2012). *Implementing the Common Core State Standards: A primer on "close reading of text."* Washington, DC: The Aspen Institute Education and Society Program.

Coleman, D., & Pimentel, S. (2012, April). *Revised publishers' criteria for the Common Core State Standards in English language arts and literacy, grades 3–12.* Available at www.achievethecore.org/stealthesetools

Cunningham, J. (2013). Research on text complexity: The Common Core State Standards as catalyst. In S. B. Neuman & L. B. Gambrell (Eds.), *Quality reading instruction in the age of Common Core State Standards* (pp. 204–218). Newark, DE: International Reading Association.

Durkin, D. (1978–1979). What classroom observations reveal about reading comprehension instruction. *Reading Research Quarterly, 14,* 481–533.

Fountas, I. C., & Pinnell, G. S. (1996). *Guided reading: Good first teaching for all children.* Portsmouth, NH: Heinemann.

Gamse, B. C., Jacob, R. T., Horst, M., Boulay, B., & Unlu, F. (2008). *Reading First impact study final report executive summary* (NCEE 2009-4039). Washington, DC: National Center for Education Evaluation and Regional Assistance, Institute of Education Sciences, U.S. Department of Education.

Garcia, G. E., Taylor, B. T., Pearson, P. D., Stahl, K. A. D., & Bauer, E. B. (2007). *Field report: Instruction of reading comprehension: Cognitive strategies or cognitive (responsive) engagement?* Submitted to the Institute of Educational Science, U.S. Department of Education, Washington, DC (Grant R305G030140). Champaign, IL: University of Illinois.

Gernsbacher, M. A. (1993). Less skilled readers have less efficient suppression mechanisms. *Psychological Science, 4*(5), 294–298.

Gersten, R., Fuchs, L. S., Williams, J. P., & Baker, S. (2001). Teaching reading comprehension strategies to students with learning disabilities: A review of research. *Review of Educational Research, 71*(2), 279–320.

Graesser, A. C., McNamara, D. S., Louwerse, M. M., & Cai, Z. (2004). Coh-Metrix: Analysis of text on cohesion and language: *Behavioral Research Methods, Instruments, and Computers, 36*, 180–193.

Guthrie, J. T., Wigfield, A., & Perencevich, K. C. (Eds.). (2004). *Motivating reading comprehension: Concept-oriented reading instruction.* Mahwah, NJ: Erlbaum.

Jacobs, J. E., & Paris, S. G. (1987). Children's metacognition about reading: Issues in definition, measurement, and instruction. *Educational Psychologist, 22*, 255–278.

Kintsch, W. (1998). The role of knowledge in discourse comprehension construction-integration model. *Psychological Review, 95*, 163–182.

McDonald, F. J. (1964). The influence of learning theories on education. In E. R. Hilgard (Ed.), *Theories of learning and instruction* (pp. 1–26.). Chicago, IL: The National Society for the Study of Education.

McKeown, M. G., Beck, I. L., & Blake, R. G. (2009). Rethinking reading comprehension instruction: A comparison of instruction for strategies and content approaches. *Reading Research Quarterly, 44*(3), 218–253.

Mesmer, H. A., Cunningham, J. W., & Hiebert, E. H. (2012). Toward a theoretical model of text complexity for the early grades: Learning from the past, anticipating the future. *Reading Research Quarterly, 47*(3), 235–258.

Meyer, B. J. F. (1985). Prose analysis: Purposes, procedures, and problems. In B. K. Britton & J. B. Back (Eds.), *Understanding expository text* (pp. 11–65). Hillsdale, NJ: Erlbaum.

Meyer, B. J. F., & Ray, M. N. (2011). Structure strategy interventions: Increasing reading comprehension of expository text. *International Electronic Journal of Elementary Education, 4*(1).

National Governors Association (NGA) Center for Best Practices & Council of Chief State School Officers (CCSSO). (2010). *Common Core State Standards for English language arts and literacy in history/social studies, science, and technical subjects.* Washington, DC: Authors.

National Institute of Child Health and Human Development (NICHD). (2000). *Report of the National Reading Panel. Teaching children to read: An evidence-based assessment of the scientific research literature on reading and its implications for reading instruction* (NIH Publication No. 00-4769). Washington, DC: U.S. Government Printing Office.

Pearson, P. D. (2013). Research foundations for the Common Core State Standards in English language arts. In S. B. Neuman & L. B. Gambrell (Eds.), *Quality reading instruction in the age of Common Core State Standards* (pp. 237–261). Newark, DE: International Reading Association.

Pressley, M., & Afflerbach, P. (1995). *Verbal protocols of reading: The nature of constructively responsive reading.* Hillsdale, NJ: Erlbaum.

RAND Reading Study Group. (2002). *Reading for understanding: Toward an R&D program in reading comprehension.* Santa Monica, CA: RAND.

Richards, I. A. (1930). *Practical criticism: A study of literary judgment.* London, UK: Kegan Paul Trench Trubner & Company Limited.

Romance, N. R., & Vitale, M. R. (2001). Implementing an in-depth expanded science model in elementary schools: Multi-year findings, research issues, and policy implications. *International Journal of Science Education, 23*(4), 373–404.

Rosenblatt, L. (1978). *The reader, the text, and the poem: The transactional theory of the literature work.* Carbondale, IL: Southern Illinois University Press.

Snow, C., & O'Connor, C. (2013). *Close reading and far-reaching classroom discussion: Fostering a vital connection.* International Reading Association policy brief. Newark, DE: International Reading Association.

Wilkinson, I. A. G., & Son, E. H. (2011). A dialogic turn in research on learning and teaching to comprehend. In M. Kamil, P. D. Pearson, E. B. Moje, & P. P. Afflerbach (Eds.), *Handbook of reading research* (Vol. IV, pp. 359–387). New York, NY: Routledge.

Williams J. P. (1993). Comprehension of students with and without learning disabilities: Identification of narrative themes and idiosyncratic text representations. *Journal of Educational Psychology, 85,* 631–641.

Williams, J. P. (1998). Improving the comprehension of disabled readers. *Annals of Dyslexia, 48*(1), 213–238.

Williams, J. P. (2002). Reading comprehension strategies and teacher preparation. In A. E. Farstrup & S. J. Samuels (Eds.), *What research has to say about reading instruction* (3rd ed., pp. 243–260). Newark, DE: International Reading Association.

Williams, J. P., Hall, K. M., & Lauer, K. D. (2004). Teaching expository text structure to young at-risk learners: Building the basics of comprehension instruction. *Exceptionality, 12*(3), 129–144.

Williams, J. P., & Pao, L. S. (2013). Developing a new intervention to teach text structure at the elementary level. In H. L. Swanson, K. R. Harris, & S. Graham (Eds.), *Handbook of learning disabilities* (2nd ed., pp. 361–374). New York, NY: Guilford Press.

Williams, J. P., Pollini, S., Nubla-Kung, A. M., Snyder, A. E., Garcia, A., Ordynans, J. G., & Atkins, J. G. (2014). An intervention to improve comprehension of cause/effect through expository text structure instruction. *Journal of Educational Psychology, 106*(1), 1.

Williams, J. P., Stafford, K. B., Lauer, K. D., Hall, K. M., & Pollini, S. (2009). Embedding reading comprehension training in content-area instruction. *Journal of Educational Psychology, 101*(1), 1.

Williamson, G. L. (2008). A text readability continuum for postsecondary readiness. *Journal of Advanced Academics, 19*(4), 602–632.

Wong-Fillmore, L., & Fillmore, C. J. (2012). What does text complexity mean for English learners and language minority students? *Commissioned papers on language and literacy issues in the Common Core State Standards and Next Generation Science Standards, 94,* 64.

CHAPTER 6

Common Core State Standards and Multiple-Source Reading Comprehension

Jay S. Blanchard and S. Jay Samuels

This chapter is about the Common Core State Standards (CCSS) requirement that K–12 students have the reading comprehension skills needed to make connections among ideas and between texts that appear in diverse media and formats, including visually, quantitatively, and orally. This chapter cleaves neatly into three parts. The first focuses on the language of CCSS with regard to multiple-source reading comprehension skills, the second on the assessment of these skills, and the third on a brief review of the most common theoretical perspective that underpins current research on multiple-source reading comprehension—namely, *constructivism*.

THE COMMON CORE STATE STANDARDS

At the outset, it is worth noting that for many years teachers have used a variety of instructional practices to help students develop and use multiple-source reading comprehension skills (see Pearson, 2009, for an in-depth review of comprehension instructional practices). Commonly, these skills were included as part of integrated or interdisciplinary curriculum approaches using multiple sources such as project-based, inquiry-based and portfolio activities in the upper grades and thematic unit activities in the lower grades. In a perfect world, these integrated approaches would occur across discipline areas such as literature, science, social studies, and history, alongside literary/language arts skills such as reading and writing (see Gavelek, Raphael, Biondo, & Wang, 2000; Shanahan, 2003; Shanahan & Shanahan, 2008, for discussion). But classrooms are not perfect worlds, and integrated approaches tended to feature or favor one or the other, that is, discipline content or literacy/language arts skills. Content teachers tended to teach content, and literacy teachers tended to teach literacy (e.g., Beane, 2000). As a result, few teachers taught "the processes for integrating across school subjects" (Gavelek et al., 2000, p. 590; see also Lipson, Valencia, Wixson, & Peters, 1993, for discussion). If the processes were taught, the instruction was provided on "as-needed basis" to complete solitary project-based or thematic-unit assignments and not as a part of any ongoing curriculum. Helping students develop and use multiple-source integration processes was just not so important, and adding to the lack of importance, historically high-stakes achievement tests did not use multiple-source test formats (see Sabatini, O'Reilly, & Albro, 2012, for discussion). That, however, has changed!

The language of the CCSS requires students to develop and use integration skills beginning in kindergarten and continuing through high school. One of those integration skills is multiple-source reading comprehension. The introductory documentation of the CCSS (Common Core State Standards Initiative, 2010) alerts the reader to the need for students to develop these comprehension skills:

> Whatever they are reading, students must also show a steady growing ability to discern more from and make fuller use of text, including making an increasing number of connections among ideas and between texts, considering a wider range of textual evidence, and becoming more sensitive to inconsistencies, ambiguities, and poor reasoning in texts. (p. 8)

Though the introduction uses the word *texts*, it is clear in the language of the College and Career Readiness Anchor Standards and the accompanying grade-level standards that the term includes not only printed matter as text but also multimedia. As we will review below, multiple-source reading comprehension skills are enumerated in CCSS for the English Language Arts (Reading, Writing, Speaking and Listening) and Literacy in History/Social Studies, Science, and Technical Subjects. (As a reminder: The CCSS contain two sets of standards: Grade-Level and College and Career Readiness Anchor Standards. Grade-Level Standards provide specificity in support of the broader Anchor Standards. All standards are grouped by grade level—namely, K–5 and 6–12.)

Grades K–5

Reading Standards. Of the 10 K–5 Anchor Reading Standards, numbers seven and nine refer to multiple-source reading comprehension. Standard 7 states that students must "integrate and evaluate content presented in diverse formats and media including visually and quantitatively, as well as in words" (Common Core State Standards Initiative, 2010, p. 10). Standard 9 says students should be able to "analyze how two or more texts address similar themes or topics in order to build knowledge or to compare the approaches the authors take" (p. 10). It follows that for each Grade-level specific standard, students must demonstrate multiple-source reading comprehension skills. There are some subtle differences between the K–5 Grade-level standards for literature and for informational text. For informational texts, the Grade-level standards clearly indicate that from kindergarten through 4th grade students are expected to integrate knowledge and ideas across two texts; however, in 5th grade the requirement is broadened to include ideas "from several texts" and "multiple print or digital sources" (p. 14). For literature texts, the grade-level standards are less clear about the number of texts but they still require students to demonstrate multiple-source reading comprehension skills. For example, in the literature standards for kindergarten, students must "compare and contrast the adventures and experiences of characters in familiar stories" (p. 11). In 2nd grade, students must "compare and contrast two or more versions of the same story by different authors from different cultures" (p. 11). By 5th grade, students are supposed to "compare and contrast stories in the same genre on their approaches to similar themes and topics" (p. 12).

Writing Standards. In the 10 Anchor Writing Standards for grades K–5, two standards (Standards 8 and 9) involve multiple-source reading comprehension skills. Anchor Standard 8 states that students should be able to "gather relevant information from multiple print and digital sources, assess the credibility and accuracy of each source, and integrate the information while avoiding plagiarism" (Common Core State Standards Initiative, 2010, p. 18). Writing Anchor Standard 9 says students must "draw evidence from literary and informational texts to support analysis, reflection, and research" (p. 18). It should be noted that the grade-level specific standards are silent about Standard 9 until 4th grade, at which point teachers are instructed to follow the reading grade-level specific standards for literature and informational texts, which of course, call for multiple-source reading comprehension skills.

Speaking and Listening Standards. In the six Anchor Standards as well as the Grade-Level standards, students are not expected to demonstrate multiple-source comprehension skills, although they *are* expected to be able to use information presented in diverse media and formats.

Grades 6–12

Reading Standards. Multiple-source reading comprehension skills can be found in Standards 7 and 9 of the 10 Anchor Standards for Reading in grades 6–12. Anchor Standard 7 calls for these skills across various formats and media. The language of the standard states that students must "integrate and evaluate content presented in diverse formats and media including visually and quantitatively, as well as in words" (Common Core State Standards Initiative, 2010, p. 35). For example, using literature texts in 7th grade, students are expected to "compare and contrast a written story, drama, or poem to its audio, filmed, staged or multimedia version, analyzing the effects of techniques unique to each medium" (p. 37). In grades 11 and 12 for informational texts, students are expected to "integrate and evaluate multiple sources of information presented in different media and formats (e.g., visually, quantitatively) as well as in words in order to address a question or solve a problem" (p. 40). Considering Anchor Standard 9, the language for grades 6–12 states that students must be able to "analyze how two or more texts address similar themes or topics in order to build knowledge or to compare the approaches the authors take" (p. 35). For example, with literature texts, 7th-grade students must "compare and contrast a fictional portrayal of a time, place, or character and a historical account of the same periods as a means of understanding how authors of fiction use or alter history" (p. 37). Using informational texts in 7th grade, students are expected to "analyze how two or more authors writing about the same topic shape their presentations of key information by emphasizing different evidence or advancing different interpretations of facts" (p. 39). Moving to literature texts for grades 11 and 12, students must be able to "demonstrate knowledge of eighteenth-, nineteenth-, and early twentieth-century foundational works of American literature, including how two or more texts from the same period treat similar themes or topics" (p. 38). Using informational texts in 11th and 12th grades, students must be able to "analyze seventeenth-, eighteenth-, nineteenth-century foundational U.S. documents of historical and literacy significance for their themes, purposes, and rhetorical features" (p. 40).

Writing Standards. Multiple-source reading comprehension skills are embedded in Standards 8 and 9 of the 10 College and Career Readiness Anchor Standards for Writing. For example, considering Anchor Standard 8, 7th-grade students are expected to "gather information from multiple print and digital sources" (Common Core State Standards Initiative, 2010, p. 44). In 11th and 12th grades, students must "gather information from multiple authoritative print and digital sources" (p. 46). Writing Anchor Standard 9 says students in 7th grade should be able to "draw evidence from literary and informational texts to support analysis, reflection, and research" (p. 44). In 11th and 12th grades, students are also expected to "draw evidence from literary or informational texts to support analysis, reflection, and research" (p. 47).

Reading Standards for Literacy in the Content Areas. Across the content areas, Standards 7, 8, and 9 enumerate multiple-source comprehension skills. Grouping the content areas and grade levels together for a simple explanation, Standard 7 requires students to integrate and evaluate visual, quantitative, and technical information from multiple sources (e.g., print, digital text, maps, experiments). Standard 8 mandates that students should be able to distinguish, assess, and evaluate evidence for fact versus opinion. Standard 9 calls for students to be able to analyze, compare and contrast, and synthesize information from multiple sources for in-depth understanding.

Writing Standards for Literacy in the Content Areas. As was the case for reading in the content areas, writing in the content areas standards include multiple-source reading comprehension skills in Standards 7, 8, and 9. Broadly stated, students are asked in Standard 7 to conduct research using multiple sources; Standard 8 expects them to gather and assess information from multiple sources; and in Standard 9, students are supposed to draw evidence for analysis, reflection, and research from multiple sources.

Speaking and Listening Standards. The second Anchor Standard states that students should be able to "integrate and evaluate information presented in diverse media and formats including visually, quantitatively and orally" (p. 48). For example, in 6th grade, students are expected to "interpret information presented in diverse media and formats (e.g., visually, quantitatively, orally) and explain how it [the information] contributes to the topic, text, or issue under study" (p. 49).

In sum, throughout the College and Career Anchor Standards as well as Grade-Level Standards, teachers are constantly reminded to provide ongoing educational opportunities that support the development and use of multiple-source reading comprehension skills, which, we might add, their students must demonstrate they possess.

ASSESSMENT OF MULTIPLE-SOURCE READING COMPREHENSION

In the United States, two federally funded assessment groups are currently developing test items for CCSS that will measure multiple-source reading comprehension skills. These groups are the Partnership for Assessment of Readiness for College and Careers (PARCC) and Smarter Balanced Assessment Consortium (SBAC). Field-testing of multiple-source comprehension items has begun, and samples from PARCC and SBAC provide ample evidence about the intended nature of these items. In general, the items require students to demonstrate reading comprehension skills that permit them to understand, integrate, synthesize, interpret, explain, and critically evaluate content from across multiple sources of information and, in some cases, multimedia.

Partnership for the Assessment of Readiness for College and Careers

Currently, PARCC intends to measure multiple-source comprehension skills through a "research simulation task," as indicated by the following samples (PARCC, 2014).

Seventh-grade task:

1. Students begin by reading an anchor text that introduces the topic. The anchor text is a biography of Amelia Earhart.
2. After discussion, to learn more, students read an article and watch a video about Amelia Earhart. Then they must answer questions about each source.
3. Finally, students write an essay "to show their reading comprehension" (p. 3). The essay directions ask them to analyze "the strength of the arguments related to Earhart's bravery in at least two of the three supporting materials" (p. 22). In particular, students must analyze how the authors shaped their presentations by offering different evidence or advancing different interpretations of the facts.

High school task:

1. Students read three texts: (1) an excerpt from a biography of Abigail Smith Adams, (2) spousal correspondence from Abigail to her husband, and (3) correspondence from John Adams to Abigail.
2. Based on the three sources, students must integrate information from each source into a coherent understanding of the Adamses' spousal relationship and its historical significance for freedom and independence.
3. As evidence of a coherent understanding, students must write an essay that explains the contrasting views between Abigail and John on freedom and independence. In particular, the essay must "make a claim about the idea of freedom and independence and how John and Abigail Adams add to that understanding and/or illustrate a misunderstanding of freedom and independence" (p. 23). The essay must contain textual evidence and inferences drawn from all three sources to support the essay's claim.

Smarter Balanced Assessment Consortium

SBAC measures multiple-source reading comprehension skills with "performance tasks," such as the following samples (SBAC, 2014).

Sample 4th-grade task:

1. On the topic of animal defenses (how animals protect themselves), students watch a video and read a short article.
2. Students are expected to answer questions and write an article based on the content of the video and article. The task directions state:

Your class is preparing a museum display that will include photos of a variety of animals and interesting facts about them. You have been asked to write an article for the museum display explaining about animal defenses. Choose one animal from the article . . . and one animal from the video. . . . In your article identify your two animals, explain how each animal protects itself from its enemies, and explain how the two animals' defenses are similar and different. Include details from your sources. (pp. 8–9)

The article must demonstrate "sufficient evidence of the ability to locate, select, interpret and integrate information within and among sources" (p. 14).

Sixth-grade task:

1. Students watch a video and read two short texts about an environmental topic.
2. Students must locate, select, interpret, analyze, and integrate information across and within the sources and demonstrate these skills through task-related questions and a writing assignment.

Eleventh-grade task:

1. Students read multiple simulated multimedia online web pages' content and judge the credibility, completeness, relevancy, and accuracy of the sources about an environmental topic.
2. As was the case in the earlier grades' tasks, students must demonstrate skills through task-related questions and a writing assignment. (Note: This performance task is similar to the online performance-based assessment in the 2016 e-PIRLS; International Association for the Evaluation of Educational Achievement, Progress in International Reading Literacy Study, 2014.)

In sum, PARCC and SBAC have begun efforts to assess multiple-source comprehension skills. Their efforts can be seen in sample test and current field-testing items on their websites. However, while PARCC and SBAC are sitting in the pole position, the race to assess multiple-source reading comprehension is just beginning, and these early efforts will likely be replaced by deeper, richer, and more authentic assessments.

A THEORETICAL PERSPECTIVE ON MULTIPLE-SOURCE READING COMPREHENSION

Despite decades of interest in the development of multiple-source or intertextual reading comprehension skills (Bakhtin, 1981; see Gavelek et al., 2000, for historical discussion), widespread interest did not come about until the 1990s. For example, in the 1992 edition of the *Encyclopedia of Educational Research*, Pearson speculated that an intertextual view of reading comprehension "may become the classic perspective of the future" (p. 1078). This, it has turned out, was a remarkably forward-looking statement conveying a sense that the reading comprehension world of one reader, one text was about to be upended. A few years later, the cognitive scientist Charles Perfetti, writing in *Discourse Processes* (1997), noted that understanding learning in intertext or multiple-text environments was a "new problem" (p. 345) and more research was needed. It could, in fact, be seen as a new problem in need of research because technology-enabled innovations were just beginning to provide widespread, easy access to information from an expanding variety of print and nonprint media sources (Blanchard, 1999). At about the same time, multiple-source reading comprehension skills began to garner the attention of educational policymakers. The changing realities of the 21st-century workplace meant that workers would be immersed in technology-enabled, multiple-source environments, and policymakers needed to ensure that schools were preparing students to meet the new reading comprehension demands inherent in those environments (see Kamil & Chou, 2009, for discussion). As a result, multiple-source reading comprehension soon became part of national and international educational policy documents as well as international large-scale assessments such as the Programme for International Student Assessment (PISA) and Progress in International Reading Literacy Study (PIRLS).

Although it is beyond the scope of this chapter to review the extant research on intertext or multiple-source reading comprehension, we will briefly review and then discuss challenges to the most commonly cited theoretical perspective that underpins a number of current research efforts—namely, constructivism.

The Constructivist Perspective

To date, the perspective of constructivism is based on Kinstch's single-text model (1988, construction-integration) as expanded to multiple sources in the Full Documents Model (Perfetti, 1997; Perfetti, Rouet, & Britt, 1999; see also Pearson & Cervetti, Chapter 1, this volume). The Full Documents Model proposes two additions to Kinstch's single-text model. Briefly described, the first addition is a subcomponent model entitled "intertext." The intertext model involves explaining how readers represent the relationships among different texts: "The intertext model links texts in terms of their rhetorical relations to each other" (Perfetti, 1997, p. 346). The second addition is a subcomponent model entitled "situations." The situations model explains how readers represent the situations described in the texts—that is, "situations described in one or more texts with links to the texts" (p. 346). According to Perfetti (1997), "when the situations model and the intertextual model are interconnected, then we have a full documents model" (p. 346). The Full Documents Model is a good reader model, and several other (not as good) models have been suggested by Perfetti and colleagues (e.g., Mush; Separate Representation; Tag All) to account for less-than-complete comprehension of texts. The Full Documents Model works this way:

- The reader understands the relevant information in each text.
- Then, the reader understands how the various information in each text is integrated (connected) across texts.
- Finally, the reader develops a global interpretation or synthesis of the relevant text information.

Originally, the model was based on inquiry-oriented tasks—that is, multiple sources presented conflicting information about a topic or subject and readers had to sort out what was and was not reliable and valid across the sources (Britt, Perfetti, Sandak, & Rouet, 1999). This type of document thinking is common in most disciplines, such as science and history, but there are also nonconflicting types of document thinking, such as locating and gathering information about a topic (Afflerbach & VanSledright, 2001; Goldman & Bisanz, 2002; Stahl, Hynd, Britton, McNish, & Bosquet, 1996; Wineburg, 1991). Today, ongoing constructivist research efforts have expanded to include nonconflicting types of document thinking as well as the study of variables such as goal direction, reader epistemic beliefs, good versus poor readers, genre, motivation, disciplinary knowledge, and prior knowledge (e.g., Anmarkud, Braten, & Stromso, 2014; Braten, Anmarkrud, Brandmo, & Stromso, 2014; Braten, Ferguson, Stromso, & Anmarkrud, 2014; Britt, Richter, & Rouet, 2014; Ferguson & Braten, 2013; Goldman, Braasch, Wiley, Graesser, & Brodowinski, 2012; Goldman & Scardamilia, 2013; Hagen, Braasch, & Braten, 2014; Maier & Richter, 2014; Richter & Rapp, 2014; Stromso & Braten, 2014; Stromso, Braten, Britt, & Ferguson, 2013).

Despite a fair number of constructivist-oriented studies since the 1990s, there are critics who challenge the usefulness of constructivist explanations given the realities of 21st-century learning environments. Chief among these critics have been researchers from the disciplines of the New Literacies (e.g., Coiro, 2014; Coiro, Knobel, Lankshear, & Leu, 2008; Leu, Kinzer, Coiro, Castek, & Henry, 2013) and Transliteracies (e.g., Thomas, 2008). However, New Literacy and Transliteracy researchers are not alone in their criticisms. Some cognitive scientists who study reading comprehension have joined the chorus as well. For example, Fox and Alexander (2009) have argued that the complexity inherent in the rapidly changing nature of today's technology-enabled thinking and learning have fundamentally altered a static, reductive model and thus must be replaced by a dynamic model. As a result, a reconceptualization of multiple-source reading comprehension is needed; simply to change a static model will not do, and there is a need to move beyond the "one reader, one text" perspective (Fox & Alexander, 2009, p. 234). Simply put, current constructivist models do not allow researchers to fully explain how students learn in today's 21st-century technology-enabled environments. Consider one example that would challenge current constructivist perspectives such as the Full Documents Model. A teacher watches and listens as a small group of her 6th-graders (11-year-olds) tries to understand the differences between U.S. poverty in the 20th century versus in the 21st century so they can write a group-authored essay. To gain an understanding they do the following:

- Watch a YouTube museum tour about the Great Depression
- Scroll through a Wikipedia text on poverty
- Click on hyperlinks that represent blue-collared accounts like *Grapes of Wrath*
- Listen to a National Public Radio (NPR) podcast about progress in the war on poverty
- Read a blog post and tweet stream from a community activist in a low-socioeconomic neighborhood

During these technology-enabled activities, the teacher observes that students are zigzagging across the sources and that much of the source content appears to be ill-structured. But the zigzagging, to-and-fro behaviors as well as the ill-structured sources are not new to the teacher; she has seen it all before. And it is not new to some researchers. For example, the zigzag, to-and-fro pattern evokes an image from

Wittgenstein's examinations of learning and knowing, in which he talks about crisscrossing the landscape of a topic, making as many connections as possible among the ideas within the topic (Wittgenstein, 1953; see also Hartman, 1995). Additionally, the notion of crisscrossing an ill-structured landscape to gather an ensemble of connections that could form knowledge representations is a key dimension of Cognitive Flexibility Theory (Spiro & DeSchryver, 2009).

In the final analysis, the challenge for cognitive scientists, educational psychologists, and literacy educators, regardless of their perspective, is the development of a model that can account for the behaviors that our 6th-grade teacher observed.

Fox and Alexander (2009) sum it up by suggesting that a model of multiple-source reading comprehension should explain how readers "form a more global, integrated representation of a topic or issue from multiple text sources should they be written or oral; linguistic, graphic, or pictorial" (p. 234). We would add that the model should also attempt to explain multiple-source reading comprehension in ill-structured sources and under ill-structured task demands.

CONCLUSION

This chapter described the Common Core State Standards with regard to multiple-source reading comprehension skills, reviewed how the two U.S. Department of Education assessment groups intend to measure the skills, and offered a brief review of one common theoretical perspective on multiple-source reading comprehension.

At the onset of efforts in the 21st century to understand multiple-source reading comprehension, Goldman and van Oostendorp (1999) reminded theorists and researchers that there would be many challenges ahead. Almost 2 decades later, Goldman and colleagues are still echoing the same reminder (Bromme & Goldman, 2014; Goldman & Scardamalia, 2013; see also Goldman, 2011). These scholars are not alone; any review of the extant literature on multiple-source reading comprehension will find a common acknowledgment by researchers from all perspectives that both better research and more complete explanations are needed. It is a testimony to the challenges ahead that several U.S. federally funded grants are currently involved in some form of multiple-source reading comprehension research (e.g., Computer Based Assessment Of, For, As Learning; Reading for Understanding [RfU]; Assessing On Line Reading Comprehension: ORCA Project).

Our claim is that the most important reason why the challenges of the 1990s have continued into the 2010s is because of the rapid expansion of technology-enabled access to clouds of information in a dazzling variety of presentation formats and from an ever-changing variety of devices. Children live and learn in a multiple-source, multimedia, and multitasking world (Atwill & Blanchard, 2013; Leu et al., 2013). As a result, it has been increasingly difficult for cognitive scientists, educational psychologists, and reading educators, regardless of perspective, to fully understand the complex, interrelated, technology-enabled variables that might or might not influence thinking, learning, and multiple-source reading comprehension skills development.

So, what does all this mean for teachers? First, just as soon as teachers have reason to believe that students can handle multiple-source tasks, they need to provide opportunities for students to read and learn from multiple sources in a variety of presentation formats and media. A good starting point for teachers is the list of "constructively responsive reading comprehension" strategies offered by Afflerbach and Cho (2009, pp. 80–84). The researchers offer almost 80 strategies that are anchored by the need for students to find links or connections between sources and prior knowledge. Simply put, students need to draw relevant and meaningful connections between multiple sources of information, including their own prior knowledge, and should be able to use that information in a meaningful way. Second, the increased complexity demands of CCSS for multiple-source reading comprehension tasks mean that teachers will need to focus some of their classroom time on helping students develop the motivation, attention stamina, and memory skills needed to meet the demands (see Guthrie, Chapter 7, this volume).

What these CCSS "needs" and many others described in this volume point toward is a new and reasonably complex curricular and instructional approach to reading comprehension skills development for American students and their teachers. We hope these needs will point toward more research and a better understanding of multiple-source thinking and learning. And, just maybe, the needs can also point toward more U.S. Department of Education funding for independent, longitudinal studies of the CCSS and their impact on teachers and students.

REFERENCES

Afflerbach, P., & Cho, B. (2009). Identifying and describing constructively responsive comprehension strategies in new and traditional forms of reading. In S. Israel & G. Duffy (Eds.), *Handbook of research on reading comprehension* (pp. 69–90). New York, NY: Routledge.

Afflerbach, P., & VanSledright, B. (2001). Hath? Doth? What? The challenges middle school students face when reading innovative history text. *Journal of Adolescent and Adult Literacy, 44,* 696–707.

Anmarkud, O., Braten, I., & Stromso, H. (2014). Multiple documents literacy: Strategic processing, source awareness, and argumentation when reading multiple conflicting documents. *Learning and Individual Differences, 30,* 64–76.

Atwill, K., & Blanchard, J. (2013). The many possible roles for technology in the reading and writing connection. In B. Miller, P. McCardle, & R. Long (Eds.), *Teaching reading and writing: Improving instruction and student achievement* (pp. 129–142). Baltimore, MD: Brookes.

Bakhtin, M. (1981). *The dialogic imagination: Four essays.* Austin, TX: University of Texas Press. (Original work published 1935)

Beane, T. (2000). Reading in the content areas: Social constructivist dimensions. In M. Kamil, P. Mosenthal, P. D. Pearson, & R. Barr (Eds.), *Handbook of reading research* (Vol. 3, pp. 629–644). Mahwah, NJ: Erlbaum.

Blanchard, J. (1999). Technology, communication, and literacy: Critical issues. In J. Blanchard (Ed.), *Educational computing in the schools: Technology, communication and literacy* (pp. 1–4). New York, NY: Haworth Press.

Braten, I., Anmarkrud, O., Brandmo, C., & Stromso, H. (2014). Developing and testing a model of direct and indirect relationships between individual differences, processing, and multiple-text comprehension. *Learning and Instruction, 30,* 9–24.

Braten, I., Ferguson, L., Stromso, H., & Anmarkrud, O. (2014). Students working with multiple conflicting documents on a scientific issue: Relations between epistemic cognition while reading and sourcing and argumentation in essays. *British Journal of Educational Psychology, 84,* 58–85.

Britt, M., Perfetti, C., Sandak, R., & Rouet, J. (1999). Content integration and source separation in learning from multiple texts. In S. Goldman, A. Graesser, & P. van den Broek (Eds.), *Narrative comprehension, causality, and coherence: Essays in honor of Tom Trabasso* (pp. 209–233). Mahwah, NJ: Erlbaum.

Britt, M., Richter, T., & Rouet, J. (2014). Scientific literacy: The role of goal-directed reading and evaluation in understanding scientific information. *Educational Psychologist, 49*(2), 104–122.

Bromme, R., & Goldman, S. (2014). The public's bounded understanding of science. *Educational Psychologist, 49*(2), 59–69.

Coiro, J. (2014, June 2). *Online reading comprehension: Challenges and opportunities.* Virtual paper presented at the Annual Meeting of the XI Encontro Virtual de Documentacao em Software Livre e VIII Congresso Internacional de Linguagem e Tecnologia online. Available at http://uri.academic.edu/JulieCoiro/Papers

Coiro, J., Knobel, M., Lankshear, C., & Leu, D. (Eds.). (2008). *Handbook of research on new literacies.* New York, NY: Erlbaum.

Common Core State Standards Initiative. (2010). *Common Core State Standards for English, language arts, & literacy in history, social studies, science and technical subjects.* Washington, DC: Council of Chief State School Officers and the National Governors Association Center for Best Practices.

Ferguson, L., & Braten, I. (2013). Student profiles of knowledge and epistemic beliefs: Changes and relations to multiple-text comprehension. *Learning and Instruction, 25,* 49–61.

Fox, E., & Alexander, P. (2009). Text comprehension: A retrospective, perspective and prospective. In S. Israel & G. Duffy (Eds.), *Handbook of research on reading comprehension* (pp. 227–239). New York, NY: Routledge.

Gavelek, J., Raphael, T., Biondo, S., & Wang, D. (2000). Integrated literacy instruction. In M. Kamil, P. Mosenthal, P. D. Pearson, & R. Barr (Eds.), *Handbook of reading research* (Vol. 3, pp. 587–607). Mahwah, NJ: Erlbaum.

Goldman, S. (2011). Choosing and using multiple information sources: Some new findings and emergent issues. *Learning and Instruction, 21,* 238–242.

Goldman, S., & Bisanz, G. (2002). Toward functional analysis of scientific genres: Implications for understanding and learning processes. In J. Otero, J. Leon, & A. Graesser (Eds.), *The psychology of science text comprehension* (pp. 19–50). Mahwah, NJ: Erlbaum.

Goldman, S., Braasch, J., Wiley, J., Graesser, A., & Brodowinski, K. (2012). Comprehending and learning from Internet sources: Processing patterns of better and poorer learners. *Reading Research Quarterly, 47,* 356–381.

Goldman, S., & Scardamilia, M. (2013). Managing, understanding, applying, and creating knowledge in the information age: Next-generation challenges and opportunities. *Cognition and Instruction, 31*(2), 255–269.

Goldman, S., & van Oostendorp, H. (1999). Conclusions, conundrums, and challenges for the future. In H. van Oostendorp, & S. Goldman (Eds.), *The construction of mental representations during reading* (pp. 323–330). Mahwah, NJ: Erlbaum.

Hagen, A., Braasch, J., & Braten, I. (2014). Relationships between spontaneous note-taking, self-reported strategies and comprehension when reading multiple texts in different task conditions. *Journal of Research in Reading, 37*(1), 141–157.

Hartman, D. (1995). Eight readers reading: The intertextual links of proficient readers reading multiple passages. *Reading Research Quarterly, 30*(3), 520–561.

Hernandez, J. (2014, June 15). Common Core, in 9-year-old eyes. *New York Times,* pp. 1, 18.

International Association for the Evaluation of Educational Achievement. (2014). *Progress in International Reading Literacy Study*. Amsterdam, The Netherlands (Secretariat): Author.

Kamil, M., & Chou, H. (2009). Comprehension and computer technology: Past results, current knowledge, and future promises. In S. Israel & G. Duffy (Eds.), *Handbook of research on reading comprehension* (pp. 289–304). New York, NY: Routledge.

Kintsch, W. (1988). The role of knowledge in discourse processing: A construction-integration model. *Psychological Review, 95*, 163–182.

Leu, D., Kinzer, C., Coiro, J., Castek, J., & Henry, L. (2013). New literacies: A dual-level theory of the changing nature of literacy, instruction, and assessment. In D. Alvermann, N. Unrau, & R. Ruddell (Eds.), *Theoretical models and processes of reading* (6th ed.) (pp. 1150–1183). Newark, DE: International Reading Association.

Lipson, M., Valencia, S., Wixson, K., & Peters, C. (1993). Integration and thematic teaching: Integration to improve teaching and learning. *Language Arts, 70*, 252–263.

Maier, J., & Richter, T. (2014). Fostering multiple text comprehension: How metacognitive strategies and motivation moderate the text-belief consistency effect. *Metacognition Learning, 9*, 51–74.

Partnership for Assessment of Readiness for College and Careers. (2014). *Test samples.* Washington, DC: Author. Available at www.parcconline.org

Pearson, P. D. (1992). *Reading.* In M. Aiken (Ed.), *Encyclopedia of educational research* (pp. 1075–1085). New York, NY: MacMillan.

Pearson, P. D. (2009). The roots of reading comprehension instruction. In S. Israel & G. Duffy (Eds.), *Handbook of research on reading comprehension* (pp. 3–31). New York, NY: Routledge.

Perfetti, C. (1997). Sentences. Individual differences, and multiple texts: Three issues in text comprehension. *Discourse Processes, 23*, 337–355.

Perfetti, C., Rouet, J., & Britt, M. (1999). Toward a theory of documents representation. In H. van Oostendorf & S. Goldman (Eds.), *The construction of mental representations during reading* (pp. 99–122). Mahwah, NJ: Erlbaum.

Richter, T., & Rapp, D. (2014). Comprehension and validation of text information: Introduction to the special issue. *Discourse Processes, 51*(1-2), 1–6.

Sabatini, J., O'Reilly, T., & Albro, E. (Eds.). (2012). *Reaching an understanding: Innovations in how we view reading assessment.* New York, NY: Rowman & Littlefield.

Shanahan, C. (2003). *Using multiple texts to teach content.* Naperville, IL: Learning Point Associates (formerly North Central Regional Educational Laboratory).

Shanahan, T., & Shanahan, C. (2008). Teaching disciplinary literacy to adolescents: Rethinking content-area literacy. *Harvard Educational Review, 78*(1), 40–59.

Smarter Balanced Assessment Consortium. (2014). *Test samples.* Olympia, WA, and Los Angeles CA: Author. Available at www.smarterbalanced.org

Spiro, R., & DeSchryver, M. (2009). Constructivism: When it's the wrong idea and when it's the only idea. In S. Tobis & T. Duffy (Eds.), *Constructivism instruction: Success or failure?* (pp. 106–124). New York, NY: Routledge.

Stahl, S., Hynd, C., Britton, B., McNish, M., & Bosquet, D. (1996). What happens when students read multiple source documents in history? *Reading Research Quarterly, 31*, 430–456.

Stromso, H., & Braten, I. (2014). Students' sourcing while reading and writing from multiple web documents. *Nordic Journal of Digital Literacy, 9*, 92–111.

Stromso, H., Braten, I., Britt, M., & Ferguson, L. (2013). Spontaneous sourcing among students reading multiple documents. *Cognition and Instruction, 31*(2), 176–203.

Thomas, S. (2008). Transliteracy and new media. In R. Adams, S. Gibson, & S. Arisona (Eds.), *Transdisciplinary digital art: Sound, vision, and the new screen* (pp. 101–109). Heidelberg, Germany: Springer-Verlag.

Wineburg, S. (1991). Historical problem solving: A study of the cognitive processes used in the evaluation of documentary and pictorial evidence. *Journal of Educational Psychology, 83*, 73–87.

Wittgenstein, L. (1953). *Philosophical investigations*. New York, NY: Macmillan.

CHAPTER 7

Growth of Motivations for Cognitive Processes of Reading

John T. Guthrie

Our notions about teaching reading are deeply grounded in what we, as reading educators, think reading is. If we believe that reading is mainly decoding written symbols to oral language, then we teach decoding. If reading is basically literary interpretation, we teach story comprehension. The Common Core State Standards for the English Language Arts (CCSS ELA) feature reading in three subject areas: literature, science, and history. If we believe that reading differs in these disciplines, then reading instruction will target subject-matter text comprehension. To progress in this direction, challenges arise more than ever before for teaching more complex reading skills, strategies, and comprehension processes. But the aims of the new teaching cannot end there.

There is no denial among literacy leaders that the CCSS are complex. There is no denial that students' reading achievement was not adequate prior to the coming of the CCSS. There is no denial that the CCSS challenge students to work harder and longer and to think more deeply about texts than they are required to do at present. Yet the standards are mute on the point of one crucial ingredient—motivation. In fact, the term is used only twice in the entire ELA standards document. This neglect is surprising in light of the substantial body of research showing that students need powerful reasons to read more and work harder, and with the increase in the level of challenge of both text and task in the CCSS, they will need even more reasons than they did previously. These reasons—the goals, values, and beliefs that undergird commitment—are motivations. Without this motivation, students will not meet the standards. Without supporting these motivations, teachers will not succeed in their endeavors to teach to these standards.

Fused with reading skills, or cognitive processes, are motivations. This chapter charts that fusion. I outline how students grow in the cognitive side of reading information texts and how motivation fuels this growth in grades 3–7. The body of research on motivation and engagement has expanded exponentially in the past 2 decades. After decades of lagging behind advances in our knowledge of cognitive processes, engagement has become a mature field of inquiry. The best evidence for this advance is the publication of a handbook, of more than 1,000 pages, that unpacks and synthesizes the empirical literature surrounding engagement (Christensen, Reschly, & Wylie, 2012).

The plan for this chapter is straightforward. I will unpack what we have learned about developments in the cognitive and motivational aspects of reading across the span of grades 3–7 (roughly ages 8–12), a span of rapid development for most readers and a time in which they fully assume the challenge of reading short informational texts that are designed to enhance their knowledge of how the world around them works. Evidence suggests that as reading comprehension for informational text increases in grades 3–7, cognitive processes also increase, as do students' motivations to read. Whereas cognition increases in proficiency, motivation strengthens in connection to cognition. Initially, I will present the prevailing cognitive systems and motivational dynamics for each grade separately. More important, I will note the changes that occur from grades 3–5 and 5–7, as it is these changes that may be regarded as progressions. The question is: What cognitive components are improving and what motivations are driving students during their development in the grade 3–7 range?

The research rationale for these progressions consists of five claims, each of which is documented by one or more reviews of empirical literature:

1. Reading comprehension—referring essentially to passage comprehension—increases during this time, and the proposed cognitive processes have been shown to be semi-independently associated with reading comprehension at primary (Walczyk et al., 2007), intermediate (van den Broek, Rapp, & Kendeou, 2005), and secondary (Cromley & Azevedo, 2007) levels.

2. Motivations develop during this period, along with their capacity to predict reading comprehension proficiency (Gottfried, Fleming, & Gottfried, 2001).

3. Reading motivation contributes significantly to longitudinal reading comprehension growth at each period (Guthrie, Wigfield, & You, 2012). This implies strongly that motivational progressions are integral to reading comprehension growth.

4. When teachers' classroom practices support motivation, students' reading comprehension increases. Such growth documents the formative role of motivation processes (Guthrie et al., 2012).

5. Support of each of these key aspects of motivation increases reading achievement, as shown by experimental tests (Guthrie & Klauda, in press).

COGNITIVE AND MOTIVATIONAL PROCESSES OF READING, GRADES 3–7

In this section, I will review the key cognitive and motivational variables that my colleagues and I have been studying over the past 2 and a half decades. For cognition, the variables include oral reading fluency, literal comprehension, inferencing, summarizing, and searching. For motivation, we have studied self-efficacy, intrinsic motivation, valuing, perceived difficulty, devaluing, avoidance, and dedication. For each of grades 3, 5, and 7, I will characterize typical readers for both cognition and motivation.

Grade 3 Cognitive and Motivational Processes

Cognition. Reading comprehension at grade 3 can be characterized as the capacity to acquire a moderate amount of factual information from grade-level text, with an emergent capability to construct the first level of conceptual knowledge evident in more advanced students at this grade level. From a descriptive passage, many students gain several facts, and a moderate proportion learn an initial level of higher-order concepts that are connected to evidence or examples of the concepts. For example, although a text may communicate six concepts about the survival of plants and animals in a wetland, this group of readers may only learn two concepts, such as predation (water scorpions eat sticklebacks) and defense (sticklebacks use grasses for cover). Third-graders are in a transition state in which factual learning from text dominates, and initial higher-order concepts may occasionally be built from text. At grade 3, a substantial number of cognitive processes contribute to this form of reading comprehension, including oral reading fluency, literal comprehension, inferencing, summarizing, and searching—all of which are typically included in instruction scope and sequence frameworks, and which I will review below.

Reading fluency refers to reading speed, syntactic processing, and full expressive reading, all three of which correlate with measures of reading comprehension (Klauda & Guthrie, 2008). Third-graders are typically capable of reading a grade-level text expressively for about 25% of the passage. Often, they read in two- or three-word phrases but seldom in larger, meaningful units (Klauda & Guthrie, 2008).

Literal comprehension consists of accurate semantic construction of simple sentence meanings. More than 50% of grade 3 students reading a grade-level passage can identify three to six facts in the passage that are relevant to a question. They can also accurately answer questions that map directly to the syntax of sentence in text. Although typical students will provide a substantial number of simple facts at a propositional level, only a small minority will provide conceptual understandings and hierarchical structures of knowledge. An example of hierarchical knowledge is that the life cycle of beetles has four stages of egg, larva, pupa, and adult, whereas the life cycle of bugs has three stages of egg, nymph, adult (Guthrie et al., 2004).

Inferencing refers to semantic connections between local units of text that enable larger meanings to be constructed. This process is integral in any of the modern Construction-Integration models of reading (see Pearson & Cervetti, Chapter 1, this volume), including the landscape model of reading comprehension (van den Broek et al., 2005) that undergirds my account of student progressions. A student who can appropriately link pairs of words or pairs of sentences with meaningful connections is inferring in crucial ways. Third-graders have typically acquired minimal levels of this proficiency. However, they show initial, rudimentary proficiency that significantly contributes to their passage comprehension (Guthrie et al., 2004).

Summarizing, which requires deep comprehension and integration of the ideas of complex text, occurs infrequently for 3rd-graders. When students are asked to write their understanding after reading a descriptive passage, they show a negligible amount of hierarchical organization that represents the knowledge conveyed in the text. Many students assemble a few facts but do not organize them well. For example, beetles and bugs differ in the number and types of stages in their life cycles. A 3rd grader's example of factually accurate but conceptually insufficient understanding of the difference between beetles and bugs is shown in the statement that "a ladybug larva looks like a caterpillar, but a nymph can sometimes give off a sticky liquid." Although mature readers can organize expository text into patterns of structured relationships with ample evidence for each pattern, 3rd-graders can typically build only the beginning of such structures. Further, their proficiencies in this process are too simple to correlate with measures of their text comprehension (Guthrie et al., 2004).

Searching for information in expository or narrative text is minimally learned at grade 3. When students are expected to read a longer, multisection text for an explicit question, they are able to identify a few, but not a majority, of text segments relevant to the stated purpose for reading. With 11 possibly relevant sections, students located an average of 3 in one study (Guthrie et al., 2004). This search competency reveals a literal level of hierarchical text perception.

Motivation. Belief in one's capacity to read successfully in the future is termed *self-efficacy*, which correlates with reading achievement from preschool through grade 3. Beyond simple associations, reciprocal causation of self-efficacy and achievement has been documented in several studies (see Morgan & Fuchs, 2007, for a review of this work). Motivation and achievement operate in a spiral, with each influencing the other. For grade 3 students, self-efficacy is highly related to performance on standardized tests and experimental reading comprehension tasks (Guthrie et al., 2004).

Intrinsic motivation refers to enjoyment of reading and is highly similar to interest, enthusiasm, and task involvement in grades K–3. At this level, intrinsic motivation correlates highly with reading comprehension, as measured by experimental tests, standardized tests, grades, or teacher ratings at grade 3 (Guthrie et al., 2004). Teachers frequently rate children highly on their level of intrinsic motivation, awarding mean scores of four on a five-point scale. Intrinsic motivation and achievement show the same reciprocity as self-efficacy and achievement.

Other motivational variables are less frequently studied in grade 3. In expectancy value theory, value refers to the belief that reading is important, useful and beneficial. Reading value predicts achievement strongly for adolescents (Guthrie, Klauder, & Ho, 2013). However, relatively little evidence regarding reading value exists for the primary grades. In grades 4–5, value did not correlate with students' amount of reading in two studies (Wigfield & Guthrie, 1997). Although students in these grades report high levels of perceived value for reading, the construct may not be well formed for them.

Both self-efficacy and intrinsic motivation are strongly positively correlated with word recognition, vocabulary, literacy comprehension, and complex text comprehension at grade 3 (Guthrie et al., 2004; Morgan & Fuchs, 2007). Both of these motivations are highly correlated with multiple-text comprehension where students are expected to read 10–12 sets of complex passages, determine which of them address previously stated questions, and summarize the answers to conceptual questions. Clearly, this qualifies as complex text comprehension, and it is connected to motivations.

Most important is mutual determination. For both self-efficacy and intrinsic motivation, motivation increases reading proficiencies over time; in turn, reading proficiencies increase motivation over time. Students who enter grade 3 relatively high in intrinsic reading motivation leave 3rd grade higher than peers in reading comprehension. In other words, motivation drives reading comprehension. Simultaneously, students who enter 3rd grade relatively adept in cognitive skills will end 3rd grade higher than peers in motivation; this means that cognitive proficiency also energizes motivation. Extensive structural equation modeling for this age group verifies these relations quantitatively (Guthrie et al., 2013): Motivation begets cognitive processing begets motivation, and so on, in a virtuous cycle of mutual reinforcement.

Grade 5 Cognitive and Motivational Processes

Cognition. By grade 5, students' oral reading fluency is moderately well developed. Typically, students will read half a passage of a grade-level text with notable expressiveness. The other half may be inaccurate, halting, word for word, or monotone. Students will often read three- to four-word phrases expressively but will not read a majority of sentences with the same level of expressiveness (Klauda & Guthrie, 2008).

Literal comprehension of simple sentences or relatively simple sentences within paragraphs of grade-level text is reasonably well formed in a majority of students. For example, if students are given a descriptive passage on an animal and asked to recount the important information, most will provide an abundance of factual, accurate statements in simple sentence form, such as: "Hyenas hunt at night. They sleep in the daytime." More than half of students will give a more conceptual rendering that consists of higher-order concepts with subordinate factual and exemplary information, such as: "Hyenas are successful nocturnal predators. They hunt at night, when their prey are vulnerable. They sleep in the daytime in carefully concealed dens." Only a small minority of students lack a basic level of literal text comprehension (Guthrie, Anderson, Alao, & Rinehart, 1999).

At grade 5, a majority of students is capable of drawing accurate inferences at the sentence level (e.g., by stating the relationship of two sentences in the same paragraph). For example, given text stating (1) that birds that fly rapidly and powerfully, like the swift, have pointed wings; and (2) that this wing shape provides the bird with enough lift without producing too much drag, the student may state that "a pointed wing has different shaped feathers that make it go fast." The typical student has progressed to providing suitable inferences at the paragraph level, which requires the integration of information across multiple sentences and relationships. For instance, the student may identify that just as wing shape (pointed vs. broad) influences flying speed and gliding, foot shape (wide, flat toes vs. narrow, clawed toes) influences feeding (herbivory vs. predation). Only a few students, however, are able to draw accurate and comprehensive inferences at the passage level that include appropriate information from multiple paragraphs and diverse sections of text (Klauda & Guthrie, 2008).

Summarizing is pivotal to deep comprehension (McNamara, Ozure, Best, & O'Reilly, 2007). Full synthesis of text information into preexisting background knowledge cannot be based on literal renderings of content at the sentence or propositional level. Students must identify the most important words or concepts. They must relate them to evidence or exemplifying information. And they must organize or structure the information set. In grade 5, when students are presented with a descriptive expository text and asked to render its main meanings, they provide a mix of simple factual information and elaborated, conceptual information (for examples, see Appendix B of Guthrie et al., 2004). Although some students are limited to learning an extended set of facts, most are capable of comprehending conceptual knowledge that is elaborated in a reasonable structure. The highest level of complex patterning and conditional elaborations are rare at this age, however.

Searching for information from extended complex texts and organizing it into a coherent framework is difficult for most students. Given the task of reading multiple passages on related topics and answering a broad integrative question, typical students will show initial levels of proficiency. They will identify about half of the information that is potentially relevant to the question, and they will render that with moderate accuracy. A typical classroom contains a substantial range of proficiency, with a few students only identifying one to two relevant passages and representing them minimally. At the other end of the scale, a few students are able to identify nearly all of the appropriate sections of text in the extended passages and to write them in their own words in an organized, compelling form.

Motivation. Grade 5 self-efficacy is associated with students' oral reading fluency according to standardized tests. Students are inclined to believe that their reading level is best gauged by their ability to read aloud. For example, in an interview study when we asked students how they determined whether they were good readers, the typical reply was that "I can get the words right" (Wigfield & Guthrie, 1997). Self-efficacy also relates to students' general reading comprehension as shown on standardized tests. Both of these are moderate relations with correlations of about .5. In this grade, self-efficacy is not connected to specific cognitive processes such as inferencing or the level of knowledge gained from reading information texts.

At this grade, an interesting aspect of self-efficacy emerges. Students become quite sensitive to the challenges of difficult text, as shown in their aversion to attempting to read a long text or one that contains long sentences or many unfamiliar words. To capture this motivation, a measure of perceived difficulty of reading was constructed from questions such as "Are the books you read in class too difficult?" Perceived difficulty correlated highly with many measures of reading, including word recognition, oral reading fluency, inferencing, knowledge gained from text, and standardized reading comprehension. Across the full spectrum of achievement, students' cognitive proficiencies were more highly related to their experiences of failing in reading than succeeding in reading. In other words, students' achievement in specific cognitive reading processes was more closely related to their sense of failure than success (Guthrie et al., 2009).

Intrinsic motivation at grade 5 continues to be highly associated with reading fluency and reading comprehension, although the absolute level of intrinsic motivation may not change from grade 3. One aspect of intrinsic motivation, curiosity, is moderately placed at the neutral point on a scale, with most students being "somewhat" curious to read. Very few students are extremely low or extremely high in intrinsic motivation (Guthrie et al., 2012).

Intrinsic motivation predicts increases in reading comprehension over time. For example, in September of an academic year, students' intrinsic motivation predicts the amount of gain students will make in reading comprehension during that school year. In one study, students with low motivation in September did not show any gain in standardized comprehension from September to April. Many of them entered at a grade level of 4.5 and ended the year at about 4.5, whereas highly motivated students gained 2.5 grade levels of comprehension (from 5.0 to 7.5) in that same year (Guthrie et al., 2007).

By grade 5, the construct of reading engagement is related to the motivational network. Engagement entails cognitive, emotional, and behavioral components (Guthrie et al., 2012). For most authors, behavioral engagement is the act of reading frequently with effort, enthusiasm, persistence, and commitment. Although behavioral engagement or "grit" has been shown to be stronger than IQ in predicting grades among secondary students (Duckworth & Seligman, 2005), grit has not been examined among students as low as grade 3.

The reverse of behavioral engagement—avoidance of reading—correlated (negatively) with two standardized tests and one performance assessment for 5th- and 6th-graders (Baker & Wigfield, 1999). In that study, students who scored below the mean of 2.5 (on a 1–4 scale of engagement) were actively avoidant of reading, and were relatively low achievers. It is fruitful to observe whether students are reading avoidant in the classroom at this age.

A body of research documents that motivation exerts its effect on comprehension through reading engagement (Schaffner, Schiefele, & Ulferts, 2013). Being highly motivated to read does not benefit reading comprehension unless such motivation translates into engagement in the form of time and energy spent reading challenging text. Some researchers claim that the best measure of reading engagement is reading volume, which is actual time spent and frequency of reading activity (e.g., Schaffner et al., 2013); others claim that self-report of effort and conscientiousness is a better a measure (e.g., Guthrie et al., 2013). Regardless, the reading material does matter. Engagement does not consist of the light perusal of magazines on fashion or sports; it must consist of deep reading of books with serious content, such as history, civics, environmental science, economics, psychology, or botany. Interestingly, reading newspapers or comics has little benefit for comprehension (PISA, 2010).

Avoidance of reading is a strong negative motivator at grade 5. Although avoidance correlates negatively with reading comprehension in a range of studies, avoidance also correlates negatively with oral reading fluency, word recognition, and inferencing, as well as standardized reading comprehension measures (Guthrie et al., 2009). When students actively avoid text (by conspiring with peers and/or exerting minimal effort), they preclude themselves from gaining fundamental reading proficiencies. For instance, some students will suggest, "Let's skip our reading assignment tonight." Regrettably, such avoidance extended over time virtually guarantees that neither basic skills nor higher-order comprehension will be attained.

Cognition and Motivation, Grade 7

Cognition. Oral reading fluency of typical young adolescents in grade 7 is quite well developed. Students can orally read grade-level passages with 75–95% expressiveness, meaning that over three-quarters of the time, their oral reading sounds like talk. As students read aloud, they make meaning from the sentences and passages. Only the lowest 25% of achievers in typical classrooms will be frustrated by a lack of oral reading fluency, and they will benefit from fluency work for important texts (Ho & Guthrie, 2013).

Literal comprehension of information texts has been examined often for this grade level (Guthrie et al., 2013; Ho & Guthrie, 2013). For instance, descriptive passages from grades 4 to 8 were used with 14 items that measure understanding of words in context, short phrases, sentences, and acquisition of very limited conceptual knowledge. Average performance was 80% correct, showing a proficient grasp of these literal reading tasks. For young adolescents, models containing vocabulary, using strategies such as predicting or evaluating, background knowledge, and inferencing, predict the vast majority of variance in text comprehension (Cromley & Azevedo, 2007). Except for the lowest achievers, oral reading proficiency and literal comprehension do not predict text reading comprehension when the other variables are used as predictors.

Although inferencing is well developed, it is not as highly assimilated as literal comprehension for 7th-graders. Using informational texts, young adolescents can do reasonably well when asked to

- form referential connections (resolve anaphoric reference and connect different words that are used to identify persons or topics);
- identify causal antecedents (Tom did well on the test because he studies hard);

- locate causal consequences (if you study hard, you will do well); and
- perceive state inferences (Tom did well on the test because he is competent).

On a substantive measure of inferencing, 7th-grade students demonstrate a mean of 70% correct (Ho & Guthrie, 2013). There is a standard deviation of about 20% on such a measure, showing that the top fifth of the students will be 95–100% accurate, while the lowest fifth may be only 55% accurate. Although most students have learned to infer regularly and accurately during reading, the lower achievers will benefit from inferencing instruction with challenging texts.

Summarizing complex text, especially science text, is achieved only by the top fifth of a typical grade 7 class; not surprisingly, it is a major challenge for the bottom fifth. Using challenging texts (excerpted and adapted from *Scientific American* articles, ranging from grade 7–12 in conventional readability—Flesch-Kincaid), students were asked to respond to tasks that required them to

1. understand higher-order concepts and relations among concepts,
2. reason across the patterns of information, and
3. construct coherent summaries of both portions of a long text and the full-length text.

Typical students performed at about 50% on these challenging tasks and exhibited a huge standard deviation: Students in the top fifth were quite proficient, while those in the bottom fifth were about 30% correct—barely higher than chance. Replicated in two studies (Guthrie et al., 2013; Ho & Guthrie, 2013) and consistent with other research (Cromley & Azevedo, 2007), these findings show that deep comprehension of complex information text is well initiated in grade 7 but requires years of additional teaching focused on summarizing and integrating multiple texts in subject matters of history and science, and practice for the lowest achievers.

Motivation. In grade 7, students' motivations shift in several respects. One widely documented change is that internal reading motivations tend to decline. For example, self-efficacy, intrinsic motivation, and value for reading decline in grades 5–8, but students make a comeback in the later secondary grades, where more constant levels are evidenced (Gottfried et al., 2005). This has been attributed to the sudden barrage of more subject-matter-driven classes, less student-centered instruction, larger classes, stronger emphasis on grades and test scores, and loss of collaborative learning opportunities in reading and English (Guthrie & Davis, 2003).

Motivational patterns also begin to differ across literary reading and information text genres. Using interviews and questionnaires, Ho and Guthrie (2013) investigated literary reading in grade 7 reading/language arts class. We discovered that the various aspects/skills of reading were highly correlated, including reading fluency, inferencing, literal comprehension, summarizing information text, passage comprehension, and class grades. This cognitive cluster of performances was highly associated with a comparable compound of motivations consisting of high levels of intrinsic motivation, self-efficacy, and prosocial interactions linked to low levels of avoidance, perceived reading difficulty, and antisocial interactions. In other words, high intrinsic motivation and its accompanying motivations for literary reading were strongly correlated with high accomplishment in a range of literary reading proficiencies.

For informational text reading in science, history, math, foreign language, and other subject matters, different motivations appeared. A pattern of three clusters stood out. The first cluster contained a large cognitive composite including reading fluency, inferencing, literal comprehension, summarizing information text, passage comprehension, and class grades. This composite was associated positively with self-efficacy and negatively with perceived reading difficulty. In other words, students' self-efficacy was connected to reading achievement in many forms.

The second cluster was a specialized form of self-efficacy. A relatively high self-efficacy for information text comprehension was significantly related to relatively high summarizing and inferencing from information text. Because information text requires specialized knowledge of particular forms of text (for example, diagrams in science texts and timelines in history texts), new alliances are formed between self-efficacy and information text comprehension. Cluster three was a weaker connection between students valuing and their grades and simple comprehension processes for diverse forms of text.

In grade 7, the construct of engagement becomes bifurcated and prominent. In a structural equation model, two forms of behavioral engagement mediated the effects of motivations on reading achievement (Guthrie et al., 2013). Dedication—which merges effort, persistence, and responsibility in reading information text—positively predicted achievement. Meanwhile, avoidance, which consists of attempts to escape reading or minimize effort and time in reading, negatively predicted achievement. These forms of engagement are semi-independent because some individuals will be low on dedication (no high effort) and avoidance (no overt reading resistance).

In the model, dedication was positively linked to self-efficacy, reading value, and prosocial goals (I want to cooperate with the teacher and help others), whereas avoidance was positively linked to perceived difficulty, devaluing reading, and antisocial goals (I try to disrupt class and enjoy teasing other students). Because some of the strongest motivations also directly improved reading achievement, this pattern is termed *partial mediation*. This finding is consistent with current structural equation models that unpack the links among motivation, engagement, and cognitive proficiency (for a summary, see Guthrie & Klauda, in press).

PROGRESSION OF COGNITION AND MOTIVATION, GRADES 3–7

A major question for all educators revolves around the progression of these important reading and motivational skills and dispositions. In this section, I'll address what we know about that trajectory of development in this crucial age period (8–12 years of age).

Cognition

In grades 3–5, students increase in each of the fundamental cognitive processes of reading comprehension described in this chapter. In oral reading fluency, students improve from being able to reading about 25% of a grade-level passage fluently to reading 50% or more fluently. Typical students increase from reading frequently in two-word phrases to three- to four-word phrases and sentences at grade 5. Of course, there is wide variability within a school, but students typically progress from initial and halting oral reading to more comfortable and expressive oral reading. Such fluency may not appear for the most difficult words and the most convoluted syntax of grade-level texts. Needless to say, text complexity has increased from grade 3 to 5, but reading fluency advances slightly in front of the decoding challenges. During grades 5–7, substantial improvement is made in each of the identified cognitive processes. Oral reading fluency for grade-level text progresses from moderate to expressive and fully formed for typical grade 7 students.

In literal comprehension of text, students improve in quantity of processing. That is, when asked to read and recall a descriptive information text (science) passage, students in grade 5 will recall more facts or propositions (6 to 12) in a grade-level text than they did in grade 3 or 4 (2 to 3). In other words, literal comprehension increases from partial to well formed. Similarly for literal comprehension, typical grade 7 students are well equipped for literal comprehension of grade-level text, although the lowest achievers will benefit from continued instructional support.

Inferencing with grade-level text progresses markedly. At grade 3, inferencing is partial, with students showing a moderate capacity to link individual words and individual sentences in a passage. But by grade 5, students are not only able to infer at simple levels but are also capable of identifying relationships between key information at paragraph levels. They can generate concepts that link several sentences in a paragraph, showing the capacity to build structured conceptual knowledge. However, their inferencing typically does not extend to being able to abstract information from multiparagraph passages and integrate text from diverse information sources (such as text and diagrams) in extended passages. By grade 7, students are able to infer at sentence and passage levels, with some adeptness at drawing inferences from multiparagraph passages.

Summarizing grade-level text increases substantially from grade 3 to 5. With a descriptive text, grade 3 students will rarely be able to discern the most important conceptual information. They will rarely be able to link subordinate information to form a coherent summary. However, grade 5 students are likely to identify central concepts in a descriptive text of one to four paragraphs. They are likely to relate one to three concepts to one another and connect supporting details to them adequately. However, only a few grade 5 students will identify all of the complex patterns with hierarchical and/or causal connections in a descriptive text. At grade 7, typical students can summarize paragraphs and short passages in grade-level text, and are able to distinguish higher-order, abstract concepts from simpler factual information and then relate them appropriately to one another.

For both inferencing and summarizing, grade 7 students show wide variance, with the top fifth of a typical school population being proficient in elaborate processing with complex texts at the level of *Scientific American* articles. Regrettably, the lowest-achieving fifth is not able to draw inferences beyond word and sentence levels of on- or below-grade text, and will not be able to summarize more than a paragraph of grade-level texts.

Searching for information to answer a complex question with an extended text requires categorical and hierarchical knowledge. Students advance in this process from grades 3 to 5. Searching for text information is rudimentary at grade 3. Typical students can identify one to two key portions of relevant text and one to two essential points in those texts. At grade 5, typical students are able to identify about half of the texts or portions of text that are relevant to a complex question on a complex text. In addition, they can extract a substantial amount (though not all) of the central information from those texts and write it with reasonable coherence. Capability for searching increases from quite primitive to moderately formed from grades 3 to 5. In grade 7, typical students are able to set learning goals, locate relevant text, comprehend text segments, and integrate segments to build complex knowledge structures. These processes grow throughout secondary school and become increasingly connected to motivations (Azevedo, 2005).

The most complex forms of processing, such as self-explanation, are beginning to form in grade 7 but require focused instructional support from grades 7 to 9. Both teacher interventions and computer systems can improve this and other forms of self-regulated reading that increase reading comprehension in the secondary grades. For both computers and teachers, vitally important instruction entails matching text difficulty to student competence, asking key questions frequently, encouraging self-explanations, and providing continual feedback on performance (McNamara et al., 2007).

Motivational Progressions in Grades 3–7

Self-efficacy and achievement in grades 3 to 5 is relatively highly correlated at about .5–.6 for these grade levels. According to interview studies at both grades, students believe that reading words is the main indicator of their reading competency. As a result, self-efficacy relates to oral reading fluency and general comprehension at both grades. However, at grade 5, self-efficacy is not related to basic cognitive processes such as inferencing or knowledge gained from text, though this has not been studied at grade 3.

Self-efficacy may be represented by its inverse, which consists of students' perception that reading is too difficult. Termed *perceived difficulty*, this side of self-efficacy is highly related to all cognitive aspects of reading at grade 5, including word recognition, oral reading fluency, inferencing, knowledge gained from text, and standardized reading comprehension (Guthrie et al., 2009). Also detrimental in the primary grades (Coddington & Guthrie, 2009), perceived difficulty is sufficiently powerful that it should be addressed in models of reading progression and instruction related to these advances.

At grade 7, perceived difficulty of reading information text is a prominent predictor of comprehension. When students think they cannot read successfully, they will avoid reading immediately and persistently. Clearly, perceived difficulty of reading at the outset of the school year precludes the learning of reading skills and severely limits the learning of subject-matter content contained in those texts. In a canonical correlation of grade 7 reading, perceived difficulty was the strongest single motivation related to a composite of reading proficiencies that included all the processes described in this chapter (Ho & Guthrie, 2013). Thus, although self-efficacy is a notable predictor of achievement in the elementary grades, perceived difficulty complements self-efficacy in the secondary grades. Because self-efficacy generates dedication and perceived difficulty fuels avoidance, it is beneficial to embrace both of these motivational attributes in painting the portrait of the motivated adolescent reader (Guthrie, Klauda, & Ho, 2013).

Intrinsic motivation continues to be a motivational force in grades 3 to 5. At both levels, it correlates with reading comprehension at substantial levels of .6–.7. Moreover, intrinsic motivation spurs the growth of reading comprehension. Students' enjoyment of reading at the start of the academic year—not their level of achievement—forecasts their level of reading achievement at the end of the academic year. Motivation spurs reading comprehension improvement for both grade levels. Thus, the contributions of intrinsic motivation are sustained from grades 3 to 5.

In grade 7, intrinsic motivation partitions into motivation for literary text versus motivation for information text. Consistent with prior grades, motivation for literary text is positively correlated with comprehension of literature and grades in reading/language arts (Ho & Guthrie, 2013). However, in an apparent anomaly, intrinsic motivation for information text correlates negatively with reading achievement on standardized tests or information text measures. Our reasoning is that the vast majority of children learn reading through fiction. The highest achievers adore the genre of fiction to the point that they become averse to nonfiction. Simultaneously, the lowest achievers may find nonfiction intrinsically motivating partly because one can learn interesting facts by reading relatively little text (Ho & Guthrie, 2013).

From grades 5 to 7, new motivations play important roles. Most prominently, valuing reading becomes a stronger predictor of achievement than it was in the elementary grades. Referring to the belief that reading is important, valuing enters as a strong correlate of dedication, which is extended, positive engagement in reading. The inverse of valuing is devaluing, which refers to the belief that reading is not beneficial. These are not simply mirror opposites because students may value reading fiction while they devalue reading information text. It appears that while intrinsic motivation prevails as a predictor of achievement in elementary school, valuing prevails in middle school. With the profusion of subject disciplines and text types in grade 7, it is not academically realistic for students to limit their reading to topics in which they are interested. On the contrary, believing that unfamiliar topics and accompanying texts are important fuels their achievement.

Referring to persistence, effort, and devotion (beyond mere time), engagement in reading correlates with achievement at grade 5 and beyond, though engagement has rarely been studied in the primary grades. Indicators of engagement have consisted of self-reported amounts of reading (Guthrie, Wigfield, Metsala, & Cox, 1999), self-reported effort and conscientiousness (Duckworth & Seligman, 2005), measures of print exposure in the form of author or title recognition (Mol & Bus, 2011), or teacher ratings of students' effort and persistence (Becker, McElvany, & Kortenbruck, 2010; Wigfield et al., 2008). All of these indicators predict not only achievement but also the growth of achievement over time.

The full set of reading motivation–engagement constructs described in this chapter, including self-efficacy, intrinsic motivation, valuing, social constructs, perceived difficulty, and devaluing, most likely exert their influence on reading achievement through engagement. Research has shown that the effects of value, intrinsic motivation, and self-efficacy on achievement are mediated by the process of literacy engagement (Guthrie et al., 2013). In other words, engagement is the bridge that links motivations to cognitive proficiency in reading.

The inverse of engagement is avoidance, which is particularly pernicious. At grade 5, students are quite capable of conspiring with friends to evade reading (e.g., not doing their reading homework). Not trying and putting forth little effort are frequent examples of avoidance. More common in grade 5 than grade 3, these behaviors are newly appearing barriers to reading improvement. This type of deliberate avoidance represents a regression rather than a progression in reading. This is a useful distinction because while valuing predicts reading dedication, devaluing predicts reading avoidance. Although dedication and avoidance predict reading achievement, avoidance is twice as strong. One explanation is that avoiding text immediately prevents any growth in reading skills. In contrast, dedication may or may not spur cognitive growth depending on students' access to texts, teacher feedback, and peer relationships.

Closely related to engagement is volume or amount of reading. Volume and engagement in reading are strongly identified with reading achievement in grade 5, though they are not visible forces in grade 3. Volume may be gauged by time spent in book reading, frequency of book reading, number of pages read per week, or number of books read per month. All of these indicators correlate with reading comprehension according to multiple studies (Schaffner et al., 2013). Further, reading volume is a link between motivations such as self-efficacy and reading achievement. Motivation raises students' depth and breadth of reading, which in turn elevates their comprehension. At grade 5 and beyond, reading volume is under the control of typical students. They can find and carry books around. They can read them at opportune moments, either for pleasure or for school. Grade 3 students are less likely to be self-initiating in this way. (See also Allington, Billen, & McCuiston, Chapter 10, this volume.)

IMPLICATIONS

This chapter charts the advances in both cognition and motivational factors across the span of grades 3–7. This analysis includes five cognitive processes that are essential to reading comprehension (oral reading fluency, literal comprehension, inferencing, summarizing, and searching/organizing). In parallel, motivation-engagement qualities of self-efficacy, intrinsic motivation, valuing, perceived difficulty, devaluing, avoidance, and dedication are charted across the same age span. And these parallel tracks interact! What I mean is that literacy growth takes the form of increasing linkage of motivational factors to reading comprehension and its underlying cognitive systems. Motivation and cognition succeed or fail together.

Imagine a 3rd-grade girl who believes she can read a three-sentence story well (self-efficacy). Then suppose that this girl advances to 7th grade without changing that self-efficacy. She would still believe she could read a three-sentence story well. Limited to this self-perception, she would not be able to tackle the reading load for any of her classes. Her 3rd-grade self-efficacy will not help her in grade 7 and may, in fact, harm her growth because she will give up when she is confronted with the challenge of middle school informational texts. Without trying, she cannot learn. In 3rd grade, the girl's self-efficacy is linked to the types of books, situations, tasks, challenges, and people she encounters in 3rd grade. Those links must shift if she is to grow her motivation.

Now imagine a 3rd-grade boy who has typical intrinsic motivation and enjoys illustrated adventure stories of three to five pages in length. Then suppose this boy advances to 7th grade with the same intrinsic motivation. He is limited to reading short illustrated stories meant for 8-year-olds. He does not enjoy age-appropriate reading in school or out, and he has not experienced the long-lived, intense involvement in a novel that deep literary comprehension depends on. With 3rd-grade intrinsic motivation, he will quickly come to dislike reading. He will decide it is not important. He will not try, will not read, and will not learn. He is headed for failure in school and perhaps beyond.

Through school, some students pick up a desire to read and to read well, but too often, they do not. Although some teachers may foster reading motivations, rarely is it systematic, as shown in research documenting that teachers' motivation support is intermittent and ineffectual unless professional development and explicit guidance is provided (Guthrie & Klauda, 2014). Fortunately, there are five teaching practices that improve reading motivation:

1. Assuring success
2. Affording choices
3. Arranging collaboration
4. Emphasizing importance
5. Empowering a high reading volume

Based on experiments, observational studies, and structural models explaining natural variation within and between classrooms, my colleagues and I have shown that each practice increases motivation (Guthrie & Klauda, 2014). Assuring success increases students' self-efficacy, affording choices fosters intrinsic motivation, arranging collaboration enhances social motivations, emphasizing importance develops value for reading, and empowering a high reading volume increases positive engagement (see Guthrie, in press, 2008, for practical examples).

Despite this compelling body of evidence, motivation is rarely taught. Few administrators ask teachers how motivated their students are, as evidenced by the lack of motivation in state-sponsored teacher evaluation rubrics. Few school personnel gauge students' literacy engagement explicitly and record the levels for decisionmaking as shown in teacher evaluation reports. There is no national committee to set standards for motivation or engagement. The nation's political and educational leaders do not see, let alone understand, the motivation side of reading.

Too many think of education through a business lens, with children as inputs and reading scores as outputs. Too often, administrators seek quality control with a test of low-level foundational skills (see Hoffman & Pearson, Chapter 14, this volume). But measuring reading quality with a low-level skill test is like gauging shirt quality with a test of the thickness of the cloth (where stitching and trim don't count). It doesn't work. Simplified cognitive measures don't work for reading because motivation and thinking count.

To measure and understand reading development, teachers must look under the hood to see what makes the engine run. In trying to promote reading education, people are not looking under the hood. In fact, it's the only hope for understanding students. Because society does not honor the inside (motivation) of reading, many students will not grow on the outside (achievement). When reading desire is missing, reading failure is everywhere. Kids can't be expected to motivate themselves; they need help.

Policy leaders too often assume that motivation will appear automatically, in response to high standards that demand achievement. By raising standards, they hope that teachers and students will try harder, and, in the process, will develop positive motivations. It hasn't happened yet. Without expanded policy for reading engagement, progress in reading achievement may never occur. Without a sea change in schools, reading as required in the CCSS won't happen. When will the nation see the inside (will) as well as the outside (skill) of reading? Probably never—unless people look under the hood.

REFERENCES

Azevedo, R. (2005). Computer environments as metacognitive tools for enhancing learning. *Educational Psychologist, 40*, 193–197.

Baker, L., & Wigfield, A. (1999). Dimensions of children's motivation for reading and their relations to reading activity and reading achievement. *Reading Research Quarterly, 34*, 452–477.

Becker, M., McElvany, N., & Kortenbruck, M. (2010). Intrinsic and extrinsic reading motivation as predictors of reading literacy: A longitudinal study. *Journal of Educational Psychology, 102*, 773–786.

Christensen, S., Reschly, A., & Wylie, C., (Eds.). (2012). *Handbook of research on student engagement.* New York, NY: Springer Science.

Coddington, C. S., & Guthrie, J. T. (2009). Teacher and student perceptions of boys' and girls' reading motivation. *Reading Psychology, 30*, 225–249.

Cromley, J., & Azevedo, R. (2007). Testing and refining the direct and inferential mediation model of reading comprehension. *Journal of Educational Psychology, 99*, 311–325.

Duckworth, A. L., & Seligman, M.E.P. (2005). Self-discipline outdoes IQ in predicting academic performance of adolescents. *Psychological Science, 16*, 939–944.

Gottfried, A. E., Fleming, J. S., & Gottfried, A. W. (2001). Continuity of academic intrinsic motivation from childhood through late adolescence: A longitudinal study. *Journal of Educational Psychology, 93*, 3–13.

Guthrie, J. T. (2008). *Engaging adolescents in reading.* Thousand Oaks, CA: Corwin Press.

Guthrie, J. T. (2015). Best practices in motivating students to read. In L. Morrow & L. Gambrell (Eds.), *Best practices in literacy instruction* (pp. 61–85). New York, NY: Guilford Press.

Guthrie, J. T., Anderson, E., Alao, S., & Rinehart, J. (1999). Influences of concept-oriented reading instruction on strategy use and conceptual learning from text. *Elementary School Journal, 99*(4), 343–366.

Guthrie, J. T., & Davis, M. H. (2003). Motivating struggling readers in middle school through an engagement model of classroom practice. *Reading & Writing Quarterly, 19*, 59–85.

Guthrie, J. T., Hoa, A.L.W., Wigfield, A., Tonks, S. M., Humenick, N. M., & Littles, E. (2007). Reading motivation and reading comprehension growth in the later elementary years. *Contemporary Educational Psychology, 32*, 282–313.

Guthrie, J. T., & Klauda, S. L. (2014). Effects of classroom practices on reading comprehension, engagement, and motivations for adolescents. *Reading Research Quarterly, 49*, 387–416.

Guthrie, J. T. & Klauda, S. (in press). Engagement and motivational processes in reading. In P. Afflerbach (Ed.), *Handbook of individual differences in reading.* New York, NY: Routledge.

Guthrie, J. T., Klauda, S. L., & Ho, A. (2013). Modeling the relationships among reading instruction, motivation, engagement, and achievement for adolescents. *Reading Research Quarterly, 48*, 9–26.

Guthrie, J. T., McRae, A., Coddington, C. S., Klauda, S. L., Wigfield, A., & Barbosa, P. (2009). Impacts of comprehensive reading instruction on diverse outcomes of low-achieving and high-achieving readers. *Journal of Learning Disabilities, 42*, 195–214.

Guthrie, J. T., Wigfield, A., Barbosa, P., Perencevich, K. T., Taboada, A., Davis, M. H., Scafiddi, N. T., & Tonks, S. (2004). Increasing reading comprehension and engagement through concept-oriented reading instruction. *Journal of Educational Psychology, 96*, 403–423.

Guthrie, J. T., Wigfield, A., & You, W. (2012). Instructional contexts for engagement and achievement in reading. In S. Christensen, A. Reschly, & C. Wylie (Eds.), *Handbook of research on student engagement* (pp. 601–634). New York, NY: Springer.

Ho, A. N., & Guthrie, J. T. (2013). Patterns of association among multiple motivations and aspects of achievement in reading. *Reading Psychology, 34*, 101–147.

Klauda, S., & Guthrie, J. T. (2008). Relationships of three components of reading fluency to reading comprehension. *Journal of Educational Psychology, 100*, 310–321.

McNamara D., Ozure, Y., Best, R. & O'Reilly, T. (2007). The 4-pronged comprehension strategy framework. In D. McNamara (Ed.), *Reading comprehension strategies,* (pp. 465–497). New York, NY: Erlbaum.

Mol, S., & Bus, A. (2011). To read or not to read: A meta-analysis of print exposure from infancy to early adulthood. *Psychological Bulletin, 137*, 267–296.

Morgan, P. L., & Fuchs, D. (2007). Is there a bidirectional relationship between children's reading skills and reading motivation? *Exceptional Children, 73*, 165–183.

PISA. (2010). Available at www.oecd.org/pisa/pisaproducts/pisa2009keyfindings.htm

Schaffner, E., Schiefele, U., & Ulferts, H. (2013). Reading amount as a mediator of the effects of intrinsic and extrinsic motivation on reading comprehension. *Reading Research Quarterly, 48*, 369–385.

van den Broek, P., Rapp, D. N., & Kendeou, P. (2005). Integrating memory-based and constructionist processes in accounts of reading comprehension. *Discourse Processes, 39*, 299–316.

Walczyk, J. J., Wei, M., Grifith-Ross, D. A., Cooper, A. L., Zha, P., & Goubert, S. E. (2007). Development of the interplay between automatic processes and cognitive resources in reading. *Journal of Educational Psychology, 99*, 867–887.

Wigfield, A., & Guthrie, J. T. (1997). Relations of children's motivation for reading to the amount and breadth of their reading. *Journal of Educational Psychology, 89*, 420–432.

Wigfield, A., Guthrie, J. T., Perencevich, K. C., Taboada, A., Klauda, S. L., McRae, A., & Barbosa, P. (2008). The role of reading engagement in mediating effects of reading comprehension instruction on reading outcomes. *Psychology in the Schools, 45*, 432–445.

CHAPTER 8

Building a Vocabulary Program That Really Could Make a Significant Contribution to Students Becoming College and Career Ready

Michael F. Graves

In 1967, 2 years after Jay Samuels began his career at the University of Minnesota, Petty, Herold, and Stoll published a book-length review of research on vocabulary in which they reluctantly concluded that "the teaching profession seems to know little of substance about the teaching of vocabulary" (p. 84). As I write this chapter, some 50 years after the publication of that review, I can say with confidence that the profession now knows a great deal about teaching vocabulary. Thus, we certainly have some information with which to address the questions that Samuels posed to frame the present volume and provide guidance for achieving the goals of the Common Core State Standards (CCSS): What has been learned about vocabulary instruction in the past 50 years? To what extent do current practices reflect that knowledge? And how could current practices better build on the evidence?

In this chapter, I will respond to each of these questions and discuss several additional topics. I begin with a review of what has been learned about the vocabulary instruction that takes place in schools. Next, I briefly describe a four-part framework for a comprehensive program of vocabulary instruction. Then, I review the existing research in nine specific areas and discuss the research that I believe is still needed in each of these areas. After that, I summarize my review of the existing research and give my recommendations for additional needed research. I conclude with my recommendations for a comprehensive vocabulary program based on current knowledge.

As will become clear as the chapter progresses, although the profession has learned a great deal about vocabulary instruction in the past 50 years, it is my judgment that building a research-based vocabulary program that can contribute significantly to students' meeting the oft-stated goal of the CCSS—becoming "college and career ready"—will require research and development efforts considerably more ambitious than educators have undertaken thus far.

WHAT HAS BEEN LEARNED ABOUT VOCABULARY INSTRUCTION IN SCHOOLS?

Content analyses of basal reading programs and classroom observation studies conducted over the past 50 years provide an all-too-consistent portrait of the vocabulary instruction that typically takes place in classrooms: In their review, Petty et al. (1967) found that classroom teachers, "if they teach vocabulary at all" (p. 19), used traditional methods such as assigning lists of words to be learned and showed little attention to research. Based on their in-depth analysis of basal reading programs, Beck, McKeown, McCaslin, and Burkes (1979) concluded that, at best, students saw a word in a meaning-revealing sentence, came across it when they read the selection, and met it again in an independent postreading activity. At worst, students simply encountered a new word in a selection. Durkin both observed classrooms (1978–1979) and conducted an analysis of basal readers (1981) and concluded that limited attention was given to new vocabulary, with typical instruction consisting of identifying a word and mentioning its meaning. Jenkins and Dixon (1983) examined basal readers and found that, at best, the basals identified words for a unit, and students were pre- and posttested on some of these words, were given definitions of the words, and perhaps completed a worksheet; at worst, students received no vocabulary instruction at all. In an analysis of two basal programs, Ryder and Graves (1994) found that vocabulary instruction varied markedly in the two, but that, in general, the instruction often was not sufficiently robust to improve comprehension.

In an observational study of 5th- and 6th-grade classrooms, Watts (1995) found that teachers usually used more than one approach to teaching words, with definitional and contextual approaches being the most frequent. Qualities associated with effective instruction in the research literature were seen rarely. In their observational study of 5th- to 7th-grade classrooms, Scott, Jamieson-Noel, and Asselin (2003) found that although more attention was devoted to networks of word meanings than had been found in past studies, "most instruction still involved mentioning and assigning rather than teaching" (p. 269). In an observational study of 3rd-grade classrooms, Carlisle, Kelcey, and Berebitsky (2013) found that "teachers rarely engaged students in cognitively challenging work on word meanings" (p. 1360). Finally, in a study of oral vocabulary instruction in kindergarten core reading programs, Wright and Neuman (2013) found large differences across the programs, that many of the words taught were too easy, and that these programs did "not reflect the current research base for vocabulary development and may not be systematic enough to influence children's vocabulary learning trajectories" (p. 386).

To summarize, research on vocabulary instruction indicates that not a lot of vocabulary instruction is taking place in our classrooms, that the instruction that does occur tends to be thin, that it does not reflect the research literature, and that it has not changed much over a 50-year period.

A FOUR-PART FRAMEWORK TO GUIDE INSTRUCTION

Over about half of this 50-year period, I have worked to develop a framework for vocabulary instruction that is quite different from the instruction depicted in these studies; moreover, it goes well beyond the curriculum suggested in the CCSS. The framework is consistent with what teachers and researchers know about vocabulary learning and instruction, although as I will note later in the chapter, there is a lot that is still not known. The framework, which is described in greater detail in Graves (2006) and Graves, August, and Mancilla-Martinez (2012), consists of four parts:

1. *Providing Rich and Varied Language Experiences* in which students are immersed in listening, discussion, reading, and writing in a positive and supportive environment
2. *Teaching Individual Words* through rich instruction, introductory instruction, and frequent reviews
3. *Teaching Word-Learning Strategies*, including the use of word parts, context clues, and the dictionary for all students; dealing with cognates for Spanish-speaking students; and dealing with idioms for all English language learners (ELLs)
4. *Fostering Word Consciousness*, students' awareness of words, their positive dispositions toward words, and their interest in learning words and learning about words

I will employ this framework in reviewing the research on vocabulary instruction just below and in making recommendations for a comprehensive vocabulary program based on our current knowledge.

STUDIES WITH DIRECT IMPLICATIONS FOR A COMPREHENSIVE PROGRAM OF INSTRUCTION

In this section, I describe the research that is presently available and the research I believe is needed on nine topics key to the development of comprehensive programs of vocabulary instruction. These are (1) the number of words students encounter in printed school English, (2) the number of words students learn, (3) variations in vocabulary size across socioeconomic and linguistic groups, (4) selecting words to teach directly, (5–8) the four parts of the framework I sketched above, and (9) multifaceted and relatively long-term vocabulary interventions.

Before continuing, however, I wish to make two apologies. First, my recommendations for future research are extremely ambitious, probably audacious, and will require commitments from funding agencies, researchers, schools, and publishers far beyond those presently available. Second, space limitations prevent me from giving adequate attention to instruction for English language learners and from giving any attention to shared book reading as an approach to building oral vocabulary and to the use of technology in vocabulary instruction.

How Many Words Are There in Printed School English?

In what I believe is the strongest attempt to get a reliable estimate of the size of printed school English, Nagy and Anderson (1984) conducted a number of calculations and arrived at the figure of 88,000 word families. In a subsequent study, Anderson and Nagy (1992) concluded that if proper words, multiple meanings of words, and idioms were included, their original figure would increase to 180,000 word families. A word family is generally defined as a root word (e.g., *laugh*), plus its common inflected (e.g., *laughed*) and derived forms (e.g., *laughable*). Other authors have suggested, however, that the number of English words is much smaller. D'Anna, Zechmeister, and Hall (1991), for example, place the figure at approximately 27,000 word families.

What is needed in order to forge a consensus on vocabulary size is a very carefully constructed word-frequency count based on a very large corpus that is clearly representative of the reading materials currently used by U.S. students. Such a count should provide the frequency of different word meanings, not just the frequency of graphic forms. It should also provide frequencies for individual forms and families of various sizes, ranging from those that include only inflected forms of words to those that include a variety of derived forms. It should provide counts with and without proper words and with and without idioms and other multiword units. And it should provide counts of prefixes, suffixes, and roots.

How Many Words Do Students Learn?

In my judgment, the most unbiased estimate of the size of students' reading vocabularies comes from work done by Nagy and Herman (1987) and reaffirmed and further explained by Stahl and Nagy (2006). Using data gathered from the Nagy and Anderson (1984) study of printed school English, Nagy and Herman (1987) recalibrated earlier estimates and concluded that 3rd-graders' reading vocabularies average about 10,000 words and that 12th-graders' reading vocabularies average about 40,000 words. Students, therefore, learn about 3,000 words each year. These figures refer to word families rather than individual graphic forms, but they do not include idioms, other multiword units, multiple meanings, or proper words, which would raise the figure considerably. As is the case with estimates of the total number of words, estimates of vocabulary size vary markedly. Snow and Kim (2007), for example, estimate that high school students have vocabularies of 75,000 words, while Goulden, Nation, and Reed (1990) have calculated that college students have vocabularies of about 17,000 words, and Dupuy (1974) has proposed that 12th-graders have vocabularies of about 8,000 words.

Although I believe that Nagy and Herman's (1987) estimate is the best one currently available, it is based on a number of older studies of varying quality, involves recalibration, and is itself nearly 30 years old. Once a comprehensive, meaning-based, up-to-date, and valid frequency count such as that described in the previous section is completed, it will be possible to move beyond recalibrations of earlier work and create tests that will provide reasonably accurate tallies of the size of students' overall vocabularies.

Variability of Vocabulary Size Across Socioeconomic and Linguistic Groups

Although a good deal of disagreement exists as to the total number of words in English and the number of words typical students learn, there is wide agreement that the size of the vocabularies of students in different socioeconomic and linguistic groups varies markedly. In one of the earlier assessments of this situation, Becker (1977) argued that the failure of the Follow Through Program to improve the reading proficiency of disadvantaged groups was largely the result of its failure to improve students' vocabularies.

Studies by Graves, Brunetti, and Slater (1982); Chall, Jacobs, and Baldwin (1990); White, Graves, and Slater (1990); Hart and Risley (1995); and Biemiller and Slonim (2001) all found that children from less advantaged socioeconomic backgrounds had substantially smaller vocabularies than did children from more advantaged backgrounds. And a recent study by Fernald, Marchman, and Weisleder (2013) found that SES differences in vocabulary size are already evident by 18 months of age. We also know that the vocabularies of ELL students are typically considerably smaller than those of students who are native English speakers (August, Carlo, Dressler, & Snow, 2005). Indeed, a recent study indicates that ELL students are 2 to 3 years behind native-English-speaking students in vocabulary knowledge, and that a large vocabulary gap remains as these students progress through school (Mancilla-Martinez & Lesaux, 2011).

What researchers know very little about is the extent of knowledge of groups of words that students from various socioeconomic and linguistic backgrounds possess. Consider for example students' knowledge of the vocabulary of 1st-grade core reading programs. It may be the case that linguistically advantaged students come to school knowing virtually all of the words that are likely to appear in their core reading programs, while linguistically less advantaged native English speakers know only about half of them, and ELLs typically know only one-fourth of them. Or it may be the case that all three of these groups know most of the words they will meet in their core readers. Or it might be that all three groups know only a small portion of the words. We simply do not know. Until we know which words appear in the materials students will be reading and what knowledge students have or lack regarding these words, it is impossible to specify what sort of vocabulary support and how much vocabulary support children of varying socioeconomic and linguist backgrounds are likely to need as they begin school. The same claim could be made for students at any grade level and with reference to any curriculum area. Not knowing what kids know or what they need to know makes designing truly research-based instruction impossible.

Selecting Words to Teach Directly

As I will discuss in the upcoming section on Teaching Individual Words, there is a good deal of information on *how* to teach words; however, much less is known about *which* words should be taught. As I noted earlier, the materials students read contain tens of thousands of words. Only a small percentage of these can be taught directly. Which ones should teachers focus on? The most widely disseminated response to this question comes from the work of Beck, McKeown, and Kucan (2002, 2013), who recommend focusing on what they call Tier 2 words, which they note are "high utility for mature language users and are found across a variety of domains" (Beck et al., 2013, p. 9). Taking a different tack, Graves, Baumann, et al. (2014) have suggested an approach they term *Selecting Words for Instruction from Texts*, which outlines procedures for selecting words to teach from the texts students are reading. Seeking a more general solution to the problem, Nagy and Hiebert (2011) have sketched a path to a theory of word selection, a theory that could provide a "principled basis for identifying the words that should be targeted for vocabulary instruction" (p. 388). More concretely, Hiebert and Cervetti (2012) have noted that the vocabulary in narrative and informational texts differs in important ways and that learning words from informational texts requires "extensive discussions, demonstrations, and experiments" (p. 341), whereas dealing with words from narratives "requires that students understand the ways in which authors vary their language to ensure that readers grasp the critical features of the story" (p. 341).

All in all, though research does provide some information about which words to teach, a lot more research is needed. In addition to a theory of word selection such as Nagy and Hiebert (2011) suggested and procedures such as Graves, Baumann, et al. (2014) suggested, educators need lists of the words that appear in various corpora. Such lists should include, for example, the vocabulary of core reading programs such as that currently being constructed by Graves, Elmore, et al. (2014); general academic word lists such as those developed by Coxhead (2000) and Gardner and Davies (2014) but based on a materials used by K–12 students in the United States; and content-specific academic word lists such as those created by Marzano (2004) from various standards' documents but based on the material in current textbooks. Following the creation of such lists, tests are needed to assess students' knowledge of these specific bodies of words, tests such as those that Pearson, Hiebert, and Kamil (2007) have called for.

Providing Rich and Varied Language Experiences

I know of no studies that have directly investigated the effects on vocabulary development of classrooms that provide students with rich and varied language experiences in a supportive and nurturing environment. However, studies of literacy development (Dickinson & Tabors, 2001), motivation (Pressley et al., 2003), reading to children (van Kleeck, Stahl, & Bauer, 2003), and the sorts of home experiences that do and do not promote word learning (Hart & Risley, 1995; Weisleder & Fernald, 2013) certainly suggest the kind of language experiences that teachers should be providing in classrooms.

Classroom studies to examine the effects of providing such experiences are sorely needed. Such studies would, I believe, prepare teachers to accomplish two complementary but quite different purposes. They would give teachers the knowledge and the skills they need to provide rich and varied experiences in listening, discussion, reading, and writing. And they would prepare teachers to create the sort of engaging and nourishing classrooms that lead students to engage eagerly in learning words, in reading and writing, and in school generally. Because such interventions are broad and have a number of outcomes, it will be challenging to decide just what to test and to isolate the effect of a particular intervention. However, by creating sufficiently robust interventions, using a variety of qualitative and quantitative measures, and extending the interventions over significant time periods, measurable results should be achievable.

Teaching Individual Words

Unlike the case for providing rich and varied language experiences, a large, robust, easily interpretable, and very consistent body of research, as well as research summaries and meta-analyses, related to teaching individual words is available. These include reviews by Petty et al. (1967), Mezynski (1983), Graves (1986), Stahl and Fairbanks (1986), Beck and McKeown (1991), Blachowicz and Fisher (2000), the National Reading Panel (NICHD, 2000), Baumann, Kame'enui, and Ash (2003), and Graves and Silverman (2010). Consideration of these reviews leads to several generalizations. To organize these, I proceed from considering effects that can be achieved by brief and relatively shallow instruction to effects that can only be achieved from more lengthy and more robust instruction.

- *Some vocabulary instruction is better than no instruction* (Petty et al., 1967). Although this is a commonsense finding, it is not a trivial one. It means that vocabulary instruction typically works. However, thin instruction—for example, giving students a set of words and asking them to look up the words in the dictionary, or giving them a set of words and their definitions—only serves to teach the basic meanings of the words and may not lead to long-term vocabulary knowledge.

- *Instruction that incorporates both a definition and the use of the word in context is likely to be more effective than instruction incorporating only one of these elements* (Mezynski, 1983; Stahl & Fairbanks, 1986). Although simply having students work with definitions of words can improve their word knowledge somewhat, giving them both a definition and the word in context has repeatedly proven to be a considerably stronger approach to promoting vocabulary growth.

- *Instruction that involves activating prior knowledge and comparing and contrasting word meanings is likely to be more powerful than simply providing a definition and the word in context* (Baumann, Kame'enui, & Ash, 2003; Beck & McKeown, 1991). Such instruction has sometimes been shown to improve comprehension of selections containing the words taught.

- *More lengthy and robust instruction that involves explicit teaching and that includes providing a definition and the word in context, multiple exposures to the word in varied contexts, and experiences that promote deep processing of the word's meaning is likely to be more powerful than less time-consuming and less robust instruction* (Beck & McKeown, 2007; Beck, Perfetti, & McKeown, 1982; McKeown, Beck, Omanson, & Perfetti, 1983; McKeown, Beck, Omanson, & Pople, 1984).

Although there is clearly a lot of information on ways to effectively teach individual words, most recent studies on vocabulary instruction employ highly effective but also very time-consuming techniques. Little information is available about the effects of less robust and therefore less time-consuming instruction, particularly the long-term effects of such instruction. Given the number of words that students need to learn, teachers simply cannot devote extensive instructional time to all of them. Thus, research is needed on the short- and long-term effects of what might be called "introductory instruction," instruction that prevents students from stumbling over words as they read and starts them on the long road to acquiring rich and full word meanings. Teachers also need information on what kinds of instruction are appropriate for what sorts of words. At the present time, most instructional programs and many research programs provide the same kinds of instruction for all the words they teach. And, as I have noted, information is needed on which words appear in the material students read, which words students with various backgrounds do and do not know, and based on these two factors, which words need to be taught to which students.

Teaching Word-Learning Strategies

The three word-learning strategies I consider here are the use of word parts, context, and the dictionary.

Use of word parts. Research findings related to teaching students to use word parts to unlock the meanings of unknown words are quite consistent and quite positive. In one study, Graves and Hammond (1980) taught a group of 7th-graders the meanings of nine common prefixes and a strategy for using the prefixes to unlock the meanings of unknown words that contained them. Results on immediate and delayed tests on a set of transfer words that contained the taught prefixes indicated that the group outperformed both a group of students who were simply taught whole words that contained the prefixes and an uninstructed control group.

In a study that involved teaching both prefixes and suffixes, White, Sowell, and Yanagihara (1989) taught nine prefixes and a procedure for suffix removal. The instruction involved teacher-led active teaching with significant amounts of practice and feedback. Results indicated that instructed students outperformed uninstructed control students on a test identifying English base words by removing a suffix, a test identifying the meaning of the prefixed word when given the base word, and a test on the meanings of the prefixes.

The most ambitious attempts to teach word parts are two studies by Baumann and his associates (Baumann et al., 2002; Baumann, Edwards, et al., 2003) that combined instruction in word parts with instruction in context clues. In the 2002 study, one group was taught 20 prefixes. Another group was taught 20 prefixes together with the use of context clues. A third group received no special vocabulary instruction. Results indicated that students in the prefix-only group and those in the prefix-context group were more skillful in deriving the meaning of transfer words that contained the prefixes taught than were students in the control group. In the 2003 study, which taught word-learning strategies in social studies classes, students in treatment classes were taught 20 prefixes and suffixes and the use of context clues, and students in control classes were taught the key vocabulary from their social studies textbook. Results indicated that the combined word-part and context-clue instruction was effective in teaching students to use word parts to unlock the meanings of new words and that students who received this instruction learned their social studies content as well as the students who were taught the social studies vocabulary directly.

In a recent review, Carlisle (2010) considered various aspects of morphological awareness, including teaching morphological awareness as a way to learn the meanings of new words. She concluded that "students generally do become more able to infer the meanings of unfamiliar words after receiving instruction in morphological awareness" (p. 478).

Though researchers have convincing information that word parts (roots, prefixes, derivational suffixes, and inflections) can be taught and used by students to unlock the meanings of unknown words, much remains to be learned. Most important, there is a lack of solid information about which word parts to teach and when to teach them. Most lists of word parts to teach are based on the compilers' intuitions, often coupled with some attention to previous lists. In fact, the only relatively recent, empirically based list of word parts I am familiar with is the list of the 20 most frequent prefixes and the 20 most frequent suffixes compiled by White et al. (1989). We need newer lists, lists based on a larger corpus of words, and lists that include roots. Additionally, research is needed on the long-term effects of teaching word parts. Although short-term studies have shown that students can learn word parts and use them to unlock the meanings of unknown words, they have not shown that students can retain and use this knowledge over time. Nor have they shown the effects of word-part instruction on students' overall vocabulary knowledge.

Use of context. Although a meta-analysis of studies examining instruction in context clues indicated that such instruction does have a positive effect on students' ability to derive word meaning from context during reading (Fukkink & de Glopper, 1998), the data testifying to the positive effect of teaching students to use context are less convincing than those for teaching word parts. In one study, Carnine, Kame'enui, and Coyle (1984) used both a rule-plus-practice and a practice-only treatment and found that either treatment facilitated students' ability to use context in a passage constructed by the experimenters. In another study, Patberg, Graves, and Stibbe (1984) used an active teaching approach to teach 5th-grade students to use synonym clues and contrast clues. Results indicated that the instructed students outperformed students in a practice-only group and students in an uninstructed control group in determining the meanings of uninstructed new words that were presented in short texts containing the sorts of clues taught. However, in a follow-up study, Patberg and Stibbe (1985) found no effects for instruction in using context clues. Buikema and Graves (1993) taught students to use descriptive context clues and found that instructed students outperformed uninstructed students on several measures, including one that required students to use natural context to infer word meanings.

The two studies by Baumann and associates (2002; Baumann, Edwards, et al., 2003) are the most ambitious studies of teaching context clues with which I am familiar. Results of the 2002 study indicated that on an immediate test, students in the context-only group and in the contextual analysis and morphological group were better able to infer the meanings of uninstructed words embedded in text that included taught context-clue types. This advantage, however, did not hold on a delayed test. Results of the 2003 study indicated that students who received the combined contextual analysis and word-part analysis treatment were more successful at inferring the meanings of contextually decipherable words on a delayed test but not on an immediate test.

All in all, though some studies have shown positive effects of learning to use context, others have not. Moreover, most of the tests used in the studies were experimenter designed and tested only immediate transfer. Only a few studies showed delayed effects or transfer to new contexts and topics. Additionally, most studies have dealt with explicit and relatively infrequent context clues such as synonym, definition, and antonym clues. Research is needed to assess learning to use less obvious, more naturalistic, and more frequent clues. Additionally, we need long-term studies of context-clue instruction.

Use of the dictionary. In this area, studies have examined the effects of revising definitions (McKeown, 1993) and of teaching students about the format of definitions (Schwartz & Raphael, 1985). And one study has examined the effectiveness of instruction in dictionary use as part of a broader vocabulary program (Graves & Sales, 2012). In this program, students who were taught to use word parts, context, and the dictionary significantly outperformed control-group students on an experimenter-constructed general test of word-learning strategies. However, I know of no studies that have isolated, directly taught, and assessed students' ability to use dictionaries effectively.

Such studies are certainly needed with both online and traditional dictionaries. It is worth adding that, unlike instruction with word parts and context, instruction in using the dictionary can probably be quite brief.

Fostering Word Consciousness

Although word-consciousness activities are frequently recommended in the literature and are major parts of several of the multifaceted and relatively long-term studies described below, I am aware of only two studies that focused specifically on word-consciousness instruction. The earlier of these was a 7-year qualitative project in which teachers and researchers collaborated in a variety of ways to build word consciousness in elementary students. Results indicated that teachers could influence their students' word consciousness, particularly "the perceptions students have about the use of words with an academic or literate tone" (Scott & Nagy, 2004, p. 206). The other study was a 3-year teacher and researcher collaborative project that was largely qualitative but did produce some quantitative data. The qualitative data showed positive results on a number of dimensions, including teachers' word consciousness and their skill in designing word-consciousness activities for students. Quantitative results on a researcher-designed test of words that were not explicitly taught showed that students in the project outperformed students who were not in the project (Scott, Miller, & Flinspach, 2012).

Additional studies are clearly needed, and these should employ a variety of quantitative and qualitative dependent measures, including quantitative measures that are independent of the researchers. Additionally, as with other facets of vocabulary instruction, studies of word consciousness need to span multiple years.

Multifaceted and Relatively Long-Term Instructional Studies

Over the past 35 years, researchers have developed and tested a small number of vocabulary programs that were well reasoned, theory- and research-based, multifaceted, and relatively long-term. Below, I briefly describe six such programs:

- In the earliest study, Beck et al. (1982) designed a program to provide 4th-grade students in an urban public school with in-depth and varied instruction on 104 words over a 5-month period. Results showed that the students who received the treatment performed significantly higher than those in a control group on a variety of experimenter-designed measures that ranged from single-word semantic decision tasks, to knowledge of the words taught, to comprehension of passages containing the words taught. A replication of the study the following year (McKeown et al., 1983) showed similar results.
- Carlo and her colleagues (2004) designed a program to enhance the vocabularies of 5th-grade ELLs and native English speakers by teaching the meanings of approximately 150 academically useful words along with strategies

for using context, morphology, knowledge about multiple meanings, and cognates to infer word meanings over a 15-week period. Both ELLs and native English speakers in the treatment group showed greater growth than did students in a comparison group on experimenter-designed tests of knowledge of the words taught, depth of vocabulary knowledge, understanding of multiple meanings, and reading comprehension.

- Snow, Lawrence, and White (2009) designed a cross-content-area program to improve the academic vocabularies of 6th- to 8th-grade ELLs and native English speakers by teaching 100 academic words and word-learning strategies over a 20-week period. Results on an experimenter-designed test indicated that students who received the treatment learned significantly more of the words taught than students in the control group. Results of a follow-up study showed that students receiving the treatment still maintained their superior knowledge of the words taught a year after the completion of the study (Lawrence, Capotosto, Branum-Martin, White, & Snow, 2012).

- Lesaux, Kieffer, Faller, and Kelley (2010) designed a program to teach academic vocabulary in middle school classrooms with high proportions of ELLs by teaching 72 academic words and word-learning strategies over an 18-week period. Results indicated positive and statistically significant effects on experimenter-designed tests of the words taught, the words taught in context, and morphological awareness with the words taught and other words. Results with a standardized test of comprehension were marginally significant, and results with a standardized test of vocabulary were nonsignificant.

- Baumann, Blachowicz, Maniac, Graves, and Olejnik (2009–2012) designed a program to improve the vocabularies of 4th- and 5th-grade students of various socioeconomic and linguistic backgrounds using the four-part model that I described earlier over approximately a 30-week period. This formative experiment, which was replicated with some modifications in Years 2 and 3, showed statistically significant and often large gains ($d = .5$ to 1.6) in each year on experimenter-designed tests of words taught, use of morphology, and use of context, as well as on the vocabulary subtest of the Gates-MacGinitie Reading Tests.

- Goldenberg et al. (2013) designed a history/social studies–based vocabulary program to improve the vocabulary and reading comprehension of struggling middle school students by teaching 450 target words and word-learning strategies over a 20- to 25-week period. Results of this study with experimenter-designed tests of the vocabulary taught and with depth of knowledge of the vocabulary taught produced strong effect sizes, whereas results with an experimenter-designed test of curriculum-based comprehension produced a weaker effect size. No significant effects were found on the vocabulary or comprehension sections of the Gates-MacGinitie Reading Tests.

In considering the additional research that is needed on multifaceted and relatively long-term vocabulary programs, I look specifically at three issues: their length, their lack of differentiation, and their central organizing principle.

None of the six research programs I have discussed—and, in fact, no vocabulary research program I am aware of—provided instruction that lasted longer than a single school year, and most lasted for a considerably shorter period of time. As I reflect upon a long line of research and best practices in teaching vocabulary, it has become clear to me that program duration matters: A vocabulary program that is at all likely to teach a substantial number of individual words, to give students a variety of durable strategies for learning words on their own, and to build students' interest in and love of words needs to continue over several years. In fact, some sort of articulated vocabulary instruction needs to span the entire 13 years of public schooling. Although a 13-year research program is not feasible at present, and although multiyear studies are extremely difficult to implement, it should be possible to design instructional research programs that span 3 to 4 years; for example, one running from kindergarten to grade 2, another for grades 3 to 5, another for grades 6 to 8, and still another for grades 9 to 12. To repeat, as difficult and demanding as such undertakings will be, shorter efforts are extremely unlikely to produce any substantial and sustainable learning gains.

In addition to being relatively brief, none of these programs I've examined differentiated instruction to accommodate students with markedly different vocabularies and/or word-learning skills. As I have noted, and as has been repeatedly documented, a substantial number of students both enter school and continue through school with markedly different stores of words (August et al., 2005; Becker, 1977; Biemiller, 2009; Chall et al., 1990; Graves et al., 1982; Hart & Risley, 1995; Mancilla-Martinez & Lesaux, 2011; Snow & Kim, 2007; White et al., 1990). To assume that all students will develop the vocabularies they need to succeed in school and the world beyond school—to become "college and career ready" in the language of the Common Core—with the same type and amount of vocabulary instruction is absurd. Different students need different types of instruction, and some students will need a lot more instruction than others.

Finally, all of the programs discussed, except that of Baumann and associates, are organized around the teaching of individual words—in four of the programs, roughly 100 words and in Goldenberg et al.'s program, 450 words. To be sure, each of the programs includes elements that go well beyond teaching individual words. Yet, in my judgment— and it is admittedly a judgment in which I have a vested interest—an effective and efficient long-term vocabulary program should be built around something much more like the four-part program I have presented; that is, it should give deliberate and substantial attention to teaching individual words, teaching word-learning strategies, and fostering word consciousness; and all of these activities should take place in a supportive environment filled with rich and varied language experiences.

SUMMARY OF CURRENT RESEARCH AND RECOMMENDATIONS FOR FURTHER RESEARCH

In summary, both studies of basal reading programs and observational studies in classrooms indicate that vocabulary instruction in schools has not changed much over the past 50 years, is often thin, and is seldom based on current research. Research on the size of the English lexicon and the number of words students learn shows wide discrepancies in estimates of the size of the word-learning task students face. Conversely, there is wide agreement that the vocabularies of different socioeconomic and linguistic groups vary markedly, with some students lacking the vocabularies they need to succeed in school. There is little information on the words that appear in specific bodies of words such as core reading programs on content-area texts (although one research groups is currently working on this task; see Graves, Elmore, et al., 2014), and consequently, there is no information available about students' knowledge of these bodies of words. I am aware of no classroom research on providing rich and varied classroom experiences. A good deal of research does exist about robust approaches to teaching individual words, but there is little research on less robust and less time-consuming approaches. There is strong support for teaching students to use word parts, but little empirical information on which word parts to teach. There is some research—though it is not totally convincing—that demonstrates the efficacy of teaching students to use context clues, but there is no research that isolates the effects of teaching students to use the dictionary. Only two studies have attempted to isolate the effects of efforts to foster word consciousness, and their results are encouraging but not conclusive. Finally, multifaceted and relatively long-term programs of vocabulary instruction have generally produced positive results on experimenter-designed, curriculum-based measures, but they have only infrequently produced results on standardized tests meant to measure transfer and have not lasted longer than a school year.

My position on the research that needs to be done in order to substantially improve vocabulary instruction in schools and markedly assist students in meeting the CCSS goal of becoming college and career ready can be captured in the following four recommendations: (1) defining the problem, (2) testing parts of the solution, (3) testing comprehensive and long-term vocabulary programs, and (4) developing comprehensive and widely available programs based solidly on research.

Defining the problem. First, studies are needed to define the size of the word-learning task students face with sufficient authority to ensure that funding agencies, researchers, teachers and administrators, and publishers all agree on the magnitude of what students need to learn. This effort should be followed with studies of the vocabulary demands of various curricular areas and for students of various ages. And following this, researchers need to study the vocabularies of students from a variety of socioeconomic and linguistic backgrounds.

Testing parts of the solution. Studies that test the various parts of a comprehensive program, such as each part of my four-part program, are the next priority. Some of these studies will necessarily be long-term. For example, teaching students to be independent and self-regulated users of naturalistic context clues will take much longer than a year. So will achieving long-term effects with virtually any type of instruction.

Testing comprehensive solutions. Taking those individual components that have been proven to be effective and combining them into long-term and comprehensive programs seems to be the next step needed. As I have noted, such programs should probably last a minimum of 3 years and might be designed for the early elementary grades (K–2), the later elementary grades (3–5), the middle grades (6–8), and high school (9–12).

Developing comprehensive and widely available programs for schools. My recommendations thus far have focused on research, but research by itself is not enough. Moving from the product of research—knowledge—to widely available, easily understood, easily used, and enticing school programs will require development efforts larger than and quite unlike the current approaches to developing reading and language arts programs. I suspect that these development efforts will involve commercial publishers because I believe that commercial publishers have the resources to produce and widely distribute attractive, well-packaged, and easily used material. However, the publishers' role will need to be very different from what it typically has been. That is, publishers will need to develop programs that are closely based on the research rather than programs based largely on the opinions of editors and the demands of the sales force.

SO WHAT DO TEACHERS DO TOMORROW?

Clearly, there is much work to be done to build research-based vocabulary programs that can make a significant contribution to students' becoming college and career ready. Equally clearly, there is a lot of work that has already been done, and there are tens of thousands of classrooms filled with students who need help building vocabularies of breadth and depth. My approach to this task has been to create the four-part framework outlined earlier in this chapter and used in discussing some of the research. I designed this approach to be logical, practical, consistent with current theory, and consistent with the research we have. As I have noted, the approach is described in detail in Graves (2006) and Graves, August, and Mancilla-Martinez (2012). The key components, in brief, include:

- *Providing Rich and Varied Language Experiences.* This part of the program includes both immersion in a word-rich environment and rich and varied experiences in listening, discussion, reading, and writing. A word-rich environment must be physically rich, a place where books and other reading material as well as words themselves are prominently displayed in the classroom, the school library, and even the halls. In addition to creating a word-rich physical environment, teachers need to make the classroom a stimulating emotional and intellectual environment that encourages and celebrates rich word usage and experimentation with words and ideas. Teachers also need to deliberately engage students at all grade levels in listening, discussion, reading, and writing. While listening and discussion may predominate with younger students and reading and writing with older students, students of all ages need to engage frequently in each of these activities.
- *Teaching Individual Words.* As I have noted, there is a great deal of information on how to teach individual words, and particularly on how to provide in-depth instruction, but not nearly as much information as we need about which words to teach. Nevertheless, teachers do need to select words to teach and to provide in-depth instruction on some words and less time-consuming introductory instruction on others. Approaches to selecting

vocabulary such as those of Beck et al. (2002, 2013) and Graves et al. (2014) can be helpful. Additionally, students' learning will be greatly facilitated if the teachers in a school or even a district can agree on at least some of the words that should be taught at each grade level—common words such as *invented* and *conversation* that most students know but that some ELLs and other students with small vocabularies may not, general academic vocabulary such as *analyze* and *require*, and content-specific academic vocabulary such as *manifest destiny* and *electrical charge*.

- *Teaching Word-Learning Strategies.* The principal word-learning strategies to teach are using word parts, using context, and using the dictionary. The approach I suggest for teaching all three is a combination of direct explanation as described by Duke and Pearson (2002) and constructivist instruction as described by Pressley, Harris, and Marks (1992). Direct explanation follows a sequence that includes (1) an explicit description of the strategy and when and how it should be used, (2) teacher and/or student modeling of the strategy in action, (3) collaborative use of the strategy in action, (4) guided practice using the strategy with gradual release of responsibility, and (5) independent use of the strategy. Constructive instruction emphasizes (1) motivating students, (2) explaining the value of strategies, (3) providing collaborative discussion of the value of strategies, and (4) deliberately and systematically working on transfer. (More details on this combined approach are available in Graves, Ruda, Sales, & Baumann, 2012). The upper elementary grades are an excellent time to focus on strategy instruction. Also, as is the case with Teaching Individual Words, students' learning will be greatly facilitated if teachers agree on which strategies to focus on at which grade levels.

- *Fostering Word Consciousness.* Although fostering word consciousness differs from grade to grade, doing so is vital at all grade levels. There are some time-consuming word-consciousness activities, but for the most part, fostering word consciousness does not take a lot of teacher or student time. For example, one very simple word-consciousness activity is to deliberately use some sophisticated words in class. For K–2 children, such words might include *alert* and *opponent*; for grade 3–5 children, words such as *acute* and *grave*; for middle school students, words like *initiate* and *prelude*; and for high school students, words such as *exacerbate* and *patriarch*. Graves and Watts-Taffe (2008) describe this and a number of other word-consciousness activities, including creating a word-rich environment, recognizing and promoting adept diction, promoting word play, fostering word consciousness through writing, and involving students in original investigations. Given the number of words that students need to learn, their becoming word conscious is an absolute must.

CLOSING REMARKS

Although researchers and teachers still have a lot to learn about vocabulary instruction, much is already known, and much can be done to help students improve their vocabularies. Building strong vocabulary programs is vitally important to helping students succeed in school. But building strong vocabulary programs is not easy. I wish to close this chapter with an endorsement of a position recently expressed by Claude Goldenberg and his colleagues (2013). In concluding a presentation on the results of their 4-year, multifaceted vocabulary program, which did not produce the strong results the researchers had anticipated, Goldenberg and his colleagues said:

> The consistency of these findings with previous research suggests that as important as vocabulary undoubtedly is, teaching vocabulary—even teaching a great deal of it—will not by itself have a substantial impact on the reading comprehension. . . . Closing the achievement gap . . . will undoubtedly require far more comprehensive and ambitious approaches that are sustained over time and, ideally, begin before students develop large gaps in vocabulary and background knowledge that compromise comprehension of academic texts. (p. 5)

I could not agree more. Furthermore, I want to stress that in addition to "more comprehensive and ambitious approaches" to vocabulary instruction, the topic of this chapter, approaches that will have a "substantial impact on reading comprehension" and that will truly lead to students' becoming college and career ready will necessarily include a variety of techniques for scaffolding students' understanding of the selections they read, instruction in reading comprehension strategies, strong elements for building students' background knowledge, and significant attention to motivating students to succeed in reading and in school more generally.

REFERENCES

Anderson, R. C., & Nagy, W. E. (1992). The vocabulary conundrum. *American Educator, 16,* 14–18, 44–47.

August, D., Carlo, M., Dressler, C., & Snow, C. (2005). The critical role of vocabulary development for English language learners. *Learning Disabilities Research & Practice, 20*(1), 50–57.

Baumann, J. F., Blachowicz, C.L.Z., Maniac, P. C., Graves, M. F., & Olejnik, S. (2009–2012). *Development of a multi-faceted, comprehensive, vocabulary instructional program for the upper-elementary grades* [R305A090163]. Washington, DC: U.S. Department of Education, Institute of Education Sciences, National Center for Education Research (Reading and Writing Program).

Baumann, J. F., Edwards, E. C., Boland E., Olejnik, S., & Kame'enui, E. J. (2003). Vocabulary tricks. Effects of instruction in morphology and context on fifth grade students' ability to derive and infer word meaning. *American Educational Research Journal, 40,* 447–494.

Baumann, J. F., Edwards, E. C., Font, G., Tereshinski, C. A., Kame'enui, E. J., & Olejnik, S. (2002). Teaching morphemic and contextual analysis to fifth-grade students. *Reading Research Quarterly, 37,* 150–176.

Baumann, J. F., Kame'enui, E. J., & Ash, G. E. (2003). Research on vocabulary instructing: Voltaire redux. In J. Flood, D. Lapp, J. R. Squire, & J. M. Jensen (Eds.), *Handbook on research on teaching the English language arts* (2nd ed., pp. 752–785). Mahwah, NJ: Erlbaum.

Beck, I. L., & McKeown, M. G. (1991). Conditions of vocabulary acquisition. In R. Barr, M. L. Kamil, P. B. Mosenthal, & P. D. Pearson (Eds.), *The handbook of reading research* (Vol. 2, pp. 789–814). New York, NY: Longman.

Beck, I. L., & McKeown, M. G. (2007). Increasing young children's oral vocabulary repertoires through rich and focused instruction. *Elementary School Journal, 107,* 251–271.

Beck, I. L., McKeown, M. G., & Kucan, L. (2002). *Bringing words to life: Robust vocabulary instruction.* New York, NY: Guilford Press.

Beck, I. L., McKeown, M. G., & Kucan, L. (2013). *Bringing words to life: Robust vocabulary instruction* (2nd ed.). New York, NY: Guilford Press.

Beck, I. L., McKeown, M. G., McCaslin, E. S., & Burkes, A. M. (1979). *Instructional dimensions that may affect reading comprehension: Examples from two commercial reading programs* (LRDC Publication No. 1979-20). Pittsburgh, PA: University of Pittsburgh, Learning Research and Development Center.

Beck, I. L., Perfetti, C. A., & McKeown, M. G. (1982). The effects of long-term vocabulary instruction on lexical access and reading comprehension. *Journal of Educational Psychology, 74,* 506–521.

Becker, W. C. (1977). Teaching reading and language to the disadvantaged—What we have learned from field research. *Harvard Educational Review, 47,* 511–543.

Biemiller, A. (2009). *Words worth teaching.* Columbus, OH: SRA/McGraw-Hill.

Biemiller, A., & Slonim, N. (2001). Estimating root word vocabulary growth in normative and advanced populations: Evidence for a common sequence of vocabulary acquisition. *Journal of Educational Psychology, 93,* 498–520.

Blachowicz, C., & Fisher, P. (2000). Vocabulary instruction. In R. Barr, M. L. Kamil, P. Mosenthal, & P. D. Pearson (Eds.), *The handbook of reading research* (Vol. 3, pp. 503–523). Mahwah, NJ: Erlbaum.

Buikema, J. A., & Graves, M. F. (1993). Teaching students to use context cues to infer word meanings. *Journal of Reading, 36,* 450–457.

Carlisle, J. E. (2010). Effects of instruction in morphological awareness on literacy achievement: An integrative review. *Reading Research Quarterly, 45,* 464–487.

Carlisle, J. E., Kelcey, B., & Berebitsky, D. (2013). Teachers' support of students' vocabulary learning during literacy instruction in high poverty elementary schools. *American Educational Research Journal, 50*(6), 1360–1371.

Carlo, M. S., August, D., McGlaughlin, B., Snow, C. E., Dressler, C., Lippman, D. N., Lively, T. J., & White, C. E. (2004). Closing the gap: Addressing the vocabulary needs of English-language learners in bilingual and mainstream classes. *Reading Research Quarterly, 39,* 188–215.

Carnine, D., Kame'enui, E. J., & Coyle, G. (1984). Utilization of contextual information in determining the meaning of unfamiliar words in context. *Reading Research Quarterly, 19,* 188–202.

Chall, J. S., Jacobs, V. A., & Baldwin, L. E. (1990). *The reading crisis: Why poor children fall behind.* Cambridge, MA: Harvard University Press.

Coxhead, A. (2000). A new academic word list. *TESOL Quarterly 34,* 213–238.

D'Anna, C. A., Zechmeister, E. B., & Hall, J. W. (1991). Toward a meaningful definition of vocabulary size. *Journal of Reading Behavior 23,* 109–122.

Dickinson, D. K., & Tabors, P. O. (Eds.). (2001). *Beginning literacy with language: Young children learning at home and school.* Baltimore, MD: Brookes Publishing.

Duke, N. K., & Pearson, P. D. (2002). Effective practices for developing reading comprehension. In A. E. Farstrup & S. J. Samuels (Eds.), *What research has to say about reading instruction* (3rd ed., pp. 204–242). Newark, DE: International Reading Association.

Dupuy, H. (1974). *The rationale, development, and standardization of a basic word vocabulary test* (DHEW Publications No. HRA74-1334). Washington, DC: U. S. Government Printing Office.

Durkin, D. (1978–1979). What classroom observations reveal about reading comprehension instruction. *Reading Research Quarterly, 14,* 481–533.

Durkin, D. (1981). Reading comprehension instruction in five basal readers. *Reading Research Quarterly, 16,* 515–544.

Fernald, A., Marchman, V. A., & Weisleder, A. (2013). SES differences in language processing skill and vocabulary are evident at 18 months. *Developmental Science, 16,* 234–248.

Fukkink, R. G., & de Glopper, K. (1998). Effects of instruction in deriving word meanings from context: A meta-analysis. *Review of Educational Research, 68,* 450–469.

Gardner, D., & Davies, M. (2014). A new academic vocabulary list. *Applied Linguistics, 35,* 305–327.

Goldenberg, C. N., Diamond, L. J., Stites, R. D., Greenberg, L., Brewer, N.J.S., & Wanf, H. (2013). *Content-rich vocabulary development to improve reading achievement of struggling adolescent readers.* Paper presented at the annual meeting of the American Educational Research Association, San Francisco, CA.

Goulden, R., Nation, P., & Read, J. 1990. How large can a receptive vocabulary be? *Applied Linguistics, 11,* 341–363.

Graves, M. F. (1986). Vocabulary learning and instruction. In E. Z. Rothkopf (Ed.), *Review of research in education* (Vol. 13, pp. 49–90). Washington, DC: American Educational Research Association.

Graves, M. F. (2006). *The vocabulary book: Learning and instruction.* New York, NY: Teachers College Press.

Graves, M. F., August, D., & Mancilla-Martinez, J. (2012). *Teaching vocabulary to English language learners.* New York, NY: Teachers College Press, International Reading Association, Center for Applied Linguistics, and Teachers of English to Speakers of Other Languages.

Graves, M. F., Baumann, J. F., Blachowicz, C.L.Z., Manyak, P., Bates, A., Cieply, C., Davis, J. R., & Von Gluten, H. (2014). Words, words everywhere; but which ones do we teach? *The Reading Teacher, 20,* 333–346.

Graves, M. F., Brunetti, G. J., & Slater, W. H. (1982). The reading vocabularies of primary grade children of varying geographic and social backgrounds. In J. A. Niles & L. A. Harris (Eds.), *New inquiries in reading research and instruction.* Rochester, NY: National Reading Conference.

Graves, M. F., Elmore, J., Bowen, K., Sanford-Moore, E. E., Copeland, M., Fitzgerald, J., Koons, H., & Stenner, A. J. (2014, December). *The vocabulary of core reading programs.* Paper presented at the meeting of the Literacy Research Association, Marco Island, FL.

Graves, M. F., & Hammond, H. K. (1980). A validated procedure for teaching prefixes and its effect on students' ability to assign meaning to novel words. In M. L. Kamil & A. J. Moe (Eds.), *Perspectives on reading research and instruction* (pp. 184–188). Washington, DC: National Reading Conference.

Graves, M. F., Ruda, M. A., Sales, G. C., & Baumann, J. F. (2012). Teaching prefixes: Making strong instruction even stronger. In E. B. Kame'enui & J. F. Baumann (Eds.), *Vocabulary instruction: Research to practice* (2nd ed., pp. 95–115). New York, NY: Guilford Press.

Graves, M. F., & Sales, G. C. (2012, December). *Teaching word learning strategies.* Paper presented at the annual meeting of the Literacy Research Association, San Diego, CA.

Graves, M. F., & Silverman, R. (2010). Interventions to enhance vocabulary development. In R. Allington & A. McGill-Franzen (Eds.), *Handbook of reading disabilities research,* (pp. 315–328). Mahwah, NJ: Erlbaum.

Graves, M. F., & Watts, S. M. (2002). The place of word consciousness in a research-based vocabulary program. In S. J. Samuels & A. E. Farstrup (Eds.), *What research has to say about reading instruction* (3rd ed., pp. 140–165). Newark, DE: International Reading Association.

Graves, M. F., & Watts-Taffe, S. W. (2008). For the love of words: Fostering word consciousness in young readers. *The Reading Teacher, 62*, 185–193.

Hart, B., & Risley, T. R. (1995). *Meaningful differences in the everyday experiences of young American children*. Baltimore, MD: Brookes Publishing.

Hiebert, E. H., & Cervetti, G. N. (2012). What differences in narrative and informational texts mean for the learning and instruction of vocabulary. In E. B. Kame'enui & J. F. Baumann (Eds.), *Vocabulary instruction: Research to practice* (2nd ed., pp. 322–344). New York, NY: Guilford Press.

Jenkins, J. R., & Dixon, R. (1983). Vocabulary learning. *Contemporary Educational Psychology, 8*, 237–260.

Lawrence, J. F., Capotosto, L., Branum-Martin, L., White, C., & Snow, C. E. (2012). Language proficiency, home-language status, and English vocabulary development: A longitudinal follow-up of the Word Generation program. *Bilingualism: Language and Cognition, 15*, 437–451.

Lesaux, N. K., Kieffer, M. J., Faller, E., & Kelley, J. (2010). The effectiveness and ease of implementation of an academic vocabulary intervention for linguistically diverse students in urban middle schools. *Reading Research Quarterly, 45*, 198–230.

Mancilla-Martinez, J., & Lesaux, N. K. (2011). The gap between Spanish-speakers' word reading and word knowledge: A longitudinal study. *Child Development, 85*, 1544–1560.

Marzano, R. J. (2004). *Building background knowledge for academic achievement*. Alexandria, VA: Association for Supervision and Curriculum Development.

McKeown, M. G. (1993). Creating effective definitions for young word learners. *Reading Research Quarterly, 28*, 16–31.

McKeown, M. G., Beck, I. L., Omanson, R. C., & Perfetti, C. A. (1983). The effects of long-term vocabulary instruction on reading comprehension: A replication. *Journal of Reading Behavior, 15*, 3–18.

McKeown, M. G., Beck, I. L., Omanson, R. C., & Pople, M. T. (1984). Some effects of the nature and frequency of vocabulary instruction on the knowledge and use of words. *Reading Research Quarterly, 20*, 522–535.

Mezynski, K. (1983). Issues concerning the acquisition of knowledge: Effects of vocabulary training on reading comprehension. *Review of Educational Research, 53*, 253–279.

Nagy, W. E., & Anderson, R. C. (1984). How many words are there in printed school English? *Reading Research Quarterly, 19*, 304–330.

Nagy, W. E., & Herman, P. A. (1987). Breadth and depth of vocabulary knowledge: Implications for acquisition and instruction. In M. C. McKeown & M. E. Curtis (Eds.), *The nature of vocabulary acquisition* (pp. 19–35). Hillsdale, NJ: Erlbaum.

Nagy, W. E., & Hiebert, E. H. (2011). Toward a theory of word selection. In M. L. Kamil, P. D. Pearson, E. B. Moje, & P. P. Afflerbach (Eds.), *Handbook of reading research* (Vol. 4, pp. 388–404). New York, NY: Longman.

National Institute of Child Health and Human Development (NICHD). (2000). *Report of the National Reading Panel. Teaching children to read: An evidence-based assessment of the scientific research literature on reading and its implications for reading instruction: Reports of the subgroups* (NIH Publication No. 00-4754). Washington, DC: U.S. Government Printing Office.

Patberg, J. P., Graves, M. F., & Stibbe, M. A. (1984). Effects of active teaching and practice in facilitating students' use of context clues. In J. A. Niles & L. A. Harris (Eds.), *Changing perspectives in research in reading/language processing and instruction* (pp. 146–151). Rochester, NY: National Reading Conference.

Patberg, J. P., & Stibbe, M. A. (1985, December). *The effects of contextual analysis instruction on vocabulary learning.* Paper presented at the annual meeting of the National Reading Conference, San Diego, CA.

Pearson, P. D., Hiebert, E. H., & Kamil, M. (2007). Vocabulary assessment: What we know and what we need to learn. *Reading Research Quarterly, 42,* 282–296.

Pressley, M., Dolezal, S. E., Raphael, L. M., Mohan, L., Roehrig, A. D., & Bogner K. (2003). *Motivating primary grade students.* New York, NY: Guilford Press.

Pressley, M., Harris, K. R., & Marks, M. B. (1992). But good strategy instructors are constructivists! *Educational Psychology Review, 4,* 3–31.

Petty, W., Herold, C., & Stoll, E. (1967). *The state of knowledge about the teaching of vocabulary.* Urbana, IL: National Council of Teachers of English.

Ryder, R. J., & Graves, M. F. (1994). Vocabulary instruction presented prior to reading in two basal readers. *Elementary School Journal, 95,* 139–153.

Schwartz, R. M., & Raphael, T. E. (1985). Concept of definition: A key to improving students' vocabulary. *The Reading Teacher, 39,* 198–205.

Scott, J. A., Jamieson-Noel, D., & Asselin, M. (2003). Vocabulary instruction throughout the day in twenty-three Canadian upper-elementary classrooms. *The Elementary School Journal, 103,* 269–286.

Scott, J. A., Miller, T. F., & Flinspach, S. F. (2012). Developing word consciousness: Lessons from highly diverse fourth-grade classrooms. In E. B. Kame'enui & J. F. Baumann (Eds.), *Vocabulary instruction: Research to practice* (2nd ed., pp. 169–188). New York, NY: Guilford Press.

Scott, J. A., & Nagy, W. E. (2004). Developing word consciousness. In J. F. Baumann & E. J. Kame'enui (Eds.), *Vocabulary instruction: Research to practice* (pp. 201–217). New York, NY: Guilford Press.

Snow, C. E., & Kim, Y. (2007). Large problem spaces: The challenge of vocabulary for English language learners. In R. K. Wagner, A. E. Muse, & K. R. Tannenbaum (Eds.), *Vocabulary acquisition: Implications for reading comprehension* (pp. 123–139). New York, NY: Guilford Press.

Snow, C. E., Lawrence, J., & White, C. (2009). Generating knowledge of academic language among urban middle school students. *Journal of Research on Educational Effectiveness, 2,* 325–344.

Stahl, S. A., & Fairbanks, M. M. (1986). The effects of vocabulary instruction: A model-based meta-analysis. *Review of Educational Research, 56,* 72–110.

Stahl, S. A., & Nagy, W. E. (2006). *Teaching word meanings.* Mahwah, NJ: Erlbaum.

van Kleeck, A., Stahl, S. A., & Bauer, E. B. (Eds.). (2003), *On reading books to children.* Mahwah, NJ: Erlbaum.

Watts, S. M. (1995). Vocabulary instruction during reading lessons in six classrooms. *Journal of Reading Behavior, 27,* 399–424.

Weisleder, A., & Fernald, A. (2013). Talking to children matters: Early language experience strengthens processing and builds vocabulary. *Psychological Science, 24,* 2143–2152.

White, T. G., Graves, M. F., & Slater, W. H. (1990). Growth of reading vocabulary in diverse elementary schools: Decoding and word meaning. *Journal of Educational Psychology, 82,* 281–290.

White, T. G., Sowell, J., & Yanagihara, A. (1989). Teaching elementary students to use word-part clues. *The Reading Teacher, 42,* 302–308.

Wright, T. S., & Neuman, S. M. (2013). Vocabulary instruction in commonly used kindergarten curriculum. *The Elementary School Journal, 113,* 386–408.

CHAPTER 9

Reading Fluency

Neglected, Misunderstood, but Still Critical for Proficient Reading

Timothy Rasinski, David Paige,
& James Nageldinger

In its review of the research related to important reading competencies and effective instruction, the National Reading Panel (National Institute of Child Health and Human Development [NICHD], 2000) concluded that sufficient evidence exists to identify fluency as one of five essential elements of reading success.

Despite this recognition of its importance, fluency continues to be misunderstood, both in research and practice. Evidence of this misunderstanding can be found in the annual "What's Hot, What's Not" survey of literacy experts (Cassidy & Grote-Garcia, 2013). In each year from 2008 through 2014, the experts concluded that fluency is not only "not hot," but that it should not be hot. Thus, the development of fluency continues to be neglected in reading classrooms around the country (Allington, 1983). An evaluation study of the Reading First initiative (Gamse, Jacob, Horst, Boulay, & Unlu, 2008) reported that of all the major components of reading instruction that were studied, fluency was given the least emphasis. Less than 5 minutes per day were devoted to reading fluency instruction. We can't help but wonder whether the disappointing results of the Reading First initiative were at least partially a result of the lack of fluency instruction it provided students.

In this chapter, we attempt to make the case for including reading fluency as an essential component of any effective reading curriculum. First, we provide a practical definition of fluency and explore why fluency continues to be neglected and misunderstood. Next, we discuss current issues in fluency that scholars and practitioners are working to resolve. We then describe proven and practical strategies for teaching students to become fluent readers and for assessing fluency.

WHAT IS FLUENCY?

Pikulski and Chard (2005) aptly describe fluency as a bridge between word-recognition accuracy (phonics) and reading comprehension, the ultimate goal of reading (see Figure 9.1). Although many students are able to cross this bridge on their own through wide

Figure 9.1. A Model of Reading Fluency

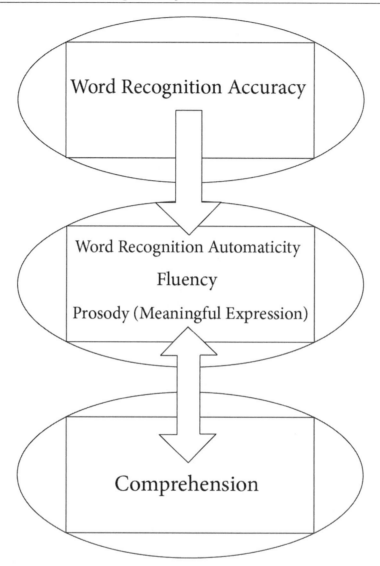

reading practice, a substantial number of students who struggle in their reading development never do, and so they remain stranded on the island of word recognition.

For years, it was conventional wisdom that accuracy in word recognition was all that was required for proficient reading. If readers could "sound out" the words they encountered in text, they were considered proficient. In their seminal 1974 paper, LaBerge and Samuels challenged the notion of word-recognition accuracy as being sufficient for good reading. They argued that good readers also need to be automatic in their word decoding. They suggested that all readers have a limited amount of cognitive resources available when reading. When readers have to apply their cognitive resources to word recognition, those resources cannot be applied to comprehension. The goal for proficient reading is automaticity, as well as accuracy in word recognition. When a task is developed to automaticity, a person is able to devote minimal cognitive resources to that task. Those unused resources can then be applied to other tasks—in reading, that other task is comprehension. Huey (1908), as well as LaBerge and Samuels (1974), noted that automaticity in reading can be viewed as a developmental process. As readers develop automaticity in text processing, they become more efficient in text processing, beginning with letters, syllables, whole words, and phrases.

Word-recognition automaticity is most often measured by reading speed or rate of reading. As readers increase their automatic recognition of words, their reading speed also tends to increase. Several studies have demonstrated a strong relationship between automaticity, as measured by reading rate, and reading comprehension (Paige, 2011a; Rasinski, Reutzel, Chard, & Linan-Thompson, 2011).

As the National Reading Panel report notes, for many years both educators and researchers assumed that fluency was the result of rapid, accurate word recognition, and so they focused instruction on developing that skill (NICHD, 2000). Newer conceptions of fluency, however, take into account another dimension of language known as *prosody*.

If fluency has been described as the most neglected area of the reading curriculum (Allington, 1983), then prosody fairly can be described as the neglected part of reading fluency. Prosody refers to expressive oral reading, or reading in which readers use and manipulate the melodic features of spoken language—stress, pitch variations, intonation, rate, phrasing, and pausing—to enhance textual meaning. If you think of fluent readers or speakers, you recognize that a critical feature of their fluency is an expressive performance that goes far beyond merely saying the words. Indeed, if fluency is a bridge from word recognition to comprehension, then prosody is the part of the bridge that links to comprehension. As readers read with appropriate expression, they enrich the meaning of the passage. However, the relationship between prosody and comprehension is reciprocal. As students construct the meaning of a text, they are able to embed appropriate prosody into their reading; the use of prosody further enhances their comprehension.

Prosody is not as easily or as precisely measured as automaticity. The most common form of classroom measurement involves the teacher simply listening to students read orally and rating the expressive quality of their reading. However, recent studies using qualitative rubrics have also shown remarkable correlations between measures of prosody and silent reading comprehension for elementary through secondary school readers (Paige, Rasinski, & Magpuri-Lavell, 2012; Rasinski, Rikli, & Johnston, 2009). Although correlation does not imply causation, studies of methods for improving prosody, many of which are teacher inspired and directed, have shown improvements in students' reading comprehension and other measures of reading proficiency (e.g., Griffith & Rasinski, 2004; Martinez, Roser, & Strecker, 1999).

WHY FLUENCY CONTINUES TO BE NEGLECTED

Interest in the role of fluency in reading instruction dates back many years. Huey (1908), for example, noted the importance of one aspect of reading fluency—automatic word recognition—that allows the reader to focus attention on the meaning of a text rather than on the mechanics of reading. However, as fluency instruction has evolved in reading curricula, it has been diminished by at least three misunderstandings.

First, as is evident in the National Reading Panel report (NICHD, 2000), fluency is often associated exclusively with oral reading; and because a primary goal of reading instruction is silent reading comprehension, fluency has been viewed as not relevant. However, the way one reads orally is a reflection of how one reads silently. Oral reading performance on informal reading inventories and running records are used to infer silent reading performance. Two large-scale studies have demonstrated that measures of oral reading fluency are consistently and positively related to proficiency in silent reading comprehension (Daane, Campbell, Grigg, Goodman, & Oranje, 2005; Pinnell et al., 1995). A growing body of scholarship has argued that fluency—both word-recognition automaticity and prosody—are manifested in silent reading (Hiebert, Samuels, & Rasinski, 2012; Samuels, Rasinski, & Hiebert, 2011). Indeed, research has demonstrated that instructional protocols in silent reading fluency result in improvements in assessments of silent reading comprehension from elementary through secondary grades (Rasinski, Samuels, Hiebert, Petscher, & Feller, 2011). Reading fluency is manifested in silent reading and is a necessary condition for proficiency in silent reading.

Fluency also has been neglected because of its association with fast reading. One aspect of fluency, automaticity in word recognition, is commonly measured in terms of reading speed or rate. As a result of several studies that have demonstrated a strong and significant correlation between readers' reading speed and their overall proficiency in reading, many manifestations of fluency instruction have emerged that focus directly and almost exclusively on increasing students' reading speed. Often, such approaches result in students who learn to read fast but fail to comprehend what they read, what Samuels (2007) calls "barking at print" (p. 563). Correlation is not causation. Reading speed is simply one observable manifestation of the underlying and critical fluency component—word-recognition automaticity. Samuels (2007) made it clear that fluency is *not* reading fast. Despite Samuels and others' attempts to clarify what fluency is not, it's likely that fluency has been neglected because of its association with fast reading. This is, indeed, ironic as LaBerge and Samuels' (1974) noted in their seminal paper—which laid the groundwork for decades of study on the role of automatic processing in reading—the point of fast and accurate word retrieval is that it allows the reader to focus attention on comprehending the text. Word-recognition automaticity is developed through practice. As students become more automatic in word recognition, through wide and repeated reading of texts, their reading speed will increase correspondingly.

Finally, the relative neglect of fluency in reading instruction can be attributed to the view that fluency is a competency that is mastered early in a student's reading development. In her developmental model of reading, Chall (1996) suggests that fluency is acquired in the primary grades. Although it may be true that students begin to acquire fluency early in their school careers, almost every reading teacher who works with students beyond the primary grades has seen many students who struggle with fluency, and, as a result, also struggle with reading comprehension. Students must continue to develop in fluency as they progress through the grades and as they encounter more complex and challenging texts.

Because fluency has been identified as fast, oral reading for the primary grades, many teachers and reading experts have rightly claimed that it should not be an instructional priority. As we noted earlier in this chapter, we feel that fluency extends well beyond these limitations and should be considered a critical component for reading success. Scholars view fluency as a base that is required for further growth in reading. There are still, however, issues that require thoughtful consideration as the concept of reading fluency continues to evolve.

FLUENCY AS A FOUNDATION FOR READING

The Common Core State Standards (CCSS; National Governors Association Center for Best Practices [NGA Center] & Council of Chief State School Officers [CCSSO], 2010) identify reading fluency, including both automaticity and prosody, as a foundational competency. We believe this is an apt designation. Any structure that is built to last needs a strong foundation. Recognizing words accurately and automatically, and reading with a level of expression that reflects the meaning of the passage, are necessary conditions for proficient reading. Thus, it is important for teachers to help students begin building this reading foundation as soon as possible in their reading careers. Without a strong foundation, the other competencies related to the close and meaningful reading of texts are likely to falter (Willingham, 2007).

When Fluency Should Be Taught

As we mentioned earlier, Chall's (1996) model of reading identifies fluency as a competency that is optimally acquired in the primary grades. We feel that such positioning may lead to a misunderstanding about when fluency should best be taught—that fluency should be taught and mastered early in a student's schooling, and then instruction should move on to other, more important reading competencies. Although we agree that fluency instruction should begin during the earliest stages of reading, as we describe later in this chapter, we feel that it must be addressed at *all* stages of the reading curriculum.

Some evidence indicates that students who struggle to get meaning from what they read have not yet developed adequate fluency to support reading comprehension. Rasinski and Padak (1998), for example, found that a lack of automaticity in word recognition was the most significant deficiency exhibited by elementary students referred for reading-intervention services. From their study of students who scored below the standard on a state-mandated silent reading test, Valencia and Buly (2004) concluded that difficulties in reading fluency were exhibited by two-thirds of these students. Similarly, Duke, Pressley, and Hilden (2004) suggest that difficulties in reading fluency are a major cause of students' reading comprehension problems. Although fluency is not the only competency required for proficient reading, lack of fluency appears to be a significant barrier to students' continued reading growth. It further appears that a significant number of students beyond grade 3 have not achieved sufficient levels of fluency to support their continued growth in reading comprehension.

Our research, however, seems to suggest that fluency does not appear to be addressed significantly beyond the primary grades, and that it remains a concern for older students. Rasinski, Rikli, and Johnston (2009) found that fluency was associated with silent reading comprehension in grades 3, 5, and 7. They also report that a significant number of 5th- and 7th-grade students still struggled with fluency. Other studies of high school students found that measures of fluency were significantly associated with reading comprehension, and a significant number of students had not yet achieved even minimal levels of fluency for their grade level (Paige et al., 2012; Paige, Rasinski, Magpuri-Lavell, & Smith, 2014; Rasinski et al., 2005).

The Increasing Difficulty of Texts

As students progress through school, the various texts they encounter generally become increasingly more difficult to comprehend and read. Textual characteristics, such as increasing syntactic complexity, new and more sophisticated vocabulary, and longer sentences and paragraphs that are often written with less coherence and cohesion, all work to make reading more difficult (O'Connor et al., 2002; O'Reilly & McNamara, 2007). A hallmark of the CCSS is their emphasis on preparing students to comprehend complex texts (that is, texts whose elements or features demand considerable thinking and interpretation by the reader). It is reasonable to assume, then, that the expectation of the CCSS is for students to read material that is difficult or challenging in terms of text processing.

Students who have not achieved adequate levels of fluency (automaticity and prosody) for their grade level will find reading materials at their assigned grade level to be a frustrating experience. How, then, might students who struggle with fluency respond to texts that are written significantly above their reading achievement level? This is a question that certainly needs to be addressed as implementation of the CCSS proceeds. Based on results of two large-scale NAEP oral reading studies (Daane et al., 2005; Pinnell et al., 1995) in which two-thirds of 4th-grade students who read texts below grade level in difficulty were found to read below the proficient level, Hiebert and Mesmer (2013) predict that an even larger proportion of students would be identified as nonproficient when reading the more challenging texts proposed by the CCSS. In their review of research on instructional texts used with struggling readers, Menon and Heibert (2011) suggest that struggling readers be given texts on which they are fairly accurate in terms of word recognition—texts that are not excessively challenging.

Stahl and Heubach (2005) did find, however, that 2nd-grade students made good progress in supportive fluency instruction when the texts were moderately challenging. On the other hand, when texts were overly difficult, progress was muted at best. The appropriate level of text difficulty in relation to the reading achievement level of the reader and the level of instructional support provided by the teacher are certainly issues that require additional research and consideration (Hiebert & Mesmer, 2013).

In summary, fluency was identified as a neglected goal of reading programs more than 30 years ago (Allington, 1983)—and it continues to be neglected and misunderstood. Unless students achieve some level of proficiency in reading fluency for the texts they must read, their comprehension will be hindered. We feel it is critical for reading education practitioners across grade levels to recognize the importance of reading fluency for proficient reading and to begin to integrate elements of fluency instruction into their reading curriculum.

PROMISING PRACTICES FOR TEACHING FLUENCY

The foundational Common Core State Standards for grades 1 through 5 address fluency directly by stating that students should read with "sufficient accuracy and fluency to support comprehension" (NGA Center & CCSSO, 2010, pp. 17–18). As the standards move to grades 6 through 12, they no longer address fluency specifically. For these levels, the CCSS require students to be able to read on-level texts independently and proficiently, although they do recognize that students may need teacher scaffolding to reach success as they read more difficult texts, thus implying that maintaining fluency beyond grade 5 is important. The CCSS developers clearly acknowledge two important criteria for successful reading. First, fluency is vital to effective reading, and second, fluency is best viewed as a developmental continuum, meaning that readers continue to develop fluency across the middle and secondary grades as they encounter new and challenging texts and text genres. In this section, we discuss research-based strategies that have been shown to encourage the development of fluent reading across this continuum.

Modeling Fluent Reading

Many protocols for developing effective fluency recommend modeling fluent reading for students. Indeed, this is a practice that can be traced back to at least the 1800s (Hoffman, 1987; Rasinski, Padak, Linek, & Sturtevant, 1994; Rasinski & Stevenson, 2005; Stahl & Heubach, 2005). In a typical modeling session, a teacher reads a text passage aloud at a conversational pace and with appropriate expression, while students listen and follow along silently in their text copies. Other renditions of modeling include the use of pre-recorded readings of texts by expert readers, which students listen to and follow as they read on their own.

The premise underlying this approach is clear: If students are to develop an understanding of fluency, they first need to know what fluent reading sounds like. Indeed, many students come to school without the developmental benefit of hearing text read aloud to them at home and consequently they possess no mental model of fluency that equates to a conversation or transaction between two speakers (Rosenblatt, 1994). In addition, although students may be fluent with known texts, they will inevitably encounter new text with unfamiliar text features. Modeling by an expert reader can help them understand what fluent reading should sound like with text that may seem difficult or even strange. The importance of modeling fluent reading becomes critical as it allows students to hear appropriately paced, expressive reading, with words correctly pronounced and phrases properly chunked, and generally teaches readers how printed text is converted to what approximates understandable speech.

The effectiveness of modeling fluent reading has research support. Rose and Beattie (1986), Rose and Sherry (1984), Dowhower (1987), Monda (1989), and Vaughn et al. (2000) all have found modeling to be beneficial to students. In a study of 20 students without reading disabilities, Rasinski (1990) compared repeated reading to listening-while-reading, which utilized a fluent reading model. Results showed that both strategies resulted in equal gains in automaticity and accuracy in 3rd-grade students.

Assisted Reading

Assisted-reading strategies provide students with the immediate scaffolding they need to read texts that may otherwise be too difficult (Dowhower, 1989). Such scaffolding or assistance typically comes from the teacher or a competent peer reader. Assisted-reading strategies can be particularly important because they can encourage the critical self-efficacy that students need to sense that they are becoming competent readers. Assisted reading can take a variety of forms. Although assisted-reading strategies are implemented during oral reading, it should be inferred that the benefits of assisted reading are manifested in both oral and silent reading.

Whole-class choral reading. One of the most popular assisted-reading strategies is whole-class choral reading (WCCR), a strategy that evolved from the neurological impress method (Heckleman, 1966, 1969; Hollingsworth, 1978). In WCCR the teacher reads a text aloud in unison with the entire class. The goal is for students to read the passage with one voice.

WCCR can be implemented either as a wide-reading rendition in which a different text is read each day, or in a repeated-reading application in which the class reads the same text across several days. As students become competent with the text, the teacher employs the gradual release of responsibility (Pearson, 1985; Pearson & Gallagher, 1983) to transfer responsibility for fluent reading to the class. Paige (2011b) conducted a study of 112 6th-grade students using a repeated-reading WCCR protocol with narrative text taken directly from the students' English language arts curriculum. The findings revealed large, statistically significant gains in reading fluency for the WCCR group, including both the struggling readers and the students who read at grade level. The power of WCCR to improve fluency exists in the anonymity of the strategy in which all students read aloud together, therefore providing "cover" for those who struggle from the embarrassment of reading aloud and alone. WCCR is an ideal strategy for exposing students to above-level texts and can be easily adapted for use in content areas and across elementary and middle grades to provide needed fluency support.

Paired reading. Paired reading matches a weaker and a stronger reader who selects a text to read based on its independent reading level—one that is above level for the tutee, yet below the level of the tutor. The two readers sit so that both of them can see the text; then they proceed to read the text aloud and in unison, with the tutor setting the reading pace to accommodate that of the tutee (Topping, 2001). A hand signal is arranged so the tutee can choose when to read alone. When the tutee mispronounces or otherwise has difficulty decoding a word, the tutor waits 4 seconds, then pronounces the word for the tutee to repeat. The pair pauses occasionally throughout the reading to discuss the meaning of what they have read.

Paired reading has extensive research to support its effectiveness at improving fluency and comprehension, both in the classroom as an adult–student or peer–peer strategy and at home as a parent–child reading strategy (Pumfrey, 1987; Topping & Lindsay, 1992; Topping, Thurston, McGavock, & Conlin, 2012). In several large-scale studies involving more than 5,000 students in over 70 schools, positive effects for paired reading were found in reading accuracy and comprehension (Topping, 1995; Topping et al., 2012).

Repeated Reading

Samuels (1979) first described this strategy in which students practice by orally rereading the same text several times until they reach a fluency criterion. An integral part of assisted repeated reading is that a teacher is present to work one-on-one with the student to correct errors and record progress over the course of the readings. As Chomsky (1976) observed, proper implementation of repeated reading can provide students with important motivation and growing self-efficacy in their ability to be competent readers. Repeated reading has been explored in several theories of reading (LaBerge & Samuels, 1974; Perfetti, 1985).

As we noted earlier, readers with poor fluency use a disproportionately large amount of their cognitive resources to process words; consequently, they have fewer resources to devote to comprehension. Repeated reading is effective because it allows students to become familiar with words, which increases automaticity and frees students to devote more attention to comprehension. Reviews of the extensive body of repeated-reading research all support its use in promoting fluency and comprehension improvement in both nondisabled and reading-disabled readers (Chard, Vaughn, & Tyler, 2002; Dowhower, 1994; NICHD, 2000; Therrien, 2004). Overall, these studies have found that repeated reading results in moderate to large gains in fluency, while comprehension gains are in the small to moderate range. Importantly, improvements in fluency and comprehension appear to transfer to the reading of texts other than those students have practiced—again, with effect sizes ranging from moderate to large and in assessments of silent reading (Kuhn et al., 2006; Therrien, 2004).

Phrasing

As we discussed earlier, one indicator of fluent reading is the ability to read with appropriate expression, or prosody (Hudson, Lane, & Pullen, 2005). Readers who exhibit prosodic reading, whether orally or silently, recognize informational units within a text and then proceed to bracket those units into phrases that mimic oral language (Sanderman & Collier, 1997). In essence, the reader adds stress to a phrase and, in doing so, makes it more prominent than the immediately surrounding text (Himmelman & Ladd, 2008). In either speaking or reading, the bracketing of phrases provides a cognitive framework in working memory that is important for maintaining comprehension (Cowie, Douglas-Cowie, & Wichmann, 2002; Frazier, Carlton, & Clifton, 2006). Readers' ability to bracket text provides a sort of rhythm to speech, and its activation during reading suggests it is an automatic skill that is evidence of appropriate reading development (Guiterrez-Palma & Palma-Reyes, 2008). Poor readers have been found to be less sensitive to the natural rhythm of speech, whereas evidence exists that proper sensitivity contributes to the development of word-reading skill (Goswami et al., 2002). Rasinski (1985) found that in normally developing 3rd- and 5th-grade readers, the ability to bracket text into meaningful phrasal units mediated the relationship between word recognition and fluency. Recent evidence suggests that the importance of prosodic reading and its subsequent contribution to comprehension extends into the secondary grades (Paige, Rasinski, Magpuri-Lavell & Smith, 2014).

One approach for helping students develop their ability to phrase text is known as the Phrased Text Lesson (Rasinski, Yildirim, & Nageldinger, 2011). In this approach, the teacher uses slash marks to highlight the phrase boundaries of a text to be read.

Integrated Fluency Lessons

Instructional routines that make fluency an integral part of the reading lesson have been shown to be highly effective for developing proficient readers (Hoffman, 1987; Rasinski, 1995; Rasinski, Homan, & Biggs, 2009; Stahl & Heubach, 2005).

Fluency Development Lesson. One such integrated routine is the Fluency Development Lesson (FDL; Rasinski et al., 1994). The FDL utilizes effective fluency instruction for 15 to 20 minutes per day. Students begin the lesson by reading aloud the text from the previous day, after which the teacher uses a new text to introduce and model fluent reading. After a brief discussion about the text, the students chorally read the text several times. Students next work in pairs, with the partners rereading the text three times to each other. This is followed by performances of the reading by student groups. Students then select several words from the text to add to the class word wall and engage in word-learning activities. After the lesson, students are encouraged to take the text home and read it again with family members. The following day, they reread the passage to either the teacher or a partner as a check for fluent reading.

Oral Recitation Lesson. Another instructional routine is the Oral Recitation Lesson (Hoffman, 1987). In this routine, the teacher models a text, emphasizing for students the characteristics of reading with prosody. For students who struggle with reading, the teacher may read aloud only a sentence or two, and then have the students chorally read the same sentences. Again, the emphasis is on fluent, expressive reading. In the final phase of the lesson, students select a small portion of the text that they practice independently and then perform for the group.

Fluency-Oriented Reading Instruction. In a routine designed to develop comprehension and fluent reading, Stahl and Heubach (2005) developed Fluency-Oriented Reading Instruction (FORI). This instructional routine begins with the teacher modeling the reading of a story to the class, which is followed by a class discussion of the story. Next, the class engages in echo reading, a version of choral reading in which students read a line of the text after hearing it read by the teacher. FORI then focuses on home practice, where students either read the next section of the text or read what they learned at school to an adult at least twice. When they return the next day, students partner-read the text, then finish up by journaling about the text they read.

The three fluency routines discussed here all include expressive teacher modeling, choral reading, and partner or paired reading as essential elements. The research on fluency instructional routines clearly suggests that these are very effective methods that accelerate fluency improvement in elementary students who struggle with reading.

Performance

Fluency instruction in the classroom can take many forms, but one approach that inspires both student confidence and motivation is performance. This approach involves the use of teacher modeling, assisted reading, and rehearsal, or repeated reading, to help students practice a targeted text over several days and eventually perform it for an authentic audience that listens for the purpose of being entertained and gaining meaning. The intent of the reading practice is to produce a prosodic or meaningful oral rendering of the text. The texts chosen are central to the performance approach—they should be texts that are meant to be performed in an expressive oral manner, such as poetry, song lyrics, and readers' theater scripts.

A typical weekly routine for teaching reading fluency in this authentic manner may look like this: On Monday, the teacher assigns each student or group of students a short text (poem, script, or other passage) that they will be expected to perform at the end of the week. Students are provided with a copy of the text, and the teacher models reading how it should be read with individual students, groups, or the entire class. A brief discussion of each text and the teacher's reading follows. On Tuesday, the students engage in assisted reading by reading the text as they simultaneously listen to a fluent rendering of the text by the teacher or other expert reader. Students continue to practice the text independently, with coaching provided by the teacher, and a dress rehearsal occurs on Thursday. On Friday, students read and perform their assigned text for an audience of classmates and other invitees. This routine is repeated on a weekly basis.

This authentic approach to fluency instruction improves not only oral reading fluency and silent reading comprehension, but student confidence and motivation as well. From across the country, teacher reports abound of reluctant readers joining the reading community after experiencing authentic fluency instruction. This is especially true in the area of performance reading, where increases in student motivation are evidenced by requests for larger performance roles and for permission to take scripts home to study (Worthy & Prater, 2002). In an urban school district in Texas, for example, researchers found significant increases in fluency, comprehension, and motivation in two 2nd-grade classes after just 10 weeks of a readers' theater program (Martinez et al., 1999). At the onset of the intervention, 75% of the students fell below the expected grade-level reading rate. After 2 and a half months, the ratio had switched, and 76% of the students were approaching or exceeding the grade-level norm; overall reading achievement gains were also noted. Motivationally, the lure of performance offered an incentive for returning to the text again and again as students worked to bring the written word to life for Friday's audience, and the infection spread into the rest of the language arts program. During their own reading time, the students chose books and wrote original plays based on characters from the books and story extensions of existing scripts. Journal comments such as "I never thought I could be a star, but I was the BEST reader today" indicate the power of authentic rehearsal performance.

Fourth-grade teacher Lorraine Griffith (Griffith & Rasinski, 2004) incorporated rehearsal and performance into her daily routine for an entire school year. It was especially effective for her Title I students. By year's end, her students achieved an average gain of over 2 years in reading achievement. Over the same period, students gained 48 words correct per minute in reading rate, nearly doubling what normally would be expected during the 4th-grade year. Ms. Griffith reported that student enthusiasm for expressive oral reading spilled over into guided reading, where her students were heard suggesting to one another during shared partner reading that they read "like characters." The performance notion spread across the curriculum, and students initiated the idea of writing content-area scripts as well.

Working in a Title I school, 2nd-grade teacher Chase Young made performance fluency instruction an integral part of his balanced literacy program (Young & Rasinski, 2009). As a result, his disfluent, reluctant readers improved in oral reading fluency and increased their comprehension, and many began to enjoy reading for the first time. His students found rehearsal and performance so motivating that they routinely were observed practicing or rehearsing their scripts before the morning bell. Although in Mr. Young's class reading rate was never an instructional goal, after implementing focused fluency instruction, the average annual gain in his class was close to double the normally expected gain.

Summing Up

"Is reading supposed to be so much fun?" asked Andy, a 2nd-grader who struggled with reading, cautiously addressing his mother after the second day of a summer reading camp that centered on the Fluency Development Lesson (FDL) and poetry. In their report of the study investigating the FDL approach, Zimmerman, Rasinski, and Melewski (2013) found that students—31 struggling readers in grades 1–4—made significant progress ($p < .001$) from pretest to posttest in word recognition, fluency, and comprehension over a period of 5 weeks. Based on a set of realistic and ambitious goals for reading-rate gains (Fuchs, Fuchs, Hamlett, Walz, & Germann, 1993), the students exceeded the realistic goal in grade 1 and the ambitious goals in grades 2, 3, and 4. Fourth-graders showed especially high gains in weekly reading-rate improvement. The ambitious goal of a .08 words per minute increase was not only met but was exceeded, with a whopping 6.2-words per minute average weekly gain. Students' comprehension across all grade levels increased an average of over 30%.

As with other effective fluency instruction, increased confidence and motivation were important by-products of this approach. Andy was typical of the students involved with the FDL, whose motivation and attitudes about reading vastly improved. Once recommended for retention because he was significantly behind his peers in reading achievement, at the end of the program he reflected on his own progress and stated, "I know how to read better, and I even *sound* like a good reader now!"

ASSESSING FLUENCY

As we mentioned earlier, fluency consists of two components that link word recognition to comprehension—automaticity in word recognition, and prosodic or expressive reading. Automaticity is most easily measured by reading rate. As students become more automatic in their word recognition, their reading speed will increase. Prosody is most easily measured in classroom settings through descriptive rubrics.

Assessing Automaticity

Deno (1985) developed an assessment of automaticity through reading called Curriculum Based Measurement (CBM), which is time-efficient, reliable, and valid. This form of oral reading fluency assessment requires readers to read a grade-level text aloud; the score is usually defined as the number of words read correctly in 1 minute (WCPM). Readers' scores are then compared against grade-level norms. Readers who are significantly and consistently below the norm for their grade level and time of year may be at risk in word-recognition automaticity and comprehension.

Assessing Prosody

Prosody develops once a degree of automaticity is established, and it is one way in which a reader constructs meaning while reading. When students read with prosody they are trying to comprehend the text (Dowhower, 1987, 1994; Schreiber, 1980, 1987, 1991;

Schreiber & Read, 1980). Because prosody does not lend itself easily to precise quantification, researchers have turned to qualitative rubrics known as prosody scales to guide its assessment (Zutell & Rasinski, 1991). Prosody scale rubrics range from word-by-word, monotonic reading (Score 1) to well-phrased and expressive reading (Score 4) (see Table 9.1).

The rubric use is simple. A reader reads a grade-level passage as a rater listens for as little as 60 seconds. At the end of the listening period, the rater consults the rubric and

Table 9.1. Prosody Scale Rubric

Score	Expression & Volume	Phrasing	Smoothness	Pace
1	Reads words as if simply trying to get them out. Little sense of trying to make text sound like natural language. Tends to read in a quiet voice.	Reads in monotone with little sense of phrase boundaries; frequently reads word-by-word.	Makes frequent extended pauses, hesitations, false starts, sound-out, repetitions, and /or multiple attempts.	Reads laboriously and with excessive slowness.
2	Begins to use voice to make text sound like natural language in some areas but not in others. Focus remains largely on pronouncing the words. Still reads in a quiet voice.	Frequently reads in two- and three-word phrases, giving the impression of choppy reading; improper stress and intonation; fails to mark ends of sentences and clauses.	Experiences several "rough spots" in text where extended pauses or hesitations are more frequent and disruptive.	Reads in a moderately slow manner.
3	Makes text sound like natural language throughout the better part of the passage. Occasionally slips into expressionless reading. Voice volume is generally appropriate throughout the text.	Reads with a mixture of run-ons, midsentence pauses for breath, and some choppiness.	Occasionally breaks smooth rhythm because of difficulties with specific words and/or structures.	Reads with an uneven mixture of fast and slow pace.
4	Reads with good expression and enthusiasm throughout the text. Varies expression and volume to match his or her interpretation of the passage.	Generally reads with good phrasing, mostly in clause and sentence units, with adequate attention to expression.	Generally reads smoothly with some breaks, but resolves word and structure difficulties quickly, usually through self-correction.	Consistently reads at conversational pace; appropriate rate throughout reading.

Source: Adapted from Zutell & Rasinski, 1991

assigns a score that most closely aligns with the prosodic characteristics of the oral reading. In using the rubric, teachers and other raters need to have a well-established sense of what constitutes appropriate phrasing and expressiveness in reading for the assigned grade level. Although it may seem that the impressionistic nature of rating oral reading fluency may challenge the reliability of such measures, a high degree of reliability with a large number of students over time has been reported in a number of studies using various forms of rubrics (Johnston, 2006; Moser, Sudweeks, Morrison, & Wilcox, 2014; Rasinski, 1985; Rasinsk, Rikli, Johnston, 2009). Moreover, these prosody rubrics have been found to be significantly correlated with students' performance on a standardized test of reading proficiency (Rasinski, Rikli, Johnston, 2009). Although prosody rubrics may not be as precise as assessments of decoding accuracy and automaticity, in the hands of knowledgeable teachers, prosody rubrics provide tools for informing instruction and give students a method for guiding their own personal fluency development.

CONCLUSION

For much of the previous century, reading fluency was obscured beneath the blanket of silent reading instruction and was thought to have little to do with overall reading ability. In this chapter, we have defined fluency as a bridge from word recognition to comprehension and discussed its relatively recent rebirth and current misunderstandings, which we maintain are a result of the emphasis on oral reading speed at the expense of understanding. We have presented evidence that reading fluency is much more than this. It is an essential element in students' reading success. Its instructional neglect has led to significant numbers of students for whom growth not only in fluency but also in general reading proficiency has been slowed. We have shown that we now have sufficient knowledge to make reading fluency an integral and authentic part of the reading curriculum. When this curricular change takes place, we feel that significant improvements in students' overall reading proficiency levels will follow.

REFERENCES

Allington, R. L. (1983). Fluency: The neglected reading goal. *The Reading Teacher, 36*, 556–561.

Cassidy, J., & Grote-Garcia, S. (2013). Common Core State Standards top the 2014 *What's Hot What's Not* survey. *Reading Today, 31*(1), 12–16.

Chall, J. S. (1996). *Stages of reading development* (2nd ed.). Fort Worth, TX: Harcourt Brace.

Chard, D. J., Vaughn, S., & Tyler, B. (2002). A synthesis of research on effective interventions for building fluency with elementary students with learning disabilities. *Journal of Learning Disabilities, 35*, 386–406.

Chomsky, C. (1976). After decoding: What? *Language Arts, 53*, 288–296.

Cowie, R., Douglas-Cowie, E., & Wichmann, A. (2002). Prosodic characteristics of skilled reading. Fluency and expressiveness in 8–10 year old readers. *Language and Speech, 45*(1), 47–82.

Daane, M. C., Campbell, J. R., Grigg, W. S., Goodman, M. J., & Oranje, A. (2005). *Fourth-grade students reading aloud: NAEP 2002 special study of oral reading*. Washington, DC: U.S. Department of Education, Institute of Education Sciences.

Deno, S. L. (1985). Curriculum-based measurement: The emerging alternative. *Exceptional Children, 52*, 219–232.

Dowhower, S. L. (1987). Effects of repeated reading on second-grade transitional readers' fluency and comprehension. *Reading Research Quarterly, 22*, 389–406.

Dowhower, S. L. (1989). Repeated reading: Theory into practice. *The Reading Teacher, 42*, 502–507.

Dowhower, S. L. (1994). Repeated reading revisited: Research into practice. *Reading and Writing Quarterly, 10*, 343–358.

Duke, N. K., Pressley, M., & Hilden, K. (2004). Difficulties in reading comprehension. In C. A. Stone, E. R. Silliman, B. J. Ehren, & K. Apel (Eds.), *Handbook of language and literacy: Development and disorders* (pp. 501–520). New York, NY: Guilford.

Frazier, L., Carlton, K., & Clifton, C. (2006). Prosodic phrasing is central to language comprehension. *Trends in Cognitive Sciences, 10*(6), 244–249.

Fuchs, L. S., Fuchs, D., Hamlett, C. L., Walz, L., & Germann, G. (1993). Formative evaluation of academic progress: How much growth can we expect? *School Psychology Review, 22*, 27–48.

Gamse, B. C., Jacob, R. T., Horst, M., Boulay, B., & Unlu, F. (2008). *Reading First impact study: Final report* (NCEE 2009-4038). Washington, DC: National Center for Education Evaluation and Regional Assistance, Institute of Education Sciences, U.S. Department of Education.

Goswami, U., Thomson, J., Richardson, U., Stainthorp, R., Hughes, D., Rosen, S., & Scott, S. K. (2002). Amplitude envelope onsets and developmental dyslexia: A new hypothesis. *Proceedings of the National Academy of Sciences of the Unites States of America, 99*(16), 10911–10916.

Griffith, L. W., & Rasinski, T. V. (2004). A focus on fluency: How one teacher incorporated fluency with her reading curriculum. *The Reading Teacher, 58*(2), 126–137.

Guiterrez-Palma, N., & Palma-Reyes, A. (2008). On the use of lexical stress in reading Spanish. *Reading and Writing, 21*(6), 645–660.

Heckleman, R. G. (1966). Using the neurological impress remedial reading technique. *Academic Therapy, 1*, 235–239, 250.

Heckleman, R. G. (1969). A neurological impress method of remedial reading. *Academic Therapy, 4*, 277–282.

Hiebert, E. H., & Mesmer, H. A. (2013). Upping the ante of text complexity in the Common Core State Standards: Examining its potential impact on young readers. *Educational Researcher, 42*, 44–51.

Hiebert, E. H., Samuels, S. J., & Rasinski, T. (2012). Comprehension-based silent reading rates: What do we know? What do we need to know? *Literacy Research and Instruction, 51*(2), 110–124.

Himmelmann, N. P., & Ladd, D. R. (2008). Prosodic description: An introduction for field workers. *Language Documentation & Conservation, 2*(2), 244–274.

Hoffman, J. (1987). Rethinking the role of oral reading. *The Elementary School Journal. 87*(3), 367–373.

Hollingsworth, P. (1978). An experimental approach to the impress method of teaching reading. *The Reading Teacher, 31*, 112–114.

Hudson, R. F., Lane, H. B., & Pullen, P. C. (2005), Reading fluency assessment and instruction: What, why, and how? *The Reading Teacher, 58*, 702–714.

Huey, E. B. (1908). *The psychology and pedagogy of reading.* Boston, MA: MIT Press.

Johnston, S. (2006). The fluency assessment system: Improving oral reading fluency with technology. In T. V. Rasinski, C. Blachowicz, & K. Lems (Eds.), *Fluency instruction: Research-based best practices* (pp. 123–140). New York, NY: Guilford.

Kuhn, M., Schwanenflugel, P., Morris, R., Morrow, L., Woo, D., Meisinger, E., Sevcik, R., Bradley, B., & Stahl, S. (2006). Teaching children to become fluent and automatic readers. *Journal of Literacy Research, 38*, 357–387.

LaBerge, D., & Samuels, S. A. (1974). Toward a theory of automatic information processing in reading. *Cognitive Psychology, 6*, 293–323.

Martinez, M., Roser, N., & Strecker, S. (1999). "I never thought I could be a star": A reader's theatre ticket to reading fluency. *The Reading Teacher, 52*(4), 326–334.

Menon, S., & Hiebert, E. H. (2011). Instructional texts and the fluency of learning disabled readers. In A. M. Franzen & R. Allington (Eds.), *Handbook of reading disability research* (pp. 57–67). New York, NY: Routledge.

Monda, L. E. (1989). *The effects of oral, silent, and listening repetitive reading on the fluency and comprehension of learning disabled students.* Unpublished doctoral dissertation, Florida State University: Tallahassee, FL.

Moser, G. P., Sudweeks, R. R., Morrison, T. G., & Wilcox, B. (2014). Reliability of ratings of children's expressive reading. *Reading Psychology, 35,* 58–79.

National Governors Association (NGA) Center for Best Practices & Council of Chief State School Officers (CCSSO). (2010). *Common Core State Standards for English language arts and literacy in history/social studies, science, and technical subjects.* Washington, DC: Authors.

National Institute of Child Health and Human Development (NICHD). (2000). *Report of the National Reading Panel. Teaching children to read: An evidence-based assessment of the scientific research literature on reading and its implications for reading instruction* (NIH Publication No. 00-4769). Washington, DC: U.S. Government Printing Office.

O'Connor, R. E., Bell, K. M., Harty, K. R., Larkin, L. K., Sackor, S. M., & Zigmond, N. (2002). Teaching reading to poor readers in the intermediate grades: A comparison of text difficulty. *Journal of Educational Psychology, 94,* 474–485.

O'Reilly, T., & McNamara, D. S. (2007). The impact of science knowledge, reading skill, and reading strategy knowledge on more traditional "high-stakes" measures of high school students' science achievement. *American Educational Research Journal, 44*(1), 161–196.

Paige, D. D. (2011a). Engaging struggling adolescent readers through situational interest: A model proposing the relationships among extrinsic motivation, oral reading fluency, comprehension, and academic achievement. *Reading Psychology, 32*(5), 395–425.

Paige, D. D. (2011b). 16 minutes with "eyes-on-text" can make a difference. Whole-class choral reading as an adolescent reading strategy. *Reading Horizons 51*(1), 1–20.

Paige, D. D., Rasinski, T. V., & Magpuri-Lavell, T. (2012). Is fluent, expressive reading important for high school readers? *Journal of Adolescent & Adult Literacy, 56*(1), 67–76.

Paige, D. D., Rasinski, T. V., Magpuri-Lavell, T., & Smith, G. (2014). Interpreting the relationships among prosody, automaticity, accuracy and silent reading comprehension in secondary students. *Journal of Literacy Research, 46*(2), 123–156.

Pearson, P. D. (1985). Changing the face of reading comprehension instruction. *The Reading Teacher, 38*(8), 724–738.

Pearson, P. D., & Gallagher, M. C. (1983). The instruction of reading comprehension. *Contemporary Educational Psychology, 8*(3), 317–344.

Perfetti, C. (1985). *Reading ability.* New York, NY: Oxford University Press.

Pikulski, J. J., & Chard, D. J. (2005). Fluency: Bridge between decoding and reading comprehension. *The Reading Teacher, 58*(6), 510–519.

Pinnell, G. S., Pikulski, J. J., Wixon, K. K., Campbell, J. R., Gough, P. B., & Beatty, A. (1995). *Listening to children read aloud.* Washington, DC: Office of Educational Research and Improvement, U.S. Department of Education.

Pumfrey, P. D. (1987). Paired reading: Promise and pitfalls. *Educational Research, 28*(2), 89–94.

Rasinski, T. V. (1985). *A study of factors involved in readertext interactions that contribute to fluency in reading.* Unpublished doctoral dissertation. Columbus, OH: The Ohio State University.

Rasinski, T. V. (1990). Effects of repeated reading and listening-while-reading on reading fluency. *Journal of Educational Research, 83*(3), 147–150.

Rasinski, T. V. (1995). Fast Start: A parental involvement reading program for primary grade students. In W. Linek & E. Sturtevant (Eds.), *Generations of literacy: Seventeenth yearbook of the College Reading Association* (pp. 301–312). Harrisonburg, VA: College Reading Association.

Rasinski, T. V., Homan, S., & Biggs, M. (2009). Teaching reading fluency to struggling readers: Method, materials, and evidence. *Reading and Writing Quarterly, 25,* 192–204.

Rasinski, T. V., & Padak, N. D. (1998). How elementary students referred for compensatory reading instruction perform on school-based measures of word recognition, fluency, and comprehension. *Reading Psychology, 19,* 185–216.

Rasinski, T. V., Padak, N. D., Linek, W. L., & Sturtevant, E. (1994). Effects of fluency development on urban second-grade readers. *Journal of Educational Research, 87,* 158–165.

Rasinski, T. V., Padak, N. D., McKeon, C. A., Wilfong, L. G., Friedauer, J. A., & Heim, P. (2005). Is reading fluency a key for successful high school reading? *Journal of Adolescent & Adult Literacy, 49*(1), 22–27.

Rasinski, T. V., Reutzel, C. R., Chard, D., & Linan-Thompson, S. (2011). Reading fluency. In M. L. Kamil, P. D. Pearson, E. B. Moje, & P. Afflerbach (Eds.), *Handbook of reading research* (Vol. 4, pp. 286–319). New York, NY: Routledge.

Rasinski, T. V., Rikli, A., & Johnston, S. (2009). Reading fluency: More than automaticity? More than a concern for the primary grades? *Literacy Research and Instruction, 48*(4), 350–361.

Rasinski, T. V., Samuels, S. J., Hiebert, E., Petscher, Y., & Feller, K. (2011). The relationship between silent reading fluency instructional protocol on students' reading comprehension and achievement in an urban school setting. *Reading Psychology: An International Quarterly, 32,* 75–97.

Rasinski, T. V., & Stevenson, B. (2005). The effects of Fast Start reading: A fluency-based home involvement reading program, on the reading achievement of beginning readers. *Reading Psychology: An International Quarterly, 26,* 109–125.

Rasinski, T. V., Yildirim, K., & Nageldinger, J. (2011). Building fluency through the phrased text lesson, *The Reading Teacher, 65,* 252–255.

Rose, T. L., & Beattie, J. R. (1986). Relative effects of teacher-directed and taped previewing on oral reading. *Learning Disability Quarterly, 9*(3), 193–199.

Rose, T. L., & Sherry, L. (1984). Relative effects of two previewing procedures on LD adolescents' oral reading performance. *Learning Disability Quarterly, 7,* 39–44.

Rosenblatt, L. M. (1994). *The reader, the text, and the poem: The transactional theory of the literary work.* Carbondale, IL: Southern Illinois University Press.

Rosenblatt, L. M. (2004). The transactional theory of reading and writing. In R. B. Ruddell & N. J. Unrau (Eds.), *Theoretical models and processes of reading* (5th ed., pp. 1363–1398). Newark, DE: International Reading Association.

Samuels, S. J. (1979). The method of repeated readings. *The Reading Teacher, 32*(4), 403–408.

Samuels, S. J. (2007). The DIBELS test: Is speed of barking at print what we mean by reading fluency? *Reading Research Quarterly, 42*(4), 563–566.

Samuels, S. J., Rasinski, T., & Hiebert, E. H. (2011). Eye movements and reading: What teachers need to know. In S. J. Samuels, & A. E. Farstrup (Eds.), *What research has to say about reading instruction* (4th ed., pp. 25–50). Newark, DE: International Reading Association.

Sandermann, A. A., & Collier, R. (1997). Prosodic phrasing and comprehension. *Language and Speech, 40*(4), 391–409.

Schreiber, P. A. (1980). On the acquisition of reading fluency. *Journal of Reading Behavior, 12*(3), 177–186.

Schreiber, P. A. (1987). Prosody and structure in children's syntactic processing. In R. Horowitz & S. J. Samuels (Eds.), *Comprehending oral and written language* (pp. 243–270). New York, NY: Academic Press.

Schreiber, P. A. (1991). Understanding prosody's role in reading acquisition. *Theory Into Practice, 30*(3), 158–164.

Schreiber, P. A., & Read, C. (1980). Children's use of phonetic cues in spelling, parsing, and—maybe—reading. *Bulletin of the Orton Society, 30,* 209–224.

Stahl, S. A., & Heubach, K. M. (2005). Fluency-oriented reading instruction. *Journal of Literacy Research, 37*(1), 26–60.

Therrien, W. J. (2004). Fluency and comprehension gains as a result of repeated reading. *Remedial and Special Education, 25*(4), 252–261.

Topping, K. J. (1995). *Paired reading, spelling & writing: The handbook for teachers and parents.* London, UK: Cassell.

Topping, K. J. (2001). Paired reading with peers and parents: Factors in effectiveness and new developments. In C. Harrison & M. Coles (Eds.), *The reading for real handbook* (2nd ed., pp. 170–185). London, UK: Routledge Falmer.

Topping, K. J., & Lindsay, G. A. (1992). Paired reading: A review of the literature. *Research Papers in Education, 7*(3), 199–246.

Topping, K. J., Thurston, A., McGavock, K., & Conlin, N. (2012). Outcomes and process in reading tutoring. *Educational Research, 54*(3), 239–258.

Valencia, S. W., & Buly, M. R. (2004). Behind test scores: What struggling readers really need. *The Reading Teacher, 57,* 520–531.

Vaughn, S., Chard, S., Bryant, D. P., Coleman, M., Tyler, B. J., Linan-Thompson, S., & Kouzekanani, K. (2000). Fluency and comprehension interventions for third-grade students. *Remedial and Special Education, 21*(6), 325–335.

Willingham, D. (2007). The usefulness of brief instruction in reading comprehension strategies. *American Educator, 30,* 39–50.

Worthy, J., & Prater, K. (2002). "I thought about it all night": Readers theatre for fluency and motivation. *The Reading Teacher, 56*(3), 294–297.

Young, C., & Rasinski, T. (2009). Implementing readers theatre as an approach to classroom fluency instruction. *The Reading Teacher, 63*(1), 4–13.

Zimmerman, B., Rasinski, T., & Melewski, M. (2013). When kids can't read, what a focus on fluency can do: The Reading Clinic Experience at Kent State University. In E. Ortleib & E. Cheek (Eds.), *Advanced literacy practices: From the clinic to the classroom* (pp. 137–160). Bingley, UK: Emerald Group.

Zutell, J., & Rasinski, T. V. (1991). Training teachers to attend to their students' oral reading fluency. *Theory Into Practice, 30,* 211–217.

CHAPTER 10

The Potential Impact of the Common Core State Standards on Reading Volume

Richard L. Allington, Monica T. Billen,
& Kimberly McCuiston

Thirty years ago, the report *Becoming a Nation of Readers,* issued by the Commission on Reading for the National Academy of Education, straightforwardly recommended that students should spend more time reading independently (Anderson, Hiebert, Scott, & Wilkinson, 1985). Basing the recommendations on the best available evidence at the time, the report's authors advocated that, by grades 3 and 4, at least 2 hours per week of in-school independent reading should be the norm in classrooms and that this time in school should be augmented with reading outside of school. But few students were receiving such opportunities, Anderson et al. (1985) concluded. Available evidence at the time suggested that typical American students spent less than 10% of their time in school (approximately 7–8 minutes daily) engaged in silent reading.

More recently, Brenner, Hiebert, and Tompkins (2009) reported a similar amount of silent independent reading in 3rd-grade classrooms. In other words, there seems to have been little improvement in the volume (amount) of silent reading that children do during the school day. What is, perhaps, most discouraging is that Brenner et al. reported that almost a quarter of the students in the classrooms studied engaged in no reading at all during their 90- to 120-minute reading instructional block.

Research evidence to date suggests, as Hiebert and Martin (2009) noted, that "even in a time when policies mandate an increase in the amount of time spent on reading instruction . . . the time students spend reading texts has not increased substantially from earlier eras" (p. 25). It remains unclear why so little time is allocated to silent independent reading in American classrooms. Furthermore, with the recent adoption of Common Core State Standards for English Language Arts (CCSS ELA), we question whether the major tenets of the standards will influence reading volume.

In this chapter, we begin by presenting research relevant to reading volume and briefly address how current literacy practices have adhered to that evidence. The second section reviews the role of reading volume in the CCSS-ELA standards and the Advice to Publishers (Coleman & Pimentel, 2012a, 2012b). The final section discusses our recommendations for improved instructional practices in light of the Common Core State Standards.

LOOKING BACK: HISTORICAL BACKGROUND OF READING VOLUME

In this section, we review the evidence that does exist, in a variety of forms, indicating that reading volume is related to reading proficiency. We argue that although researchers have long known about the correlation between reading volume and reading achievement, a growing body of evidence now asserts a causal relationship between the two, not just a correlational relationship. In other words, we argue that accumulated evidence indicates that students' reading proficiency can be improved by increasing the volume of their reading.

The question we address in this section is: How do current practices build on the evidence we have gained over the past 50 years? Current practice seems to allocate little time for students to participate as readers, responsible for their own texts during the school day (Hiebert & Martin, 2009). One explanation for this state of affairs may lie with the conclusions of the National Reading Panel (NRP, 2000). We begin by summarizing the NRP's conclusions regarding independent reading. Following this description, we describe the meta-analyses of experimental research that have been conducted, subsequent to the review of the NRP. Finally, we present an overview of the types of research that the NRP did not consider because of NRPs emphasis on experiments with random assignment.

The Report of the NRP

The NRP acknowledged that correlational evidence showed the value of independent reading. In most domains of life, the more individuals participate in a set of activities, the greater their expertise (Ericsson, Krampe, & Tesch-Romer, 1993). The same would appear to be true with reading, according to correlational data. Students who read more have better fluency, vocabulary, and comprehension (e.g., Cipielewski & Stanovich, 1992; Foorman et al., 2006; Kuhn, 2005; Swanborn & DeGlopper, 1999). But the group of astute researchers who were members of the National Reading Panel held out the possibility that this effect can be explained in alternative ways. For example, better readers may simply choose to read more. After all, the outcomes were correlational, and correlations do not imply causation.

When the panel looked at experiments aimed to increase students' independent reading, it was unable to find strong evidence either for or against the efficacy of independent reading. The panel concluded that "even though encouraging students to read more is intuitively appealing, there is still not sufficient research evidence obtained from studies of high methodological quality to support the idea that such efforts reliably increase how much students read or that such programs result in improved reading skills" (NRP, 2000, pp. 12–13).

Numerous scholars raised questions about this interpretation of the research (e.g., J. W. Cunningham, 2001). Krashen (2001), in particular, criticized the NRP report for failing to distinguish between studies that lasted for 10 days and studies that lasted for a much longer period of time (e.g., a full school year). Krashen argued that the evidence supporting the role of increasing volume is far more powerful when only the longer-term studies are included. He also argued that the NRP's finding that there were no significant differences in reading growth between treatment students (increased reading volume) and control students (business-as-usual students with no attempt to increase reading volume) should be interpreted as demonstrating that extensive reading activity is as powerful as whatever tasks the control students were engaged in during the school day.

An example of a long-term study was conducted by Fader and McNeil (1968) with incarcerated youth. Though both groups were enrolled in an English class, one group received a supplementary supply of trade books, magazines, and newspapers that they were encouraged to read, while a second group received neither texts nor encouragement to read. After a year, those in the text group had higher reading comprehension scores by more than a grade level on a standardized reading assessment. The increase in reading achievement of the treatment students was more than twice as large as the increase in reading achievement of those students in the second group who were not provided the various texts to read.

Meta-Analyses Following the NRP Conclusions

Following the NRP's conclusion regarding the lack of experimental evidence for in-school, independent reading, several research teams have revisited the existing literature on independent reading. One of these meta-analyses was conducted by Lewis and Samuels (2005). They arrived at several conclusions from their analyses of 48 studies on in-school, independent reading. First, not a single study in the sample produced a negative achievement outcome for in-school, independent reading. Second, there was a moderately strong, positive relationship between reading volume and reading outcomes based on experimental studies. That is, students who have in-school independent reading time, in addition to regular reading instruction, do significantly better on measures of reading achievement than peers who have not had independent reading time. Third, the effects for in-school, independent reading time appeared to be strongest for students in the lower grades, struggling readers, and English language learners.

Mol and Bus (2011) also carried out a meta-analysis of 99 studies of print exposure (reading volume) and components of reading growth with students from preschool to high school. Noteworthy was their finding that weaker readers seem to benefit more from increased reading volume than better readers. In other words, "Leisure time reading is especially important for low-ability readers. We found that the basic reading skills of children in primary and middle school with a lower ability level were more strongly related to print exposure as compared with higher ability readers" (p. 271). They also noted that while print exposure explains 12% of the variance in oral language skills among primary grade readers, by high school print exposure explains 30% of the variance. This finding, Mol and Bus indicated, suggests an upward spiral of causality, with more extensive reading experiences leading to a longer-term payoff for academic reading.

Lindsay (2013) conducted a meta-analysis focused on increasing book access. In examining the outcomes of rigorous experimental studies (where students were randomly assigned to conditions), Lindsay found that the impact of increasing book access on reading achievement produced a moderate effect size of $d = .435$. Access also increased students' motivation to read, with a large effect size of $d = .967$. Lindsay's conclusion was that increasing students' access to text produces effects that are one to four times as large as those in the average intervention, depending on the outcome variable of focus. This meta-analysis indirectly addressed reading volume by looking at the results of improving children's access to books they could elect to read, finding that studies that experimentally improved access to reading materials resulted in gains in reading achievement that were far superior to the gains produced by other changes to the instructional environment. In effect, schools in search of a reform strategy focused on enhancing reading achievement could simply expand the number of books available that students could read with a reasonable level of accuracy and understanding and also that students wanted to read for student selection.

Correlational Analyses

Finally, there are the correlational studies that the NRP deemed inappropriate for inclusion. As Stanovich (2007) has pointed out, just because a correlation has limited value as a causative inference does not mean that correlation studies are not important to science. There are areas of instructional practice where it is difficult, if not impossible, to manipulate particular variables. Opportunity to read is one such area. We are hard-pressed to identify areas of learning in virtually any human endeavor where some practice is not required. Similarly, in reading, it would be difficult (if not impossible) to conduct a school-based study where one group of students is not allowed to read in order to determine the effects of independent reading. Correlational analyses in an area such as opportunity to practice a skill like reading are important for considering the degrees of differences or variables that make independent reading more effective.

Topping, Samuels, and Paul (2007) analyzed data from the Accelerated Reader database, using computerized records of reading activity from more than 45,000 students in grades 1 through 12, although most of the data were derived from the records of readers in grades 1 through 6. The researchers examined the effects of two predictor variables: (1) volume of reading (an analysis of the numbers of books read) and (2) quality of reading (based on the comprehension of the books read) and their interaction. Only when the comprehension assessment scores reached the 80–85% correct range was volume of reading linked to reading growth. In addition, the effect of the volume measures was mediated by what occurred in the classrooms where students were reading the self-selected books. Topping et al. concluded that time spent reading without guidance (which they assumed was more likely to be the case when comprehension was low) had only a modest influence on reading achievement. Merely allocating time for independent reading is not sufficient in classrooms, at least when reading achievement is the focus.

In a follow-up analysis, Topping, Samuels, and Paul (2008) noted that when students read substantially challenging texts, little reading growth was observed. Similarly, reading texts with low levels of challenge also had little effect on reading development. This finding suggests that students benefit most from increases in reading volume only when the selected texts offer a modest level of challenge (akin to a Goldilocks effect—not too hard, not too easy), thus supporting research on the effects of text difficulty in developing proficiency (Allington, McCuiston, & Billen, in press).

Braten, Lie, Andreassen, and Olaussen (1999) reported on the role that reading volume played in the development of word recognition. They summarized their findings by noting that phonological processing and nonverbal intelligence did not correlate with reading experience; however, the amount of leisure-time reading—part of one's volume of reading—directly influenced the development of students' orthographic processing skills. Reading volume, they surmised, seems to correlate with the skills associated with word recognition. Unsurprisingly, students who read more showed better word recognition than their peers who did less voluntary reading.

A study of the impact of instructional practices by Foorman et al. (2006) provides additional insights into learning. They observed 107 grade 1 and 2 teachers and used hierarchical linear modeling (HLM) to examine how tasks, teachers, and initial reading ability related to reading growth. They found that the time allocated to text reading loaded positively on its own factor, while time spent in preparation to read and giving directions loaded negatively. Only time allocated to text reading explained any of the variance on any of the outcome measures, including word recognition, decoding, and passage comprehension. No other time factor, including time spent on phonemic awareness, word recognition, or decoding, was related to reading growth.

Using an innovative procedure for predicting reading achievement, A. E. Cunningham and Stanovich (1991) examined the relationship between performance on an assessment that they called the Title Recognition Test (an unobtrusive and indirect measure of reading volume) and the reading achievement of a group of students from grades 4, 5, and 6. Knowledge of book titles was significantly correlated with decoding, spelling, knowledge of word meanings, and general knowledge. A. E. Cunningham and Stanovich also demonstrated that the quantity of students' reading significantly contributed to their verbal abilities, including growth in both vocabulary and overall knowledge, even when general ability and phonological coding skill—both potential contributing variables to vocabulary and knowledge—were controlled. The results of this study suggest that reading supports students in building vocabulary and knowledge.

In a second study, A. E. Cunningham and Stanovich (1997) examined the relationship among reading achievement at grade 1, volume of independent reading, and later reading achievement. They concluded that "individual differences in exposure to print can predict differences in growth in reading comprehension ability throughout the elementary grades and thereafter" (p. 940). Grade 1 reading achievement (as well as grade 3 and 5 reading achievement) was reliably linked to exposure to print, as assessed at grade 11, even after parsing out grade 11 reading comprehension ability.

Similarly, a study conducted by Guthrie, Wigfield, Metsala, and Cox (2000) led to the conclusion that the volume of reading that students did predicted their reading comprehension in grades 3, 5, 8, and 10, even when pupil factors such as past reading achievement, prior knowledge, and motivation were controlled statistically. Guthrie et al. reported a positive correlation between reading volume and reading comprehension achievement. This was true even after removing a number of variables that might influence reading comprehension.

Guthrie, Schafer, and Huang (2001) provided additional evidence from an engaged reading perspective based upon student reports of reading activity and reading achievement on the National Assessment of Educational Progress (NAEP). They concluded that the opportunity to read increased the amount of engaged reading despite demographic differences such as ethnicity or mother's educational background. The authors determined that reading achievement was increased by reading engagement, which was influenced by having the opportunity to read. They noted that these data support in-class independent reading as a way to indirectly improve reading achievement.

Examining survey data that had been collected as part of the NAEP from 1971 to 1999, Campbell, Hombo, and Mazzeo (2000) found that those students who reported that they typically read six or more pages daily had higher reading achievement scores than students who reported reading five or fewer pages in the same time period. By 12th grade, students who described themselves as reading more than 20 pages daily had the highest level of achievement.

A variety of correlational studies has linked reading volume and reading achievement. Although this does not necessarily indicate a causal relationship, the substantial pool of studies should be seriously considered in any thinking about the potential role of reading volume on reading development. We will, as did J. W. Cunningham (2001), point to the simple fact that correlational data illustrating a relationship between tobacco use and lung cancer led to the U.S. government's decision to require warning labels on tobacco products. For literacy development, we might consider a similar warning label: *Caution: Failure to read extensively may result in more limited development of reading proficiencies.*

Multiple Perspectives on Reading Volume

In addition to the meta-analyses and correlational analyses that suggest reading volume in schools is highly related to achievement, other studies—not directly attending to reading volume in school—suggest that students need sufficient opportunities to read to become proficient.

One such study is the diary study conducted by Anderson, Wilson, and Fielding (1988). In that project, 5th-graders completed daily diaries detailing how they spent their out-of-school time for periods of 8 and 26 weeks. Anderson et al. concluded that reading books predicted several measures of reading achievement, including gains in reading achievement between 2nd and 5th grade.

Another study suggesting the importance of reading opportunities was done by Shany and Biemiller (1995), who experimentally studied the effects of teacher-assisted reading and tape-assisted reading on reading achievement. One experimental group received extra reading practice with adult assistance (pronouncing any mispronounced words), while the other experimental group received extra reading practice with audiotapes of the texts to assist the reading. Students in both experimental groups read more books in and out of the classroom than the control group. Treatment students read five to ten times as many words as control group readers during this 16-week study. The differences between the two experimental groups were staggering. The tape-assisted group had 70% more practice than the experimental group with adult assistance. Most students in the tape-assisted group read through 2.5 years' worth of basal stories in 64 days (32 hours) of practice! Students in both experimental groups performed better on measures of reading comprehension, listening comprehension, reading speed and accuracy, and verbal efficiency. Comparing the treatments, the tape-assisted group scored significantly better in listening comprehension. Students in the two treatment groups had similar scores on reading comprehension, reading speed and accuracy, and verbal efficiency. Neither treatment, however, improved students' word identification in isolation or their ability to decode on the Woodcock Reading Mastery Test. Shany and Biemiller (1995) surmised that increasing students' reading volume increased their reading competence. The study also supported the idea that increasing reading volume itself, without continuous active teacher support, could benefit students' reading achievement.

Increased reading of text in a tutoring context has also proven to be influential in increasing young readers' word reading and spelling. Vadasy, Sanders, and Peyton (2005) experimentally compared two forms of instruction: word study with scaffolded oral reading of text and word study alone. Spending part of a tutoring session on oral text reading resulted in significantly higher fluency, word reading, and spelling than spending an entire tutoring period on word study. In other words, younger readers benefited more from lessons that extended the volume of reading as opposed to expanding the number of minutes of skills work, specifically word study.

Another area of research that shows the effects of independent reading on achievement comes from research on summer reading. Allington et al. (2010) conducted an experiment where low-income, minority children in grades 1 and 2 were randomly selected to participate in a summer reading program while a comparable group served as the control group. Each student in the intervention group could pick 15 titles from more than 600 trade book selections for each of three summers. The distribution of self-selected trade books was the sole intervention. Control students received no books for summer reading.

After receiving the summer books for three consecutive summers, the intervention students exhibited statistically significant better reading achievement than children from the control group. Distributing summer books to these low-income children resulted in roughly an additional year's worth of reading growth when compared with the control-group children.

Randomized controlled experimental comparisons directly link increased reading volume to improved reading achievement. These studies have taken multiple forms, but in each case children who engaged in a greater volume of reading outperformed control-group children in reading proficiency on standardized tests of reading achievement. Thus, we think it is safe to say, contrary to the conclusions of the NRP report, that increasing the volume of reading that children do will result in improved reading achievement.

LOOKING FORWARD: CCSS CRITERIA AND READING VOLUME

Considering these findings from key research studies, we might anticipate that the priority in educational standards would be to emphasize reading volume. Within the CCSS ELA, however, the relationship between reading proficiency and opportunities to read is not addressed directly. Even in Standard 10, which addresses students' capacity to read increasingly more complex texts across the school years, the issue of reading volume is not mentioned directly. To achieve the worthy goal of Standard 10, the CCSS call for students to read a vast array of classic, contemporary, and challenging informational texts in order to develop bodies of knowledge and broaden their insights and perspectives. Another element of the CCSS ELA is the incorporation of seminal reading materials, including myths and stories from around the world, foundational U.S. documents, and works of English literature. The focus of the CCSS is not just on reading greater amounts of literature. Students are also expected to read critical texts in content areas, including mathematics, science, technology, and social studies.

The CCSS are a set of standards—proficiencies that students are supposed to display at particular levels. They are not a curriculum; in fact, the CCSS writers were clear that curriculum development was not their purview. However, the situation changed considerably with the release of the Publishers' Criteria for ELA, written by the two principal architects of the ELA section of the CCSS—David Coleman and Sue Pimentel (2012a,

2012b). These documents were intended to guide publishers and curriculum developers to ensure that the materials used for instruction in ELA aligned to the standards. Coleman and Pimentel produced two related but separate sets of criteria: one for grades K–2 and the second for grades 3–12. The Publishers' Criteria gave rather specific suggestions regarding what materials are appropriate instantiations of the CCSS and what materials are not. The explicitness of the documents and the credentials of the authors have resulted in substantial interest in their contents. As states and districts draw on these documents to generate curriculum aligned with the standards and/or use the guidelines to evaluate the materials and programs available in the marketplace (and, in the case of some states, mandate materials based on the guidelines) the Publishers' Criteria promise to have a strong influence on the materials that teachers have and, as a result, affect teaching practice. This expected outcome goes beyond Coleman and Pimentel's intention for the Publishers' Criteria guidelines to support teachers in obtaining effective and appropriate tools, not dictate classroom practice.

Publishers' Criteria for CCSS-ELA—Grades K–2

The Publishers' Criteria document for grades K–2 is organized into three sections, each of which identifies key criteria for a particular component of classroom learning and instruction: (1) reading foundations (e.g., curriculum), (2) text selections, and (3) questions and tasks.

Reading foundations. Coleman and Pimentel (2012a) noted that the first 3 years of classroom instruction (K–2) are critical for later success in education and that it is important to set a solid literacy foundation during these early grades. Reading foundation includes deciphering words so that students can be prepared to independently read complex text closely. Also included in the reading foundation section of the Publishers' Criteria is the need for flexible materials for students at various levels, the need for materials that include foundational principles (such as concepts of print, phonological awareness, and phonics), the need for fluency and vocabulary instruction, and frequent assessments to measure students' progress.

Text selection. Coleman and Pimentel (2012a) discussed the importance of text selection in the second section of the document, especially the need for school texts to have the overall goal of containing meaningful content that supports (and requires) comprehension. This underlying goal applies to both informational and narrative texts, which are to be equally distributed in primary classrooms.

Some of these texts should be ones that teachers read aloud, according to the Publishers' Criteria, but there should also be opportunities for students to confront and comprehend grade-level texts. Two elements of the statement bear consideration, especially from the perspective of struggling readers: first, that opportunities to confront and comprehend grade-level texts should be consistent and, second, that this goal is for all students.

The amount of text that students should read is not addressed directly, but there is an indirect reference in the statement about independent reading. According to Coleman and Pimentel (2012a), students should also have opportunities to read additional materials independently. These additional materials should be ones that appeal to students' interests and that simultaneously develop their knowledge and joy of reading. The proportion of an ELA block of time that should be devoted to independent reading is left unspecified, but Coleman and Pimentel note that the presence of additional materials (from publishers) is intended to "increase the regular independent reading" (p. 6). Does *regular* imply a daily event? Or does *regular* mean a once-a-week event, such as the typical Friday afternoon recreational reading period? The definition of *regular* is left up to classroom teachers to determine.

Questions and tasks. For the third key criterion for implementing CCSS in grades K–2—questions and tasks connected to high-quality texts—the emphasis is on the need for text-dependent questions. Rather than using generic or knowledge-based questions, such as those that might ask students to identify experiences similar to that in the text, these text-dependent questions should ask students to think about text carefully and find evidence from the text itself. The questions that publishers and curriculum developers are asked to provide engage students directly with the text and don't avoid challenging texts or segments. Guidance provided by publishers for teachers should support them in engaging students directly with the text as they use the text to answer questions about specific content. Teachers' questions should also move students to acquire knowledge from texts. Through this process of interacting with the text, it is assumed that students will improve their ability to deal with challenging texts. However, there is little evidence to support this assumption.

Publishers' Criteria for CCSS-ELA, Grades 3–12

Similar to the Publishers' Criteria for grades K–2, Coleman and Pimentel (2012b) have offered criteria on the most significant elements of CCSS for grades 3–12 with the aim of providing guidelines for publishers and curriculum developers in developing curricula that will provide teachers with the kind of support that ensures instruction that is aligned with and supportive of the standards. The Publishers' Criteria for grades 3–12 include two of the foci of the grade K–2 document—text selection and questions and tasks. They also attend to academic vocabulary and writing based on sources and research.

Text selection. In regard to text selection for grades 3–12, Coleman and Pimentel (2012b) reiterated the suggestion from the grade K–2 document that complex, grade-level texts are needed for all students, even those who are behind their peers. The authors also mentioned that additional materials (e.g., books, magazines, newspapers, websites) should be used to increase students' independent reading of texts.

Additionally, the Publishers' Criteria say there is a need for shorter, challenging texts at each grade. We assume the criteria suppose that shorter complex texts may be easier to use in instructional contexts than longer complex texts would be. Also unique to upper grades is the inclusion of novels, plays, and other full-length texts. During the period of middle school and beyond (beginning with grade 6), the criteria indicate that the balance between narrative and informational texts should shift substantially in favor of literary nonfiction texts that merit close reading. These texts, the document argues, will help students become college and career ready.

Questions and tasks. Similar to the elements discussed for grades K–2, high-quality questions and tasks are key criteria in the CCSS for upper grades. These high-quality questions and tasks should be text-dependent and should require use of textual evidence, while not encouraging students to rely on their existing knowledge from experiences or other texts. In classrooms where students know that text-dependent questions are emphasized, the anticipation is that students will be motivated to read texts carefully. Additionally, students in the upper grades should compare and synthesize information from multiple sources. However, making "connections between texts . . . should not supersede the close examination of each specific text" (p. 8). Students in grades 3–12 should also be required to "demonstrate their independent capacity to read at the appropriate level of complexity and depth" (p. 8). Coleman and Pimentel (2012b) also have warned publishers to avoid offering activities that are not grounded in the text that students have read.

Academic vocabulary. Academic vocabulary is emphasized to a greater extent in the Publishers' Criteria for the upper grades than for lower ones. In particular, the criteria note that the guidance teachers receive with materials and lessons should focus on the academic vocabulary that characterizes complex text. This vocabulary should be used in all forms of language instruction—reading, writing, listening, and speaking. Instead of highlighting technical terms that may be unique to a particular discipline, words that are used in a wide range of complex texts should be emphasized in the ELA classroom. In addition, students should be asked to analyze the impact of the words in texts.

Analysis of Publishers' Criteria

Although there are differences among the upper and lower grade CCSS, there are some foundational similarities across all grades. One such similarity is the focus on the use of complex texts for all students. However, decades of research make quite clear that primary grade readers, at least, need a lot of experience with high-success texts (e.g., Allington et al., in press). High-success texts are those that can be read with 98% accuracy and 90% comprehension. Likewise, Mesmer and Hiebert (submitted) report that few grade 3 students would be able to read the kind of texts that the CCSS suggest are appropriate. Students would experience difficulties both because of the difficulty level and the length of the texts. In other words, when texts contained a larger number of infrequent words and as sentences and texts got longer, the numbers of students who could successfully read the texts dropped. Both Allington et al. (in press) and Mesmer and Hiebert (submitted) cautioned that a heavy diet of texts with which particular students struggle could result in even higher levels of failure—and consequent frustration—than already exist. Spending time on difficult texts—or even listening to more capable readers (through audio, the teacher, or peers) read the text—may discourage literacy engagement and development in the very students for whom national initiatives such as the CCSS would seem to be intended (Corno & Snow, 1986). In addition to using more complex texts, the CCSS hold that all grade levels should focus on complex questions and tasks that are grounded in texts.

In the Publishers' Criteria, Coleman and Pimentel (2012b) acknowledge that students also need to read independently on a daily basis. They note that these texts are to be in addition to those that anchor the instructional program. Precisely how much independent reading should be done is not specified, but Coleman and Pimentel do note that these additional texts should appeal to students' interest, and should, at the same time, cultivate their knowledge base along with a joy of reading.

Should these texts for independent reading be self-selected? The Publishers' Criteria leave that dimension uncertain. There is, however, substantial research documenting the consistently large positive impact of student self-selection of texts, on both the development of reading comprehension and motivation for reading (Guthrie & Humenick, 2004; Lindsay, 2013).

In sum, although the CCSS' emphasis on engaging children with high-quality texts is heartening, we find other aspects of the standards worrisome, as detailed above.

RECOMMENDATIONS FOR READING-VOLUME PRACTICES

This chapter has introduced much of the key research that has been done on reading volume. Generally, this research has found that reading volume strongly influenced reading achievement. Although the CCSS ELA "focus on what is most essential" (Key Design Consideration, 2012), reading volume is not a major component of the standards. Independent reading is included in CCSS, but it is considered an additional component. We do not believe that independent reading or increasing reading volume should be pushed to the back burner.

In light of decades of research on reading volume, we recommend that practitioners find ways to incorporate more independent reading into their curriculum. This will prepare students to engage in the additional CCSS-mandated complex text passages and to answer the complex questions and tasks. Teachers should consider the following research-based recommendations in developing their independent reading programs.

Select Texts That Students Can Read Accurately

Generally, it does not seem to make sense to give students classroom time to read texts that they are not able to read with accuracy and automaticity. When they are reading independently, students need to be able to read texts accurately.

However, there may be an important difference between beginning and mature readers. Primary grade readers are still developing their reading proficiencies. The evidence currently available indicates that reading with high levels of accuracy is particularly important for beginning readers (c.f., Allington et al., in press; Brophy & Evertson, 1981; Fisher et al., 1980).

With older students, the number of unknown words in a text remains important. Pressley and Allington (2015) note that research suggests that texts that present a modest challenge do seem to be more motivating to students than are texts where students recognize every word easily. The problem is determining just how many previously unknown words might be in a text without undermining students' motivation to read. Likewise, interest in the topic of a text, as well as prior knowledge of the topic, seem to be important factors when considering a text's appropriateness for older students. Finally, the amount and type of teacher support that is available influences a text's appropriateness. In other words, determining how appropriate texts are for use with students is a complicated process.

Teachers should be conscious of a progression that includes opportunities for students to be supported in reading increasingly harder texts. However, there is little evidence available to provide guidance about the amount of scaffolding students will need as well as what types of scaffolding are appropriate. Similarly, we know too little about the degree of difference between a reader's reading level and the optimum difficulty of a text to be read. Concerns around text difficulty may be more important in the primary grade classroom than in the middle school classroom. However, there is far too little research to help educators decide just how wide the gap might be between a student's reading level and the difficulty of appropriate text.

The Publishers' Criteria suggest that the classroom should emphasize challenging texts more than texts with which students have sufficient facility to read with automaticity and meaningfulness. Yet, at the present time we lack descriptions of classrooms where teachers have been able to provide the appropriate diet of texts to challenge students while also supporting them in attaining word-recognition automaticity and comprehension while also fostering students' motivation to continue reading.

In contexts where there is little support (from teachers, peers, or electronic supports) for students to read on their own, as in the independent segment of a reading class, it is important that texts not be so challenging that students cannot make sense of what they are reading on their own. Access to books *that can be read* has been shown to be a powerful factor in fostering both voluntary reading and reading development (Krashen, 2004; Lindsay, 2013; McQuillan & Au, 2001). The Publishers' Criteria recognize that classroom experiences should include times when students can read texts that are enjoyable and do not require effortful and tedious word recognition and that such times should not be forgotten as teachers and administrators move to implement the CCSS.

Offer High-Interest Texts

In addition to improving access to texts generally, it is important for teachers to enhance students' access to books they want to read, books they find interesting (e.g., Guthrie & Humenick, 2004). Of course, students are more likely to read if they care about what they are reading. Although including complex texts is a major tenet of the CCSS, teachers cannot forget that interest is also recognized within the standards and in the Publishers' Criteria (Coleman & Pimentel, 2012b). Though the CCSS may focus on complex texts more heavily than has been the case with previous reform efforts, teachers cannot forget how important it is to support students in finding books that engage them and develop areas of interest and knowledge.

Increase Reading Time During the School Day

Given how little research supports the use of workbooks and test preparation activities, it is surprising that upwards of 70% of reading instructional time is currently spent using such materials or engaged in such activities (Osborn & Decker, 1993; Pianta et al., 2007; Turner, 1995). Recently, Connor (2009) reported that when primary grade teachers in high-poverty schools had students engaged in reading and writing activity during the school day, children made more progress than when they were engaged in other activities commonly found as components of daily reading lessons. Her data suggest that when teachers reduce the time children spend on workbook pages and skill drills, and replace that time with actual reading activity, teachers can expect students' reading proficiency to improve.

Teachers have known for a long time that reading growth is related to the amount of instructional time allocated for reading lessons (e.g., Guthrie, Martuza, & Seifert, 1979), but it has been less clear what exactly should occur during the time allocated for reading lessons. What does seem to be emerging as an important aspect of reading lessons is the volume of reading children are expected to do. However, as Topping et al. (2008) noted, simply allocating more time for independent reading may not be sufficient, especially for some students. Even Connor (2009) noted that children enter classrooms with an array of proficiencies as well as an array of limitations. Some children need greater amounts of teacher-managed reading instruction than others. Other students need greater amounts of child-managed reading activity in order to thrive (see also Connor et al., 2013). At the same time, in school today, all students seem to benefit when teachers allocate greater amounts of time to actual reading or rereading activity. For example, Miller (2009) noted that "Any activity that substantially replaces extensive reading, writing, and discourse in the classroom needs to be better than the activity it replaces, and nothing, not even test prep, is better for students' reading ability than just plain reading, day after day" (p. 134).

Provide Opportunities to Engage in Thoughtful Literacy

Thoughtful literacy is quite different from the usual interrogations that occur during reading lessons. Interrogations ask students to simply supply a word or phrase answer to a low-level literal question. This common interrogation pattern has been described as an Initiate, Respond, Evaluate (IRE) sequence (Cazden, 2001). There may be misinterpretations of what is meant in the CCSS by "text-dependent" questions (see Pearson & Hiebert, 2013). In the standards themselves and in Coleman and Pimentel's descriptions in the Publishers' Criteria, the focus is on asking provocative questions that require readers to go into the text—what Langer (1984) referred to as high-level comprehension. However, it may well be, as curriculum developers and publishers work quickly to create new materials, that the term *text-dependent* will be misinterpreted in a more trivial manner (e.g., Where was Mary going when the lamb followed her?). Teachers, in turn, may feel pressure to include questioning practices in their curriculum materials simply because they are in the teachers' manuals. It is also possible that professional development, quickly conceived and provided, may foster this sense of text-dependent in the manner in which text-dependency has historically been defined.

In contrast, thoughtful literacy involves dialogic interaction between pupils or between pupils and teachers. Taylor, Pearson, Peterson, and Rodriguez (2003) reported year-long observational data from a study of 88 elementary teachers in nine schools in three regions of the United States. Using HLM, the most consistent variable related to achievement growth was teacher emphasis on higher-order thinking either through the questions they asked or the sorts of tasks they assigned students. But a focus on higher-order questions was relatively rare. The most common comprehension activities were responding to teacher-generated questions, usually of a literal nature, and completing workbook pages that elicited responses about story recall.

Almasi and Garas-York (2009) reviewed studies of opportunities to engage peers in a discussion of what has been read. They concluded that "findings from these studies suggest that discussion, as a general instructional activity, fosters higher literacy performance in terms of level of abstraction and elaboration, significantly higher levels of literal understanding of text, and significantly higher levels of both literal and inferential comprehension for students of all levels of language proficiency" (p. 478). In other words, increasing the volume of reading in which students engage across the school day and beyond, when coupled with opportunities to talk with peers about the text being read, is a potentially powerful instructional tool, one that is substantially missing from children's school experiences (Nystrand, 2006; Taylor et al., 2003).

The finding that discussion rarely occurs in elementary classrooms (Taylor et al., 2003) may be related to the use of commercial core reading programs. The teachers' manuals that accompany these products are filled with low-level, text-explicit questions but only rarely include recommendations for discussion (Dewitz, Jones, & Leahy, 2009). When discussion is largely absent from the advice that teachers follow, it is not surprising that few teachers engage students in peer discussions. However, with many teachers adhering to CCSS, discussion can be used to teach students how to gather evidence, knowledge, and insight from what they read. The CCSS emphasize that students need to become strong when it comes to drawing on the text for evidence and being able to explain their evidence orally, including in peer discussion. We can only hope that those who have read the Publishers' Criteria document have also read the CCSS.

CONCLUSION

There is sufficient research evidence that reading volume is very important for the reading development of students. As Stanovich (1986) so boldly stated, "the evidence available, I believe, supports my 30-year-old argument that reading volume matters" (p. 383). This important factor cannot be forgotten with the initiation of CCSS. Although many indicators in the CCSS might discourage reading volume, there are, indeed, elements of the standards that support reading volume. These elements need to be highlighted as much as, or more than, any other elements of the CCSS. Adams (2008) contended, "Beyond the basics and whether the focus is fluency, vocabulary, or knowledge, the most important activity for developing literacy is inducing students to read independently" (p. 295). In summary, we hope that teachers who implement the CCSS use the standards to support increases in students' reading volume, rather than focusing on those elements of CCSS that could potentially decrease reading volume.

REFERENCES

Adams, M. J. (2008). The limits of the self-teaching hypothesis. In S. B. Neuman (Ed.), *Educating the other America: Top experts tackle poverty, literacy, and achievement in our schools* (pp. 277–300). Baltimore, MD: Brookes Publishing.

Allington, R. L., McCuiston, K., & Billen, M. T. (in press). What research says about text complexity and learning to read. *The Reading Teacher.*

Allington, R. L., McGill-Franzen, A. M., Camilli, G., Williams, L., Graff, J., Zeig, J., Zmach, C., & Nowak, R. (2010). Addressing summer reading setback among economically disadvantaged elementary students. *Reading Psychology, 31*(5), 411–427.

Almasi, J. F., & Garas-York, K. (2009). Comprehension and peer discussion. In S. Israel & G. G. Duffy (Eds.), *Handbook of research on reading comprehension* (pp. 470–493). Mahwah, NJ: Erlbaum.

Anderson, R. C., Hiebert, E. H., Scott, J. A., & Wilkinson, I.A.G. (1985). *Becoming a nation of readers: The report of the Commission on Reading.* Washington, DC: The National Academy of Education, National Institute on Education, Center for the Study of Reading.

Anderson, R. C., Wilson, P. T., & Fielding, L. G. (1988). Growth in reading and how children spend their time outside of school. *Reading Research Quarterly, 23,* 285–303.

Braten, I., Lie, A., Andreassen, R., & Olaussen, B. S. (1999). Leisure time reading and orthographic processes in word recognition among Norwegian third- and fourth-grade students. *Reading and Writing: An Interdisciplinary Journal, 11*(1), 65–88.

Brenner, D., Hiebert, E. H., & Tompkins, R. (2009). How much and what are third graders reading? In E. H. Hiebert (Ed.), *Read more, read better* (pp. 118–140). New York, NY: Guilford.

Brophy, J. E., & Evertson, C. M. (1981). *Student characteristics and teaching.* New York, NY: Longman.

Campbell, J. R., Hombo, C. M., & Mazzeo, J. (2000). *NAEP 1999 Trends in Academic Progress: Three Decades of Student Performance.* (No. NCES 2000–469). Washington, DC: U.S. Department of Education, Office of Educational Research and Improvement, National Center for Education Statistics.

Cazden, C. B. (2001). *Classroom discourse: The language of teaching and learning* (2nd ed.). Portsmouth, NH: Heinemann.

Cipielewski, J., & Stanovich, K. E. (1992). Predicting growth in reading ability from children's exposure to print. *Journal of Experimental Child Psychology, 54*(1), 74–89.

Coleman, D., & Pimentel, S. (2012a). *Revised publishers' criteria for the Common Core State Standards in English language arts and literacy, grades K–2.* Available at www. corestandards. org/assets/Publishers_Criteria_for_3-12.pdf

Coleman, D., & Pimentel, S. (2012b). *Revised publishers' criteria for the Common Core State Standards in English language arts and literacy, Grades 3–12.* Available at www.corestandards. org/assets/Publishers_Criteria_for_3-12.pdf

Common Core State Standards Initiative. (2012). Available at www.corestandards.org/assets/KeyPointsELA.pdf

Connor, C. M. (2009). Instruction, student engagement, and reading skill growth in Reading First classrooms. *Elementary School Journal, 109*(3), 221–250.

Connor, C. M., Morrison, F. J., Fishman, B., Crowe, E. C., Al Otaiba, S., & Schatschneider, C. (2013). A longitudinal cluster-randomized control study on the accumulating effects of individualized literacy instruction on students' reading from 1st through 3rd grade. *Psychological Science, 24*(8), 1408–1419.

Corno, L., & Snow, R. E. (1986). Adapting teaching to individual differences among learners. In M. C. Wittrock (Ed.), *Handbook of research on teaching* (pp. 605–629). New York, NY: Macmillan.

Cunningham, A. E., & Stanovich, K. E. (1991). Tracking the unique effects of print exposure in children: Associations with vocabulary, general knowledge, and spelling. *Journal of Educational Psychology, 83*(2), 264–274.

Cunningham, A. E., & Stanovich, K. E. (1997). Early reading acquisition and its relation to reading experience and ability 10 years later. *Developmental Psychology, 33*, 934–945.

Cunningham, J. W. (2001). The National Reading Panel report. *Reading Research Quarterly, 30*(3), 326–335.

Dewitz, P., Jones, J., & Leahy, S. (2009). Comprehension strategy instruction in core reading programs. *Reading Research Quarterly, 44*(2), 102–126.

Ericsson, K. A., Krampe, R. T., & Tesch-Romer, C. (1993). The role of deliberate practice in the acquisition of expert performance. *Psychological Review, 100*(3), 363–406.

Fader, D. N., & McNeil, E. B. (1968). *Hooked on books: Program and proof.* New York, NY: Berkley Publishing.

Fisher, C. W., Berliner, D. C., Filby, N. N., Marliave, R., Cahen, L. S., & Dishaw, M. M. (1980). Teaching behaviors, academic learning time, and student achievement: An overview. In C. Denham & A. Lieberman (Eds.), *Time to learn* (pp. 7– 32). Washington, DC: National Institute for Education, U. S. Department of Education.

Foorman, B. R., Schatschneider, C., Eakins, M. N., Fletcher, J. M., Moats, L., & Francis, D. J. (2006). The impact of instructional practices in grades 1 and 2 on reading and spelling achievement in high poverty schools. *Contemporary Educational Psychology, 31*(1), 1–29.

Guthrie, J. T., & Humenick, N. M. (2004). Motivating students to read: Evidence for classroom practices that increase motivation and achievement. In P. McCardle & V. Chhabra (Eds.), *The voice of evidence in reading research* (pp. 329–354). Baltimore, MD: Brookes Publishing.

Guthrie, J. T., Martuza, V., & Seifert, M. (1979). Impacts of instructional time in reading. In L. B. Resnick & P. A. Weaver (Eds.), *Theory and practice of early reading* (Vol. 3, pp. 153–179). Hillsdale, NJ: Lawrence Erlbaum Associates.

Guthrie, J. T., Schafer, W. D., & Huang, C. (2001). Benefits of opportunity to read and balanced instruction on NAEP. *Journal of Educational Research, 94*(3), 145–162.

Guthrie, J. T., Wigfield, A., Metsala, J. L., & Cox, K. E. (2000). Motivational and cognitive predictors of text comprehension and reading amount. *Scientific Studies of Reading, 3*(3), 231–256.

Hiebert, E. H., & Martin, L. A. (2009). Opportunity to read: A critical but neglected construct in reading instruction. In E. H. Hiebert (Ed.), *Reading more, reading better* (pp. 3–29). New York, NY: Guilford.

Key Design Consideration. (2012). Available at www.corestandards.org/ELA-Literacy/introduction/key-design-consideration

Krashen, S. (2001). More smoke and mirrors: A critique of the National Reading Panel report on fluency. *Phi Delta Kappan, 83*, 119–123.

Krashen, S. (2004). *The power of reading: Insights from the research* (2nd ed.). Portsmouth, NH: Heinemann.

Kuhn, M. R. (2005). A comparative study of small group fluency instruction. *Reading Psychology, 26*(2), 127–146.

Langer, J. A. (1984). Literacy instruction in American schools: Problems and perspectives. *American Journal of Education, 83*(1), 107–132.

Lewis, M., & Samuels, S. J. (2005). *Read more, read better? A meta-analysis of the literature on the relationship between exposure to reading and reading achievement.* Minneapolis, MN: University of Minnesota.

Lindsay, J. J. (2013). Impacts of interventions that increase children's access to print material. In R. L. Allington & A. McGill-Franzen (Eds.), *Summer reading: Closing the rich/poor reading achievement gap* (pp. 20–38). New York, NY: Teachers College Press.

McQuillan, J., & Au, J. (2001). The effect of print access on reading frequency. *Reading Psychology, 22*(3), 225–248.

Mesmer, H.A.E., & Hiebert, E. H. (submitted). How far can third graders be "stretched"? Exploring the influence of text difficulty and length. *Journal of Literacy Research.*

Miller, D. (2009). *The book whisperer: Awakening the inner reader in every child.* San Francisco, CA: Jossey-Bass.

Mol, S. E., & Bus, A. G. (2011). To read or not to read: A meta-analysis of print exposure from infancy to early adulthood. *Psychological Bulletin, 137*(2), 267–296.

National Reading Panel (NRP). (2000). *Teaching children to read: An evidence-based assessment of the scientific research literature on reading and its implications for reading instruction.* Available at www.nichd.nih.gov/research/supported/Pages/nrp.aspx/

Nystrand, M. (2006). Research on the role of classroom discourse as it affects reading comprehension. *Research in the Teaching of English, 40*, 392–412.

Osborn, J., & Decker, K. (1993). Ancillary materials: What's out there? In B. Britton, A. Woodward, & M. Binkley (Eds.), *Learning from textbooks: Theory and practice* (pp. 161–185). Hillsdale, NJ: Lawrence Erlbaum Associates.

Pearson, P. D., & Hiebert, E. H. (2013). Understanding the Common Core State Standards. In L. M. Morrow, T. Shanahan, & K. Wixson (Eds.), *Common Core Standards for English language arts,* (pp. 1–21). New York, NY: Guilford.

Pianta, R. C., Belsky, J., Houts, R., Morrison, F., & NICHD Network. (2007). Opportunities to learn in America's elementary classrooms. *Science, 315*(5820), 1795–1796.

Pressley, M., & Allington, R. L. (2015). *Reading instruction that really works: The case for balanced teaching.* New York, NY: Guilford.

Shany, M. T., & Biemiller, A. (1995). Assisted reading practice: Effects on performance for poor readers in grades 3 and 4. *Reading Research Quarterly, 30*(3), 382–395.

Stanovich, K. E. (1986). Matthew effects in reading: Some consequences of individual differences in the acquisition of literacy. *Reading Research Quarterly, 21*, 360–407.

Stanovich, K. E. (2007). *How to think straight about psychology.* Boston, MA: Pearson.

Swanborn, M. S. L., & DeGlopper, K. (1999). Incidental word learning while reading: A meta-analysis. *Review of Educational Research, 69*(3), 261–286.

Taylor, B. M., Pearson, P. D., Peterson, D. S., & Rodriguez, M. C. (2003). Reading growth in high-poverty classrooms: The influences of teacher practices that encourage cognitive engagement in literacy learning. *Elementary School Journal, 104*(1), 4–28.

Topping, K. J., Samuels, S. J., & Paul, T. (2007). Does practice make perfect? Independent reading quantity, quality and student achievement. *Learning and Instruction, 17*, 253–264.

Topping, K. J., Samuels, S. J., & Paul, T. D. (2008). Independent reading: The relationship of challenge, nonfiction and gender to achievement. *British Educational Research Journal, 34*(4), 505–524.

Turner, J. C. (1995). The influence of classroom contexts on young children's motivation for literacy. *Reading Research Quarterly, 30*(3), 410–441.

Vadasy, P. F., Sanders, E. A., & Peyton, J. A. (2005). Relative effectiveness of reading practice or word-level instruction in supplemental tutoring: How text matters. *Journal of Learning Disabilities, 38*(4), 364–380.

CHAPTER 11

Formative Assessment

An Evolution or Revolution for Classroom Teachers?

Robert Calfee, Barbara Kapinus,
& Kathleen M. Wilson

For the past half-century, standardized, year-end tests have exerted an increasingly dominant influence in measuring student achievement, determining the effectiveness of schools and teachers, and promoting the skills-based reading programs that are presently the core of K–5 schooling. Many groups and individuals (e.g., Gordon, 2013; Piety, 2013; Rothman, 2011) have discussed the deleterious effects of these narrow approaches to assessment. The time for fundamental change is certainly right. The world is in the midst of a paradigm shift, variously labeled as digitalized, globalized, or simply "flat" (Friedman, 2006; Marx, 2014; Zhao, 2009). Whatever the label, it seems clear that future graduates will require schooling of a different sort than is being offered under the current model (Darling-Hammond, 2013), and we will undoubtedly need a different model of student assessment—one more compatible with the digital-global world—if the needs and aspirations of the next generations of students are to be met.

Into this context have come suggestions for the increased use of formative assessment for marking and guiding student progress (Heritage, 2010a; Popham, 2008; Shepard, 2008; Wiliam, 2011). Formative assessment is a tool used in some classrooms, taught in some education courses, and embraced by a few states and districts as an essential part of what takes place in classrooms. Formative assessment is a process that involves tasks integrated with instruction, provides teachers with specific information on where to go next with instruction, allows students to be aware of their achievement and needs in the process of doing activities, and is part of an ongoing sequence of activities to monitor and direct instruction for individuals as well as groups.

This chapter provides an overview of formative assessment and the promise it holds for supporting the goals of the Common Core State Standards for English Language Arts (CCSS ELA; National Governors Association for Best Practices [NGA] & The Council of Chief State School Officers [CCSSO], 2010). We begin with an in-depth definition and description of formative assessment. We then offer a historical review of classroom assessment practices that, in our view, provide the perfect context for understanding formative assessment. We close with a discussion of the manner in which formative assessment offers new opportunities for student learning in CCSS classrooms. In particular, we describe how formative assessment can be a tool for improving teaching and learning in reading, although it can be used across the curriculum (Brookhart, 2010; Heritage, 2013; Wiliam, 2011).

FORMATIVE ASSESSMENT: DESCRIPTION AND DISTINCTIONS

Formative assessment is a relatively new development in reading assessment in class-rooms, even though some of its basic elements and principles have been a part of class-room life for a long time. Those principles include:

- Directly assessing students' ability to use what has just been taught
- Using data from classroom activities to guide individual pathways for students (to differentiate instruction and practice activities) and to evaluate the quality and effectiveness of lessons (so that they can be revised and retaught)
- Engaging students in the assessment process so they can learn to evaluate their own progress
- Regarding assessment as an ongoing part of the instructional program that is intimately integrated with curriculum (what we teach and hold kids accountable to) and pedagogy (how we teach)

There are several definitions of formative assessment that come from the community of educators who have expertise in and a deep commitment to this process. From among these definitions, we want to highlight McManus's (2008) description of formative assessment as a "process used by teachers and students during instruction that provides feedback to adjust ongoing teaching and learning to improve students' achievement of intended outcomes" (p. 3).

This definition was the result of several years of work by a group of state assessment leaders, researchers, experts, and teacher practitioners of formative assessment in an initiative called the Formative Assessment of Teachers and Students (FAST) State Collaborative on Assessment and Student Standards (SCASS; FAST/SCASS, 2012). The Council of Chief State School Officers (CCSSO) facilitated this group, as well as several others, to support states in improving their education systems. Because McManus's definition of formative assessment reflects a consensus among professionals with a wide range of experiences who were endeavoring to communicate a complex concept to policymakers and the public, we have chosen it as the basis for further exploration.

Critical Features of Formative Assessment

Our definition articulates critical features of formative assessment. First, formative assessment is a *process*, not an event or a test. It is critical to acknowledge this feature because federal policy documents as well as publishers of testing and instructional materials have used the term *formative assessments* to refer to interim tests administered at the end of units or during the school year. Interim assessments are not integrated with instruction and usually look like shorter versions of the summative assessments used for accountability and grades. Indeed, use of the term *formative assessments* in the plural is incorrect because it connotes a set of discrete tasks that are not integrated with classroom activities. In reality, there are no such sets of tasks according to the definition we provide above, because formative assessment is a process. The process is continuous and involves activities, observations, and reflections that are integral to the classroom curriculum.

A second critical feature of formative assessment is that it provides useful information to both teachers and students. By virtue of activities and tools used as part of formative assessment, both groups are informed of what has been accomplished and what needs to be learned next. The participants—teachers and students—do not need to wait for something to be scored to see what learning has occurred and what still remains to be addressed.

A third essential feature of formative assessment is that it occurs as an integral part of instruction and classroom-based activities. Students do not stop and put their books away to "take" a formative assessment. It occurs as an almost seamless part of classroom learning, even when it is planned.

The fundamental purpose of formative assessment is to adjust and guide teaching and learning, the fourth critical aspect of the definition. Formative assessment instances mark points on a continuum rather than a summary of teaching outcomes. Those outcomes must be clear and specific for classroom activity, and they guide formative assessment. As part of the increasing understanding and practice of the process of formative assessment, the constructs of learning progressions and learning targets have been introduced and integrated with the process of formative assessment.

Formative Assessment and Learning Progressions

Over the past 20 years, learning progressions have become a major part of the process of building assessments (e.g., Misleavy & Riconscente, 2006; Wilson, 2005). Learning progressions have been described as a "sequenced set of subskills and bodies of enabling knowledge that it is believed, students must master en route to mastering a more remote curricular aim" (Popham, 2008, p. 24). Following an extensive review of research on learning progressions, Heritage (2013) said that learning progressions attend to the manner in which "learning is envisioned as a process of increasing sophistication in understanding and skills within a domain, beginning with novice levels and moving through increasingly complex stages of competence" (p. 40).

It makes sense that a process of continuously gathering information on student progress and adjusting instruction accordingly requires a clear map of the steps in that progress. However, there are caveats to using learning progressions. Popham (2008) points out that they are not completely accurate, especially when differences between individual students are considered. Few sequences are research-based (Pearson, 2013), and some are not necessarily the most effective paths to the achievement of end goals. Nevertheless, some versions of learning progressions are needed for guiding formative assessment, which Heritage (2013) warns cannot be a "series of ad hoc events" (p. 6).

Learning targets are useful in applying learning progressions and are the specific learning goals—not instructional objectives—that guide daily classroom learning so that students progress toward achieving standards. They are the connective goals that link standards and learning progressions to the specific activities that students and teachers perform in classroom. Moss and Brookhart (2012) emphasize certain characteristics of learning targets that distinguish them from instructional objectives. The main distinction is that the targets guide learning as well as teaching, and to do so, they must be shared with students and written in student language. Learning targets place the focus of observation and evidence gathering in formative assessment on what students are doing rather than what teachers are doing. One feature of formative assessment is not an explicit part of the definition but is instead implied in the notion of learning being a general term not assigned solely to students. That feature is the sharing of information and insights among groups of teachers to develop and enhance their understanding of their practice. These communities of practice or professional learning communities are key to the success of formative assessment in improving learning (DuFour, 2004; Heritage, 2013; Herrington, Herrington, Kervin, & Ferry, 2006).

Formative Assessment Activities

There is a long list of activities for use in formative assessment. Some are relatively traditional, while others are less frequently used in classrooms. Some recommended examples include (1) quick checks of knowledge using every pupil response with hand signals; holding up fingers for one, two, or three when given multiple possible answers; individual whiteboards; or holding up papers with responses; (2) student peer evaluations with guidelines provided; (3) classroom discussions with probing questions that clarify student thinking; and (4) teacher–student interviews (Heritage, 2010b, 2013; Popham, 2008; Wiliam, 2011). The critical aspect of these activities is that they follow closely after instructional activities and they provide both the teacher and students with information about learning.

Evidence for Formative Assessment

Formative assessment is supported by evidence from both research and practice (e.g., Black & Wiliam, 1998; Hattie & Timperley, 2007). The best-known synthesis of research on formative assessment was done by Black and Wiliam (1998). From an initial group of 250 international sources that covered students from preschool through college, Black and Wiliam selected 40 studies as valid for the analysis. They concluded that formative assessment led to some of the largest gains in achievement of any reported classroom strategies. A later study by Wiliam, Lee, Harrison, and Black (2004) showed that students whose teachers used formative assessment approaches in their classrooms made almost twice the yearly progress on standardized tests as similar students from classrooms where those approaches were not used.

Darling-Hammond and Wood (2008) used descriptions of the assessment systems in high-performing countries as evidence of the effectiveness of including performance assessment and classroom-based, curriculum-embedded assessment in a complete assessment system. In 2010, Darling-Hammond strengthened the case for assessment systems that include curriculum-embedded and performance assessments by summarizing and outlining the characteristics of an effective system based on evidence from parts of the United States as well as other nations.

Even a brief review such as the present one indicates that formative assessment offers substantial possibilities and is particularly germane to the goals of the CCSS. For these possibilities to become part of practice in thousands of classrooms, it is also necessary to understand the potential challenges for a set of new practices related to assessment. A brief overview of teacher assessment in the United States over the past 50 years provides a context for understanding these potential challenges. The underlying theme of this volume is to draw on our knowledge and experiences of the past to inform changes or embellishments in instruction that support the next-generation standards. Formative assessment has not emerged from a vacuum. There is a long tradition of classroom assessment that predates formative assessment and, in many ways, that predated many of the elements commonly viewed as part and parcel of formative assessment (see Calfee & Hiebert, 1991). We turn next to a brief history of teacher assessment practices to understand what has come before and the types of challenges that formative assessment might face.

EVOLUTION OF TEACHER ASSESSMENT PRACTICES: A SHORT HISTORY

There is a long tradition of classroom assessment that predates formative assessment and, in many ways, includes at least some of the elements commonly associated with it (see Calfee & Hiebert, 1991). Factors related to changes in classroom reading assessment include (1) changes in the teacher's role from directing a private decisionmaking endeavor behind a closed classroom door to implementing heavily outside-directed curriculum and instruction and then moving back again to more complex and autonomous orchestrating of activities; (2) the rise of mandated testing and the primacy of results on tests developed from outside the classroom rather than classroom-based tests and instructionally related assessments; and (3) changes in the definition of reading. In the following sections, we elaborate on each of these factors.

Teachers' Roles

Changes in teachers' roles over the past 50 years do not necessarily follow a straight path but rather meander along different routes at different times. At some points, teachers had a great deal of autonomy in their classrooms, especially during the early 1960s. There were other times when teachers had to follow highly prescriptive instructional plans, as during the NCLB era (e.g., Bond & Dykstra, 1997). At any given time, some schools, districts, or states emphasized one or the other, but there were periods when certain approaches prevailed.

One place where the teacher's role can be gauged is in published instructional materials. The period from 1955 to 1975 marked a major transition in the materials used by teachers for reading instruction. Before this transition, the basal readers provided to students included brief sections advising the teacher about ways in which the materials might be used, offering both pedagogical and philosophical recommendations, but giving few specifics. After the transition, basal reading series became massive systems that included student readers but were dominated by the spiral-bound manual designed to fit into the teacher's lap and directing virtually every action and activity. Worksheets and workbooks ensured that student time was fully occupied, and end-of-unit tests served as precursors to the benchmark and progress-monitoring tests that emerged some 30 years later as part of the NCLB accountability process. A correlate of this movement was a shift from a situation in which teachers were largely *responsible* for decisions regarding the planning, sequencing, and timing of instruction to one in which policy levers such as tests and standards held teachers *accountable* for students meeting particular performance levels. The shift from responsibility to accountability was also a shift from internal to external standards regarding what counts as evidence of expected progress.

Basal reading programs of the 1960s through 1980s gave some inkling of what was to come later. The 1957 Houghton-Mifflin Reading for Meaning series (McKee, Harrison, McCowen, & Lehr, 1957), for example, included "seatwork exercises" at the end of each unit, with sections on vocabulary recognition and sentence completion. These appeared to be optional, and there were no instructions for grading or otherwise using the information. The lessons in Scott Foresman's *Curriculum Foundation Series* (Robinson et al., 1965), on the other hand, were more heavily scripted than the 1950s series had been. The 1960s program had multiple-choice tests at the end of the teachers' manual, but provided no guidance about how to use them. *Reading to Learn* (Early, 1970) from Harcourt-Brace Jovanovich (HBJ) provided assessment guidance that had much in common with today's ideas about formative assessment, emphasizing questioning, observations, and attention to student discussion. There were no tests in the series. In the same decade, the Open Court Basic Readers (Trace & Carus, 1971) provided quarterly tests of language, vocabulary, and meaning, "designed strictly as a diagnostic," with no end-of-unit tests. A decade later, all the popular series included extensive testing materials, and computer-based management systems were becoming options for district administrators (e.g., Aaron, Jackson, Riggs, Smith, & Tierney, 1981; Clymer, Indrisano, Johnson, Pearson, & Venezky, 1982; Durr et al., 1986; Smith & Wardhaugh, 1980).

During the 1980s and 1990s, the whole-language movement opened the door momentarily for teachers to take more responsibility for designing instruction to build students' affinity for reading and writing as well as their skills and knowledge for literacy achievement (see Pearson, 1989, for a historical account of these developments). Teachers and students chose the books to be read, and teachers interviewed students about their reading and replaced worksheets from basal materials with journals and writing activities. One approach to classroom assessment espoused by the whole-language movement was the use of portfolios of student work to demonstrate progress over time. Portfolios also gave teachers and students more discretion in choosing what demonstrated progress.

Then, sometime in the early 1990s, dissatisfaction with the reading achievement of students as indicated in National Assessment of Educational Progress (NAEP) trends as well as some questionable classroom practices led to a backlash against whole language and the teacher's role as the primary decisionmaker in the classroom. The National Reading Panel (NRP) was instrumental in the move toward highly scripted reading programs for primary students. The panel was convened at the request of Congress by the National Institute of Child Health and Human Development (NICHD). Its purpose was to examine "research-based knowledge about the effectiveness of various approaches to teaching children to read" (NICHD, 2000, p. 1). The panel's report led to the promotion of specific research approaches that focused on reading instruction and prescriptions for classroom teachers to follow.

The Reading Excellence Act (REA) of 1998 and the Reading First legislation in the 2002 Elementary and Secondary Education Act (ESEA) increased pressure from the federal government and states on districts to implement specific programs based on "scientific reading research," which essentially meant carefully controlled experimental research. As a result, teachers have experienced much greater pressure to follow the basal scripts that are supposedly based on this research.

From Informal Inventories to Standardized Tests

With roots in the 1940s (Betts, 1946), one well-known tool for classroom reading assessment that rose to popularity in the 1960s and 1970s was the informal reading inventory

(IRI). IRIs were widely used for a range of assessment purposes: (1) to determine students' appropriate reading levels in instructional books, (2) to monitor their progress over time, and (3) to determine whether they could recognize and decode words. IRIs were available and known to teachers, but it is uncertain exactly how much they were used. The inventories required time to administer and were only useful when teachers had access to alternative materials for students. To identify appropriate texts for students, teachers had to gather information on their students' independence, instructional, and frustration levels and then used these designations to select materials for students to use (Farr, 1969; Farr & Carey, 1986; Pikulski & Shanahan, 1982). At least, teachers did this some of the time, when they had access to textbooks that allowed for this kind of differentiation. Those teachers who took the time and had the expertise also tracked oral reading errors to mark students' skills and needs in word recognition, phonics, and fluency. These assessments were used mainly for diagnostic purposes and assigning texts at appropriate reading levels for reading tasks

Although these practices continued to be employed in classrooms, new approaches and ideas were developing. Goodman (1969) began his work with miscue analysis as a window into students' knowledge and thinking about words and language. It moved classroom assessment beyond a number score on components of inventories to a qualitative focus on what students do when they are reading. Later, Clay's (1982) work in New Zealand with running records and Taylor's (1990) work in the United States also began to focus on patterns and qualitative aspects of reading. These qualitative approaches required teachers to use their own observations to record student progress.

At the same time that the use of a whole-language approach to reading instruction was growing in some places, an opposite trend growing as well, at least in pockets of schools around the country. By the 1980s, many teachers didn't have to accept responsibility for conducting classroom assessment because results on state exams were becoming the more widely accepted indicators of students' reading achievement. Basal skills management systems, complete with progress tests, replaced teacher-developed and teacher-directed forms of classroom assessment. Summarizing the situation in this context, Johnston (1984) reported on the development and increased use of tests of reading achievement over the 20th century. He also noted that by the 1980s, commercial tests were often used for placement in special programs (such as ESEA and special education).

The Impact of No Child Left Behind

The use of tests developed by commercial groups beyond the classroom to determine classroom progress and overall achievement rose with the ESEA legislation of 2001, No Child Left Behind (NCLB). Along with a demand for accountability for student achievement in reading based on summative, large-scale assessments, there was a growing conviction on the part of policymakers that teachers needed to be controlled and directed. This led states and districts to adopt commercial assessment tools for classrooms that not only marked achievement and progress but also provided what was considered both diagnostic and summative information. This culminated in what, by the early years of NCLB, became the single most widely used of any of these specific skill assessments. Dubbed DIBELS, for Dynamic Indicators of Basic Early Literacy Skills (Good & Kaminski, 2005), it is a prime example of this genre of tools. This easy-to-administer tool yielded scores to track progress in beginning reading skills but provided little explanation for what students were actually doing while reading. It also gave little instructional guidance beyond what skill needed to be addressed next.

At the end of the 1980s, a different approach to assessment began to grow in some areas. Some reading educators recognized that teachers did not have much autonomy and involvement in making instructional decisions in many classrooms. Publishers were giving teachers all the tools, and teachers didn't have to make choices and decisions. Calfee and Hiebert (1991) explored several issues surrounding the teacher's role as an "applied social scientist" (p. 291). They pursued the notion of classroom assessment as inquiry, discussing observations and questioning as methodologies, and suggesting the need to reconceptualize the reliability and validity of this task. They concluded that "the concept of critical literacy, coupled with a view of informed teacher judgment as the key to effective assessment, provides the foundation for a significant agenda for the next generation" (p. 302).

The term *authentic assessment* came into vogue, at least as a concept, as educators tried to determine whether students could use literacy skills in real-world situations. Hiebert, Valencia, and Afflerbach (1994) defined *authentic assessment* as "especially appropriate to signify assessment activities that represent literacy behavior of the community and workplace, and that reflect the actual learning and instructional activities of the classroom and out of school worlds" (p. 7). These activities often involved the application of reading skills to complex tasks such as gathering information for a research report.

At about the same time that authentic assessment was gaining attention as a concept, the notion of *performance assessment* was also achieving some popularity. Indeed, Goodman's (1969) miscue analysis was a form of performance assessment: Teachers noted what students did when they actually read aloud. Open-ended writing tasks that required the selection, use, and interpretation of information from text were one type of performance assessment, although the production of complex products was also included in the definition (Afflerbach, 2007). Maryland and Kentucky developed large-scale state assessments that used open-ended tasks, contextualized to provide a somewhat authentic aspect to the assessment tasks. Maryland established a consortium of districts that convened teachers to develop and share classroom tasks similar to the ones on the assessment. These tasks called for combining the assessment of skills in reading, writing, mathematics, science, and social studies; emphasizing open-ended responses and lots of writing in response to reading; and, like good instruction, spanning several days. The coming of federal requirement for individual scores for all students beginning in the 2005–2006 school year (Goertz & Duffy, 2003) ended the use of assessments like those in Maryland, which reported data at the school rather than student level.

Moving to the present era, the September 9, 2013, issue of *Education Week* recounted how teachers and administrators in Washington, D.C., prepared for the 2013–2014 school year (Gewertz, 2013). Two weeks before classes were set to begin, teachers from 111 district schools dug into individual scores; "emotional ups and downs permeate the mid-August dive into the data . . . . They're analyzing performance . . . by grade level, subject, student subgroup, right down to the academic standards. . . . Tiny detail by tiny detail, they completed the color-coded grid that would guide the work of the coming year" (p. 1). The details were instructional plans that were frequently based on student responses on only two to four test items on specific skills such as finding the main idea. Data at that level can be little more reliable than chance and certainly don't have more reliability than student performance across several classroom activities observed by the teacher. Year-end standardized tests remain the focus for planning as schools enter the third year of the CCSS. Teacher-to-teacher discussion is usually not about student learning now but about percentages. Efforts to make sense of "tiny details" go against every word of advice that has been offered by major educational testing companies and psychometricians. The activities described, well intended though they may be, provide less guidance for the work of the coming year than watching August fireflies blinking on lawns.

THE COMMON CORE STATE STANDARDS FOR ENGLISH LANGUAGE ARTS

In 2010, the National Governors Association with the Council of Chief State School Officers released a set of common standards in English language arts and mathematics—the Common Core State Standards (NGA/CCSSO, 2010)—to be used by those states that adopted them for developing curriculum and assessments. By the end of 2012, 46 states, the District of Columbia, and the Department of Defense had adopted the CCSS (Rothman, 2013). Since then, some states have changed course and decided not to adopt the standards (Gewertz, 2014; Ujifusa, 2014). Currently, 37 states and territories have adopted and retained the standards as the focus for their state curriculum and assessment. Two consortia—PARCC and Smarter Balanced—of states have been funded by the federal government to develop assessments of student progress with respect to the standards.

With the emergence of the Common Core State Standards, the conception of literacy took yet another turn (NGA/CCSSO, 2010). The CCSS do not provide an explicit definition of reading, but they do offer a list of tasks that able readers at each grade level should be able to perform. These tasks emphasize the gathering, synthesis, and use of information from text and the analysis of text construction and content. The standards also list broad aspects of reading such as building content knowledge and exhibiting independence, and they include the use of media in the digital age as an essential aspect of reading. It seems that an all-encompassing definition of reading has become more difficult to construct now that not only the processes and products of competent readers but also their habits and dispositions are being considered.

What the Standards Say

Elaborating on points about the standards that others in this volume (e.g., Kapinus & Long, Pearson & Cervetti) have made, we (Calfee, Wilson, Flannery, & Kapinus, 2014) have proposed six points that we believe are the essence of the CCSS-ELA:

- The standards are a work in progress: "The Standards are intended to be a living work: as new and better evidence emerges, the Standards will be revised accordingly" (NGA/CCSSO, 2010, p. 3).
- The standards portray a compelling image of future graduates from 2020 and beyond: "students who meet the Standards develop the skills in reading, writing, speaking, and listening that are the foundation for any creative and purposeful expression in language" (NGA/CCSSO, 2010, p. 3).

- The standards propose a bold image of project-based learning coupled with the primary disciplines through an integrated literacy program: "To be ready for college, workforce training, and life in a technological society, students need the ability to gather, comprehend, evaluate, synthesize, and report on information and ideas, to conduct original research in order to answer questions or solve problems, and to analyze and create a high volume and extensive range of print and nonprint texts in media forms old and new" (NGA/CCSSO, 2010, p. 4).
- The standards call curriculum, instruction, and assessment to be intertwined: "While the Standards delineate specific expectations in reading, writing, speaking, listening, and language, each standard need not be a separate focus for instruction and assessment, [and] several standards can often be addressed by a single rich task" (NGA/CCSSO, 2010, p. 5).
- The standards lay out fundamentals and broad goals, and are not intended to serve as a curriculum: "While the Standards focus on what is most essential, they do not describe all that can or should be taught. A great deal is left to the discretion of teachers" (NGA/CCSSO, 2010, p. 6).
- The standards propose that all students can and should achieve the standards through teacher support and scaffolding: "Students advancing through the grades are expected to meet each year's standards, retain or further develop skills and understandings mastered in preceding grades, and work steadily toward meeting the more general expectations described by the CCR standards" (NGA/CCSSO, 2010, p. 4).

The CCSS-ELA clearly call for a fundamental departure from a factory model of schooling that consists of marching students through instruction to achieve a set of basic skills. For emphasis, we repeat the following paragraph from the CCSS Introduction, titled "Research and media skills blend into the Standards *as a whole*" (NGA/CCSSO, 2010, p. 4), because it is a real headliner:

> [To be ready for] life in a technological society, students need the ability to gather, comprehend, evaluate, synthesize, and report on information and ideas, to conduct original research in order to answer questions or solve problems, and to analyze and create a high volume and extensive range of print and nonprint texts in media forms old and new. The need to conduct research and to produce and consume media is embedded into every aspect of today's curriculum. In like fashion, research and media skills and understandings are embedded throughout the Standards rather than treated in a separate section. (NGA/CCSSO, 2010, p. 4)

The connection between the acquisition of literacy and immersion in the disciplines and other academic experiences ensures that students learn to read and write (and speak, listen, think, and communicate) about knowledge and experience that has lifelong value. The images of learning and achievement are quite dramatic, calling for (1) a shift to integrated literacy, (2) an emphasis on academic language (Snow & Uccelli, 2009; Zacarian, 2013; Zwiers & Crawford, 2011), and (3) reliance on an extension of project-based learning. These elements call for changes in curriculum and instruction, but also for the implementation of a version of formative assessment that is consistent with the image of powerful, challenging learning embedded in the CCSS.

Formative Assessment Under the CCSS

This final section presents a conceptual model for formative assessment integrated with implementation of the CCSS, along with initial thoughts about implementation of the model. It assumes that the CCSS will be implemented as they were originally written. Our model calls for a multilevel system of ongoing inquiry into student learning, orchestrated by the classroom teacher in collaboration with students, where, from kindergarten through graduation, learning follows paths established by the standards that support acquisition of 21st-century literacy skills interwoven with disciplinary strands from the school curriculum. The model of formative assessment is designed to support full implementation of the standards, provide a framework for the professional development of teachers, and guide policy and information for the public. In this context, teachers become experts in "seeing learning" as they monitor, provide feedback, shape and guide progress, and document student achievements. In presenting the model, we concur with Brookhart (2013) and Haertel (2013) that, for the CCSS, a balanced approach to evaluating student achievement is one in which formative assessment plays a dominant role, placing the emphasis on growing rather than grading.

In this model, teachers guide students along learning progressions by engagement in project-based activities, during which formative assessment is an ongoing process of inquiring into students' progress during these encounters. The professional role of teachers is pivotal in the move from a traditional, prescriptive coverage of piecemeal objectives toward inquiry-based projects of significant scope and depth. Our description of formative assessment in support of the CCSS will address three questions: (1) What is it? (2) How is it done? and (3) When does it take place?

Earlier in this chapter, we began to describe what formative assessment is. The diagram in Figure 11.1 lays out the elements of our model relating formative assessment to the CCSS. It emphasizes inquiry as the driver of formative assessment, in which the goal is to *see* what students are thinking and learning. The model is framed with the teacher in mind, but the goal is also for students to internalize the process of assessment of learning. The process begins with participants in the learning and thinking process defining the problem and developing a plan for responding to it. As the plan is put into action, evidence is gathered (e.g., comments in discussions, written responses). This evidence is analyzed and evaluated, which results in reflection and review. Have the learning objective been achieved? Are there other issues that have arisen during the course of the learning activity that require additional instruction? Answers to questions like these lead to actions and decisions. The action may require an iteration of the learning cycle. Whether a single or multiple cycle of learning occurs, both teachers and students have ways to document what has been achieved. In some cases, documentation can take the form of a simple annotation in a notebook. In other cases, it might take the form of a student logbook, journal, or vocabulary record.

Although instruments and templates of various sorts can support this process, it is designed to be "test-free." In fact, you can imagine situations in which an activity might not include any traditional assessment tools. To illustrate, here is an activity that is completely "test-free." Toward the end of a week-long project on conservation of energy, a

Figure 11.1. An Inquiry Model for Formative Assessment

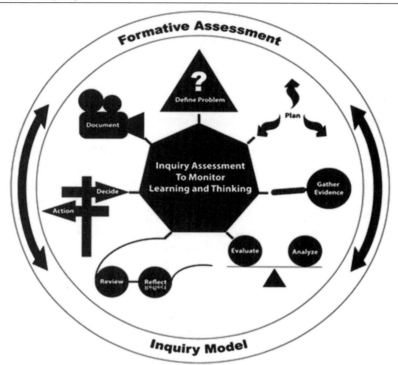

5th-grader remarks in the middle of a discussion that sometimes energy disappears: "When two cars crash, there is noise and things are broken and smashed, but then everything is quiet and the energy is all gone—right?" What has this student been thinking during the week? What has he learned? What about other students? This is not the time for a quick quiz or a benchmark test, even if one were readily available. A problem has emerged—a serious one. Evidence is required immediately; students need to assist with analysis and evaluation. Perhaps they think that conservation happens sometimes, but not always. Perhaps they do not fully understand the different forms of energy. Perhaps they need some additional examples. Perhaps an answer can be found by searching the Internet.

Each of these hunches provides a possible starting point for formative assessment, where collecting evidence, reviewing what the evidence implies, and revising instruction or framing further questions may be done in a matter of minutes, with each aspect leading to a new variant of the original problem: "I heard that the sun will run out of energy in a few billion years. That doesn't sound like conservation to me!" This sort of student statement may contain extremely valuable evidence about what students are thinking and learning.

When the teacher is the master of all knowledge, then students' questions can be bothersome, and even challenging. But when the teacher is the guide and facilitator of learning, then students' questions can be valuable starting points for investigating thoughts and understandings about a topic. One point is clear: Unlike the interim/benchmark tests that are part of today's NCLB practices, formative inquiry is not a routine assembly-line task for the teacher. Instead, the teacher is continuously monitoring where students' efforts at learning and application have taken them most recently, and after reflecting on students' progress or problems, asking what actions might need to be taken.

When to use formative assessment requires consideration of grain size or depth and degree of knowledge learned and cycle time—within lesson or unit of study or across a semester or academic year. These dimensions of the formative assessment process may appear simple at first glance, but they bring order to an otherwise complex question and support the teacher in managing a complex task. As shown in Figure 11.2, cycle time ranges from momentary activities to spans of 2 or 3 months and can include a year-end evaluation.

Running in parallel with cycle time is grain size. Grain size refers to whether the focus of an assessment activity is a single discrete skill/concept or the orchestration of multiple skills/concepts to solve some sort of real-world problem. For practical implementation of formative assessment, it is important to conduct assessments on a regular schedule, much like the maintenance schedule for your automobile. However, the need for data in the teacher's ongoing inquiry about student learning must drive the timing of formative assessment activities more than a schedule. Consider the differences in grain size between these cycles:

- *Moment by moment:* Spontaneous interactions are based on questioning, observations, and student queries. These cannot be fully planned in advance but can follow well-defined strategies (Heritage, 2013; Wiliam, 2011) and can be tailored to specific activities. These moment-by-moment interactions occur quickly and are typically focused on a particular literacy strategy and/ or interpretation of text. These interactions then inform "teachable moments" and instructional planning, with the teacher adding notes along the way in a journal or teacher logbook for future/further action.
- *Daily/weekly lessons:* Lessons that are typically a 15- to 50-minute time slice with a definite beginning, middle, and end represent the foundation for instructional planning across the grades. Lessons are generally planned with specific purposes and objectives, and hopefully, learning targets are shared with students (e.g., to develop a new concept, begin a new project, review progress, enable students to evaluate others' presentations, and so on). Lessons can vary in grain size from focusing on a single skill to applying multiple skills and concepts during a discussion. Lessons lend themselves to a variety of assessment activities, including quick quizzes or learning checks, warm-up questions, discussions, homework review, small-group assignments, and every-pupil-response activities, many of which can be designed in advance and may even be appear to be test-like.
- *Unit:* Developing student skills in a cluster of the CCSS such as Writing Standards 6–12, "Research to build and present knowledge (NGA/CCSSO, 2010, p. 44)" requires extended inquiry-based projects that last 1–3 weeks. The grain size of the project or unit is fairly large—pertaining to students' ability to ask questions and define problems, to gather appropriate resources, to integrate information from across resources, and, finally, to organize and share information with others. Assessment activities focus on monitoring

Figure 11.2. Cycle Time and Grain Size for Conducting Formative Assessment

Grain Size		Cycle Time
	*Quarter/Annual* Weeks - Months Portfolio Review Parent, Teacher, & Student Meeting	
	*Project/Unit* Days - Weeks Problem, Process, Product. Build and Present	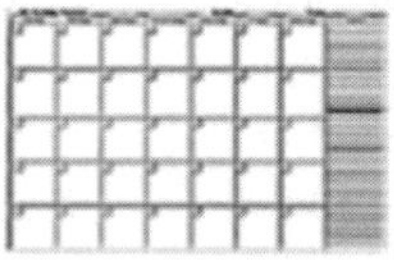
	*Lesson* Minutes - Class Period Episodic: Beginning, Middle and End. Set Outcomes Review Learning	
	*Moment by Moment* Seconds - Few Minutes Interactions, Questions, Discourse and Instant Action	

and guidance for both students and teachers, as well as end-of-unit products, covering both process and creation.

- *Quarter/Year:* Assessments at the end of the quarter and the school year are important events for benchmarking student accomplishments against the standards. The interim tests called for under Race to the Top (RttT) grant guidelines and those being developed by the Smarter Balanced Assessment Consortium (SBAC) and the Partnership for Assessment of Readiness for College and Careers (PARCC) are typically linked to summative tests in both content and task design and are seldom directly relevant to classroom instruction (see also Blanchard & Samuels, Chapter 6, this volume).

At this point in the formative assessment process, the grain size used to view student learning has grown to match particular standards. For example, a demanding standard such as Grade 5 Reading Standards for Informational Text, Standard 9 "Integrate information from several texts on the same topic in order to write or speak about the subject knowledgeably" (NGA/CCSSO, 2010, p. 14), calls for a substantial amount of evidence.

The basis for summarizing students' accomplishments with respect to a rigorous standard like this one draws on the full range of instructional experiences and student activities during the preceding time period. These assessment activities are conducted by teachers, not as tests, but as reviews of and inquiries into the full range of student performances. Templates can provide an important support for teachers in making these assessments and for establishing comparability across teachers and schools. They can also be designed to support adequate documentation of formative assessment for long-term activities. At the later grades, these summative evaluations can be collaborations between teacher and student.

Each cycle-time/grain-size slice has a unique character and can be used to elaborate on the stack of books and papers on formative assessment that have been accumulating over the past several years, offering a broad range of ideas and practices for formative assessment: questioning strategies, student–teacher dialogues, reviews of homework, and in-class writing activities.

The matrix in Table 11.1 suggests how the Inquiry Process and cycle-time/grain-size dimensions can be combined to create a comprehensive design for formative assessment. The full potential of the design comes into play when we take a look at *formative assessment in action*, where assessment is a film rather than a snapshot. Imagine a videotaped lesson in which formative assessment activities appear at several different cycle-time/grain-size intervals and times during the lesson. For a professional development exercise, participants could identify these events and trace out the details of the process for each on the matrix as the inquiry moves through time. With today's technologies, resources for conducting such an exercise would be a "piece of cake," compared with the situation even 10 years ago.

CONCLUSION

Our hope in writing this chapter is that this review of research and development on classroom assessment could provide a starting point for addressing the creation of a formative assessment program designed to complement other facets of the larger package required for full implementation of the CCSS. In the years since the working definition of formative assessment first appeared (McManus, 2008), numerous books and papers on formative assessment have been released, none of which provides a comprehensive "working model" built upon the definition. Instead, educators are falling back on formative "tests," much like the Bloom, Madaus, and Hastings (1981) approach. The result is that teachers are using tests with no understanding of the process and with little impact on student learning (Herman, Osmundson, Ayala, Schneider, & Timms, 2006).

A new vision of literacy—that of the Common Core State Standards for English Language Arts—is not explicitly grounded in the past half-century of research, but after a careful and critical reading, we have concluded that this new view is consistent with much of the best of scholarship and practice from earlier eras. The CCSS articulate the goals of teaching and learning as complex, highly related capacities, not simple skills. In order to implement the CCSS in classrooms, teachers must move away from directing simple, canned instruction in small, unrelated steps and assessing progress with summative tasks, then moving students on to whatever step is listed next in instructional

Table 11.1. Matrix for Combining Inquiry Methods with the Cycle-Time/Grain-Size Dimensions of Formative Assessment

Grain Size	Cycle Time			
	Moment	**Lesson**	**Unit**	**Quarter/Year**
Identify question				
Develop plan				
Collect evidence				
Analyze & evaluate				
Review and reflect				
Take action				
Review & document				

guides—regardless of their need or readiness. Instead, teachers need to reflect on the major foci of the CCSS. Clearly, one of those foci involves gathering and using evidence as teachers conduct continuous inquiry into the learning of their students. Students need to see that their learning involves their own inquiry into their progress. This focus on inquiry, for all of us involved in this grand reform (students, teachers, administrators, and researchers) holds promise for teaching and learning that will truly help prepare students for the ever-changing world of the future.

REFERENCES

Aaron, I. E., Jackson, D., Riggs, C., Smith, R. G., & Tierney, R. J. (1981). *Scott Foresman Reading.* Glenview, IL: Scott Foresman.

Afflerbach, P. P. (2007). *Understanding and using reading assessment.* Newark, DE: International Reading Association.

Betts, E. A. (1946). *Foundations of reading instruction.* New York, NY: American Book Company.

Black, P., & Wiliam, D. (1998). Assessment and classroom learning. *Assessment in Education: Principles, Policies and Practice, 5*(1), 7–73.

Bloom, B. S., Madaus, G. F., & Hastings, J. T. (1981). Evaluation to improve learning. *Journal of Educational Measurement, 20*(1), 93–95.

Bond, G. L., & Dykstra, R. (1997). The Cooperative Research Program in first-grade reading instruction. *Reading Research Quarterly, 32*(4), 348–427.

Brookhart, S. M. (2010). *How to assess higher order thinking skills in your classroom.* Alexandria, VA: Association for Supervision and Curriculum Development.

Brookhart, S. M. (2013). Comprehensive assessment systems in service of learning: Getting the balance right. In R. W. Lissitz (Ed.), *Informing the practice of teaching using formative and interim assessment* (pp. 165–184). Charlotte, NC: Information Age Publishing.

Calfee, R. C., & Hiebert, E. H. (1991). Classroom assessment of literacy. In R. Barr, M. Kamil, P. Mosenthal, & P. D. Pearson (Eds.), *Handbook of research on reading* (2nd Ed., pp. 281–309). New York, NY: Longman Publishers.

Calfee, R. C., Wilson, K. M., Flannery, B., & Kapinus, B. A. (2014). Formative assessment for the Common Core literacy standards. *Teachers College Record, 116*(11).

Clay, M. (1982). *Observing young readers: Selected papers.* Portsmouth, NH: Heinemann Educational Books.

Clymer, T., Indrisano, R., Johnson, D. D., Pearson, P. D., & Venezky, R. L. (1982). *Ginn Reading Program.* Lexington, MA: Ginn & Company.

Darling-Hammond, L. (2010). *Performance counts: Assessment systems that support high quality learning.* Paper prepared for the Council of Chief State School Officers.

Darling-Hammond, L. (2013). *The flat world and education: How America's commitment to equity will determine our future.* New York, NY: Teachers College Press.

Darling-Hammond, L., & Wood, G. H. (2008). *Refocusing accountability: Using performance assessments to enhance teaching and learning for higher order skills.* Paper presented at the Forum for Education and Democracy, Washington, DC.

DuFour, R. (2004). What Is a "Professional Learning Community"? *Educational Leadership, 61*(8), 6–11.

Durr, W. K., Pikulski, J. J., Bean, R. M., Cooper, J. D., Glaser, N. A., Greenlaw, M. J., . . . Mason, P. A. (1986). *Houghton Mifflin Reading.* Boston, MA: Houghton Mifflin Company.

Early, M. (1970). *Reading to learn.* New York, NY: Harcourt, Brace, Jovanovich.

Farr, R. (1969). *Reading: What can be measured?* Newark, DE: International Reading Association.

Farr, R., & Carey, R. F. (1986). *Reading: What can be measured?* (2nd ed.). Newark, DE: International Reading Association.

FAST/State Collaboratives on Assessment and Student Standards (SCASS). (2012). *Distinguishing formative assessment from other educational labels.* Washington, DC: Council of Chief State School Officers.

Friedman, T. L. (2006). *The world is flat: A brief history of the 21st century.* New York, NY: Farrar, Straus and Giroux.

Gewertz, C. (2013, September 9). One district's Common-Core bet: Results are in. *Education Week, 33*(3), 1, 18–20.

Gewertz, C. (2014, July 9). Lawmakers assert role in standards Common Core sparks bills. *Education Week, 33*(36), 1, 32–33.

Goertz, M., & Duffy, M. (2003). Mapping the landscape of high-stakes testing and accountability programs. *Theory Into Practice, 42*(1), 4–11.

Good, R., & Kaminski, R. A. (2005). *Dynamic indicators of basic early literacy skills* (6th ed.). Eugene, OR: Institute for Development of Educational Achievement.

Goodman, K. S. (1969). Analysis of reading miscues: Applied psycholinguistics. *Reading Research Quarterly, 5*(1), 652–658.

Gordon, E. (2013). *To assess, to teach, to learn: A vision for the future of assessment.* Princeton, NJ: Educational Testing Service.

Haertel, E. (2013). *A vision for the future.* Paper presented to the Symposium on the Reports of the Gordon Commission on the Future of Assessment in Education. UCLA, June 12, 2013.

Hattie, J., & Timperley, H. (2007). The power of feedback. *Review of Educational Research, 77,* 81–112.

Heritage, M. (2010a). *Formative assessment and next generation assessment systems: Are we losing an opportunity?* Washington, DC: Council of Chief State School Officers.

Heritage, M. (2010b). *Formative assessment: Making it happen in classroom.* Thousand Oaks, CA: Corwin.

Heritage, M. (2013). *Formative assessment in practice: A process of inquiry and action.* Cambridge, MA: Harvard Education Press.

Herman, J. L., Osmundson, E., Ayala, C., Schneider, S., & Timms, M. (2006). *The nature and impact of teachers' formative assessment practices.* Los Angeles, CA: UCLA/CSE Tech Report 703.

Herrington, A., Herrington, J., Kervin, L., & Ferry, B. (2006). The design of an online community of practice for beginning teachers. *Contemporary Issues in Technology and Teacher Education, 6*(1), 120–132.

Hiebert, E. H., Valencia, S. W., & Afflerbach, P. P. (1994). Definitions and perspectives. In E. H. Hiebert, S. W. Valencia, & P. P. Afflerbach (Eds.), *Authentic reading assessment: Practices and possibilities* (pp. 6–21). Newark, DE: International Reading Association.

Johnston, P. H. (1984). Assessment in reading. *Handbook of reading research,1,* 147–182. White Plains, NY: Longman.

Marx, G. (2014). *Twenty-one trends for the 21st century: Out of the trenches and into the future.* Bethesda, MD: Education Week Press.

McKee, P., Harrison, M. L., McCowen, A., & Lehr, E. (1957). *Reading for meaning.* Boston, MA: Houghton Mifflin.

McManus, S. (2008). *Attributes of effective formative assessment.* Paper prepared for the Council of Chief State School Officers.

Mislevy, R. J., & Riconscente, M. M. (2006). Evidence-centered assessment design: Layers, concepts, and terminology. In S. Downing & T. Haladyna (Eds.), *Handbook of test development* (pp. 61–90). Mahwah, NJ: Erlbaum.

Moss, C. M., & Brookhart, S. M. (2012). *Learning targets helping students aim for understanding in today's lesson.* Alexandria, VA: Association for Supervision and Curriculum Development.

National Assessment of Educational Progress (NAEP). (1989). *Reading Objectives for the 1990 National Assessment of Educational Progress.* Princeton, NJ: Educational Testing Service.

National Governor Association/The Council of Chief State School Officers (NGA/CCSSO). (2010). *Common Core State Standards for English language arts and literacy in history, social studies, science and technical subjects.* Washington, DC: Authors.

National Institute of Child Health and Human Development (NICHD). (2000). *Report of the National Reading Panel. Teaching children to read: An evidence-based assessment of the scientific research literature on reading and its implications for reading instruction* (NIH Publication 00-4754). Washington, DC: Author.

Pearson, P. D. (1989). Reading the whole-language movement. *Elementary School Journal, 90*(2), 231–241.

Pearson, P. D. (2013). Research foundations for the Common Core State Standards in English language arts. In S. Neuman & L. Gambrell (Eds.), *Quality reading instruction in the age of Common Core State Standards,* (pp. 237–262). Newark, DE: International Reading Association.

Piety, P. J. (2013). *Assessing the educational data movement.* New York, NY: Teachers College Press.

Pikulski, J. J., & Shanahan, T. (1982). Informal reading inventories: A critical analysis. In J. J. Pikulski & T. Shanahan (Eds.), *Approaches to the informal evaluation of reading,* (pp. 94–117). Newark, DE: International Reading Association.

Popham, W. J. (2008). *Transformative assessment.* Alexandria, VA: Association for Supervision and Curriculum Development.

Robinson, H. M., Monroe, M., Artley, A. S., Huck, C. S., Jenkins, W. A., & Weintraub, S. (1965). *Curriculum foundation series.* Glenview, IL: Scott Foresman.

Rothman, R. (2011). *Something in Common: The Common Core Standards and the next chapter in American education.* Cambridge, MA: Harvard Education Press.

Rothman, R. (2013). *Fewer, clearer, higher: How the Common Core State Standards can change classroom practice.* Cambridge, MA: Harvard Education Press.

Shepard, L. A. (2008). Formative classroom assessment: Caveat emptor. In C. A. Dwyer (Ed.), *The future of assessment: Shaping teaching and learning,* (pp. 279–303). New York, NY: Erlbaum.

Smith, C. B., & Wardhaugh, R. (1980). *Series R: Macmillan Reading.* New York, NY: Macmillan.

Snow, C. E., & Uccelli, P. (2009). The challenge of academic language. In D. R. Olson & N. Torrance (Eds.), *The Cambridge handbook of literacy* (pp. 112–133). New York, NY: Cambridge University Press.

Taylor, D. (1990). Teaching without testing: Assessing the complexity of children's literacy learning. *English Education,* February, 4–74.

Trace, A. S., Jr., & Carus, M. (1971). *Open Court Basic Readers.* Chicago, IL: Open Court.

Ujifusa, A. (2014, July 9). Louisiana standards showdown: Governor vs. state chief, board. *Education Week, 33*(36), 1, 32–33.

Wiliam, D. (2011). *Embedded formative assessment.* Bloomington, IN: Solution Tree Press.

Wiliam, D., Lee, C., Harrison, C., & Black, P. J. (2004). Teachers developing assessment for learning: Impact on student achievement. *Assessment in Education: Principles, Policy and Practice, 11*(1), 49–65.

Wilson, M. R. (2005). *Constructing measures: An item response modeling approach.* Mahwah, NJ: Erlbaum.

Zacarian, D. (2013). *Mastering academic language: A framework for supporting student achievement.* Thousand Oaks, CA: Corwin.

Zhao, Y. (2009). *Catching up or leading the way.* Alexandria, VA: Association for Supervision and Curriculum Development.

Zwiers, J., & Crawford, M. (2011). *Academic conversations: Classroom talk that fosters critical thinking and content understandings.* New York, NY: Stenhouse.

PART III

THE CONTEXT OF LITERACY INSTRUCTION

CHAPTER 12

Grounding Common Core Teaching in Proven Practices

Schoolwide Efforts to "Close the Achievement Gap"

Barbara M. Taylor

This chapter focuses on research regarding effective schoolwide programs and reform efforts that enhance students' literacy abilities and achievement to help close the achievement gap. Knowledge of the research regarding reform and effective practices will help educators as they implement the Common Core State Standards (CCSS; National Governors Association Center [NGA Center] for Best Practices & Council of Chief State School Officers [CCSSO], 2010). The chapter begins by describing the current state of affairs related to school reform in the United States. It then goes on to review effective schoolwide practices related to reading and effective teachers of reading before concluding with a discussion of the research on collaborative school reform in reading.

THE CONTEXT OF SCHOOL REFORM

In *Reign of Error: The Hoax of the Privatization Movement and the Danger to America's Public Schools*, Ravitch (2013) discusses misconceptions about the health of our public schools today as well as practices based on government mandates and what she calls the "corporate reform movement" that she believes are undermining efforts to close the achievement gap and improve students' achievement in reading and math.

The media often report that the test scores of students in the United States are poor and falling and that our public schools are broken. Thus, we have government mandates for testing and accountability, plus federal and corporate calls for school reform via school choice. However, Ravitch presents extensive data showing that U.S. students do not have weaker national tests scores than they did in the past and are generally performing well on international tests. In the 2011 data from the Progress in International Reading Literacy Study (PIRLS), based on 48 nations, 4th-grade students in the United States ranked behind Hong Kong, Russia, Finland, and Singapore (Mullis, Martin, Foy, & Drucker, 2012). In math and science on the 2012 tests from the Trends in International Mathematics and Science Study (TIMSS), U.S. students in grades 4 and 8 performed well above the international average (National Center for Education Statistics, 2012).

Ravitch, who served for 7 years on the National Assessment Governing Board (NAGB) under President Clinton, points out that in 2011, two-thirds of grade 4 students and three-fourths of grade 8 students were at or above the basic (average) level in reading. Ravitch cites the results of the National Assessment of Educational Progress (NAEP) 2011 data on U.S. students in reading and math from 1992 to 2011 for grades 4 and 8 and the 1973–2008 NAEP data in reading and math for grades 4, 8, and 12: Scores have increased slowly but steadily in reading and even more dramatically in math for students in grades 4, 8, and 12 and for White, Black, and Hispanic students (National Center for Education Statistics, 2011). However, Ravitch (2013) explains that although the scores of all groups and age levels of students have increased over the years, the achievement gap remains a serious problem. The achievement gap between more and less affluent students, as well as between White students and students of color, has not closed a great deal because the scores of *all* groups of students are improving. Also, because the lowest achievement is found in the most segregated, predominantly non-White, highest-poverty schools, Ravitch makes an evidence-based claim that schools alone cannot close the achievement gap. Our society also needs to work on reducing the extent of child poverty in the United States.

Ravitch posits that federal mandates focusing on testing and accountability under No Child Left Behind (NCLB) and Race to the Top (RttT) have dramatically affected the role of the federal government in education. She argues that the use of standardized tests to judge the effectiveness of schools and teachers, in addition to assessing growth in students' reading and math achievement, has led to a host of problems, including low teacher morale, teaching to the test, and narrowing of the curriculum. Clearly, our national emphasis on standardized testing for more than 20 years has not helped close the achievement gap or substantially reform schools.

NCLB's expectation that all students would be proficient in reading and math by 2014 led to the push for an approach to school reform focused on school choice, competition, and charter schools as alternatives to public schools. Ravitch explains that this push came from federal and state governments, as well as from corporate reformers. Special interest groups or businesses, often supported by foundations and the corporate world, sprang up to establish and/or manage charter schools or to allow the use of vouchers for students to enroll in private schools. In some cases, staffs were replaced or schools were closed. Unfortunately, as Ravitch discusses, charter schools do not have better records of achievement than public schools (see also Bryant, 2013).

The Common Core movement that has swept across (most of) the United States in recent years has become a focal point for current literacy instruction and is a major driving force behind the curriculum of K–12 literacy instruction in the future. The CCSS movement has the potential to significantly improve K–12 students' literacy learning and abilities. The focus on higher-order (as opposed to low-level or rote) cognitive abilities and the integration of literacy and content-area processes are encouraging aspects of the CCSS. However, there are many challenges that must be addressed if schools and students are going to succeed.

How to measure literacy abilities that require some level of complex thinking effectively is one major area of challenge. Teaching that covers all standards, especially those that require higher-level thinking—which is traditionally difficult to measure—is another challenge. Conscious action by teachers and principals to avoid overreliance on commercial materials and externally provided professional learning to drive instruction is a third. Teaching well and covering the standards in the process of excellent literacy instruction, as opposed to teaching more narrowly simply to cover the standards, is perhaps the biggest challenge of all.

Fortunately, effective literacy instruction—most specifically, reading instruction—is a field of study with a rich research base. The research-validated practices described in this chapter for the most part do not support the unproven practices of the contemporary reform movement described by Ravitch: excessive testing, charter schools, online schools, for-profit schools, vouchers, school closures, or the shift toward privatization of schooling in America. Instead, research over the past 5 decades points to the importance of a collaborative school community made up of professional educators and parents. Such communities are found in schools that are "beating the odds" or in schools with a proven reform agenda that results in substantial improvement in students' reading abilities and progress in closing the achievement gap over time. The research-based information on effective schools and effective school reform presented in this chapter can help guide principals and teachers within schools to implement effective instructional practices as they also work to incorporate the CCSS into their teaching and to manage the requisite standardized tests.

EFFECTIVE SCHOOLWIDE PRACTICES RELATED TO READING

Numerous studies of school factors contributing to high reading performance in high-poverty schools have been conducted over the years. This research points to important factors that must be in place at the building level for all children to achieve at high levels in reading. Hoffman (1991) summarized research on effective schools and reading achievement from the 1970s and early 1980s (Venezky & Winfield, 1979; Weber, 1971; Wilder, 1977). He uncovered eight recurring attributes of effective schools: (1) a clear school mission; (2) effective instructional leadership and practices; (3) high expectations; (4) a safe, orderly, and positive environment; (5) ongoing curriculum improvement; (6) maximum use of instructional time; (7) frequent monitoring of student progress; and (8) positive home–school relationships. Many of these factors are *not* stressed in today's current national reform agenda. However, they still remain important factors for schools to address when they engage in reform efforts.

Effective High-Poverty Schools

During the late 1990s, five important large-scale research studies were conducted (Charles A. Dana Center, 1999; Lein, Johnson, & Ragland, 1997; Puma et al., 1997; Taylor, Pearson, Clark, & Walpole, 2000). These studies, all of which focused on effective, high-poverty elementary schools, reported strikingly similar findings that both supported and extended earlier research on effective schools from the 1970s and 1980s (Taylor, Pressley, & Pearson, 2002). Six recurring building-level characteristics found in these reports follow:

- *Primary emphasis on improved student learning.* In four of these studies, improved student learning was cited as schools' overriding priority. Schools had a strong, collective sense of responsibility for school improvement. The principal, teachers, other school staff members, and parents worked as a team to achieve their goal of substantially improved student learning and achievement.

- *Strong building leadership.* Three studies identified the importance of strong building leadership. For example, the principal may have worked to redirect the staff's time and energy, to develop a collective sense of responsibility for school improvement, to secure resources and training, to provide opportunities for collaboration, to create additional time for instruction, and/or to help the school staff persist despite difficulties. Also, the principals typically served as instructional leaders, energized the change process, and built a strong staff by hiring thoughtfully and providing regular assistance to teachers to improve instruction.

- *Strong teacher collaboration.* In addition to strong leadership, strong staff collaboration was highlighted in four of the studies. Teachers planned and taught together with a focus on how best to meet students' needs. Teachers reported a strong sense of building communication, talking and working across as well as within grades, to better understand one another's curricula and expectations.

- *Consistent use of data on student performance to improve learning.* Four of the studies found that teachers in effective schools systematically shared student assessment data, usually on curriculum-embedded measures, to make instructional decisions and to improve pupil performance. Teachers also worked together to carefully align instruction to standards and state or district assessments.

- *Focus on professional development and innovation.* Four of the studies stressed the value of ongoing professional development and the implementation of new, research-based practices. Often, there was an emphasis on sustained professional development in which teachers learned together within a building and collaborated to improve instruction.

- *Strong links to parents.* All five studies reported strong efforts from teachers and principals within schools to reach out to parents. Schools worked to win the confidence of parents, to treat them as valued members of the school community, and to build effective partnerships to support student achievement. Schools also reported a positive school climate, good relations with the community, and high levels of parental support.

In addition to the these six recurring factors, one additional effective school-level factor resulting from research on beginning reading surfaces again and again—the implementation of research-based early reading interventions for children in 1st grade who are at risk of experiencing reading difficulties (Hiebert & Taylor, 2000; Taylor et al., 2000). Schools in which faculty and administrators have collectively made the decision to provide early reading intervention programs typically subscribe to the notions of supplemental instruction for children who are in need of additional support and the acceleration of children's learning to read. Successful intervention programs share a set of common characteristics: repeated reading of stories, systematic instruction in word recognition, carefully selected texts, guided writing, regular assessment of pupil progress, one-on-one reading practice, home connections, and ongoing staff development (e.g., Hiebert, Colt, Catto, & Gury, 1992; Hiebert & Taylor, 2000; Invernizzi, Juel, & Rosemary, 1997; Pinnell, Lyons, DeFord, Bryk, & Seltzer, 1994; Taylor, Short, Frye, & Shearer, 1992).

Drawing on several characteristics itemized earlier is the concept of teachers as a community of learners. Research from the 1990s and early 2000s on effective school reform and teacher professional development stressed the importance of teachers learning and changing together over an extended period of time as they reflect on their practice and implement new teaching strategies (Fullan, 1999; Fullan & Hargreaves, 1992; Louis & Kruse, 1995; Richardson & Placier, 2001). In successful schools, which typically operated as strong professional learning communities, teachers systematically studied student assessment data, related this to their instruction, and worked with others to refine their teaching practices (Fullan, 1999). Reflective dialogue, deprivatization of practice, and collaborative efforts enhanced shared understandings and strengthened relationships within a school (Louis & Kruse, 1995).

Effective Teachers of Reading

Research on effective schools and effective school reform has consistently identified the importance of effective teachers, especially in the elementary grades (Taylor et al., 2000). From the research of the 1960s and 1970s, we learned that effective teachers maintained an academic focus, had a high incidence of pupils on task, and provided direct instruction (Brophy, 1973; Dunkin & Biddle, 1974; Flanders, 1970; Soar & Soar, 1979; Stallings & Kaskowitz, 1974). Effective direct instruction included making learning goals clear, asking students questions as part of monitoring student understanding of what was being covered, and providing feedback to students about their academic progress.

In the 1980s, Duffy and Roehler began to uncover the cognitive processes used by excellent teachers of reading. Effective teachers used modeling and explanation to teach students strategies for decoding words and understanding texts (Duffy et al., 1987). Knapp (1995) found that effective teachers stressed higher-level thinking skills more than lower-level skills. Taylor et al. (2000) found that accomplished primary grade teachers in high-poverty schools provided more small- than whole-group instruction, elicited high levels of pupil engagement, preferred coaching over telling when interacting with students, and engaged students in higher-level thinking related to reading (Pressley et al., 2001).

The National Reading Panel report (National Institute of Child Health and Human Development, 2000) concluded that instruction in systematic phonics, phonemic awareness, fluency, and comprehension strategies were important parts of a complete reading program. The panel's conclusions regarding the balance that outstanding primary grade teachers achieved in their classroom reading programs were consistent with the findings of Pressley et al. (2001), Puma et al. (1997), and Taylor et al. (2000). Pressley et al. (2001) also found that outstanding teachers directly taught skills, had their students read and write more than other teachers in the study, and fostered self-regulation in students' use of strategies. In addition, effective primary grade teachers had excellent classroom management skills (Pressley et al., 2001; Taylor et al., 2000). Additional studies also found support for a focus on high-order thinking (Puma et al., 1997).

Conclusions from Research on Effective Reading Instruction

Research on effective schools and teachers from the 1970s through 2000 is surprisingly convergent. Effective schools are typically characterized as collaborative learning communities in which teachers assume a shared responsibility for all students' growth and achievement, monitor progress and plan effective instruction for groups and individuals, help one another learn more about the art and science of teaching, and reach out to the families they serve.

Effective teachers maintain an academic focus, provide balanced instruction that meets individual student needs, teach basic skills, stress high-level thinking, model and coach while students are actively engaged in learning experiences, and monitor student learning to assess their progress and adjust instruction. Generally, the schools in these studies did not necessarily view packaged reforms and materials as required for improving student achievement. The common denominator seemed to be commitment and hard work that focused on the classroom-level and school-level practices that the research consistently identified as effective.

COMPREHENSIVE SCHOOL REFORM

A major push for whole-school reform began in the late 1990s with the Comprehensive School Reform (CSR) movement. (For additional information, see Taylor, Raphael, & Au, 2010.) Nationally disseminated CSR models sprang up in response to concerns that large-scale federal programs such as Title I of the Elementary and Secondary Education Act had only minimally affected growth in student achievement (Borman & D'Agostino, 1996). The CSR movement was based on externally developed and validated models of school reform in reading that were focused primarily on changes in curriculum, and concomitantly, effective research-based teaching strategies developed through ongoing professional development for teachers.

One prominent CSR model from the 1980s, Accelerated Schools, focused on accelerated learning for disadvantaged students through constructivist teaching and challenging learning activities rather than skills-based learning (Levin, 1987). This reform model, in which reading was an important component, stressed the importance of a common school vision shared by educators, parents, and the community, as well as shared decisionmaking related to changes in curriculum and instruction. However, the program was more philosophical than concrete in terms of curriculum and instructional practices, and, perhaps because of this, it led to few changes in teaching practices and minimal gains in students' test scores (Bloom, Ham, Melton, & O'Brien, 2001; Correnti & Rowan, 2007).

Success for All (SFA) is another national CSR reading reform model that has been evaluated extensively (Slavin & Madden, 2001). First implemented in 1987, the program focuses on phonics and literal comprehension delivered in 90-minute reading periods in which teachers use scripted or highly controlled lessons in reading groups organized by student achievement levels (Slavin & Madden, 2001). Student progress is assessed every 8–9 weeks, and students who need additional support may be moved to a different group or receive tutoring. The model focuses on procedural controls to maintain the fidelity of implementation.

Research on SFA has documented that many teachers value the ongoing professional learning they received regarding how to implement the program successfully (Correnti

& Rowan, 2007). Even so, some were dissatisfied with the lack of flexibility in the highly prescriptive program (Klinger, Cramer, & Harry, 2006). Some studies have shown non-significant or inconclusive effects of SFA on students' reading achievement (Ross et al., 2004; Sterbinsky, Ross, & Redfield, 2006). However, other studies have shown positive effects (Borman & Hewes, 2002; Borman et al., 2007; Skindrud & Gersten, 2006), and there is more evidence for the effectiveness of this CSR model than for any other (Taylor et al., 2010).

America's Choice schools, established in 1998, focused on standards-based assessments, instructional materials and strategies aligned to those standards, and a focus on readers' and writers' workshops and independent reading (Consortium for Policy Research in Education, 2002). Like Accelerated Schools, the America's Choice model stressed the importance of parental and community engagement and also emphasized strong instructional leadership and ongoing professional learning in the form of professional learning communities. The program was found to have a positive impact on students' writing abilities (Correnti & Rowan, 2007) and reading performance (May & Supovitz, 2006). However, issues of variability in implementation and of sustainability, typical challenges in school reform, have been reported (May & Supovitz, 2006).

These three CSR models share features with the effective schools reviewed in the research mentioned earlier. The focus of all three models is ongoing professional learning to enhance teacher effectiveness and to promote curriculum improvement. All three models are predicated on high expectations for students' learning and achievement. Two of the programs stress collaboration and connections to parents and the community. Two stress the importance of monitoring pupil progress frequently. One stresses the importance of strong instructional leadership. Another urges schools have a clear mission set in place.

However, the top-down nature of these externally developed models—and, in the case of two of them, a primarily prepackaged curriculum—may negatively impact the ability of these kinds of models to be sustained over time and to meet the specific needs of particular schools, teachers, students, and parents (Taylor et al., 2010). The school reform in literacy models described in the next section build on the research of effective schools and, in part, on the CSR models, but they also focus on university and school partnerships that help individual schools develop reading literacy improvement models over which principals and teachers feel ownership. These models focus on ongoing teacher professional learning and balance teacher autonomy with public accountability.

RESEARCH AND COLLABORATIVE SCHOOL REFORM

During the 2000s, various university literacy educators across the United States partnered with principals and teachers within K–12 schools to engage in research-based professional learning and schoolwide improvement in literacy. The primary purpose of the university partners was to help schools develop research-validated, sustainable school improvement models and resources with the goals of producing highly qualified literacy teachers and improving literacy achievement for all students in meaningful ways.

The research on effective school improvement coming out of these university–school partnerships reveals striking similarities across sites and with earlier research on effective schools and schoolwide reform. Research stemming from these university–school partnerships has found that successful school improvement in literacy requires support for organizational change, support for individual teacher change, and a focus on sound instruction that emphasizes complex thinking as well as basic skills. Research reveals that a framework for school improvement that helps schools focus on these three key elements can be effective in improving students' reading ability. Within each element, certain common features emerged, as discussed below. (For additional information, see Taylor et al., 2010.)

Support for Organizational Change

Vision and commitment. Members of a school community must develop a shared vision and establish a long-term commitment to literacy improvement. Langer (2000) found that successful high school English programs with locally developed reform agendas had highly coordinated efforts to increase student performance. As students' scores increased, teachers set higher goals. All of the successful schools with locally developed reform agendas that Lipson, Mosenthal, Mekkelsen, and Russ (2004) studied had a history of long-term commitment to literacy improvement (8–10 years) and a stable school administration. Also, everyone within these successful schools appeared to be working toward a shared vision for students' literacy learning. The Standards-Based Change Process helps schools establish a vision and set a direction for change but also helps teachers and administrators understand that they must stay the course for 3 years or more to make the improvements needed to achieve substantial gains in student learning (Au, Raphael, & Mooney, 2008).

Buy-in and leadership. A structure or model for school improvement is essential, and most staff members within a school must consciously select a particular school improvement model if it is to be successfully implemented. For example, the School Change Framework encourages schools to have at least 75% buy-in across teachers (Taylor, Pearson, Peterson, & Rodriguez, 2005). Once a school has commitment, strong leadership is needed to keep the reform effort moving forward. Taylor et al. (2005) found that high-reform schools, which were in turn seeing accelerated growth in students' reading, had an effective teacher leader, an enthusiastic leadership team, and a supportive principal.

Data-driven reform. Use of data at the student, teacher, and school level is needed to promote change. The successful schools that Lipson et al. (2004) studied used external standards and data to help focus their efforts and evaluate their progress. In the Standards-Based Change Process, teachers set targets for student performance and collect evidence to examine students' progress toward meeting these benchmarks three times a year (Au, Hirata, & Raphael, 2004). Teachers met by grade levels to score evidence according to rubrics, and as student scores rose, teachers developed more challenging benchmarks and rubrics. In the School Change Framework, each school received an annual school report with data not only on students' progress in reading, but also on teachers' changes in teaching and their perceptions of school-level collaboration and leadership (Taylor et al., 2005). These data in turn helped schools improve the following year.

Collaborative school community. To be successful with a school improvement effort, teachers and administrators must become a collaborative school community. Langer

(2000) found that teachers in successful schools were members of teaching and learning communities that reportedly sustained them in their efforts. Lipson et al. (2004) found that teachers in successful schools had built a collaborative community with high expectations and a climate of commitment. Teachers felt they were collectively responsible for all of their school's students. This positive school culture was missing in the less successful schools that Lipson et al. studied. In another study of elementary schools that were beating the odds, teachers reported that collaboration in teaching was a major reason for their success. Peer coaching, teaming, and program consistency were mentioned as aspects of collaboration that teachers valued (Taylor et al., 2000).

Support for Individual Change in the Development of Effective Teachers

Professional learning. Teachers benefit from opportunities to engage in ongoing, focused, challenging, job-embedded professional learning. Lipson et al. (2004) found that successful schools had extensive professional development and that teachers spoke with confidence about their learning. Also, teachers were eager to receive feedback and new ideas from their external professional development partners. At schools that were successful with the Standards-Based Change Process, leaders had developed a multiyear plan for school-based professional development that was tied to specific goals for curriculum development designed to improve students' achievement (Au et al., 2004). Teachers in schools that were successful with the School Change Process engaged in weekly study groups that focused on substantive literacy topics such as comprehension strategies and higher-level thinking (Taylor et al., 2005). Teachers engaged in video sharing and looked at student work to improve their practice.

Change in teaching. Teachers' professional learning must focus on reflection and changes in thinking and teaching. The Schools for Thought reform effort supported teachers as they shifted from having students memorize facts to learning with understanding (Zech, Gause-Vega, Bray, Secules, & Goldman, 2000). Teachers engaged in classroom-based inquiry with a facilitator and other teachers with a focus on comprehending students' understanding in specific content domains. Similarly, reflection on and change in teaching is at the heart of the professional development model used in the School Change Framework project (Taylor, Pearson, Peterson, & Rodriguez, 2003). Study groups focus on research-based changes in reading instruction. In addition, facilitators visit classrooms to model and coach, and teachers reflect on their teaching through video sharing and personal analysis of observation data. Taylor et al. (2005) found that teachers in high-reform schools, those that succeeded with this model, made more positive changes in their teaching than teachers in low-reform schools.

A Focus on Coherent, Balanced, Challenging Instruction

Curriculum coherence and balanced instruction. To help all students achieve at high levels in reading and writing, teachers need to develop a coherent curriculum and provide sound, balanced instruction. In the Standards-Based Change Process, teachers in successful schools developed a coherent curriculum across grade levels with a shared understanding of goals for student learning, instruction, and assessment (Au et al., 2004). Lipson et al. (2004) found that in successful elementary schools with locally developed reform agendas, teachers provided balanced literacy instruction regardless of the type of reading program the school had adopted.

Complex thinking. To help all students achieve at high levels in reading and writing, teachers need to teach with an instructional emphasis on complex thinking as well as basic skills. Langer (2001) found that in successful secondary schools, teachers moved students from initial skill acquisition or basic understandings to deeper understandings and the generation of ideas. Taylor et al. (2000, 2003, 2005) found that students who showed greater reading growth had teachers who engaged them in more high-level talk and writing about text.

Student thinking and learning. To help all students achieve at high literacy levels, teachers need to reflect on how their students are thinking and learning rather than simply on what they, as teachers, are teaching. Langer (2001) found that English teachers in high-performing schools taught students procedural or metacognitive strategies in addition to content or skills, whereas teachers in more typical schools focused on content or skills alone. Similarly, Zech et al. (2000) helped teachers focus on a question about students' learning (e.g., How do my students develop an understanding of summarizing?) and then examined student work or student responses to answer their question. This focus on student learning processes improved teachers' teaching.

Through university–school partnerships, research-validated school improvement models were developed along with resources that could be used by schools in their own reform efforts to improve students' literacy abilities. External partners, such as the university members who engaged in the research described above, assisted schools in this important work by providing initial knowledge and support. However, the drive and hard work necessary for long-term change ultimately had to come from within individual schools.

CONCLUSION

Based on the review of research in this chapter, ideal models of collaborative school reform stress the following:

- A locally developed vision for change that includes parent partnerships
- Strong building-level leadership
- Opportunities for teachers to engage in ongoing, collaborative professional learning and support to teach well and broadly
- Challenging instruction that engages all students in high-level thinking as well as basic skills
- Ongoing testing not only to assess students' growth but also to assess students' strengths, weaknesses, and day-to-day learning

Lessons for the Common Core

Reflecting on the possible interface between this work on reform and the Common Core movement, I believe the lesson is that school context matters. Thus, any state or district that thinks it can achieve the higher-order learning goals of the Common Core simply by mandating that schools adopt the standards and attend a "hire the hall" professional development series is in for disappointment. My experience with reform—which is consistent with a much larger body of research on school reform—suggests that external mandates and even earnest professional development efforts are doomed to failure unless they take the lessons of this impressive body of research seriously. Unless school personnel are willing to follow the agenda of the contemporary national reform movement, their chances of implementing the Common Core State Standards, let alone promoting student achievement with them, are slim to none. They will stand a better chance of success if they embed the Common Core as part of a broader, multiyear process of collaborative school reform.

REFERENCES

Au, K. H., Hirata, S.Y., & Raphael, T. E. (2004). *Improving achievement through standards.* Paper presented at the annual meeting of the National Reading Conference, San Antonio, Texas.

Au, K., Raphael, T., & Mooney, K. (2008). Improving reading achievement in elementary schools: Guiding change in a time of standards. In S. B. Wepner & D. S. Strickland (Eds.), *Supervision of reading programs* (4th ed., pp. 71–89). New York, NY: Teachers College Press.

Bloom, H. S., Ham, S., Melton, L., & O'Brien, J. (2001). *Evaluating the Accelerated Schools approach: A look at early implementation and impacts on student achievement in eight elementary schools.* New York, NY: Manpower Demonstration Research Corporation.

Borman, G. D., & D'Agostino, J. V. (1996). Title I and student achievement: A meta-analysis of federal evaluation results. *Education Evaluation and Policy Analysis, 18,* 309–326.

Borman, G. D., & Hewes, G. M. (2002). The long-term effects and cost-effectiveness of Success for All. *Educational Evaluation and Policy Analysis, 24*(4), 243–266.

Borman, G. D., Slavin, R., Cheung, A., Chamberlain, A., Madden, N., & Chambers, B. (2007). Final reading outcomes of the national randomized field trial of Success for All. *American Educational Research Journal, 44*(3), 701–731.

Brophy, J. (1973). Stability of teacher effectiveness. *American Educational Research Journal, 10,* 245–252.

Bryant, J. (2013). The charter school lie: Market-based education gambles with our children. Available at www.salon.com/2013/11/04/the_charter_school_lie_market_based_education_gambles_with_our_children/

Charles A. Dana Center, University of Texas at Austin. (1999). *Hope for urban education: A study of nine high-performing, high-poverty urban elementary schools.* Washington, DC: U.S. Department of Education, Planning and Evaluation Service.

Consortium for Policy Research in Education. (2002). *America's Choice school design: A research-based model.* Washington, DC: National Center on Education and the Economy.

Correnti, R., & Rowan, B. (2007). Opening up the black box: Literacy instruction in schools participating in three comprehensive school reform programs. *American Educational Research Journal, 44*(2), 298–338.

Duffy, G. G., Roehler, L. R., Sivan, E., Rackliffe, G., Book, C., Meloth, M. S., Vavrus, L. G., Wessleman, R., Putnam, J., & Bassiri, D. (1987). Effects of explaining the reasoning associated with using reading strategies. *Reading Research Quarterly, 20,* 347–368.

Dunkin, M., & Biddle, B. (1974). *The study of teaching.* New York, NY: Holt, Rinehart, & Winston.

Flanders, N. (1970). *Analyzing teacher behavior.* Reading, MA: Addison-Wesley.

Fullan, M. (1999). *Change forces: The sequel.* Philadelphia, PA: Falmer.

Fullan, M., & Hargreaves, A. (1992). *What's worth fighting for in your school?* New York, NY: Teachers College Press.

Hiebert, E. H., Colt, J. M., Catto, S. L., & Gury, E. C. (1992). Reading and writing of first-grade students in a restructured Chapter 1 program. *American Educational Research Journal, 29,* 545–572.

Hiebert, E. H., & Taylor, B. M. (2000). Beginning reading instruction: Research on early interventions. In M. L. Kamil, P. B. Mosenthal, P. D. Pearson, & R. Barr (Eds.), *Handbook of reading research* (Vol. III, pp. 455–482). Mahwah, NJ: Lawrence Erlbaum Associates.

Hoffman, J. V. (1991). Teacher and school effects in learning to read. In R. Barr, M. L. Kamil, P. B. Mosenthal, & P. D. Pearson (Eds.), *Handbook of reading research* (Vol. II, pp. 911–950) . New York, NY: Longman.

Invernizzi, M., Juel, C., & Rosemary, C. A. (1997). A community volunteer tutorial that works. *Reading Teacher, 50(4),* 304–311.

Klingner, J., Cramer, E., & Harry, B. (2006). Challenges in the implementation of Success for All in four high-need urban schools. *Elementary School Journal, 106*(4), 333–349.

Knapp, M. S. (1995). *Teaching for meaning in high-poverty classrooms.* New York, NY: Teachers College Press.

Langer, J. A. (2000). Excellence in English in middle and high school: How teachers' professional lives support student achievement. *American Educational Research Journal, 37*(2), 397–439.

Langer, J. A. (2001). Beating the odds: Teaching middle and high school students to read and write well. *American Educational Research Journal, 38*(4), 837–880.

Lein, L., Johnson, J. F., & Ragland, M. (1997). *Successful Texas schoolwide programs: Research study results.* Austin, TX: Charles A. Dana Center, University of Texas at Austin.

Levin, H. M. (1987). Accelerated schools for disadvantaged students. *Educational Leadership, 44*(6), 19–21.

Lipson, M. L., Mosenthal, J. H., Mekkelsen, J., & Russ, B. (2004). Building knowledge and fashioning success one school at a time. *The Reading Teacher, 57*(6), 534–542.

Louis, K. S., & Kruse, S. (1995). *Professionalism and community in schools.* Thousand Oaks, CA: Corwin.

May, H., & Supovitz, J. A. (2006). Capturing the cumulative effects of school reform: An 11-year study of the impacts of America's Choice on student achievement. *Educational Evaluation and Policy Analysis, 28*(3), 231–257.

Mullis, I.V.S., Martin, M. O., Foy, P., & Drucker, K. T. (2012). *PIRLS 2011 international results in reading.* Chestnut Hill, MA: TIMSS and PIRLS International Study Center, Boston College.

National Center for Education Statistics (NCES). (2011). *The nation's report card: Reading 2011*; Washington, DC: Institute of Education Sciences, U.S. Department of Education.

National Center for Education Statistics (NCES). (2012). Trends in international mathematics and science study. Available at http://nces.ed.gov/timss/

National Governors Association (NGA) Center for Best Practices & The Council of Chief State School Officers (CCSSO). (2010). *Common Core State Standards for English language arts and literacy in history/social studies, science, and technical subjects.* Washington, DC. Available at www.corestandards.org/the-standards

National Institute of Child Health and Human Development (NICHD). (2000). *Report of the National Reading Panel: Teaching children to read: An evidence-based assessment of the scientific research literature on reading and its implications for reading instruction* (NIH Publication No. 00-4769). Washington, DC: U.S. Government Printing Office.

Pinnell, G. S., Lyons, C. A., DeFord, D. E., Bryk, A. S., & Seltzer, M. (1994). Comparing instructional models for the literacy education of high-risk first graders. *Reading Research Quarterly, 29,* 8–39.

Pressley, M., Wharton-McDonald, R., Allington, R., Block, C. C., Morrow, L., Tracey, D., Baker, K., Brooks. G., Cronin, J., Nelson. E., & Woo, D. (2001). A study of effective first-grade literacy instruction. *Scientific Studies of Reading, 5,* 35–58.

Puma, M. J., Karweit, N., Price, C., Ricciuiti, A., Thompson, W., & Vaden-Kiernan, M. (1997). *Prospects: Final report on student outcomes.* (Title I). Washington, DC: U.S. Department of Education, Planning and Evaluation Service.

Ravitch, D. (2013). *Reign of error: The hoax of the privatization movement and the danger to America's public schools.* New York, NY: Alfred A. Knopf.

Richardson, V., & Placier, P. (2001). Teacher change. In V. Richardson (Ed.), *Handbook of research on teaching* (4th ed., pp. 903–947). Washington, DC: American Educational Research Association.

Ross, S. M., Nunnery, J. A., Goldfeder, E., McDonald, A., Rachor, R., Hornbeck, M., et al. (2004). Using school reform models to improve reading achievement: A longitudinal study of Direct Instruction and Success for All in an urban district. *Journal of Education for Students Placed At Risk, 9*(4), 357–388.

Skindrud, K., & Gersten, R. (2006). An evaluation of two contrasting approaches for improving reading achievement in a large urban district. *Elementary School Journal, 106*(5), 389–407.

Slavin, R., & Madden, N. (Eds.). (2001). *Success for All: Research and reform in elementary education.* New York, NY: Routledge.

Soar, R. S., & Soar, R. M. (1979). Emotional climate and management. In P. L. Peterson & H. J. Walberg (Eds.), *Research on teaching: Concepts, findings, and implications* (pp. 97–119). Berkeley, CA: McCutchan.

Stallings, J., & Kaskowitz, D. (1974). Follow through classroom observation evaluation 1972–73 (SRI Project URU-7370). Palo Alto, CA: Stanford Research Institute.

Sterbinsky, A., Ross, S. M., & Redfield, D. (2006). Effects of comprehensive school reform on student achievement and school change: A longitudinal multi-site study. *School Effectiveness and School Improvement, 17*(3), 367–397.

Taylor, B. M., Pearson, P. D., Clark, K., & Walpole, S. (2000). Effective schools and accomplished teachers: Lessons about primary grade reading instruction in low-income schools. *Elementary School Journal, 101*(2), 121–166.

Taylor, B. M., Pearson, P. D., Peterson, D. S., & Rodriguez, M. C. (2003). Reading growth in high-poverty classrooms: The influence of teacher practices that encourage cognitive engagement in literacy learning. *Elementary School Journal, 104,* 3–28.

Taylor, B. M., Pearson, P. D., Peterson, D. S., & Rodriguez, M. C. (2005). The CIERA School Change Framework: An evidenced-based approach to professional development and school reading improvement. *Reading Research Quarterly, 40*(1), 40–69.

Taylor, B. M., Pressley, M., & Pearson, P. D. (2002). *Research-supported characteristics of teachers and schools that promote reading achievement.* Washington, DC, National Education Association.

Taylor, B. M., Raphael, T. E., & Au, K. H. (2010). Reading and school reform. In M. L. Kamil, P. D. Pearson, P. Afflerbach, & E. Moje (Eds.), *Handbook of reading research* (Vol. 4, pp. 594–628). New York, NY: Routledge.

Taylor, B. M., Short, R., Frye, B., & Shearer, B. (1992). Classroom teachers prevent reading failure among low-achieving first-grade students. *The Reading Teacher, 45,* 592–597.

Venezky, R. L., & Winfield, L. (1979). *Schools that succeed beyond expectations in teaching reading* (Technical Report No. 1). Newark, DE: Department of Educational Studies, University of Delaware.

Weber, G. (1971). *Inner city children can be taught to read: Four successful schools* (CGE Occasional Papers No. 18). Washington, DC: Council for Basic Education. (ERIC Document Reproduction Service No. Ed 057 125.)

Wilder, G. (1977). Five exemplary reading programs. In J. T. Guthrie (Ed.), *Cognition, curriculum, and comprehension* (pp. 57–68). Newark, DE: International Reading Association.

Zech, L. K., Gause-Vega, C. L., Bray, M. H., Secules, T., & Goldman, S. R. (2000). Content-based collaborative inquiry: A professional development model for sustaining educational reform. *Educational Psychologist, 35*(3), 207–217.

CHAPTER 13

Changes in the Texts of Reading Instruction During the Past 50 Years

Elfrieda H. Hiebert and Leigh Ann Martin

By definition, reading is "the activity of looking at words and understanding them" (Longman Dictionary of American English, 2007, p. 553). Comprehending single words or small groups of words in the environment can be both functional and essential (e.g., *stop*, *in*, *out*, *exit*), but reading generally refers to a process of comprehending connected text in a range of media—books, magazines, digital environments, and the like. The model of the Rand Reading Study Group (Snow, 2002) described reading as the interaction between reader and text within a context (see Pearson & Cervetti, Chapter 1, this volume).

The nature of attention given to the text portion of the reading interaction has ebbed and flowed within the research community during the past 50 years, which Pearson and Cervetti (Chapter 1, this volume) confirm. During the 1970s and 1980s, cognitive scientists produced a sizable body of research on the nature and impact of rhetorical (genre and macrostructures), syntactic (sentence structure), and semantic (word meaning) manipulations on comprehension. In contrast, during the 1990s and the first decade of the 2000s, researchers focused on the discourse between teachers and students surrounding the reading of text, with less attention paid to the features and content of texts themselves.

The appearance of the Common Core State Standards (CCSS; National Governors Association Center for Best Practices [NGA Center] & Council of Chief State School Officers [CCSSO], 2010a) has changed the game, leading to a renewed interest in the texts that students read in school—positioning text as more important than the reader and the context. The writers of the CCSS stressed the importance of students' capacity to read increasingly more complex texts as they move through the grades. This focus has generated particular attention to text complexity because of the CCSS writers' assertion that texts since 1960 have trended downward in difficulty (NGA Center & CCSSO, 2010b). Further, because high school texts had been described as less complex than those used in college and the workplace (Stenner, Koons, & Swartz, 2010), the CCSS writers reasoned that text complexity levels needed to be augmented across the entire span from grades 2–12 in order for students to be college and career ready when they graduate from high school.

The CCSS writers recommended a tripartite method for establishing text complexity, which requires educators to consider readers and tasks, qualitative rubrics, and quantitative systems. Even though Appendix A of the CCSS suggests that all three categories are equal in importance, the size of the steps in the staircase of text complexity, was described, at least in the initial version of Appendix A, with a single quantitative system—the Lexile® Framework (NGA Center & CCSSO, 2010b). The Lexile® Framework, similar to other readability systems (Klare, 1984), establishes a text's complexity with an algorithm that uses an indirect measure of syntactic difficulty (mean sentence length [MSL]), and an indirect measure of semantic challenge (mean log word frequency [MLWF]). MLWF indexes the average frequency of occurrence in written English of individual words in text samples. The framework uses Lexiles rather than grade levels as a unit of text complexity; a Lexile is defined as "1000th of the difference between the comprehensibility of the primers and the comprehensibility of the encyclopedia" (Stenner, Burdick, Sanford, & Burdick, 2007, p. 6). In other words, the Lexile scale posits 1,000 steps between easy and challenging texts within our culture.

The magnitude of the increase in text complexity across grades 2 through College and Career Ready (CCR) is depicted in Figure 13.1. The dotted line represents the pre-CCSS level for Lexiles of texts, while the gray line represents the Lexile levels presented in the staircase of text complexity in Appendix A of the CCSS. These levels were increased, as evident in the black line shown in Figure 13.1, in a supplement to the CCSS (NGA Center & CCSSO, 2012). By the end of elementary school (grade 5), students are expected to read texts that were previously read by exiting 8th-graders.

The changes in expectations represented by the staircase of text complexity are of epic proportions. The two consortia responsible for creating CCSS-compatible assessments, the Partnership for Assessment of Readiness for College and Careers (PARCC) and Smarter Balanced Assessment Consortium (SBAC), have committed to using the staircase of text complexity to select texts for assessments. Pilot tests of the new assessments (Hernandez & Baker, 2013) show that even students who were proficient on their state assessments can do poorly on assessments where texts come from the high end of their grade-level band on the staircase of text complexity. Clearly, educators need to understand the consequences of the new mandates in the CCSS on text complexity.

The premise of this chapter, as is the case with the entire volume, is that solutions to the problems of the present can benefit from an understanding of the efforts of the past. The current policy to ramp up text levels illustrates a problem where all existing knowledge needs to be brought to bear—whether that knowledge comes from theoretically derived research, tried-and-true practice, or common sense. The contexts of classrooms in the 1960s may not be exactly the same as those of the 2010s, but in any reading interaction, the fundamental participants remain the same: students reading texts with the support of teachers.

We begin by comparing texts over the past 50 years. Then we examine curricular and policy events that have influenced the elementary texts used during the period. The final section of the chapter provides recommendations for how teachers might employ evidence-based practices to respond to increasing demands for more challenging texts.

AN EXAMINATION OF TEXTS: 1960s AND 2000s

For our examination of reading texts from the 1960s and the 2000s, we chose examples from a single core reading program—Scott Foresman (SF), largely because of its popularity and longevity throughout this period. The majority of American elementary

Figure 13.1. Lexiles for Five Grade Bands at Three Points in Time: Prior to CCSS, in CCSS Appendix A, and in CCSS Supplement

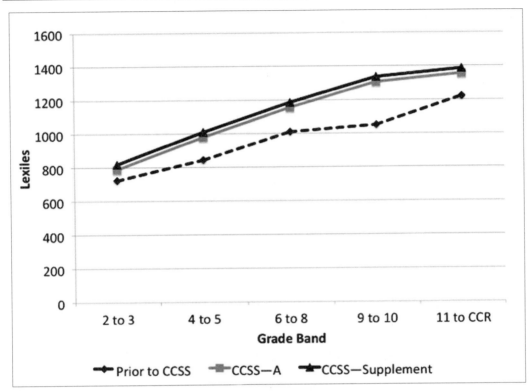

classrooms in the early 1960s used textbook series, either the SF program or one with a similar philosophy (Austin & Morrison, 1963). The 1960s SF edition is the prototypical text of the era—the series starring Dick, Jane, and their collection of relatives, friends, and pets. The SF program is also one of the two mainstream programs that Chall (1967/1983) reviewed in her seminal study of textbook difficulty. This program has particular significance in that Chall's study was one of only two empirical investigations of text difficulty (the other was Hayes, Wolfer, & Wolfe, 1996) on which the CCSS writers based their conclusions that texts had decreased in difficulty from 1960 to 2010.

Core reading programs (CRP) were not as dominant in American reading instruction in the 2000s (Bauman, Hoffman, Duffy-Hester, & Ro, 2000; Fitzgerald, Hiebert, Bowen, Relyea-Kim, Kung, & Elmore, 2014) as they had been in the 1960s. However, as will become evident in the review of texts representing the 2000s, the trade selections and magazine articles that were part of the CRP in 2008 are typical of the materials that teachers report using (Bauman et al., 2000; Fitzgerald et al., 2014) whether they use CRPs or some personal collection of books and articles. The CRPs of the 2000s have many components, including decodable and leveled texts, consumable workbooks and reproducibles, plus other supplemental materials. However, when a state or district purchases a CRP for classrooms, the anthologies for each grade typically account for the bulk of the cost of textbooks. In both the 1960s and the 2000s, most instruction occurs within these anthologies (or basals, as they were called in the 1960s).

The Analysis

Our analysis focused on the 1st-grade texts (Robinson, Monroe, Artley, & Huck, 1962) and 4th-grade texts (Gray, Monroe, Artley, & Arbuthnot, 1962) for the SF 1962 copyright and on 1st- and 4th-grade texts for the SF 2008 copyright (Afflerbach et al., 2008), which was published just prior to the appearance of the CCSS. Our choice of the 2008 program reflected our interest in considering the texts that were available when CCSS writers drew their conclusions about the decline in text complexity over the past half-century.

The materials we reviewed from the 1962 program included five 1st-grade texts and two 4th-grade readers. The materials from 2008 included five 1st-grade texts and two 4th-grade texts. Each of the five 1st-grade texts, for both editions, was treated as a unit. When the number of units differed (which was the case for grade 4, where there were eight units in 1962 and six in 2008), we formed an equivalent number of units and used the middle third of the texts from those units. Our sample, then, consisted of one-third of the selections in two editions (1962, 2008), each of which represented an entire grade level (grades 1 and 4) for a school year.

Numerous text features can be analyzed to determine complexity, and readers are directed to a variety of sources to learn about analytic systems, including ones related to CCSS' tripartite model (Hiebert & Pearson, 2014). In the current analysis, we focused on three word-level features of texts that have been linked to student proficiency:

1. *Quantity of words in text*—the number of unique words, the total number of running words, and the ratio of unique words to total words (Justice, Bowles, Pence, & Gosse, 2010)
2. *Vocabulary distributions*—proportions of highly, moderately, and rarely occurring vocabulary (Hayes et al., 1996)
3. *Repetition of vocabulary*—two indices, one anchoring the low end of the repetition continuum (the number of single-appearing words) and the other anchoring the high end of that continuum (the number of words repeated 10 times or more) (Mesmer, Cunningham, & Hiebert, 2012)

Lexiles were also obtained on texts, including the two components that make up the overall score: average sentence length (Mean Sentence Length), and average word frequency (Mean Log Word Frequency).

The analyses described to this point focus on the word-level demands of texts. We were also interested in changes in the quality of the selections the programs used over this period. Systems used for analyzing the quality of texts—one of the three parts of the CCSS model of text complexity—are less transparent than the other two text complexity systems (quantitative and reader-task) (Pearson & Hiebert, 2014). For the present analysis, we focused on the authenticity of the texts. Authentic texts were considered those that had been written and published either as trade books or magazine articles and then repurposed by publishers for the CRP. Texts that appeared for the first time in the program were regarded to have been written specifically for the CRP and were classified as CRP-only texts. The authenticity of a text, we reasoned, was indexed by whether or not permissions were noted in the acknowledgments of the textbooks: Did they seek and receive permission to reprint the selection, in unabridged or adapted form, from other sources?

The Findings

To offer a short but vivid example of what these texts that we analyzed look like, we offer excerpts from a 1st- and 4th-grade text from each of the programs in Table 13.1. Summaries of the quantity, vocabulary, and repetition of words within the programs and grades, along with Lexile information, appear in Table 13.2.

First-grade texts. The 1962 program had substantially fewer *different* or unique words than the 2008 program but almost twice as many total words. This pattern of fewer unique words and more total words means that the type/token ratio (i.e., the number of different words to the total words in text) was lower for the 1962 grade 1 texts than it was in 2008. What this pattern means is that the 2008 1st-grade students were expected to read almost four times the number of new, unique words for every 100 words of text, compared with 1st-graders in 1962.

With so many new words in the 2008 edition, it is not surprising that many unique words appear a single time (42%) and less than 10% of the unique words are repeated the 10 or more times that is considered necessary for gaining fluency with a word's meaning (McKeown, Beck, Omanson, & Pople, 1985; Reitsma, 1988). The pattern in word repetition was almost exactly the opposite in 1962: 11% of the words appeared a single time and 46% of the unique words appeared 10 times or more.

Regarding vocabulary, in this analysis, rare words are defined as those words that are predicted to occur nine or fewer times within a million words of text (Hiebert, 2005a; Zeno, Ivens, Millard, & Duvvuri, 1995). Nine repetitions was chosen as the indicator of rareness in vocabulary because, from the best available research (McKeown et al., 1985; Reitsma, 1988), a reader needs approximately 10 repetitions of a word to become facile with a word's meaning and use. First-graders reading the 2008 edition would encounter 2.3 times as many rare words as students exposed to the 1962 edition.

On measures of quantity, repetition, and vocabulary, these comparative results lead to the prediction that the 2008 texts would be considerably more challenging for 1st-graders than the 1962 texts were. With respect to the source of texts (magazines, trade books, adapted, or written especially for the textbook), approximately three-quarters of the texts were specially written for both programs (see Table 13.3). The texts that came from other sources (i.e., permissioned texts), however, came from different sources: The permissioned texts in 1962 primarily came from magazines, while the 2008 texts came from trade books. To illustrate the differences across the decades, we identified three of the permissioned texts from each of the time periods to determine whether the permissioned texts appeared in their original form or had been adapted for the CRP. The text of the trade books that had been permissioned for use in the 2008 program remained intact. For example, the reproduction of *Dot and Jabber and the Great Acorn Mystery* (Walsh, 2003) in the 2008 CRP retains all of the text, although all the original illustrations do not appear in the student textbook. The form of the permissioned texts in the 1962 programs is quite different. None of the illustrations from the original story *The Merry-go-round and the Griggses* (Emerson, 1927) was retained. The changes in the text are drastic, as illustrated in Table 13.4, where a single excerpt from the original text and the parallel text from the CRP appear. A 1,139-word text was condensed into just 256 words in the 1962 CRP. Sentences in the CRP version are short, and vocabulary consists of high-frequency

Table 13.1. Prototypical Texts for Grades 1 and 4 In 1962 and 2008 Editions of Core Reading Program

Grade Level	1962	2008
Grade 1	"Oh, Father," said Dick. "Do you want the car?" "I do," said father. Jane said, "Sally! Sally! Father wants the car. Come and help Dick and me." (Robinson et al., 1962)	Do not be afraid to start a garden. It is not hard. Read how. 1. Plant a few seeds. 2. Let the sun shine on them. (Afflerbach et al., 2008, p. 146)
Grade 4	Grandpa Toggle sat by his new roadside stand. On it, arranged in neat rows, were fruits and vegetables from Grandpa's farm. Grandpa Toggle was feeling discouraged. (Gray et al., 1962)	Warren Faidley is a storm chaser. Beginning in April and continuing through November, he can be found on the trail of tornadoes, thunderstorms, and hurricanes, photographing their spectacular beauty and power. (Kramer, 1998, p. 1)

words. There is scarcely any resemblance between the CRP version and the original one. If our examples typify these two periods—and we believe they do—then the differences are dramatic.

Fourth-grade texts. The 4th-grade texts in the 1962 and 2008 programs differed on the quantitative variables (number of words, presence of rare words, repetition of words). In all cases, the direction of the difference pointed to potentially more challenge for the 2008 edition than for the 1962 edition. These differences, however, were not as substantial as they were for the 1st-grade texts.

With respect to the authenticity of the text, a similar percentage of texts in the 4th-grade components from 1962 and 2008 came from trade books and magazines (see Table 13.3). The two programs differed, however, in the nature of changes made to texts from original sources. The words in the texts of the trade book selections in the 2008 edition were not manipulated, although all illustrations in the original texts were not included in the CRP.

In contrast, editors for the 1962 texts took considerable license in adapting them. An illustration of the adaptations made to original texts in the 1962 fourth-grade text is given in Table 13.4. We chose three texts from each program to compare the original and CRP

Table 13.2. Features of Grade 1 and 4 Texts from 1962 and 2008 Editions on Quantity, Repetition, Vocabulary, and Lexiles

Grade & Copyright	Quantity			Repetition		Vocabulary		Lexile		
	Unique Words (#)	Total Words	Types/ Tokens	Single-Appearing (% of Total Unique Words)	10+ Times (% of Total Unique Words)	Rare (% of All Unique Words)	Moderately Frequent (% of All Unique Words)	Overall	MSL	MLWF
Grade 1 (1962)	344	6,480	.05	11.33	46.22	4.7	23.26	260	6.21	3.69
Grade 1 (2008)	763	3,301	.23	42.29	9.30	11.66	32.63	400	6.83	3.52
Grade 4 (1962)	3,441	26,644	.13	38.36	12.21	24.67	44.20	640	10.02	3.62
Grade 4 (2008)	4,597	30,841	.15	43.59	10.68	31.39	41.22	820	11.86	3.48

Table 13.3. Sources of Texts (Percentage)

	No Permissions	Permissions from Magazines	Permissions from Trade Book Publishers
Grade 1/1962	.76	.21	.03
Grade 1/2008	.75	0	.25
Grade 4/1962	.42	.33	.25
Grade 4/2008	.40	0	.60*

*This is based on the word count, rather than on the selections. In the 2008 4th-grade texts there is one main selection, averaging 1,851 words, for a week. Three magazine-like articles that average approximately 415 words in length accompany each main selection. Main selections come from trade books, while the pre- and post-articles that are magazine-like in nature have been written to accompany the selections.

versions. Across the three texts that were adapted in the 1962 edition, the original texts were 197L higher than the adapted texts. The original texts averaged 2.5 words more in sentence length than the adapted texts. The original texts also had lower word-frequency averages (i.e., more challenging vocabulary) than adapted texts.

This review of changes in reading texts during the past 50 years, although not exhaustive by any means, provides a glimpse into the texts that students read in 1962 and 2008. The CCSS writers claim that the challenge of texts has decreased over the last 50 years, but our analysis suggests that either the text challenge has remained the same (grade 4) or has dramatically increased (for grade 1). And even at grade 4, the quality and content of texts have changed, rendering them, on balance, more challenging in terms of length and opportunities to encounter new words.

These data—provided for illustrative reasons—are consistent with recent research demonstrating that the purported dumbing-down of texts claimed by CCSS writers is inaccurate. In a comprehensive study of elementary texts over a century, Gamson, Lu, and Eckert (2013) showed that 3rd-grade texts used just prior to the writing of the CCSS were more challenging than the texts of the 1960s and that 6th-grade texts of the 2000s were at least as challenging as those of 1960s. Thus, the widely held belief that the texts of the current period reflect dramatically less linguistic and cognitive challenge is, at best, a misguided conjecture.

LANDMARK EVENTS IN READING TEXTS DURING THE PAST 50 YEARS

In this section, we identify several of the landmark events that led to shifts that were likely responsible for the differences between the 1962 and 2008 readers. Often, as Kim (2008) has stated, research serves as the incentive for a change in policy, but the content of the policy may have tenuous connections to the research, if it has any at all. There is evidence of at least a modicum of research in the four landmark events that have influenced texts from the 1960s through the 2000s, but often interpretations of the research have been selective or ideological, reflecting the wishful thinking of the interpreters (Tyson-Bernstein, 1988). The four landmark events are:

Table 13.4. Examples of Original and Adapted Texts at Grades 1 and 4: 1962 Core Reading Program

Grade	Original Text	Basal Text
1	"I have been doing just what that merry-go-round man has told me to do ever since I was a child," said the merry-go-round. "To-day for once I'm going to do what I want to do. I don't care if I have given them a five cent ride. I'm not going to stop!" (Emerson, 1927)	The merry-go-round did not stop. It called to the fathers and mothers, "Go away! Go away! I'll run all day." (Robinson et al., 1962)
4	So he hopped wildly from one spot to another, dodged a chicken sandwich, a pot of coffee, a basket of spinach, and two bowls of soup and finally gave one great leap over the head of a puffing old woman who was thrusting a rice pudding at him (Sharp, 1940)	When the bunny looked up, he saw apples, carrots, beets, tender young turnips, small squashes, and even lamb chops come flying at him. (Robinson et al., 1962)

1. Chall's (1967/1983, 1977) critiques of textbook programs;
2. perspectives and findings from cognitive psychology and their reporting in *Becoming a Nation of Readers* (Anderson, Hiebert, Scott, & Wilkinson, 1985);
3. policies on decodable texts in the era just prior to NCLB (California English/ Language Arts Committee, 2000; Texas Education Agency, 1997); and
4. the CCSS (NGA Center & CCSSO, 2010a, 2012) themselves.

Chall's Critique of the Complexity of Texts: 1967 and 1977

Chall's (1967/1983) critique of 1st-grade reading textbooks in *Learning to Read: The Great Debate* captured the interest of the public, scholars, and policymakers. The degree to which Chall's analysis influenced reading textbooks from 1967 through the 2000s is difficult to establish, but her 1967 report and a follow-up on middle and high school textbooks (Chall, 1977) were among the handful of studies cited by the CCSS (NGA Center & CCSSO, 2010a) writers as evidence for a need to increase text complexity. To understand Chall's critique, it is helpful to put the school texts in the decades prior to her analysis into context.

Context for Chall's critique. Before the 1930s, a typical primer for beginning readers consisted of selections that contained rhymes and poems and lyrics from songs. For example, a page in the Stickney (1885) primer has the rhyme (with a picture of a child and dog): "Beg for it! Beg, sir! See! It is a bun! But you cannot have it if you do not beg." This is followed by five sets of words with rhymes for each vowel (e.g., *beg, leg, keg, peg*).

The foundation for changes in beginning texts was laid with Gray's (1925) report on the National Committee on Reading. In this document, Gray presented a perspective that became the foundation for instructional texts, especially for beginning readers, for at least a 40-year period. Gray's model was based on the behaviorist perspective (Thorndike, 1903). The reasoning behind the perspective was that repetition of a core group of high-frequency words—especially the 300 words that accounted for almost 50% of the words in texts (Thorndike, 1921)—would lead to successful reading acquisition. Because many of these frequently used words have vowel patterns (e.g., *the, of, one, some*) that do not follow the most common and consistent patterns of English, Gray's instruction encouraged beginning readers to use a "look-say," or memorization strategy, rather than sounding out words.

In 1930, Gray became the second author of an existing reading series—the Elson Basic Readers (Elson & Gray, 1930). By 1936, Gray's perspective was prominent in the series (and his role was reflected in a change of the name—the Elson-Gray Basic Readers; Gray & Elson, 1936)): The text emphasized high-frequency words that were repeated in stories about Dick and Jane and their family members, friends, and pets. By the late 1950s, when Chall began examining textbooks, SF's Dick and Jane series (formally labeled the Curriculum Foundation Series, with Gray as the lead author from the early 1940s through the late 1950s) dominated the marketplace, along with that of another publisher, Ginn. The first-grade texts of the Ginn program featured characters Tom and Susan, who encountered similar scenarios as those experienced in the Dick and Jane readers of the SF program.

The rate of introducing and repeating vocabulary followed a formulaic pattern in the 1st-grade texts. The model of repetition was described explicitly in the back pages of the student texts, as illustrated in the 1962 SF primer (Robinson et al., 1962) in which each of the 101 new words in the primer were repeated at least 10 times. Beginning in 2nd grade for the 1962 series, readability formulas influenced the design and selection of texts. Readability formulas became part of the institutional machinery as states established acceptable readability levels for their textbook adoption lists (Tyson-Bernstein, 1988). In these mandates, readability requirements were stipulated across the grades. The effect of readability-formula requirements beyond 1st grade was evident in the analysis of the 1962 4th-grade textbook where orginal stories were altered to satisfy the requirements of the readability formulas, with complex words changed to simpler ones and conjunctions or other connections removed to create shorter, less complex sentences, and so forth. Researchers (e.g., Pearson, 1974) empirically confirmed the negative impact on comprehension of text adaptations. Texts with higher readability scores could elicit superior comprehension, while those with shorter sentences and more generic vocabulary could hinder comprehension.

Chall's critique. Among the components of Chall's (1967/1983) landmark study was a review of the features of two of the mainstream programs in the educational marketplace at the time: Scott Foresman (Gray, Monroe, Artley, Arbuthnot, & Gray, 1956) and Ginn (Russell, Gates, & McCullough, 1961). These two programs were compared to a phonics program, Lippincott (McCracken & Walcutt, 1963). Chall also included a summary of the features of the 1920, 1930, and 1940 SF series. Chall did not include any empirical analyses of students' actual text reading; rather, she summarized five features of passages within texts: total number of words, new words, new words per 100 running words (vocabulary load, according to Chall), pictures, and pictures per 100 running words (picture load). From 1920 to 1956, the number of unique words had increased. However, from Chall's perspective, the number of new words was simply not enough to challenge most readers.

Chall (1977) continued to develop the argument of what came to be called the dumbing-down of text in a report that attempted to explain why scores on the Scholastic Aptitude Test (SAT), the most widely used college admissions test at the time, had declined from 1963 to 1976. Based on an analysis of the readability of content-area textbooks from 1945 to 1975 at grades 6 and 11, Chall concluded that the difficulty of texts had declined during this period. Chall suggested that the decline in SAT scores might well be accounted for by the decline in the complexity of texts. Chall, Conard, and Harris-Sharples (1991) extended Chall's 1977 report with additional analyses from the 1974–1982 and 1985–1989 editions of social studies and science textbooks for grades 4, 6, 8, and 11, and from reading textbooks for grades 4, 6, and 8. Chall et al. concluded that the reading textbooks were the easiest, considerably less difficult than social studies and science textbooks. Further, at 4th grade, most of the science and social studies textbooks were above the reading levels of most students. By 6th and 8th grade, the content-area textbooks were more closely matched to students' reading levels. But, at the 11th-grade level, content-area texts were below the reading levels of most students.

A frequent assumption is that Chall's (1967/1983) critique precipitated substantial changes in reading programs, especially in beginning reading programs. It is true that the 1971 edition of the Scott Foresman program (Aaron et al., 1971) did change course in the primary grades, dropping the Gray (1925) model and increasing the number of unique words (but not the number of phonetically regular words). When that program fared poorly in the marketplace (Chall & Squire, 1991), the next edition (and those of other publishers) returned to the look-say instructional approach. Chall's critique in *Learning to Read; The Great Debate* did appear to have prompted substantial changes in the teachers' manuals that accompanied beginning readers (see Pearson, 2000). These manuals almost doubled in size as publishers responded to recommendations for increased phonics instruction. This phonics instruction, however, appears to have been tenuously associated with the words in texts for students (Beck & Block, 1979).

Research from Cognitive Psychology and Linguistics

Cognitive scientists and psycholinguists brought frameworks from their disciplines to the analysis of text in the 1970s and early 1980s, resulting in considerable criticism of the look-say model. The Commission on Reading's report *Becoming a Nation of Readers* (Anderson et al., 1985) used research evidence to develop two themes about instructional texts. The first theme drew heavily on Chall's 1983 reissue of *Learning to Read: The Great Debate*, in which she concluded that beginning reading texts continued to emphasize high-frequency words rather than easily decodable (predictable letter-to-sound correspondences) words. The commission recommended that beginning texts should be engaging, comprehensible, and decodable (i.e., children should be provided with opportunities to apply letter-sound knowledge) (Anderson et al., 1985). The commission gave *Green Eggs and Ham* (Dr. Seuss, 1960) as an exemplar of a beginning text that had all three features of engagingness, comprehensibility, and decodability.

The report's "Extending Literacy" chapter summarized research on the obstacles to comprehension created by manipulations performed to make text comply with readability formulas. This message was translated into policy over the next several years, as the states of California and Texas called for authentic texts in their state textbook adoptions, eschewing texts that had been manipulated to comply with readability formulas (California English/Language Arts Committee, 1987; Texas Education Agency, 1990). Even though proponents of whole language as a movement would never choose to be associated with any state policy initiative, among teachers and the public, this instructional perspective was often associated with the whole-language approach—to the point that the term *whole-language basal* was used to characterize these new programs.

These state mandates did not distinguish between texts for beginning reading and those for subsequent grade levels. As a result, the vocabulary of the 1st-grade texts in the next editions of major core reading programs (see Hiebert, 2005b) was no longer controlled according to the model that had been put forward by Gray (1925) 65 years earlier. Instead, the new beginning reading texts used predictable text structures, in which key words were substituted within repeated phrases or sentences (as in the song, *I know an old lady who swallowed a fly*). A prototypical predictable text, *Brown Bear, Brown Bear* (Martin, 1967), differed substantially from *Green Eggs and Ham* (Dr. Seuss, 1960) in the amount and repetition of vocabulary.

Decodable Texts

When the results of the first state-by-state comparison of the National Assessment of Educational Progress (NAEP) were released in 1996 (Campbell, Donahue, Reese, & Phillips, 1996), the poor performances of California's 4th-graders were interpreted as an indictment of the whole-language approach (Levine, 1996). A widespread demand for a return to reading instructional methods that stressed "the basics"—most specifically, phonics and decodable texts—followed (see Pearson, 2004, for an account of the "reading wars" of this period).

Texas (Texas Education Agency, 1997) preceded California (California Reading/Language Arts Committee, 2000) in mandating that programs should provide increased phonics instruction accompanied by decodable texts. From numerous types of texts emphasizing decodability, Texas chose the individual phoneme-grapheme as the focus of text creation. A decodable text was defined as one where all of the phoneme-grapheme correspondences of all of the new words in a text had been taught previously. High-frequency words were considered acceptable if they had been introduced in a lesson as sight words. The implicit theory seems to be that the more elements that had been taught (either as sight words or as predictable orthographic patterns), the greater the likelihood that the text could be accurately and readily decoded.

These policies began to exert their influence in the late 1990s, but they were all given a boost by the orientation to fundamentals within the NCLB legislation that became law in January 2002. Although these perspectives influenced texts in the primary grades, they had little if any influence on texts beyond grade 2. It should be noted that kindergarten texts came to be treated in the same category as 1st- and 2nd-grade texts during this era. By the mid-2000s, the components of kindergarten programs, as well as expectations for student performance, were not very different than those of 1st-grade students and texts in 1988 (Hiebert & Martin, 2008).

The Common Core State Standards

The CCSS represent the fourth milestone in views of text within the past 50 years. As pointed out earlier in this book (Kapinus & Long, Chapter 2, this volume), 46 states, the District of Columbia, 3 territories, and the Department of Defense Education Activity originally adopted the CCSS for English Language Arts. Even the states that did not participate in the CCSS have accepted the policies about text complexity and, as states move out of the CCSS or at least the CCSS-aligned assessment consortia, there is no indication that text complexity has lost any momentum whatsoever. With one fell swoop, policies about text complexity have been implemented without any empirical evidence that the levels that have been mandated at different grade bands can be either attained or sustained throughout the grades.

Unlike previous efforts that have served as watersheds for changes in text complexity (e.g., Anderson et al., 1985; Chall, 1967/1983), the CCSS were accompanied by neither a research synthesis nor a report. The intent was to create a set of standards that states would adopt in an effort to reform reading instruction by upping the ante for text and task challenge. The CCSS made several assumptions about text complexity. The most critical is the assumption that texts have trended downward in difficulty over time (CCSS, 2010b). As discussed previously, the basis for this statement was Chall's analyses (1967/1983, 1977; Chall et al., 1991) and that of Hayes et al. (1996)—analyses of editions of programs from decades prior to the 1990s and 2000s. Based on their perception that overall text difficulty had decreased, the CCSS writers recommended that the levels of texts, beginning with grade 2, should increase in complexity.

We can all agree that attention to text complexity is critical and that there needs to be a progression in text complexity across the school years. We can disagree, however, about where to begin to accelerate text complexity. Should Grade Two be the point of acceleration as suggested in the CCSS's staircase of text complexity (NGA Center & CC-SSO, 2010b)? Should levels at Grades K–One be accelerated? The CCSS's staircase of text complexity may not begin until grade 2, but the identification of 450L as the beginning of the Grade Two–Three text complexity band in the staircase of text complexity implies an expectation for end of grade-one reading. Prior to the CCSS, the ability to read texts at 450L had not been articulated as an expectation for end of Grade One reading, either in Standards documents or by publishers of core reading programs. Hiebert and Mesmer (2013) have raised numerous reasons to start the acceleration at higher grades rather than the primary grades. For example, a comparison of comprehension-based levels of reading rate shows that Grade Two levels have remained steady from 1960 to 2011 (Spichtig, Hiebert, Pearson, & Radach, 2013). In the Spichtig et al. study, the period where reading levels have declined most during the 50-year period from 1960 to 2011 is the middle-school grades. Might these grades be a more appropriate focus for acceleration than the primary grades?

Further, we might not agree that any one of the dimensions identified by CCSS writers for establishing text complexity—quantitative, qualitative, or reader and task—should be emphasized more than other dimensions. The CCSS writers implied in Appendix A that the three elements ought to be treated equally; however, when it comes to implementation, reader and task and qualitative indices have taken a back seat to the quantitative face of text complexity. The staircase of text complexity in Appendix A is defined solely by quantitative measurement of text complexity. In fact, the CCSS writers assumed that second-generation readability systems, such as the Lexile® Framework (Stenner et al., 2007), provide measures of text complexity that can guide instruction.

Limitations to quantitative assessments of text complexity have long been recognized (Anderson et al., 1985; Gray & Leary, 1935). Additional limitations are evident in digital systems such as the Lexile® Framework that use averages (e.g., MLWF) to measure vocabulary load. The problem with a metric like MLWF lies in the distribution of words in written English. Of the approximately 300,000 words in written English, approximately 2,500 words and their morphological relatives (approximately 11,000 words in all) account for 90% of all the words appearing in the entire corpus of text (Hiebert, 2014). The remaining words in written English—approximately 289,000—appear infrequently. In the *Educator's Word Frequency Guide* (Zeno et al., 1995), which reports on frequencies of more than 150,000 words, 52% of unique words are predicted to appear once in every 10 million words of text. A skewed distribution of words means that average scores, even when statistical procedures are employed to correct for the skewed distribution, are limited in range because of the high frequency of common words.

The range for sentence lengths, in contrast to vocabulary, is extensive. What this means is that the correlation between the Lexile and the mean sentence length is high (.94), while that between the Lexile and the word-frequency mean is substantially lower (−.53, with the negative correlation reflecting the fact that harder vocabulary has a lower word frequency) (Hiebert, 2012).

A Lexile score for a text can be changed quite easily by combining sentences (increasing the Lexile) or dividing sentences (decreasing the Lexile). Manipulating the complexity of texts by changing sentence length creates its own set of problems, among them a lack of knowledge as to how syntactic patterns can be taught. Even more troubling is the fact that, when sentence length is easy to manipulate, superficial changes can be made to texts that do not necessarily make texts easier to comprehend. Several linguistic (Davison & Kantor, 1982) and empirical (Pearson, 1974) analyses suggest that shorter sentences do not always make text easier. Short sentences tend to have fewer context clues and fewer explicit connectives between ideas, thus requiring readers to make more inferences.

GROUNDING CURRENT PRACTICES ON EVIDENCE

Texts are not as readily malleable as some aspects of classroom instruction. Scholars in other chapters in this volume have identified practices that teachers can adopt or adapt in their classrooms, such as engaging students in discussion (Horowitz, Chapter 4, this volume), teaching particular words as morphological families (Graves, Chapter 8, this volume), or focusing on different features of instruction (Pearson & Cervetti, Chapter 1, this volume; Williams, Chapter 5, this volume). But changes in texts require districts (or states) to invest funds in buying new materials.

Within the CCSS context, the press is to increase the level of text complexity that all students encounter in their school reading programs. However, there is precious little in the way of research to support these momentous policy changes. We know little about the efficacy of forcing more challenging text on students, nor do we know that using largely quantitative indices of difficulty to gauge complexity is more valid than employing either of the other two legs of the CCSS model of complexity (qualitative or reader and task indicators). Especially in the face of policies and recommendations that texts need to be accelerated based on quantitative indices, educational leaders need to have solid bases for designing instruction with appropriate texts. We identify three responses that build on evidence related to the complexity of texts.

Keep the Focus on Selecting Texts for Students' Learning About Content

In the push for complex text, all of those involved in the educational enterprise—policy-makers, publishers, district and state leaders, and teachers—need to keep in mind that the purpose of reading is for students to gain knowledge and insight about the natural and social world. Therefore, the right question isn't whether a text fits into the right level of text complexity band but rather, "What will my students learn from this text?" Another way to phrase this critical question is to ask whether a text is worthy of students' time. If this criterion is satisfied, then educators can consider what to focus on in terms of text (what effect the styles, structures, and words of a text will have on students' comprehension) and the instructional scaffolding surrounding the reading.

When CCSS writers describe texts as having been dumbed-down or as not sufficiently complex, they mean that the content is either inconsequential or inappropriate for students at a particular grade level. An excerpt of such a text follows:

> My phone rang today. A man said, "Is Finch there?" "No, there is no Finch here. You might have the wrong number," I said. "Have a nice day!" Then I went to eat lunch with a pal. I got an itch, so I stood up to scratch. At the same time, my arm hit a man. (Scarella, Rivera, Rivera, Beck, McKeown, & Chiappe-Collins, 2010)

This excerpt comes from an intervention program for struggling readers in middle school. The Lexile of the text—930—places it solidly in the grade 4–5 band recommended by the CCSS (Lexiles from 740–1010). The ideas and vocabulary, however, fail to support students in developing either critical vocabulary or background knowledge. As is the case with many intervention texts, the content of this text is trivial. Students' time would be better spent with texts of equivalent complexity but dealing with content that furthers the goals of the curriculum. Finding texts that support critical content learning goals should be the driving factor in text selection, not the number obtained from applying either a traditional or modern readability formula.

Ensure That Texts Provide a Steady Progression in Demands for Knowledge About Words and Literary Features

To increase capacity in any domain requires that there be a progression in learning. For example, in learning to play the piano, novices typically start with ditties such as "Row, Row, Row Your Boat" or "Twinkle, Twinkle, Little Star," not Bach's *Minuet in G*. Similarly, in learning to read, a progression would be expected in the texts that students read. In the Dick and Jane era (i.e., the texts of the early 1960s), the progression was based on an algorithm that presented the most frequently used words earliest and generated texts that, while providing opportunities to read these words repeatedly, resulted in tedious reading experiences. In the decodable books of the early 2000s, prior instruction in learning how to decode particular phoneme-grapheme patterns replaced frequency as the standard for sequencing words in grade 1. The assumption was that, once a lesson on a phoneme-grapheme pattern had been presented, students had learned that element. Words where all the phoneme-grapheme patterns had been covered in lessons were judged to be decodable. Features such as these are assumed to influence complexity, but the degree to which the presence of many, different words with a particular phoneme-grapheme makes a text easier or harder has yet to be proven.

Overall text length can be important, especially when the text contains numerous different words within the text, few of which are repeated. Even when length is kept consistent, having fewer unique words means that students receive more exposure to those words. For example, *Hop on Pop* (Dr. Seuss, 1963) may have many pages, but the number of different words in the text is few, the words are short, and almost all the words are repeated often. Once beginning readers have unlocked a word in the book, they have the chance to apply that discovery again. The situation is quite different with the texts in 1st-grade anthologies, as our earlier review documents, where there are lots of unique words (e.g., *tuxedo, gargoyle*), few of which are repeated.

For all students, instructional texts need to offer the opportunity to increase capacity on some element of text comprehension. For high school students, the opportunity may lie in becoming fluent with the use of dialects by writers (e.g., *The Grapes of Wrath* [Steinbeck, 1939]), *Their Eyes Were Watching God* [Hurston, 1937]). With beginning and struggling readers, the opportunity may be to get the chance to practice with texts where the majority of words have been encountered previously and are repeated regularly.

Resist the Push to Select Texts on the Basis of Omnibus Measures

Overall or omnibus measures of a given text's complexity—whether gained from human judgments such as guided reading levels (Fountas & Pinnell, 2012) or an algorithm developed by humans and executed by a computer such as Lexiles (Stenner et al., 2007)—fail to give teachers enough specific information to know why a text receives the designation it does. Without more descriptive information, teachers cannot identify texts appropriately or create appropriate instructional experiences for their students.

These omnibus measures are readily obtained from Internet databases and give a straightforward designation of a text's complexity. But these results should be viewed only as a starting point, much like a measure of blood pressure on a medical exam alerts physicians that additional analysis and diagnosis might be needed. Teachers need to understand that overall evaluations of texts such as Lexiles or guided reading levels give general information and need to be followed with evaluations of the specific features of texts. To establish which texts are appropriate for particular students and how best to use texts to increase students' capacity to comprehend increasingly more complex texts, teachers need guidance on which features of texts contribute to making comprehension challenging for students.

Particular problems with quantitative text complexity systems such as Lexiles have long been recognized (Anderson et al., 1985; Klare, 1984). For example, because sentence length influences readability formulas and narratives often have dialogues, there is a tendency for these systems to underestimate the difficulty of a text. The difficulty of informational texts is often overestimated because every instance of a specialized word (e.g., *zygote, gamete*) adds to the word-frequency load. As has already been described, a new wrinkle in the measurement of readability arises when, as is the case with Lexiles (or Advantage/TASA Open Standard [ATOS]; Milone, 2009), vocabulary is assessed as an average of the frequencies of words in a text. When the average frequency of the vocabulary in a text is difficult to change (Hiebert, 2012) but changes in sentence length can be made easily and with substantial consequences on the measure of text complexity, texts can be manipulated so that they fit into the specifications on the staircase of text complexity. This kind of manipulation was precisely what Anderson et al. (1985) cautioned against in *Becoming a Nation of Readers.*

Sets of texts are now available commercially that use this manipulation of sentence length to provide a range of texts. For example, the same news article may be available at a number of different Lexile levels. A sample of texts on one topic from one of these programs appears in Table 13.5. Many of the changes reflect variations in sentence length, not vocabulary. Even a text at the lower end of the Grade Two–Three text band (e.g., 660L) has challenging vocabulary (a 3.37 word-frequency average is on the harder end of the word-frequency range). Texts with lower Lexiles are also consistently shorter, which means that students who are reading texts at the lower levels read considerably less text than their peers, potentially contributing to the Matthew effect, where the poor get poorer and the rich get richer, as readers (Stanovich, 1986).

Programs that promise texts with different levels of the same content should be evaluated carefully. It is possible to create texts with similar content but variations in text complexity. To maintain the integrity of ideas and also ensure accessibility at the lower levels is a challenging task for writers. The task is possible (see readworks.org), but the commercial programs available currently that claim to provide sets of texts with similar content that vary in complexity have typically achieved these differences by manipulating the length of sentences and by eliminating challenging ideas at lower levels of complexity.

CONCLUSIONS

Expectations for text complexity have increased with the CCSS. This increase has occurred despite the presence of more complex text in the primary grades over the past 50 years and texts that are at least as difficult at the end of elementary school (Gamson et al., 2013; Hiebert, 2005b). Even so, because of the guidelines set forth in the CCSS, there is a push for texts that are more complex at all levels.

There is much that is still not known about text complexity. The size of the steps in the staircase of text complexity, both those in the original iteration of the staircase in Appendix A and the revised staircase in the Supplement to the Common Core (NGA Center & CCSSO, 2012), are based on hypothetical models, such as those described in Williamson, Fitzgerald, and Stenner (2014). To date, there has been no validation that the majority of students can attain the high ends of the grade-band levels or even that attainment of these levels at grades 2–3 or 4–5 leads to successful reading of CCR-level texts at high school graduation.

Table 13.5. Same Content Across Four Lexile Levels: A 2014 Version of Text Manipulations[1]

Lexile Level	Excerpt	Mean Sentence Length	Mean Long Word Frequency	# of Words in Text
250 (below level)	This past winter, Florida had cold weather. On many days, there was a freeze. The weather is usually warmer.	5.61	3.53	213
660 (approaches level)	On a cold day in December, helicopters whirred above Florida's valuable veggie crops. Farmers had sent for the helicopters. They wanted the helicopters to push warmer air closer to the plants.	9.38	3.37	694
980 (at level)	On an unseasonably cold day in December, helicopters whirred above Florida's valuable and sensitive veggie crops. . . . Farmers had sent the helicopters on their mission in a desperate attempt to push warmer air closer to the plants.	13.34	3.29	774
1,280 (exceeds level)	On an unseasonably cold day in December, helicopters whirred above Florida's valuable but sensitive veggie crops. . . . Farmers had sent the choppers on their mission in a desperate attempt to push warmer air closer to the plants after it became clear that the freeze could ravage their harvests.	15.66	3.21	830

[1]Text excerpts come from achieve3000.com

The perspective that we have developed in this chapter is for educators to ground practices in the underlying aims of Standard 10. The goal of Standard 10 is to increase students' capacity in reading over the grades. We need to understand on what dimensions this capacity needs to be increased and, to make this happen, how the features of particular texts support particular goals. Presumably, a primary goal of reading instruction is to increase students' capacity with texts that represent more challenging content, structures, and genres. However, previous standards and also state assessments (and even the NAEP) have been relatively silent about the complexity of texts that form the basis for establishing students' reading proficiency. Bringing this central aspect of reading development and instruction to the forefront is a substantial contribution of the CCSS.

As is often the case, unique interpretations accompany a policy document such as the CCSS and these unique interpretations have taken center stage, often leaving the goal in the background. For example, the presentation of explicit Lexiles for exit levels at different grades has been interpreted to mean that all students should be reading texts at these levels for instruction. When primary-level students who are developing vocabulary and automaticity in reading texts are asked to read texts that have been designated as "grade-level" without consideration of the students' proficiency levels, the underlying goal of increasing students' capacity in reading more and more complex texts is lost. To ensure that students receive the texts that support them in increasing their capacity to read more complex text, educators need to build on what we know and to move with alacrity.

LITERATURE

Emerson, C. D. (1927). *A merry-go-round of modern tales*. New York, NY: E. P. Dutton & Company.

Kramer, S. (1998). *Eye of the storm: Chasing storms with Warren Faidley*. New York, NY: Scholastic.

Martin, B., Jr. (1967). *Brown bear, brown bear, what do you see?* New York, NY: Henry Holt.

Hurston, Z. N. (1937). *Their eyes were watching God*. New York, NY: Harper.

Seuss, Dr. (1960). *Green eggs and ham*. New York, NY: Random House.

Seuss, Dr. (1963). *Hop on pop*. New York, NY: Random House.

Sharp, C. J. (1940). Auntie Grumble meets the wizard. In R. Lawson (Ed.), *Just for fun: A collection of stories & verses* (pp. 8–19). Chicago, IL: Rand McNally.

Steinbeck, J. (1939). *The grapes of wrath*. New York, NY: Viking Press.

Walsh, E. S. (2003). *Dot and Jabber and the great acorn mystery*. New York, NY: Scholastic.

REFERENCES

Aaron, I., Artley, A. S., Goodman, K. S., Huck, C. S., Jenkins, W. A., Manning, J. C., Monroe, M., Pyle, W. J., Robinson, H. M., Schiller, A., Smith, M. B., Sullivan, L. M., Weintraub, S., & Wepman, J. M. (1971). *Scott Foresman Reading Systems*. Glenview, IL: Scott Foresman.

Achieve3000. (2011, March 16). Trying to take the chill off. Available at portal.achieve3000.com/kb/lesson/?lid=15911&step=11&c=58&asn=1

Afflerbach, P., Blachowicz, C., Dawson Boyd, C., Cheyney, W., Juel, C. (2008). *Reading Street*. Glenview, IL: Scott Foresman.

Anderson, R. C., Hiebert, E. H., Scott, J. A., & Wilkinson, I.A.G. (1985). *Becoming a nation of readers*. Champaign: University of Illinois, Center for the Study of Reading.

Austin, M. C., & Morrison, C. (1963). *The first R: The Harvard report on reading in elementary schools*. New York, NY: Macmillan.

Baumann, J. F., Hoffman, J. V., Duffy-Hester, A. M., & Ro, J. M. (2000). The First R yesterday and today: U.S. elementary reading instruction practices reported by teachers and administrators. *Reading Research Quarterly, 35*(3), 338–377.

Beck, I. L., & Block, K. K. (1979). An analysis of two beginning reading programs: Some facts and some opinions. In L. B. Resnick & P. A. Weaver (Eds.), *Theory and practice of early reading* (Vol. 1, pp. 279–318). Hillsdale, NJ: Erlbaum.

California English/Language Arts Committee. (1987). *English-language arts framework for California public schools (kindergarten through grade twelve).* Sacramento, CA: California Department of Education.

California English/Language Arts Committee. (2000). *English-language arts framework for California public schools (kindergarten through grade twelve).* Sacramento, CA: California Department of Education.

Campbell, J. R., Donahue, P. L., Reese, C. M., & Phillips, G. W. (1996). *NAEP 1994 reading report card for the nation and the states: Findings from the National Assessment of Educational Progress and trial state assessments.* Washington, DC: National Center for Education Statistics.

Chall, J. S. (1977). *An analysis of textbooks in relation to declining SAT scores.* Princeton, NJ: Educational Testing Service & College Board.

Chall, J. S. (1983). *Learning to read: The great debate.* New York, NY: McGraw-Hill. (Original work published 1967)

Chall, J. S., Conard, S. S., & Harris-Sharples, S. (1991). *Should textbooks challenge students? The case for easier or harder textbooks.* New York, NY: Teachers College Press.

Chall, J. S., & Squire, J. R. (1991). The publishing industry and textbooks. *Handbook of reading research, 2*, 120–146.

Davison, A., & Kantor, R. N. (1982). On the failure of readability formulas to define readable texts: A case study from adaptations. *Reading research quarterly, 17*, 187–209.

Elson, W. H., & Gray, W. S. (1930). *The Elson Basic Readers.* Chicago, IL: Scott Foresman.

Fitzgerald, J., Hiebert, E. H., Bowen, K., Relyea-Kim, J., Kung, M., & Elmore, J. (2014). Text complexity: Primary teachers' views. *Literacy Research and Instruction*, 1–26.

Fountas, I. C. & Pinnell, G. S. (2012). *The F & P text level gradient: Revision to recommended grade-level goals.* Portsmouth, NH: Heinemann. Available at www.heinemann.com/fountasandpinnell/pdfs/WhitePaperTextGrad.pdf

Gamson, D. A., Lu, X., & Eckert, S. A. (2013). Challenging the research base of the Common Core State Standards: A historical reanalysis of text complexity. *Educational Researcher, 42*(7), 381–391. doi:10.3102/0013189X13505684

Gray, W. S. (1925). A modern program of reading instruction for the grades and high school. Report of the National Committee on Reading. *24th yearbook of the National Society for the Study of Education*, part 1, 21–73.

Gray, W. S., & Leary, B. E. (1935). *What makes a book readable.* Chicago, IL: University of Chicago Press.

Gray, W. S., & Elson, W. S. (1936). *Elson-Gray basic readers: Curriculum foundation series.* Chicago, IL: Scott Foresman.

Gray, W. S., Monroe, M., Artley, A. S., Arbuthnot, M. H., & Gray, L. (1956). *The new basic readers: Curriculum foundation series.* Chicago, IL: Scott Foresman.

Gray, W. S., Monroe, M., Artley, A. S., & Arbuthnot, M. H. (1962). *The new basic readers: Curriculum foundation series* (Grade 4). Chicago, IL: Scott Foresman.

Hayes, D. P., Wolfer, L. T., & Wolfe, M. F. (1996). Schoolbook simplification and its relation to the decline in SAT-Verbal Scores. *American Educational Research Journal, 33*(2), 489–508.

Hernandez, J. C., & Baker, A. (2013, April 19). A tough new test spurs protest and tears. *The New York Times*, p. A24.

Hiebert, E. H. (2005a). In pursuit of an effective, efficient vocabulary curriculum for the elementary grades. In E. H. Hiebert & M. Kamil (Eds.), *The teaching and learning of vocabulary: Bringing scientific research to practice* (pp. 243–263). Mahwah, NJ: Erlbaum.

Hiebert, E. H. (2005b). State reform policies and the task textbooks pose for first-grade readers. *Elementary School Journal,105,* 245–266.

Hiebert, E. H. (2012, December). *Readability and text complexity.* Paper presented at the annual meeting of the Literacy Research Association, San Diego, CA.

Hiebert, E. H. (2014, July 19). *Development and application of a morphological family database in analyzing vocabulary patterns in text.* Paper presented at the annual meeting of the Society for the Scientific Study of Reading, Santa Fe, NM.

Hiebert, E. H., & Martin, L. A. (2008). Repetition of words: The forgotten variable in texts for beginning and struggling readers. In E. H. Hiebert & M. Sailors (Eds.), *Finding the right texts for beginning and struggling readers: Research-based solutions* (pp. 47–69). New York, NY: Guilford.

Hiebert, E. H., & Mesmer, H. A. E. (2013). Upping the ante of text complexity in the Common Core State Standards: Examining its potential impact on young readers. *Educational Researcher, 42*(1), 44–51.

Hiebert, E. H., & Pearson, P. D. (2014). Understanding text complexity: Overview of the special issue. *Elementary School Journal, 115*(2), 153–160.

Justice, L. M., Bowles, R., Pence, K., & Gosse, C. (2010). A scalable tool for assessing children's language abilities within a narrative context: The NAP (Narrative Assessment Protocol). *Early Childhood Research Quarterly, 25*(2), 218–234.

Kim J. S. (2008). Research and the reading wars. In F. M. Hess (Ed.), *When research matters: How scholarship influences education policy* (pp. 89–111). Cambridge, MA: Harvard Education Press.

Klare, G. R. (1984). Readability. In P. D. Pearson, R. Barr, M. L. Kamil, & P. Mosenthal (Eds.), *Handbook of reading research,* (Vol. 1, pp. 681–744). New York, NY: Longman.

Levine, A. (1996). America's reading crisis: Why the whole language approach to teaching reading has failed millions of children. *Parents, 16,* 63–65, 68.

Longman Dictionary of American English (4th ed.). (2007). Harlow, UK: Pearson Education Limited.

McCracken, G., & Walcutt, C. C. (1963). *Basic reading.* Philadelphia, PA: J. B. Lippincott.

McKeown, M. G., Beck, I. L., Omanson, R. C., & Pople, M. T. (1985). Some effects of the nature and frequency of vocabulary instruction on the knowledge and use of words. *Reading Research Quarterly, 20*(5), 522–535.

Mesmer, H. A., Cunningham, J. W., & Hiebert, E. H. (2012). Toward a theoretical model of primary-grade text complexity: Learning from the past, anticipating the future. *Reading Research Quarterly, 47*(3), 235–258.

Milone, M. (2009). *The development of ATOS: The Renaissance readability formula.* Wisconsin Rapids, WI: Renaissance Learning.

National Governors Association (NGA) Center for Best Practices & Council of Chief State School Officers (CCSSO). (2010a). *Common Core State Standards for English language arts and literacy in history/social studies, science, and technical subjects.* Washington, DC: Authors. Available at www.corestandards.org/assets/CCSSI_ELA%20Standards.pdf

National Governors Association (NGA) Center for Best Practices & Council of Chief State School Officers (CCSSO). (2010b). *Common Core State Standards for English language arts and literacy in history/social studies, science, and technical subjects: Appendix A.* Washington, DC: Authors. Available at www.corestandards.org/assets/Appendix_A.pdf

National Governors Association (NGA) Center for Best Practices & Council of Chief State School Officers (CCSSO). (2012). *Supplemental information for Appendix A of the Common Core State Standards for English language arts and literacy: New research on text complexity*. Washington, DC: Author. Available at www.corestandards.org/resources

Pearson, P. D. (1974). The effects of grammatical complexity on children's comprehension, recall, and conception of certain semantic relations. *Reading Research Quarterly*, 155–192.

Pearson, P. D. (2000). Reading in the 20th century. In T. Good (Ed.), *American education: Yesterday, today, and tomorrow. Yearbook of the National Society for the Study of Education* (pp. 152–208). Chicago, IL: University of Chicago Press.

Pearson, P. D. (2004). The reading wars. *Educational Policy, 18*(1), 216–252.

Pearson, P. D., & Hiebert, E. H. (2014). The state of the field: Qualitative analyses of text complexity. *The Elementary School Journal, 115*(2), 161–183.

Reitsma, P. (1988). Reading practice for beginners: Effects of guided reading, reading-while-listening, and independent reading with computer-based speech feedback. *Reading Research Quarterly, 23*(2), 219–235.

Robinson, H., Monroe, M., Artley, A. S., & Huck, C. S. (1962). *The new basic readers: Curriculum foundation series* (Grade 1). Chicago, IL: Scott Foresman.

Russell, D. H., Gates, D., & McCullough, C.M. (1961). *The Ginn Basic Readers*. Boston, MA: Ginn & Company.

Scarella, R., Rivera, H., Rivera, M., Beck, I. L., McKeown, M., & Chiappe-Collins, P. (2010). *Decodable reader (Steck-Vaughn California gateways)*. Austin, TX: Steck-Vaughn.

Snow, C. (2002). *Reading for understanding: Toward an R&D program in reading comprehension*. Santa Monica, CA: RAND Corporation.

Spichtig, A. N., Hiebert, E. H., Pearson, P. D., & Radach, R. (April 29, 2013). *Comprehension-based silent reading rates: How well are American students ascending the staircase of text complexity?* Paper presented at the annual meeting of the American Educational Research Association, San Francisco, CA.

Stanovich, K. E. (1986). Matthew effects in reading: Some consequences of individual differences in the acquisition of literacy. *Reading Research Quarterly, 21*(4), 360–407.

Stenner, A. J., Burdick, H., Sanford, E. E., & Burdick, D. S. (2007). *The Lexile framework for reading* (Technical report). Durham, NC: MetaMetrics.

Stenner, A. J., Koons, H., & Swartz, C. W. (2010). *Text complexity and developing expertise in reading*. Durham, NC: MetaMetrics.

Stickney, J. (1885). *A primer*. Boston, MA: Ginn.

Texas Education Agency. (1990). *Proclamation of the State Board of Education advertising for bids on textbooks*. Austin, TX: Author.

Texas Education Agency. (1997). *Proclamation of the State Board of Education advertising for bids on textbooks*. Austin, TX: Author.

Thorndike, E. L. (1903). *Educational psychology*. New York, NY: Lemcke & Buechner.

Thorndike, E. L. (1921). *Teacher's word book*. New York, NY: Teachers College Press.

Tyson-Bernstein, H. (1988). *A conspiracy of good intentions: America's textbook fiasco*. Washington, DC: Council for Basic Education.

Williamson, G. L., Fitzgerald, J., & Stenner, A. J. (2014). Student reading growth illuminates the Common Core text-complexity standard. *The Elementary School Journal, 115*(2), 230–254.

Zeno, S., Ivens, S., Millard, R., & Duvvuri, R. (1995). *The educator's word frequency guide*. Brewster, NY: Touchstone Applied Science Associates.

CHAPTER 14

Teachers or Programs?

A Historical Perspective on Where Trust Is Placed in Teaching Reading

James V. Hoffman and P. David Pearson

Trust lies at the heart of a successful relationship between professionals and those they serve. When strong levels of trust exist, professionals are able to make decisions that are informed and responsive to individual needs. Teaching, as a profession, is no exception. Trust is necessary for teaching to be effective, but trust in teachers as professionals is not common—which contributes to instructional practices and student achievement levels that are below expectations. It is not parental trust of teachers that is in question; in fact, parental trust in teachers is quite high (Mendes, 2010). It is within the educational system where trust in teachers—the trust that allows teachers to practice their profession—falls short. Nowhere are the complex trends surrounding trust within the teaching profession more clearly revealed than in the teaching of reading. Trust in the teaching of reading from a historical perspective has typically been framed as a choice between trusting teachers or trusting programs. Should teachers be trusted to make important and consequential decisions about their students, or should we trust the programs and materials used to shape practices and insist that teachers follow guidelines and teachers' manuals faithfully? In this chapter, we will explore moments in the history of teaching of reading that reveal a lack of trust in teachers as professional decisionmakers and an equally deferential faith that programs and materials can solve the challenges faced in the teaching of literacy. We will argue that, within the educational system, trust in teachers to make decisions and shape a curriculum that is responsive to learners and contexts has been soft in comparison to trust in programs. The current movement toward the implementation of the Common Core State Standards may be one more step toward trusting programs instead of teachers. We will argue that this imbalance in trusting programs/materials over teachers is not in the interest of learners. In the end, we will suggest an alternative future that has the potential to transform reading programs and materials from mechanisms of technical control into tools that serve as resources for trusted, professional teachers to enact effective instruction.

We have adopted a historical lens for the treatment of this topic, with a particular focus on the past 50 years in the United States—the very period adopted by the authors of this volume to characterize trends in reading theory and practice (see Preface, this volume). We will analyze this question of trust across five periods of educational practice leading up to the present. We label these periods Utility, Accessibility, Efficiency, Effectiveness, and Accountability. In adopting this historical framework, we suggest something of a grand narrative for the imbalance in levels of trust we have identified. We document this imbalance by focusing on moments of disruption or discontinuity in our history that are revealing forces that shape institutional policies. The time periods we offer are, at best, rough estimates that are tied not to particular historical events but to our reading of the broader forces that have shaped education more generally and the particular approaches to materials and programs that prevailed in each period. We hope the treatment of these periods will serve to ground the implicit appraisals of teacher and program trust.

UTILITY: 1630–1830

In colonial America, schools were formed out of social needs and cultural practices. Monaghan (2005) has carefully documented the emergence of schools as institutions and the qualities of reading instruction in America during the colonial period. Reading instruction was largely shaped by local circumstances, especially the dominant influences of local religious authorities. The nation was mostly rural, and access to schools was very limited. Individual families were left to their own resources in planning for the education of their children. "Dame schools" or home schooling were often the only options for instruction. Because the goals for reading instruction were limited—firmly focused on the spiritual, with some attention to the economic and social (e.g., contracts, laws)—the demand and resources needed for reading programs in schools were also limited (Smith, 1965). Teachers were seldom prepared for their role beyond their own experiences and expertise in reading and sometimes writing. Given its very limited goals (e.g., an ability to read the Bible), reading instruction tended to focus on the technical dimensions of reading. According to Smith (1965), instruction relied on restricted materials (e.g., hornbooks and primers) and limited methodologies (e.g., repetition, memorization, and recitation).

In 1647, a law was passed in the colony of Massachusetts that related to the responsibilities of communities to educate youth and in particular to teach children to read. This law became known as the Old Deluder Satan Law. The law described ignorance as a "satanic ill" to be addressed through education so that "ye ould deluder, Satan, could not use illiteracy to keepe men from the knowledge of ye Scriptures." The law required every town with more than 50 families to hire a teacher and towns with more than 100 families to establish a grammar school (for boys only). These kinds of laws were also passed in other colonies to ensure that children were being taught to read following "The Ordinary Road" from the hornbook, to the primer, to the Psalter, to the New Testament, and finally to the entire Bible (Monaghan, 2005). Monaghan points to this period and these laws specifically as the first steps toward the institutionalization of public education as a responsibility of the government. With this shift came the responsibility for government to both shape the goals and monitor the quality of education.

As goals began to expand in the revolutionary period (toward citizenship and moral character), shifts in instruction and programs soon followed (Smith, 1965). Noah Webster (1797) was a key figure in this period, developing a three-part instruction series: *A Grammatical Institute of the English Language*. Webster's "Blue-Back Speller" was the most popular of the books in this series. Webster's attention to spelling and to the use of a phonic method (tied to the teaching of letter-sound relationships) would challenge the dominance of the "alphabet spelling" method (tied to letter naming and spelling) and would radically reshape reading instruction because there was a more transparent relation between the letter and its sound in helping students unlock new words.

Perhaps even more important was Webster's attention to stories that exemplified moral behavior, for this would mark the beginning of a movement away from the dominant religious function of instructional text. All of these shifts that impacted practice were tied to institutional and societal influences. Webster (1848) was less concerned about pedagogy than about the standardization of oral and written English that was uniquely American. Letter-sound work would support Webster's goal of standard pronunciation in a country that was divided by dialects. Standardized spelling would ensure a common written language; thus, Webster's lifework on the dictionary of the English language. The focus on moral stories reflected his strong belief in the future of democracy and the forces that would bind the nation rather than divide it. Moral character became a safe middle ground that would appeal to the diverse array of religions in the country, while avoiding the question of whose religious beliefs would take precedence in whatever materials might be developed (Bynack, 1984; Kendall, 2011; Rollins, 1980). In a sense, this new tradition of materials for beginning reading, like so much in the rest of the new nation, championed the separation of church and state.

From its infancy, American reading instruction has adapted to shifts in utility. Shifts in practice followed shifts in societal goals, needs, and structures. Schools and practices were shaped by these shifts and relied on commercial reading materials and a "teacher" who had no formal preparation to teach. Crises, as in the moral imperative to learn to read the Bible for salvation or the need to standardize English pronunciation for the preservation of the nation, were used as leverage to reshape curriculum and teaching. It was widely believed that anyone who possessed strong moral character and the ability to read could be trusted to transfer these skills to others using the materials that embodied core values around language, religion, and citizenship. In this manner, schools (or, perhaps more aptly, schooling) would play a critical role in promoting religious homogeneity, economic prosperity, and national unity. At least until the awareness of a need to expand access to literacy became a part of the American conscience, utility held sway in shaping the teaching of reading. And teachers were the purveyors, not the shapers, of that utility; they did society's bidding.

ACCESS: 1830–1890

The period of education between the late 1830s through the 1880s is often characterized as the period of the Common School Movement (Kaestle, 1983). The population of the United States was growing rapidly, largely as a result of waves of immigration, and there was an accompanying expansion of territory to the west. With this rapid growth came a perceived need to extend literacy both for an expanding range of occupations and because of a desire to extend the rights of citizenship to a broader segment of (the White male) society; thus, the demands for schooling increased dramatically.

The Common School Movement was famously led by politician and educational reformer Horace Mann and focused on the goal of providing free, compulsory, and public primary education for all citizens (Cremin, 1957). Mann, from his leadership position in the state of Massachusetts, aggressively modeled the ways in which state governments could promote education for all citizens. He believed education was essential for instilling a spirit of democracy and hope in all citizens for a better life. Mann was concerned that educating only the elite would not bode well for the future of democracy. He founded *The Common School Journal* in 1838 and used his widely circulated annual reports on the state of education as a platform to raise attention to the inadequacies of schools in the state of Massachusetts around a range of issues from disdain for corporal punishment and punitive teaching to advocacy for graded schools that would meet the needs of greater numbers of students and school libraries (Filler, 1965).

Influenced by the reforms in education that were taking place in Europe, Mann advocated for reading instruction that focused on the word method, to replace the dreaded drill of alphabetic methods. A flurry of reading materials based on the word method, beginning with Ward's rational method in 1896, competed in the marketplace. McGuffey's readers, relying on the word method, appeared and gained prominence throughout the country (Ruggles, 1950).

As with the previous period, shifts in practice were influenced by institutional changes (within state educational systems, in particular), creating a new set of tools to shape educational practices through public policy at both the state and district levels. From the Common School Movement came the first significant attention to the preparation of teachers, but the teacher's role in shaping the curriculum was not clear. Mann valued investment in teacher preparation, but his work suggests that he envisioned a role for teachers as deliverers of a curriculum rather than as initiators or innovators. The training—not the education—of teachers was emphasized (see Hoffman & Pearson, 2000, for more on this distinction). There was an envisioned role for teachers revealed, in particular, in the positioning of women as elementary teachers by the leaders of the Common School Movement.

Preston (1989) offers a critical analysis of the work of teachers as constructed by leaders in the Common School Movement, with a particular focus on the feminization of teaching. Mann, for example, during his tenure as the Massachusetts secretary of education from 1837 to 1841, put forward numerous arguments for the employment of female teachers, including the curious point that women were superior to men as teachers because of the qualities they possessed "by nature": Mild and gentle manners were considered consistent with "true women's" docility. The feminization of the elementary teaching workforce that took place during this time period is complex and is not the focus of this chapter. However, it is important to note this major disruption in teaching and in society as women moved into professional roles that were then constructed as being docile and nonintellectual.

Again, as in the previous period, we see the use of crisis rhetoric to prompt public action. In the Common School Movement, the crisis was the lack of education for the growing masses, guided by the assumption that ignorance could potentially destroy a democratic society. Whom did our society trust? Teachers, but with qualifications: Society could trust those who were trained in what and how to teach—those who would do what was expected and do it well.

EFFICIENCY: 1890–1970

The Progressive Era in American history was a time of rapid change, social activism, and economic expansion (Buenker, Burnham, & Crunden, 1977; Flanagan, 2007; Gould, 1974). Historians typically frame this era as somewhere between the 1890s through the end of the 1920s and the start of the Great Depression. The "Efficiency Movement," or the "Economy of Time" reform effort, was a significant part of the Progressive Era (Tyack & Cuban, 1995). The Efficiency Movement emphasized the application of scientific principles to the accomplishment of human work. Efficiency became a centering theme for the Progressive Era. The assembly line, used in mass production, was a driving metaphor for the movement. Determine the desired characteristics of a product and then find the way to produce the product with the smallest allocation of resource costs—both human and material. The "stopwatch" (Taylor, 1913) became the tool that symbolized the movement. Scrutiny over the efficiency of schools in response to rapid population growth soon appeared.

Joseph Rice (1893), a pediatrician, provides a rich example of this fascination with efficiency. He conducted a year-long study of education in school systems across the country during this period and published his findings in serial form in magazine articles and later as a book. Rice employed both observation and student assessments as tools in his inquiry into schools and teaching practices. Although the results of his inquiry are complex, a few generalizations can be offered. First, Rice claimed that, with few exceptions, schools across the country were failing in their responsibility to educate American youth. Second, Rice found that the quality of the teaching in most schools was poor and disorganized and that teachers were largely unsupervised and unsupported. Rice saved his harshest criticism for leadership (at the school and district levels). The failure of the system should not be blamed on the teachers, Rice argued, but on the system that has failed them and their students. Rice (1913) called for massive reforms in school organization and leadership that echoed the principles of the Efficiency Movement for clear goals, measurable outcomes, and close supervision and support.

The Efficiency Movement, however, was not just about managing resources. It was accompanied by a particular vision of society. Just as everyone has a place in the manufacturing of a product (e.g., workers, managers, owners), everyone has a place and role in society. Do your part. Accept your role. Both individuals and the society would thrive as a result. The capacity of individuals to fill certain roles was not distributed equally. Some individuals are suited for menial tasks or physical labor, others for intellectual work, and still others for creative endeavors. Schools should prepare individuals for their role in life—and the sooner a given individual's future role could be ascertained, the sooner schools could get him or her into an educational track that would offer apt preparation for pursuing that role. Less education, and education focused on the technical and vocational, would suit the less intelligent, those who were destined for factory roles and service occupations. Higher levels of education would be required for the more intelligent, who were bound for professional roles and responsibilities. This sorting would take place at an early stage in educational systems based on scientific assessments of intelligence and aptitude. Over the full range of the 20th century, tracking, grouping, and limiting access to schools with high standards would serve as the mechanisms to achieve this end (Oakes, 2005).

William S. Gray, commonly regarded as the father of reading education, was active in this period. Like many of his colleagues, he advocated for the scientific management of schools through testing. He guided periodic reviews of schoolwide reading programs to assess their quality. Standardized measures, with measures of reading rate prominent, were used to assess outcomes, and the system was examined for the efficient and scientific management of resources toward outcomes. The "whole-word" or "look-say" method, distinguishable from the word method in the previous period that was focused on meaning, emphasized rapid and automatic word recognition through repeated exposure. Speed, efficiency, and practice mattered (Carver, 1990). In the quest for efficiency there was a strong push toward standardization of reading programs during this time through the mechanism of state laws and regulations for the purchasing of core textbooks across the country. During the 1920s, there was a dramatic rise in attention to state textbook adoption policies that promised free textbooks to schools (Tidwell, 1928). Though there were many motivations for state textbook adoptions (e.g., cost savings or guarantees of equal access to good pedagogy across districts within the state), the primary goal was standardization and control over the curriculum (Tulley & Farr, 1985). Basal readers fit neatly into this scheme of state procurement and control. From the publishers' viewpoint, this movement toward state adoptions offered the promise of reward and a fairly stable target for content. Basal reader systems became identified with efficient and organized programs that would promote learning to read. Gray et al.'s own Scott Foresman basal series, the Curriculum Foundation series (1940–1948; 1951–1957) featuring Sally, Dick, and Jane, became the standard for the field as an organized reading program.

In line with the goal of efficiency and sorting, the reading community began to promote a view of reading programs as serving different kinds of students in different ways. A school reading program consisted of a developmental program (designed for the majority of the children—"normal"), the corrective program (for children who were falling behind—with a shared responsibility for the classroom teacher and the reading specialist), and the remedial program (for children who were very behind and required the support of a reading specialist in one-on-one settings). Occasionally—but only occasionally—there might be commercial programs that paralleled these classifications, and sometimes even programs for gifted students as well. For example, in the 1960s, Scott Foresman published, in addition to a foundational program (the New Basic Readers: Curriculum Foundation Series; Robinson, Monroe, Artley, & Greet, 1960–1962), a remedial program with the label of *Open Highways* (Robinson et al., 1967) and a gifted program entitled *Wide Horizons* (Robinson et al., 1965). Publishers Lyons and Carnahan offered a different twist on this same theme of differentiation. In their 1962 Companion Readers (Bond & Cuddy, 1962), the same story was written in three different versions—one *at* grade level for most students, one *below* grade level for struggling readers, and one *above* grade level for gifted readers. The bet was that a teacher could hold a whole-class discussion around the core ideas in a story because all the students had versions that they actually stood a chance of reading on their own. But the logic of differentiation and getting students placed properly was the same as for the Scott Foresman approach.

The drive toward efficiency can certainly be framed from an economic argument and the scarcity of resources principle. However, it can also be framed from a sociological perspective around schools working toward an envisioned society with emphasis on the American dream that hard work leads to progress and economic well-being when everyone plays their role. As Rice (1913) noted, the crisis (failure) in schools was not the fault of teachers but the fault of administrators who failed to apply proper organizational structures and guidance. Where was trust placed during this era? In scientific management that would guide teachers to do their job—with materials defining the track they should follow.

EFFECTIVENESS: 1965–1985

In her classic book, *Learning to Read: The Great Debate*, Jeanne Chall (1967) described the period of reading instruction from the turn of the 20th century up through the 1960s as a period of gathering consensus around practice. This consensus was embodied in the leading basal reading programs during this time, with a focus on readiness, leveled texts, word selection based on a meaning-frequency principle, sight-word ("look-say") methods with supporting word repetition in the readers, and ability grouping within the classroom. There was widespread agreement throughout the first half of the 20th century that reading goals were being met through this consensus approach. This view was disrupted by the scrutiny placed on schools as the "Sputnik era" emerged and questions regarding effectiveness and equity bolted onto the scene. Concurrent with the Sputnik wake-up call were national reports, such as the Coleman Report (J. S. Coleman et. al., 1966), documenting patterns of achievement in reading and other areas that showed large and growing discrepancies between White and African American youth, and Flesch's (1955) scathing critique in *Why Johnny Can't Read*, decrying the very same methods that Chall documented as prevalent in her 1967 book. President Johnson, through his Great Society programs, poured money into federal programs and research to address issues of effectiveness. This period marked the first significant involvement of the federal government in education, including shaping educational research, based on civil rights.

During this time period, there were four particular research efforts focused on program issues and the teaching of reading that are important to consider: the Effective Schools studies, the First-Grade studies, the Follow-Through studies, and the Rand Change Agent studies.

Effective Schools Studies

A number of researchers during this period challenged the general characterization of schools as having a minimal influence on achievement based on the findings from the Coleman Report (J. S. Coleman et al., 1966). They questioned the assertion that achievement was determined by qualities (e.g., intelligence and SES) outside the control of schools. These researchers often examined the interaction of achievement and context in outlier schools where school and program characteristics did make a difference (Hoffman & Rutherford, 1984; Purkey & Smith, 1983). Drawing on the work of Weber (1971) in schools in Harlem and other researchers who examined high-success schools in the context of poverty, Edmonds and Frederiksen (1978) documented the qualities of programs (in urban schools in particular) that made a difference despite individual and community characteristics—schools that were "beating the odds" predicted by their demographic makeup. These qualities ranged from an orderly and safe climate conducive to teaching and learning and principal leadership to a clear instructional focus (on reading), high expectations for all learners, and systematic plans for assessment. One strong assertion that came out of this literature is that these effective schools were not places that had gathered together a large number of outstanding teachers. In fact, many of the research reports went out of their way to describe the teachers and teaching as not particularly creative or impressive—in fact, these were described as rather "businesslike" (Rosenshine & Furst, 1971).

First-Grade Studies

A second research effort, specifically focused on reading instruction, took the form of a national comparison study of effective programs supported by the federal government. It was officially known as the Cooperative Research Program in First-Grade Reading Instruction (Bond & Dykstra, 1967) and commonly referred to as the First-Grade studies. Twenty-seven different research projects around the country were coordinated to address three questions:

1. To what extent are various pupil, teacher, class, school, and community characteristics related to pupil achievement in 1st-grade reading and spelling?
2. Which of the many approaches to initial reading instruction produces superior reading and spelling achievement at the end of the 1st grade?
3. Is any program uniquely effective or ineffective for pupils with high or low readiness for reading?

The studies compared various approaches, methods, and materials for the teaching of beginning reading, including traditional basals, language experience, a "linguistic" approach , systematic phonics-based methods, and the "*ita*" (initial teaching alphabet). The questions that guided the study reveal the widely held view of the time that programs (i.e., approaches, materials, and methods) were at the heart of effective teaching. In some sense, the notion that methods and program comparison studies were the focus for the study of effectiveness reflects trust in programs rather than teachers as the critical variable. The fact that none of the programs or approaches showed any great advantage in student outcomes (both student success and failure were documented across all programs) led the researchers to speculate that teacher quality was the variable that was most responsible for achievement differences. Because teachers were not included as a variable in the study and few of the studies even monitored the level of implementation, this assertion was left as nothing more than conjecture.

The Follow-Through Studies

A third research effort that focused on the teaching of basic skills in the early grades was the Follow-Through studies (Egbert, 1981). The Follow-Through Program (1968–1977) was initiated in response to findings from evaluation studies that showed the academic gains realized through the introduction of Head Start programs in schools serving low-income communities seemed to wash out as students entered formal schooling (Maccoby & Zellner, 1970; Stebbins, St. Pierre, Proper, Anderson, & Cerva, 1977). Follow-Through was designed to provide academic support to bridge the movement of students from Head Start into early primary education. Rather than specifying a particular program for implementation and using a randomized-control model for evaluation, the federal government gave local school districts the choice to select from a range of programmatic options. The purpose was to increase community control and investment in the outcomes (Egbert, 1981). The included programs were as diverse in their philosophy and execution as Direct Instruction (DISTAR) and the Behavioral Analysis Model, which anchored the scripted-structured end of the programmatic continuum, to the Bank Street Model and Open Education Model, which were the least constrained and structured of the programs. Most of the program models, outside of DISTAR and the Behavioral Analysis Model, were rather vague, underdeveloped, and barely field-tested (Elmore, 1977).

The intervention and research model for the Follow-Through studies is referred to as planned variation. Stallings took a leadership role in evaluating the effects of the Follow-Through Program and the features of these programs that were associated with positive learning outcomes (Stallings, 1976; Stallings & Kaskowitz, 1974). As with the First-Grade studies, there was no clear winner; rather, there was variation across sites and programs in implementation and success. In general, the research revealed that the features associated with effective programs included:

- a clear focus on academic outcomes and academic engaged time;
- time spent working in textbooks and academic workbooks (as opposed to time spent with puzzles, games, toys, and the like);
- grouping and whole-class instruction;
- high program structure and sequence;
- carefully prescribed teaching practices; and
- academic-focused feedback (acknowledgment, praise, and positive and negative corrective feedback).

Overall, there was general support for direct instruction with clearly specified learning outcomes. Although the results and claims surrounding Follow-Through were widely questioned (see Elmore, 1977; House, Glass, McLean, & Walker, 1978), the findings continued to be used for at least another 3 decades to support program effectiveness in reading that positions teachers in a delivery role (Carnine, Silbert, Kame'enui, & Tarver, 2009).

The Rand Change Agent Studies

A fourth research effort focused on reform at the programmatic level related to the federal government's support for the creation and transfer of effective programs. The Elementary and Secondary Education Act (in particular, the Education Amendments of 1974) provided support for innovative and exemplary projects that provide creative or imaginative solutions to problems in curriculum and teaching. Some of these grants were designed to support development work, while other grants were designed to support institutions working to adopt programs that had been created through development grants. The National Diffusion Network (NDN; 1974–1995) was the first federally sponsored effort to identify and spread innovative educational programs. The NDN would conduct an evaluation of the data on the effectiveness of innovative programs and certify those that passed the demonstration of effectiveness for diffusion. The program was administered through the Office of Education and was designed to make use of the best ideas from the innovative programs. A large number of these programs focused on improving reading achievement.

The federal government sponsored an independent evaluation of this process, designed to spread innovation. The Rand Corporation was contracted to study the effective transport of innovative programs from one site to the next with a particular focus on replication of the outcomes related to student achievement. Paul Bermann and Milbrey McLaughlin directed this study, which was eventually reported as the Rand Change Agent studies, undertaken from 1973 to 1978 (McLaughlin, 1976, 1990). It was built on a framework for change constructed by Berman and McLaughlin (1976). They examined four federal programs and 293 projects in 18 states. Overall, they found the level of implementation of programs to be very low and uneven. They identified a set of characteristics that seemed to be very ineffective in supporting program adoption and a set of strategies that they associated with success.

Some factors associated with limited implementation:

- Reliance on outside consultants
- Packaged management approaches
- One-shot, pre-implementation training
- Pay for training
- Formal, summative evaluation
- Comprehensive systemwide projects

Some strategies associated with effective implementation:

- Concrete, teacher-specific, and extended training
- Classroom assistance from local staff
- Teacher observation of similar projects in other locations
- Regular project meetings that focused on practice
- Teacher participation in project decisions
- Local development of project materials
- Principals' participation in training

This report concluded that effective change in schools does take place through adoption, but also through mutual adaptation: the adaptation of a project or policy and the organizational setting to each other. Too much emphasis on fidelity to the original program could undermine the entire effort to effect positive programmatic changes that would lead to increased student achievement (Elmore & McLaughlin, 1988).

The effectiveness era was characterized by a belief that research could provide answers to the important questions surrounding teaching and literacy achievement—in particular, the disparity of achievement related to socioeconomic factors—through the careful study of programs (i.e., approaches, materials, and sometimes training) as they are implemented and evaluated. Despite the mixed results and the failure to demonstrate transfer, faith remained strong that the answers to questions of equity would be found in trust at the program level and the training of teachers who could follow programs with a high degree of fidelity. Who was trusted during this period? Not teachers. "Teacher-proofing" the curriculum became the ideal.

ACCOUNTABILITY: 1985–????

The start of the accountability movement in education is often associated with the publishing of the report *A Nation at Risk* (National Commission on Excellence in Education,

1983). Echoing the Sputnik era critics of the previous period, the authors and sponsors of the *Nation at Risk* report claimed that educational system in the United States was failing its citizens to such an extent that it had become a matter of national security. The document, spearheaded by Secretary of Education Terrel Bell, advised educational systems to model themselves after businesses, including the advice to hold people accountable for results in return for the resources being allocated. In particular, the report called for the application of more rigorous and measurable standards—and the report explicitly cited the success of the measurable standards movement in business and industry.

The tools for reform and accountability evolved in the years following *A Nation at Risk*. The first big enhancement came at the end of the 1980s, with the influential Charlottesville National Governors Conference in 1989 (Bill Clinton, then governor of Arkansas, convened the conference). Out of that meeting came all of the apparatus to encourage all disciplines to follow the lead of the National Council of Teachers of Mathematics (NCTM) in developing highly rigorous and specific *content* standards (specifying what students should know and be able to do), as well as standards for *assessment* (what cut scores on what tests would tell us whether individual students or teachers or schools were achieving the content standards?). (See National Research Council, 1999, for a compelling account of the evolution of the standards movement.) The tools of standards-based reform were standards, assessments to measure their achievement, and the stakes or consequences that come with an accountability system. These consequences took the form of rewards or sanctions for good or poor performance, particularly at the school level, but there were—and are—examples where the onus falls at the student level—for example, with state and district retention policies.

Some progress in implementing these new policy tools was achieved during Clinton's presidential years, mainly through the auspices of the Improving America's Schools Act of 1994; however, these various tools were not finally brought together legislatively until the No Child Left Behind Act of 2001. This act established an accountability system for states, school districts, and schools receiving federal funding. The law required states to establish academic standards, tests to measure their mastery, and an accountability architecture that would require schools to make annual progress toward having every student achieve the standards until, in 2014, all students in every school would achieve the mastery cut score—a policy version of "Lake Wobegone," where all children are above average! Schools also had to make annual progress toward closing the achievement gaps between various demographic groups, particularly groupings based on race, language, income, or intellectual status. The law also required states to identify schools and school districts that were not making adequate yearly progress and to mandate that these low-performing schools follow a step-by-step process for either turning themselves around or risk closure. Although neither NCLB nor its reading section, Reading First, was a "program," the context of these mandates shaped programs in clear and powerful ways. The accountability legacy of this era for reading can be characterized by our version of the "big five" in literacy policy: standards, stakes, scripts, sorts, and supervision.

Standards

The standards movement that began in the late 1980s has been gaining momentum ever since. States such as Texas have spirited the movement with variations that began as "opportunity standards" around curriculum areas and have moved toward performance standards that are mostly grade-level bound. We have already alluded to the two lynchpins of the standards movement—content standards (what students know and can do) and performance standards (what scores on which tests indicate whether they have achieved standards). But there was the third key standard that, while part of the original conceptualization of standards, has lost its punch since the early days of the standards movement—namely, opportunity to learn standards. They were supposed to be the "quid pro quo," the resources that schools, districts, and states would offer in return for schools and teachers holding themselves and their students to account for the content and performance standards. Alas, they seem to have dropped out of the standards equation, so what we are left with is teachers, schools, and students being held accountable for particular standards without a reciprocal allocation of curricular and material resources to achieve those standards.

Stakes

The rise of high-stakes assessments across the country was (and continues to be) fast and furious (see critiques by Linn, 2000, and Nichols, 2012). These high-stakes assessments typically take a census approach (everyone gets assessed on the very same test) rather than a sampling approach (samples of students get assessed on different facets of the learning goals and overall performance at the school or district level on each of these facets is inferred from the performance of the samples). The choice of a census model is certainly not driven by economics (a state report based on sampling could be conducted on a much wider range of reading standards at a fraction of the cost of the current census model), but rather by the intent to shape compliance with the standards through the logic of accountability (i.e., make the stakes for low performance high for everyone, including students!). It should be noted that this "every student takes the very same test" approach to state-level testing comes at a very high cost, not only in terms of the actual dollars spent but also in terms of content covered by the test: Only a very small sample of all the important curricular outcomes can be assessed in the hour or 2 allocated for a reading or a writing assessment. In the case of reading comprehension, this means that only a very small sample of passages can be used from which to draw a conclusion about students' collective performance.

This accountability mechanism allows stakes to affect players at all levels in the system. Students' lives are affected in terms of promotion, graduation, immediate rewards, or placement in mandatory tutoring programs. Teachers are subject to bonus pay, contract probation, or even termination. Schools get labeled on a continuum from exemplary to failing, threatened with closure, and subjected to involuntary faculty reassignment. Even communities and neighborhoods suffer or benefit from the impact of school test scores on property values. The high-stakes assessments are tied to the standards in a structure that is criterion-referenced, although the scores are often interpreted on normative grounds (e.g., what percentage of students should achieve the magical mastery cut score).

Scripts

The third piece of the accountability puzzle takes the form of scripts, where the script metaphor is intended to capture the concept of program fidelity. The No Child Left Behind Act required program resources to be used only to support teaching strategies and materials that had been shown effective through scientific research. These commercial programs suggested that the teacher's role was to follow the manual instructions without deviation. Scripted programs were not new phenomena in the 2000s. In fact, they are as old as basal programs themselves, which have, at least since the 1920s, offered teachers explicit directions for how to teach skills. For example, the DISTAR (Bereiter & Engleman, 1966) program of the 1960s championed the notion of scripted instruction as reflecting research on effective teaching, along with a trust in materials and practices. But the surge in popularity and use of scripted programs through NCLB and Reading First was unprecedented. Although scripts were found only in a few programs during the Effectiveness period, now scripts are found in the most popular core reading materials (such as the McGraw-Hill/SRA version of Direct Instruction). In fact, state adoption policies called for districts to ensure that teachers followed the scripts and pacing guides that align with the standards and stakes.

Sorts

In the Accountability era, attention to grouping and tracking operates in ways that still reflect the efforts initiated in the Efficiency period. But some of the grouping plans and tracking have resulted from ad hoc efforts in response to the pressures of high-stakes assessments. "Bubble Kids" or "Triage for Testing" have become a common part of the discourse in programs across the country. Because most high-stakes tests are criterion based, passing (i.e., reaching the magical cut score) or not passing is the only thing that matters. Students who are going to pass the test regardless of the instruction they receive become a low priority for resources. Likewise, students who will *not* pass the test regardless of the support offered also become a low priority for instructional resources. "Bubble Kids," or those who may be able to pass with intense support, receive the bulk of the attention—all directed at the targeted outcome (i.e., achieving a passing score on the test).

As with instructional programs, during the reign of NCLB/Reading First, assessment tools underwent an official review by a federally funded technical assistance center. And assessment tools that survived the review process, including classroom assessments designed to monitor progress and diagnose individual needs, were strongly recommended (with the moral force of mandate) for use by districts and schools receiving NCLB funds. No assessment tool received more uptake for Reading First than DIBELS (Good & Jefferson, 1998; Good & Kaminski, 2002), at least in part because of its blessing as an officially validated tool. Even through DIBELS was designed as a progress monitoring tool (taking a reading on student performance at regular intervals), it became widely used as a diagnostic tool used to shape instruction in school settings. The net effect of DIBELS use was to focus corrective and remedial efforts on the low-level fundamental skills of phonemic awareness and phonics that it measured, thus relegating low-performing students to a steady diet of basic skills in their reading programs, with no opportunity to engage in advanced comprehension or critical thinking.

Supervision

The final policy tool in the NCLB toolkit was supervision, especially supervision enacted as classroom observation to ensure that the scripts and pacing guides were being followed with a high degree of fidelity. Program fidelity has become a key theme in the accountability period, with the goal of every teacher enacting programs in exactly the same manner. Here again, NCLB and Reading First took the lead in enacting this fifth element by supporting coaches in observing and supporting teachers toward successful implementation. This is not a coaching model that takes a reflective stance toward teacher learning, but rather one that emphasizes compliance and fidelity of implementation.

The Aggregate Effect of These Levers

Taken together, these five elements of the accountability movement, particularly as the movement reached its acme in the NCLB era, have come to define what counts as a reading program. Alignment is seen as the key process in program development. Align your goals, the materials and assessments you use, the professional development you receive, and the guidance you get from coaches in your classroom. Sort students into tracks using assessment tools. Provide scripts and pacing guides for teachers to follow, and supervise implementation according to the goals of the program. Trust the program and insist that teachers follow the plan—that's the formula for success. Who is trusted in such a system? Programs—not teachers. The freedom for teachers to become responsive to learners had reached a low point in history as Obama took office and the era of the CCSS began. But has anything really changed since the CCSS came into being? That is the topic to which we now turn.

THE ROLE OF READING PROGRAMS IN THE COMMON CORE STATE STANDARDS

It is hard to characterize the post-NCLB era ushered in by the one-two punch of the Obama administration's Race to the Top initiative (U.S. Department of Education, 2009) and the appearance of Common Core State Standards (National Governors Association Center for Best Practices [NGA Center] & Council of the Chief State School Officers [CCSSO], 2010). One reason why it is difficult to characterize the movement is that these initiatives are at once both a critique of the NCLB Bush policies and a continuation of them. What continued from the Bush years was the accountability apparatus—standards for what students should know and be able to do; assessments to measure progress toward achieving them at the school, district, and state level; and rewards or sanctions for achieving or failing to achieve the standards. The critique focused on the standards and the assessments to measure them, implying, of course, that it was not the accountability construct that was the problem in NCLB but rather the fact that our curriculum and pedagogy were being guided by flawed, low-level standards and misguided assessments. The remedy, according to the logic of the Obama administration, was better (i.e., higher and more rigorous) standards and better (i.e., more challenging) assessments to measure students' mastery of the higher standards. The promise of the CCSS was to bring rigorous curriculum to all students.

This current logic hearkens back to the beginning of the standards movement in the early 1990s, when the motto was something like "If we are going to teach to the test, then let's have tests worth teaching to" (Resnick, 1993). In the 1990s, this logic drove the development of performance assessments (e.g., the California Learning Assessment System, 1994). Such tasks required students to respond to complex, challenging, multistage tasks that emphasized integrating knowledge and insights across multiple sources and using that knowledge to address some sort of pressing complex social, scientific, or literary issue, such as whether global warming is real, whether Martin Luther King's reliance on the nonviolent strategies of Gandhi served the interests of civil rights reform in the United States, or how O. Henry achieved irony in his short stories. In 2010, this same logic drove the Obama administration to invest over $365 million in two national consortia, Partnership for Assessment of Readiness for College and Careers (PARCC) and the Smarter Balanced Assessment Consortium (SBAC), to develop assessments that would do justice to the higher standards mandated by the CCSS.

The CCSS, which have been voluntarily adopted by each of the 44 participating states (making them a state and not federal initiative), promise a rigorous curriculum for students of precisely the sort that will earn them entry into higher education and/or a solid, secure career in the workforce. In the bargain, they will be prepared to do well on the new tests that are being developed, somewhat ironically, with federal support. The vision of student excellence is exemplary, almost inspiring:

> Students who meet the Standards readily undertake the close, attentive reading that is at the heart of understanding and enjoying complex works of literature. They habitually perform the critical reading necessary to pick carefully through the staggering amount of information available today in print and digitally. They actively seek the wide, deep, and thoughtful engagement with high-quality literary and informational texts that builds knowledge, enlarges experience, and broadens worldviews. (NGA Center & CCSSO, 2010, p. 3)

The CCSS developers' view of the role that standards should play in the classroom reflects progressive moral and ethical values about teachers and teaching. The body politic has the right to set the ends or goals for our schools and students, but teachers must have the prerogative to determine the means of achieving those ends:

> By emphasizing required achievements, the Standards leave room for teachers, curriculum developers, and states to determine how those goals should be reached and what additional topics should be addressed. (NGA Center & CCSSO, 2010, p. 4)

Again, in discussing the implementation of criteria for judging the complexity of text, the developers of the CCSS ceded the right to moderate quantitative assessments (e.g., readability scores) of complexity to teacher judgment:

> While the prior two elements of the model focus on the inherent complexity of text, variables specific to particular readers (such as motivation, knowledge, and experiences) and to particular tasks (such as purpose and the complexity of the task assigned and the questions posed) must also be considered when determining whether a text is appropriate for a given student. Such assessments are best made by teachers employing their professional judgment, experience, and knowledge of their students and the subject. (NGA Center & CCSSO, 2010, Appendix B, p. 4)

There is hope in some camps (for glimpses of this guarded optimism, see Pearson, 2013; Pearson & Hiebert, 2013) that the new CCSS will be a game changer in that they will provide a different vision of what it means to meet high and rigorous standards and what it means for states and districts to come through with the right curricular and material resources to help schools help teachers help students meet the standards. Whether all this will happen remains to be seen. On paper, it appears that in contrast to earlier policies that privileged programs over teacher prerogative, the CCSS are willing to trade teacher accountability to high and rigorous standards for at least a modicum of teacher choice in curricular and pedagogical matters.

We can't yet know whether the standards will be implemented in a manner that will allow them to remain true to these lofty aspirations. There is already reason to believe that some of the documents guiding implementation of the CCSS betray these aspirations. For example, Pearson (2013) has pointed out that the highly influential Publishers' Criteria, written by the very authors who wrote the CCSS-ELA (D. Coleman & Pimentel, 2012), put forward a model of reading comprehension instruction, dubbed "close reading," that undermines the emphasis on interpretation, integration, and critique that characterizes two-thirds (Standards 4–9) of the CCSS for reading. In the same paper, Pearson (2013) points out that the same Publishers' Criteria, because they offer such highly specific instructional guidance, can quickly erode teacher prerogative. That is, when teacher manuals offer fine-grained, step-by-step guidance (very much like the scripts used during the NCLB accountability era), they leave teachers with few choices to make, rendering the promise of prerogative a hollow sham. These possibilities provide room for skepticism on the question of teacher trust as educators begin the arduous process of implementation.

BUILDING TRUST ALL AROUND: A CHALLENGE FOR PROGRAM DEVELOPERS AND A NEW GENERATION OF TEACHERS

Thirty years may be a very short span of time in an historical sense, but 30 years of life with accountability is surely enough in the face of the failure of this movement to serve students well. We look forward to the time when we can put an end date on the Accountability period. We close our chapter with a focus on two shreds of hope that we have identified in the current and somewhat discouraging state of affairs. One lies in the consideration of a movement situated in the very teacher guides that we have decried for their complicity in foisting scripts on teachers to achieve a high level of fidelity in program implementation. Beginning with the influential essay of Ball and Cohen in 1996, several scholars have undertaken the study of "educative materials" for teachers (Davis et al., 2014; Krajcik & Davis, 2005). With all these manuals available to teachers, the fundamental idea is, why can't educators exploit their ubiquitous use to promote deeper and broader teacher knowledge of curriculum and pedagogy, with the proviso that those who design educational materials for teachers undergo an elaborate iterative design process in which evidence is used to refine materials at every step in the development process? The hope—indeed, the expectation—is that when teachers use materials developed in such a process, they actually learn more about their craft. To our knowledge, we have yet to witness an empirical test of the claim that teachers can refine their craft with well-designed materials, but the concept is so eminently sensible that it seems almost compelling.

A second, and perhaps more absorbing, shred of hope comes in considering teachers—in particular, in the consideration of the young teachers who are entering or have just entered the profession. This new generation of teachers is the first to have personally experienced the weight of accountability throughout their lives as students in schools. They know the system from the inside and may, therefore, be the ones who are best equipped to topple the Accountability era and replace it with a new vision for the teaching profession. We challenge these young professionals to consider the virtue of responsibility as a stance that can lead to meaningful reform. Teachers who take responsibility for their learning, for the quality of their service to children, and for the shaping of their profession would be a formidable force for change and would usher in a new era of Responsibility.

The simple fact is that accountability sets a much lower bar for excellence than responsibility. Educators have decades of evidence that trying to raise the quality of schooling by raising accountability only distorts teachers' efforts to be responsible for their work. There is no evidence that raising accountability standards has, as promised, driven less effective teachers from the classroom. The performance standards associated with accountability reflect an easily rendered mimicking of what real teaching involves. Teachers who take on responsibility for their professional lives would mark a shift toward trust that enables the design of materials and programs that can serve as tools for achieving the goal of all students becoming literate. We are not suggesting that the evaluation of teachers would not be a part of this movement; rather, evaluation under a Responsibility stance would begin with self-evaluation, leading to peer evaluation, and would find ultimate accountability in the determination of students and parents, and not in the actions of supervisors or managers.

Perhaps our efforts in the past—both ours personally and the profession's at large—to argue for change through policy reform at the top have failed following Ben Goldacre's (2009) caution that "you cannot reason people out of positions they didn't reason themselves into" (p. xii). We have come to believe that the audience we are writing for in this chapter is not the old guard who stand at the top of the accountability hierarchy and find their power within it, but the new generation of teachers who have been burdened by lives in classrooms dulled by standards and testing. Knowing the history as it is represented in this chapter may inform strategies for this new generation to move forward in unlocking its future into a transformative period of trust and excellence. Starting at the grassroots level, these dedicated professionals can inspire parents, colleagues, and administrators to adopt the spirit of responsibility in their own roles as the key to success. An appreciation for shared responsibility across communities of practice emerging out of these local interactions can become the hallmark for excellence. Perhaps, then, the policymakers who shape context and the publishers who craft tools for teaching will be convinced that the time is ripe for a new approach and a new era in literacy education. Jeanne Chall (1967) recognized this same tension when she asked which is better: a good teacher or a good method (e.g., phonics, look-say, or language experience)? She wrote: "Good teaching is always needed. But a good method in the hands of a good teacher—that is the ideal" (p. 308). We wonder, in the end, whether the question we posed in the title regarding trust in teachers or trust in programs may come to be answered: both! If it ever becomes necessary to make a forced choice between the two, as teachers, we know which side we will choose.

REFERENCES

Ball, D. L., & Cohen, D. K. (1996). Reform by the book: What is—Or might be—The role of curriculum materials in teacher learning and instructional reform. *Educational Researcher, 25*(9), 6–8, 14.

Bereiter, C., & Engelmann, S. (1966). *Teaching disadvantaged children in the preschool.* Englewood Cliffs, NJ: Prentice-Hall.

Berman, P., & McLaughlin, M. W. (1976). Implementation of educational innovation. *Educational Forum, 40*(3), 345–370.

Bond, G. L., & Cuddy, M. (1962). *Good time for us, Companion first reader.* Chicago, IL: Lyons & Carnahan.

Bond, G. L., & Dykstra, R. (1967). *Coordinating Center for first-grade reading instruction programs* (Final Report of Project No. X-001, Contract No. OE-5-10-264). Minneapolis, MN: University of Minnesota.

Buenker, J. D., Burnham, J. C., & Crunden, R. M. (1977). *Progressivism.* Cambridge, MA: Schenkman.

Bynack, V. P. (1984). Noah Webster and the idea of a national culture: The pathologies of epistemology. *Journal of the History of Ideas 45*(1), 99–114.

California Learning Assessment System. (1994). *Elementary performance assessments: Integrated English-language arts illustrative material.* Sacramento, CA: California Department of Education.

Carnine, D., Silbert, J., Kame'enui, E., & Tarver, S. (2009). *Direct instruction reading* (5th ed.). New York, NY: Pearson.

Carver, R. P. (1990). *Reading rate: A review of research and theory.* San Diego, CA: Academic Press.

Chall, J. (1967). *Learning to read: The great debate.* New York, NY: McGraw-Hill.

Coleman, D., & Pimentel, S. (2012). *Revised publishers' criteria for the Common Core State Standards in English language arts and literacy, grades 3–12.* Washington, DC: National Governors Association Center for Best Practices & Council of Chief State School Officers. Available at www.corestandards.org/assets/Publishers_Criteria for_3-12.pdf

Coleman, J. S., Campbell, E. Q., Hobson, C. J., McPartland, F., Mood, A. M., Weinfeld, F. D., et al. (1966). *Equality of educational opportunity.* Washington, DC: U.S. Government Printing Office.

Cremin, L. A. (1957). *The republic and the school: Horace Mann on the education of free men.* New York, NY: Teachers College Press.

Davis, E. A., Palincsar, A. S., Arias, A. M., Schultz, A., Bismack, L. M., & Iwashyna, S. K. (2014). Designing educative curriculum materials: A theoretically and empirically driven process. *Harvard Educational Review, 84*(1), 24–52.

Edmonds, R., & Fredericksen J. R. (1978). *Search for effective schools: The identification and analysis of city schools that are instructionally effective for poor children.* Cambridge, MA: Harvard University, Center for Urban Studies.

Egbert, R. L. (1981). *Some thoughts about Follow Through thirteen years later.* Lincoln, NE: Nebraska University. (ERIC Document Reproduction Service No. ED244733)

Elmore, R. F. (1977). *Follow Through: Decision-making in a large-scale social experiment.* Unpublished doctoral dissertation, Harvard Graduate School of Education.

Elmore, R. F., & McLaughlin, M. W. (1988). *Steady work: Policy, practice and reform in American education.* Santa Monica, CA: Rand.

Filler, L. (1965). *Horace Mann on the crisis in education.* Yellow Springs, OH: Antioch Press.

Flanagan, M. A. (2007). *America reformed: Progressives and progressivisms, 1890s–1920s.* New York, NY: Oxford University Press.

Flesch, R. (1955). *Why Johnny can't read.* New York, NY: Harper and Row.

Goldacre, B. (2009). *Bad science.* London, UK: Fourth Estate.

Good, R. H., & Jefferson, G. (1998). *Contemporary perspectives on curriculum-based measurement validity*. New York. NY: Guilford Press.

Good, R. H., & Kaminski, R. A. (2002). *DIBELS oral reading fluency passages for first through third grades* (Technical Report, No. 10). Eugene, OR: University of Oregon.

Gould, L. L. (1974). *The Progressive era*. Syracuse, NY: Syracuse University Press.

Gray, W. S., Arbuthnot, M. H., et al. (1940–1948). *Basic readers: Curriculum foundation series*. Chicago, IL: Scott Foresman.

Gray, W. S., Arbuthnot, M. H., Artley, A. S., Monroe, M., et al. (1951–1957). *New basic readers: Curriculum foundation series*. Chicago, IL: Scott Foresman.

Hoffman, J. V., & Pearson, P. D. (2000). Reading teacher education in the next millennium: What your grandmother's teacher didn't know that your granddaughter's teacher should. *Reading Research Quarterly, 35*(1), 28–44.

Hoffman, J. V., & Rutherford, W. (1984). Effective reading programs: A critical review of outlier studies. *Reading Research Quarterly, 20*(1), 79–92.

House, E. R., Glass, G. V., McLean, L. D., & Walker, D. F. (1978). No simple answer: Critique of the Follow Through evaluation. *Harvard Educational Review, 48*, 128–160.

Improving America's Schools Act. (1994). Washington, DC: Government Printing Office. Available at www.ed.gov/legislation/ESEA/index.html

Kaestle, C. (1983). *Pillars of the republic: Common schools and American society, 1780–1860*. New York, NY: Hill and Wang.

Kendall, J. (2011). *The forgotten founding father: Noah Webster's obsession and the creation of an American culture*. New York, NY: G.P. Putnam's Sons.

Krajcik, J. S., & Davis, E. A. (2005). Designing educative curriculum materials to promote teacher learning. *Educational Researcher, 34*(3), 3–14.

Linn, R. L. (2000). Assessments and accountability. *Educational Researcher, 29*(2), 4–16.

Maccoby, E. E., & Zellner, M. (1970). *Experiments in primary education: Aspects of Project Follow-Through*. New York, NY: Harcourt Brace Jovanovich.

McLaughlin, M. W. (1976, February). Implementation as mutual adaptation: Change in classroom organization. *Teachers College Record, 77*, 339–351.

McLaughlin, M. W. (1990, December). The Rand Change Agent study revisited: Macro perspectives and micro realities. *Educational Researcher, 19*, 15.

Mendes, E. (2010). *U.S. Parents want teachers paid on quality, student outcomes. Gallop Politics*. Available at www.gallup.com/poll/142664/parents-teachers-paid-quality-student-outcomes.aspx

Monaghan, J. E. (2005). *Learning to read and write in colonial America*. Amherst, MA: University of Massachusetts Press, in association with the American Antiquarian Society.

National Commission on Excellence in Education. (1983). *A nation at risk: A report to the nation and the Secretary of Education, by the National Commission on Excellence in Education*. Washington, DC: Author.

National Governors Association (NGA) Center for Best Practices & Council of Chief State School Officers (CCSSO). (2010). *Common Core State Standards for English language arts and literacy in history/social studies, science, and technical subjects*. Washington, DC: Authors. Available at www.corestandards.org/assets/CCSSI_ELA%20Standards.pdf

National Research Council (NRC). (1999). Testing, teaching, and learning: A guide for states and school districts. Committee on Title I Testing and Assessment, Richard F. Elmore and Robert Rothman, editors. Board on Testing and Assessment, Commission on Behavioral and Social Sciences and Education. Washington, DC: National Academy Press.

No Child Left Behind Act of 2001, Pub. L. No. 107-110, 115 Stat. 1425. (2002). Available at www. ed.gov/offices/OESE/esea

Nichols, S. (2012). High-stakes testing: Does it increase achievement? *Journal of Applied School Psychology. 23*(2), 47–64.

Oakes, J. (2005). *Keeping track: How schools structure inequality* (2nd ed.). New Haven, CT: Yale University Press.

Pearson, P. D. (2013). Research foundations of the Common Core State Standards in English language arts. In S. Neuman & L. Gambrell (Eds.), *Quality reading instruction in the age of Common Core State Standards* (pp. 237–262). Newark, DE: International Reading Association.

Pearson, P. D., & Hiebert, E. H. (2013). Understanding the Common Core State Standards. In L. Morrow, T. Shanahan, & K. K. Wixson (Eds.), *Teaching with the Common Core Standards for English Language Arts: What Educators Need to Know, Grades PreK–2* (pp. 1–21). New York, NY: Guilford Press.

Preston, J. (1989). Female aspiration and male ideology: School-teaching in nineteenth-century New England. In A. Angerman, G. Binnema, A. Keunen, V. Poels, & J. Zirkzee (Eds.), *Current issues in women's history* (pp. 171–182). New York, NY: Routledge.

Purkey, S. C., & Smith, M. (1983). Effective schools: A review. *The Elementary School Journal, 83*(4), 426–452.

Resnick, L. (1993). as cited in J. O'Neil, On the New Standards Project: A conversation with Lauren Resnick and Warren Simmons. *Educational Leadership, 50*(5), 17–21.

Rice, J. M. (1893). *The public-school system of the United States.* New York, NY: Century.

Rice, J. M. (1913). *Scientific management in education.* New York, NY: Hinds, Noble & Eldredge.

Robinson, H. M., Monroe, M., Artley, A. S., & Greet, W. C. (1960–1962). *The new basic readers: Curriculum foundation series.* Chicago, IL: Scott Foresman.

Robinson, H. M., et al. (1967). *Open highways readers.* Chicago, IL: Scott Foresman.

Robinson, H. M., et al (1965). *Wide horizons readers.* Chicago, IL: Scott Foresman.

Rollins, R. (1980). *The long journey of Noah Webster.* Philadelphia, PA: University of Pennsylvania Press.

Rosenshine, B., & Furst, N. (1971). Research on teacher performance criteria. In B. O. Smith (Ed.), *Research in teacher education,* (pp. 37–72). Englewood Cliffs, NJ: Prentice Hall.

Ruggles, A. M. (1950). *The story of the McGuffeys.* New York, NY: American Book.

Smith, N. B. (1965). *American reading instruction.* Newark, DE: International Reading Association.

Stallings, J. (1976). How instructional processes relate to child outcomes in a national study of follow-through. *Journal of Teacher Education, 27*(1), 43–47.

Stallings, J. A., & Kaskowitz, D. H. (1974). *Follow Through classroom observation evaluation (1972–1973).* Menlo Park, CA: Stanford Research Institute.

Stebbins, L. B., St. Pierre, R. G., Proper, E. C., Anderson, R. B., & Cerva, T. R. (1977). *Education as experimentation: A planned variation model, Volume IV—A, An evaluation of Follow Through.* Cambridge, MA: Abt Associates.

Taylor, F. W. (1913). *Principles of scientific management.* New York, London: Harper & Brothers.

Tidwell, C. J. (1928). *State control of textbooks.* New York, NY: Columbia University Press.

Tulley, M. A., & Farr, R. (1985). Textbook adoption: Insight, impact and potential. *Book Research Quarterly, 1*(2), 4–11.

Tyack, D., & Cuban (1995). *Tinkering toward utopia: A century of public school reform.* Cambridge, MA: Harvard University Press.

U.S. Department of Education. (2009). *Race to the top: Executive summary.* Washington, DC. Available at www2.ed.gov/programs/racetothetop/executive-summary.pdf

Weber, G. (1971). *Inner city children can be taught to read: Four successful schools* (CBE Occasional Papers No. 18). Washington, DC: Council for Basic Education. (ERIC ED 057 125)

Webster, N. (1797). *The American spelling book: Containing an easy standard of pronunciation. Being the first part of a grammatical institute of the English language. In three parts* (19th ed.). New York, NY: Durham.

Webster, N. (1848). *An American dictionary of the English language.* Springfield, MA: George and Charles Mirriam.

About the Contributors

P. David Pearson is a professor in the areas of Language and Literacy and Human Development at the University of California, Berkeley, where he works on issues of pedagogy, assessment, and policy related to literacy development across the K–12 continuum. He began his educational career in 1964 as a 5th-grade teacher in Porterville, California, so he has been involved in education throughout the period covered by this volume.

Elfrieda "Freddy" H. Hiebert is president and CEO of TextProject, a nonprofit that provides open-access resources to support higher reading levels, and a research associate at the University of California, Santa Cruz. Dr. Hiebert received her Ph.D. in educational psychology from the University of Wisconsin–Madison. She has worked in the field of early reading acquisition for over 45 years, first as a teacher's aide and teacher of primary-level students in California and, subsequently, as a teacher educator and researcher at the universities of Kentucky, Colorado–Boulder, Michigan, and California–Berkeley. Her research addresses how fluency, vocabulary, and knowledge can be fostered through appropriate texts. Dr. Hiebert's research has been published in numerous scholarly journals. She has also authored or edited ten books. Through documents such as *Becoming a Nation of Readers* (Center for the Study of Reading, 1985) and *Every Child a Reader* (Center for the Improvement of Early Reading Achievement, 1999), she has contributed to making research accessible to educators. Dr. Hiebert's model of accessible texts for beginning and struggling readers—TExT—has been used to develop numerous reading programs that are widely used in schools. Dr. Hiebert was the 2008 recipient of the William S. Gray Citation of Merit (awarded by the International Reading Association). She is also a member of the Reading Hall of Fame, a Fellow of the American Educational Research Association, and the 2013 recipient of the American Educational Research Association's Research to Practice (Interpretive) award. Hiebert chaired an advisory group on early childhood for the Common Core and serves on the Item Quality Review Panel of Smarter Balanced.

Richard L. Allington is a professor of literacy studies at the University of Tennessee. He is past-president of the International Reading Association and the Literacy Research Association.

Monica T. Billen and **Kimberly McCuiston** are doctoral candidates at the University of Tennessee. Both are completing their dissertations as this paper is submitted for publication.

Jay S. Blanchard is a former board member of the International Reading Association and has focused research and writing efforts on technology as well as emergent reading issues for language and culturally diverse children including American Indian children.

Robert Calfee was a cognitive psychologist with research interests in the effect of schooling on the intellectual potential of individuals and groups. His interests focused on assessment of beginning literacy skills and the broader reach of the school as a literate environment. He was a professor emeritus from Stanford University and the University of California, Riverside.

Gina N. Cervetti is an assistant professor of literacy, language, and culture at the University of Michigan. Her research focuses on literacy learning in content areas, especially science, at the elementary level.

Michael F. Graves is professor emeritus of Literacy Education at the University of Minnesota and a member of the Reading Hall of Fame. His research and writing focus on vocabulary learning and instruction. His books on vocabulary include *Teaching Vocabulary to English-Language Learners* (2012, with Diane August and Jeannette Mancilla-Martinez), *Essential Readings on Vocabulary Instruction* (2009), *Teaching Individual Words: One Size Does Not Fit All* (2009), and *The Vocabulary Book* (2006). His current research focuses on selecting vocabulary to teach.

John T. Guthrie, Ph.D., is the Jean Mullan Professor of Literacy Emeritus in Department of Human Development and Quantitative Methodology at the University of Maryland at College Park. In 2011, he was elected to the National Academy of Education to address research to national policy. In 2012, he was appointed to the Literacy Research Panel of the International Reading Association that investigates literacy policy.

James V. Hoffman is professor of language and literacy studies at The University of Texas at Austin. Dr. Hoffman's research interests are focused on teacher education, the text environment, and international development work in literacy.

Rosalind Horowitz is chair of the American Education Research Association, Special Interest Group (SIG) on Research in Reading and Literacy. She is a National Academy of Education Spencer Fellow and a University of Minnesota Twin Cities Campus distinguished alumni, among 100 selected for the centennial, *Inspiring Minds for a Century, 1905–2005*. Horowitz serves on the research advisory board to the President at The University of Texas at San Antonio, federally designated as a Hispanic-serving institution, one of the fastest growing universities in the Americas.

Michael L. Kamil is professor emeritus, Stanford University Graduate School of Education. He has written extensively on models of reading, effects of technology on literacy, and the relationship of recreational reading to reading ability. Another line of his work has included extensive syntheses of research in reading, second language, and technology.

Barbara Kapinus has been a classroom teacher, reading teacher, researcher, policy analyst, and assessment developer. She has worked for Prince George's County, Maryland Schools, Maryland State Department of Education, The Council of Chief State School Officers and the National Education Association. She has also taught graduate courses at several colleges and universities.

Richard Long is the president of Literate Nation, an advocacy group focused on changing education public policy to ensure that all high need students get the evidence-based instruction they need to become effective readers and learners. Long has worked on literacy policy for over 35 years. Prior to working with Literate Nation, Long worked for the International Reading Association, the National Title I Association, as well as on the staff of Congressman James W. Symington (D-MO) on federal and state literacy education policy.

Leigh Ann Martin is a research associate with TextProject.org. Her current work focuses on digitizing and analyzing historical 1st-grade texts.

James Nageldinger is an assistant professor of literacy education at Elmira College. His research interests include reading fluency, emphatic prosody, hybrid text, readers who struggle, and the impact of theatre activities on reading. James has taught literacy in classrooms in Washington State, Ohio, and Hawaii.

David Paige is associate professor of education at Bellarmine University in Louisville, Kentucky. Paige's research interests focus on literacy issues in K–12 education, particularly those concerning reading fluency.

Timothy Rasinski is a professor of literacy education at Kent State University. His scholarly interests include reading fluency and word study, readers who struggle, and parental involvement. His research has been published in journals such as *Reading Research Quarterly* and *The Reading Teacher*. A former classroom and reading intervention teacher, Tim has served on the board of directors of International Reading Association as well as co-editor of *The Reading Teacher* and the *Journal of Literacy Research*.

S. Jay Samuels has written widely on a number of literacy and reading topics across a long career in educational psychology, most importantly fluency.

Barbara M. Taylor is professor emerita of literacy education, University of Minnesota, where she focused on research on the elements of effective instruction that contribute to children's success in reading. She directed a large national study on school change in reading in high-poverty schools through CIERA (Center for the Improvement of Early Reading Achievement) from 1997–2003, headed up the professional learning for REA and Reading First elementary schools in Minnesota from 2002–2008, and was the founder and past director of the Minnesota Center for Reading Research at the University of Minnesota. She received the 2005 Albert J. Harris Award for outstanding research from the International Reading Association, the 2005 Outstanding Teacher Educator Award from the International Reading Association, and the Oscar Causey Award from the National Reading Conference for outstanding contributions to reading research in 2009.

Joanna P. Williams is professor emerita of psychology and education at Teachers College, Columbia University. Her research interests include reading comprehension, text structure, learning disabilities, and learning problems of young children at risk for academic failure. She was a member of the National Reading Panel and the RAND Reading Study Group and has edited the *Journal of Educational Psychology* and *Scientific Studies of Reading*.

Kathleen M. Wilson is a founding director of the University of Nebraska–Lincoln's Schmoker Reading Center where she is an associate professor of teaching, learning, and teacher education. She studies teacher professional development in the formative process, especially when instructing children experiencing difficulty with literacy acquisition. Her current interests center on teachers' integration of digital technologies into literacy instruction and assessment.

Index